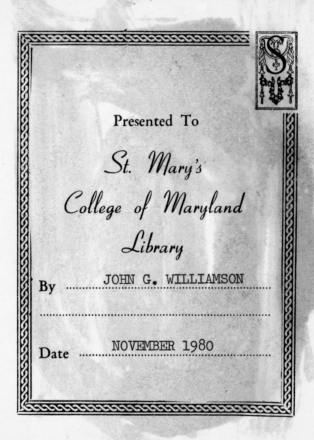

The Sudeten Problem, 1933–1938

The Sudeten Problem
1933-1938

Volkstumspolitik and the Formulation
of Nazi Foreign Policy

by

RONALD M. SMELSER

Wesleyan University Press

MIDDLETOWN, CONNECTICUT

The publisher gratefully acknowledges the support of the publication of this book by Alma College, the Earhart Foundation, and The Andrew W. Mellon Foundation.

Library of Congress Cataloging in Publication Data

Smelser, Ronald M., 1942–
  The Sudeten problem, 1933–1938.

  Bibliography: p.
  1. Germans in the Czechoslovak Republic. 2. Czechoslovak Republic—Foreign relations—Germany. 3. Germany—Foreign relations—Czechoslovak Republic. I.
Title.
DB205.8.G4S55   327.43′0437   74–5912
ISBN 0–8195–4077–3

Manufactured in the United States of America
First edition

TO MARY

Contents

Acknowledgments

THIS book could not have been researched and written without the generous assistance and advice of a large number of individuals and institutions both in this country and in Europe. I am particularly grateful to my friend and adviser Professor Robert Koehl, whose support and careful criticism helped me through a sometimes formidable topic. The Graduate School, the History Department, and the Memorial Library staffs of the University of Wisconsin were also invaluable in their assistance.

I should like to express gratitude to the Deutscher Akademischer Austauschdienst and especially to Mr. Martin Mruck as well as to the University of Wisconsin Graduate School, for so generously supporting my research abroad. I am also deeply indebted to Professor Hans-Adolf Jacobsen of Bonn for making otherwise inaccessible materials available to me and for sharing his experience and contacts in the area of German foreign policy; and to Dr. Vilém Prečan, formerly of the Historical Institute of the Czech Academy of Sciences in Prague, whose selfless, indefatigable efforts enabled me to do research in Czechoslovakian archives.

The directors and personnel of the following archives and institutes gave freely of their time and expertise, in addition to allowing me to use their materials: the Politisches Archiv des Auswärtigen Amtes in Bonn; the Bundesarchiv in Koblenz; the Sudetendeutsches Archiv, Collegium Carolinum and Institut für Zeitgeschichte in Munich; the Berlin Document Center; Institut für Auslandsbeziehungen in Stuttgart; Johann-Wolfgang-Herder Institut in Marburg; the Czechoslovak Central State Archives in Prague, Bratislava, and Litoměříce. The following individuals also were most generous in consenting to share their personal experiences regarding this period: Dr. Günther Altenburg, Dr. Walter Brand, Friedrich Bürger, Dr. Hans Neuwirth, Dr. Hans Steinacher, and Dr. Franz Wehofsich.

I also wish to thank the Alma College Institutional Grants Committee and the Earhart Foundation of Ann Arbor for their generous support in the publication of this book.

A personal word of gratitude is due our friends the Georg Wagenbach family, whose understanding and assistance made some potentially difficult days of research abroad much more rewarding and enjoyable.

My wife Mary has shared this labor from the beginning. Without her tireless aid and encouragement as well as her patient, skilled editing, this book might never have reached fruition. I dedicate it, affectionately, to her.

Ronald M. Smelser

Alma, Michigan
May, 1974

The Sudeten Problem, 1933–1938

I

Introduction

AS a case study in international politics, the events leading to the Munich crisis of 1938 have long exerted their own special appeal—and justifiably so. The road to Munich is a fascinating one, but one not easily charted. In attempting to answer the elusive question "why Munich," historians have explored a wide variety of perspectives: among them the political machinations of Hitler in his pursuit of European, and world, hegemony; the appeasement policies of Britain and France; as well as the "fifth column" role played by the Sudeten German population of Czechoslovakia. In many respects it might seem that the whole question has been exhausted. And yet despite the wealth of scholarly literature on the subject, there is much about the very nature of the Munich crisis which remains unanswered.

The controversy seems to center particularly around the role the Sudeten German political parties played in the ultimate destruction of the Czechoslovakian state. Was one of the most well known nationalist Sudeten leaders, Konrad Henlein, merely a tool of Hitler throughout the 1930s, systematically but secretly leading his countrymen down the path to *Anschluss* with the Reich? Some historians have defended this interpretation to one degree or another. Sudeten German apologists, on the other hand, have maintained that Henlein was not working hand-in-hand with Hitler in order to betray the Czech state so odious to many segments of the Sudeten population. Although many historians would reject either of these stereotypes, for the most part scholars still tend to argue that the Sudeten German national movement had, by 1933, become essentially "Nazi" oriented: that while there may have been some differences between the goals of Hitler and the Sudeten German national camp, these differences were so slight as to make any real distinctions purely academic.[1] The often intense rivalry within the Sudeten camp, raging so hotly even as the crisis in Czechoslovakia neared its peak, could be construed, then, as merely peripheral squabbling which had little bearing on the development of Hitler's actions toward the whole Czech situation.

If either of these extreme interpretations of the Sudeten German crisis is not satisfactory, and if perhaps the "differences" between Reich National Socialism and Sudeten nationalism are more significant than even the most moderate studies have suggested, then where and how is such evidence for a reevaluation of Hitler's relations with the Sudeten Germans to be found? Part of the difficulty may lie in the fact that whatever their point of view, most studies of the Sudeten crisis eventually take as their framework a diplomatic approach.[2] This approach, although in itself rewarding, is not without serious limitations: for in the Third Reich, "official" channels were all too often merely the tip of the iceberg. Thus, studies that stress official contacts between Germany and her antagonists, however unorthodox the form these relations often took, frequently seem to run aground on the problem of the intricacies of power allocation in the Third Reich and the effect such power allocation had on Hitler's foreign policy. In some respects Hitler's foreign policy goals may have influenced the way in which the Sudeten crisis developed. But there is evidence that suggests the reverse might also be valid. The key to Munich might lie in the interpretation that Hitler's concrete goals vis-à-vis Czechoslovakia were sufficiently vague and open ended that the activities of Sudeten German as well as those of Reich nationalists, not merely "National Socialists," were able to shape the Munich crisis, and in the process, to help mold Hitler's foreign policy toward Czechoslovakia.

This, basically, is the thrust of my study: to explore the question of Munich and the Sudeten Germans on a subdiplomatic level, within the context of ethnic German politics (*Volkstumspolitik*). But beyond this limited goal, I believe that the whole problem of ethnic German politics and the Sudeten question can reveal much about the nature of the Nazi state and the mechanics of Hitler's foreign policy formulation.

Though *Volkstumspolitik* apparently did much to shape Nazi foreign policy, it was not in itself a Nazi creation. Long before the Nazis came to power, Reich Germans and Germans abroad had been involved in something known as "Germandom work" (*Deutschtumsarbeit* or *Volkstumsarbeit*), which on the surface did not seem to have much at all to do with politics, much less with National Socialism. *Volkstumsarbeit*, can be defined as an intense concern for the welfare of ethnic German groups and an attempt to foster closer ties between these groups and the Reich German population through social, economic, and cultural assistance. The reasons for this concern for Germandom were many. Partly it was a matter of defensiveness, born of the fact that Germans not only achieved national unity at a rather late date, but then not the kind of unity in which language boundaries and geographic boundaries coincide, as was the case in England and France. Despite the existence of a German national state, there were large numbers of Germans who had been scattered in a centuries-old diaspora over Eastern Europe and who were not part of the new German polity.³ The resulting ethnic defensiveness became especially strong at the end of the last century, as the Germans gradually lost their once dominant political and cultural position vis-à-vis the awakening Slavic peoples. Finally, the disastrous defeat of Germany and Austria in the First World War; the additional loss of power and prestige as many ethnic Germans became "minorities" in new countries now run by other nationalities; and the steadily worsening economic position of these minority groups led to an unprecedented growth in activity on the part of the organizations concerned with maintaining the cultural integrity and improving the material welfare of ethnic Germans everywhere.⁴

For the most part, on the surface at least, aid and counsel to ethnic Germans represented a completely legitimate Reich German enterprise. Schools were opened and libraries kept stocked. Educators would travel among the German ethnic groups promoting closer cultural ties with the Reich. Economic aid was given to hundreds of firms, large and small, in German communities abroad. Through it all, it was emphasized that these German communities shared a common cultural tradition with Germandom as a whole. The fact that each of these ethnic groups had developed a unique identity through centuries of autonomous growth was viewed not as a threat to German cultural unity, but rather as a means of strengthening and giving new vitality to Germandom because of the diversity of experience each ethnic settlement had to offer. The great danger underlying *Volkstumsarbeit*, however, was that the ideology behind it made its thrust not primarily cultural and social, but rather political and potentially revolutionary. *Völkisch* ideology was and had been for decades antidemocratic and antiliberal, as well as anti-Slav. It tended also to be authoritarian and racist. Above all, *völkisch* thought emphasized loyalty to the *Volk* above any loyalty to the state within which a given *Volk* happened to live.[5] This placement of loyalty could either mean toleration of a particular state if its policies did not violate *völkisch* sensibilities too much, or outright rejection of a polity if it did. In extreme cases *völkisch* loyalty might even lead to an aggressive imperialism: to a militant search for a new kind of state that would have boundaries contiguous with the *Volk.* In pre-World-War-I Europe this *völkisch* ethos was not so explosive politically. There were no democratic states to speak of; the Slavs were, with some minor exceptions, safely ensconced as second class citizens in the old monarchies. Most important, the existence of the old Habsburg and Hohenzollern thrones created a kind of dynastic loyalty that bridged the gap between *Volk* and state, and that made the tension arising from lack of contiguity between *Volk* and state bearable.

The year 1918 changed all this. After 1918 both Reich and ethnic Germans were forced to live in initially democratically constituted states; many ethnic Germans also found themselves compelled to live in states dominated by the Slavs. All of this was, of course, an affront to *völkisch* antidemocratic and racial biases. As a result, *völkisch* thinking suddenly came out into the open in political, not just "cultural" and "social," form: among both Reich and ethnic Germans, there was a widespread feeling of hostility toward, if not outright rejection of, the political status quo. Sudeten Germans, for the most part, did not sanction their inclusion in the newly formed Czechoslovak state; Germans in Posen and West Prussia likewise had no desire to be included in the Polish state. In short, *völkisch* ideology, so long a "respectable" form of nationalist protest, was now leading in a politically revolutionary direction. The situation became even more dangerous because of the fact that an important restraining force, the old dynasties of the Habsburgs and Hohenzollerns were now gone. Deprived of these outlets for their loyalties, many ethnic Germans turned to attempts to unite the *Volk* in order to express nationalist political feelings.[6] Symptomatic of this sudden mass expression of *völkisch* loyalty was the spate of utopian books, like Othmar Spann's *Der wahre Staat* (1921) or Arthur Moeller van den Bruck's *Das Dritte Reich* (1923), many of which posited a mythical polity which would finally bring Germans together under one system. Another sign of the widespread concern for *völkisch* loyalty was the development of new categories by which ethnic Germans identified themselves. Older regional-tribal designations rooted in the past and tradition began to be replaced by new unitary concepts, whereby German ethnic groups in each of the new successor states saw themselves as a united German community circumscribed by the border of each of those states. The Saxons of Siebenbürgen and the Swabians of the Banat suddenly began to think of themselves as *Ungarndeutsche* or *Rumänendeutsche*. Likewise in Czechoslovakia the unitary concept of *Sudetendeutsch* began to replace the more traditional terms *Deutschböhmen* and *Deutschmähren*.[7] Needless to say, this new identity did not imply loyalty *to* those states, but was a step away from the old parochialism toward pan-Germanism.

Neither the utopian theories nor the new ethnic designations were in themselves all that subversive, but they do betray a climate growing ever more conducive to wholesale irredentism and imperialism. The atmosphere of defeat and humiliation that accompanied all these changes only served to exacerbate an already explosive *völkisch* renaissance. The carnage of war gave an already militant movement a truly military language. *Völkisch* adherents spoke of the *Volkstumskampf*, the "national struggle"; they spoke of converging lines of German and Slavic settlements as "fronts," as if a village or town succumbing here or there to a Slavic majority represented battlefield skirmishes. The *völkisch* movement absorbed both the idiom and the psychology of war. In light of this mentality it is not surprising that *völkisch* loyalty became not only outwardly aggressive, but also inwardly exclusive. Although many *völkisch* adherents admitted that other peoples, too, had a right to their own identity and integrity—to their own *Volkstum*—they seldom honored this principle in practice. Particularly since the struggle of the Slavic peoples for national identity had begun in the middle of the last century, the confrontation between German and Pole or German and Czech had largely been one of hostility and competition, not of understanding and mutual respect. Faced now with the loss of their long time political and cultural dominance, many German groups felt the need to assert their ethnic superiority that much more vehemently. Not even the one powerful remaining German state gave them reason for encouragement. The Weimar regime, it seemed, was more interested in developing good relations with neighboring successor states than with looking after the interests of ethnic Germans living within those states.[8] Thus, both Reich and ethnic German *völkisch* adherents tended to reject the Weimar state, not only out of distrust of democracy, but perhaps even more from a sense of betrayal.

The outcome was that for all the "nonpolitical" social and charitable work they performed, the *Volkstum* organizations were, for the most part, inherently political in nature. If money were given to Sudeten German schools in which children were taught that the Versailles settlement was an abomination which Germany would one day eliminate through *Anschluss* or if funds were channeled to firms that hired and fired a worker according to whether he was sympathetic to *völkisch* ideas, where indeed did cultural and social activities stop and political concerns begin? On a deeper level, in countries where all life—social, political, and cultural—is organized along ethnic lines, any attempt to separate cultural and social from political activity is practically impossible.

Nowhere were the political implications of *Volkstumsarbeit* greater than among the Sudeten German population of Czechoslovakia, for nowhere else was there more resentment against the Versailles settlement and the changes it brought. For centuries the Germans had dominated Bohemia, politically, economically, and culturally. Suddenly in 1918, as a result of a disastrous and unexpected military defeat, they found themselves a minority in a new country dominated politically by an ethnic group—the Czechs—they themselves had long suppressed. Ill-considered remarks and untoward incidents accompanying the founding of the new state only compounded the resentment and widened the gulf between the two peoples. In his address to that nation on December 22, 1918, Thomas Masaryk, founder and soon-to-be first president of the Czech republic, made an unfortunate reference to the Germans as "immigrants" and "colonists." [9] Many Germans, pointing to their centuries-long presence in Bohemia, reacted bitterly to the statement and never forgot it. On May 27, 1920, as Masaryk was about to take the presidential oath, Rudolf Lodgman von Auen, the leader of the Sudeten German nationalists, ostentatiously left the hall where the oath was being administered with the protest: "the German 'colonists' and 'immigrants' are leaving the hall." [10] Somewhat later Auen again indicated where his loyalties lay when he asserted that "high treason is now a duty." [11] Not only words, but deeds, too, poisoned relations between Czechs and Germans, alienating many Sudeten Germans from the new polity even further. The Sudeten Germans had voted in the majority not to enter the new state at all, but rather to become a part of German-Austria. When on March 4, 1919, Sudeten Germans in many towns gathered to protest their inclusion in the new Czech state instead, nervous Czech police opened fire, leaving fifty-four dead, many of them in the town of Kaaden. The "massacre of Kaaden" later became a symbol for many Sudeten Germans on the Right of the enmity which had to exist between the two peoples.[12]

As the years passed, larger, impersonal developments also conspired to prevent a healing of the breach between the Czechs and the Sudeten Germans. Although the Germans continued in their position of preeminence economically, this brought them little consolation amidst the ruin which accompanied the postwar period. The economic dislocation was largely a product of the greatly shrunken market which the Sudeten Germans faced after the destruction of the Habsburg empire, but it was all too easy to attribute it to Czech malevolence, especially when the government in Prague took certain steps such as the granting of contracts to Czech firms in an effort to redress imbalances that resulted from long-time German domination. Another related bone of contention was the continuous exodus of Czechs from rural areas into cities, where most of the Germans lived. This was a natural development, a by-product of modernization and industrialization. To the Sudeten Germans, however, conditioned for decades to the "nationality struggle," it looked like Czech attempts to "denationalize" traditionally German areas.[13]

These suspicions were strengthened by a number of other sensitive issues which developed after 1918. In a number of areas of public life—including language, finance, and education—Czech attempts at redressing long standing inequities were regarded by many Sudeten Germans as part of a conscious policy aimed at undermining the German ethnic group in Czechoslovakia. It was an impression scarcely mitigated by the many cases of petty Czech chauvinism which often accompanied the implementation of specific policies. One could easily quote statistics giving ample support to both sides. The Czechs could point out with justice that the Germans still administered 21.4 percent of all elementary schools, just below their per capita allotted portion of 22.3 percent, hardly a sign that ethnic Germans were being systematically discriminated against in education.[14] The Germans, in turn, could counter with the argument that Czechs would build brand new schools for just a few Czech children in German areas, leaving the more numerous German children in crowded, outdated facilities. The intent, as the Germans saw it, was to lure the German children into the new schools in order to "Czech-ify" them.[15]

But one can quote statistics at will. In the end it is not such "facts," but what people believe to be the facts, which count. And many Sudeten Germans seem to have honestly believed that their very ethnic existence was being threatened. They reacted accordingly, turning away from the new state and its politics. *Volkstumsarbeit* was rapidly on the way to becoming overt *Volkstumspolitik*. Ultimately this brand of "nonpolitical" Germandom work would also bring large segments of the Sudeten German population into contact with those in the Reich who themselves were placing their hopes in or building their careers on the whole area of *Volkstumsarbeit*.

The burgeoning interest in *Volkstum* work—and all the revolutionary potential it represented—had particularly grave implications for the Czech state. The Sudeten Germans were the largest German ethnic minority group in Europe; they were also the closest in proximity to the Reich. More important, their settlement areas included the strategically significant Bohemian mountain rim on Germany's border.[16] A dissatisfied Sudeten German population would seem to have offered an ideal tool for the Nazis to "coordinate," mold, and use as they pursued an aggressive, expansionist foreign policy. In 1933, however, directly after Hitler's seizure of power, there could be no question of such a militant foreign policy. The new regime had first to consolidate its power internally, a task which called for quiescence in Germany's international relations.[17] All of Germany's neighbors, especially those to the east and southeast, had considerable German minorities, and if these countries were to suspect that National Socialism was an export commodity, they were conceivably in a position to end the Thousand Year Reich before it even began.

At this point, as Hitler attempted to keep Germany's relations with its neighbors correct if not cordial, the ethnic Germans represented more of a problem than an opportunity. It was a problem, however, that Hitler had no time to solve or even to consider. Apart from an insistence that nothing dare happen which might compromise the new regime's peaceful image, the führer left the fate of the ethnic Germans pretty much to the groups themselves and to those *Volkstum* organizations, not all of them National Socialist in orientation, which had already concerned themselves for decades with these people. The old-timers still remained in the game; they were soon joined by all sorts of political parvenus who took advantage of the Nazi rise to power in order to carve out spheres of influence for themselves. Neither wasted any time pursuing their individual brands of *Volkstumspolitik* with regard to Czechoslovakia and the Sudeten Germans. The result, as might be expected, was the growth of intense competition—both personal and ideological—in the realm of Germandom work.

Ultimately, understanding the course these ethnic rivalries took during the 1930s is essential to interpreting what happened at Munich and how the whole crisis over Czechoslovakia came about. As evidence will show, the struggles over Sudeten politics were far from mere personal quarrels which pale in light of Hitler's ultimate desire for conquest. On the contrary, the *Volkstum* conflict seems to have had a profound impact on the development of the Sudeten crisis and on the leadership role Hitler was to play in the solution of that crisis. In a sense, Munich and the events leading up to it reflect the most revolutionary application of means Hitler ever used in his foreign policy. At other times, and in other crises, whatever his long range goals might have been, Hitler relied for the most part on traditional means (although often somewhat overapplied): that is, on using and threatening to use state and military power. It was only in the crisis over Czechoslovakia that the Nazis made use of a new and quite novel foreign policy tool—exploiting an ethnic German population as a fifth column to undermine a country from within.[18] Yet, as we look at the development of the fifth column in the Sudetenland, it will become apparent that this foreign policy tool was not a consciously fashioned weapon with its impetus and control coming from the führer in Berlin. There was no fifth column in 1933, nor did Hitler envision one at that time, when Czechoslovakia and the Sudeten Germans were of no concern to him. Rather the fifth column only very gradually came into being, primarily as a result of political struggles in the Sudetenland and in the Reich, as well as the reciprocal relationship between the two—struggles in which Hitler often played little if any role at all.

But *Volkstumspolitik* did not merely create a tool for Hitler to utilize in implementing his foreign policy goals. There is also evidence that ethnic German politics in no small way helped determine *how* Hitler would use that tool: that is, *Volkstumspolitik* helped determine what the führer's foreign policy position would be. By the time the struggle over Czechoslovakia and the Sudeten Germans had reached a crisis point, Hitler seems to have been aware of a number of alternatives. There is evidence, for example, that Hitler personally by this time was favorably inclined toward a violent, military solution to the whole question. Yet, he was to revise this view. From a diplomatic point of view, the actions of Britain and France, as well as Italy's intervention, go a long way toward explaining why Hitler was to turn away from this course. Diplomatic considerations, however, do not seem to fully account for this gradual reversal. The *Volkstum* conflict, as we shall see, had by this time developed sufficient dynamic and momentum that Hitler's violent solution was perhaps no longer necessary. If a radicalized Sudeten population, if a fifth column exerted enough pressure, causing Czechoslovakia to collapse into its component regional-ethnic segments, then the pieces—particularly the Sudeten German areas—might be fair game for German political control. "Chemical dissolution" the German State Secretary Ernst Weizsäcker was to call it at one point; and this was precisely what was to come about, despite Hitler's predilections and initial projections.

The Germandom struggle and its role in conditioning and shaping much of what Hitler did in his foreign policy decision-making ultimately reveals a great deal about the führer's political style. During the course of the struggle, Hitler emerges as a pragmatic improviser. Although he leaned toward a violent restructuring of Europe under revolutionary German leadership, he never laid out a detailed program for implementing this open-ended goal.[19] Thus, as those involved in ethnic German politics presented him with viable alternatives, violent or not, he was not loath to capitalize on them. In fact, he seems to have encouraged his subordinates to behave precisely along these lines: by delegating the same power and assignments to several groups or individuals simultaneously, by refusing to make binding decisions in matters of personal quarrels and in questions of official competencies in many areas of public life, and by keeping his thoughts on policy matters to himself.

This pragmatic style of leadership in the development of the Sudeten crisis in turn seems to give credence to the theory that one of the most striking characteristics of the Nazi state was the fragmentation of power.[20] Underneath the apparent *Gleichschaltung* of public life in Germany, underlying the formal hierarchy of power leading toward Hitler the dictator, the National Socialist state appears to have operated from day to day primarily on the basis of a bewildering duplication of competencies, personal rivalries on the highest levels, and incredible confusion in every aspect of public life. As a result a number of virtually independent power centers developed, each trying to determine policy and the direction that the national *Erhebung* would take. The resulting fragmentation of power allowed various political forces within the Reich a great deal of latitude and considerable political "free enterprise" in their activities. And nowhere was this more striking than in the realm of *Volkstumspolitik*.

Ethnic German politics, in short, emerges not as a tempest in a teapot or as a trifling over semantics. Rather, *Volkstumspolitik* apparently both contributed to and reflected the nature of Hitler's leadership. By allowing, and, in fact, encouraging the competition of different personalities and organizations over what would eventually become Germany's foreign policy toward Czechoslovakia, Hitler—the dictator—did not "make" his foreign policy directly and consequently. Instead he put himself into the position of having to react to situations created by others. As the Sudeten problem approached the crisis stage, Hitler's subordinates—and others as well—who had long been independently struggling for supremacy in the *Volkstum* question, presented the dictator at the critical hour both with a unique opportunity and with a controlled set of options. It is ironical that the Hitlerian "program" culminating in the crisis at Munich seems to have been largely a function of men trying to determine, and act upon, what that so-called program might be.

II

Germandom Organizations in the Reich

THE very structure of Reich Germandom work during the early 1930s is in itself evidence that the Nazi regime was characterized by a lack of clear competencies, by a duplication of official functions, by rampant political free enterprise, and by ideological confusion. There were almost as many interpretations of *Volkstum* work in Hitler's Reich as there were people active in this area. Various new Germandom groups, as well as some which had been concerned with ethnic Germans for decades prior to 1933, not only survived, but competed fiercely with one another for influence and power. Among the plethora of organizations, it is possible to distinguish three basic approaches to *Volkstumsarbeit* during the 1930s: traditionalists, official National Socialist organizations, and radical "splinter" groups at work on the fringes of political life (*see* Appendix B).

The first type of Germandom group, here lumped under the term "traditionalist," includes an admixture of orthodox conservatives and right-wing but non-Nazi "conservative revolutionaries." [1] During the twenties, men of this persuasion often quite unwittingly contributed to the rise of the Nazi movement through their vague but strongly *völkisch* way of thinking, their acute sense of malaise and dissatisfaction with the republic, their "respectable" anti-Semitism, and their mindless enthusiasm for a national revival. Many of them saw in Hitler a useful tool and survived to be active in the new regime: some because they still had not seen behind the malevolence of National Socialism, others because they desired to mitigate that malevolence. To the extent that such traditionalists were aware of the potential dangers of the new Reich, they could and did function as a kind of resistance to the extremes of many Nazis in the regime. In the end, however, the traditionalists were bamboozled not just once, but yet a second time. They found not only that Hitler could not be used as they had originally hoped; they also ultimately discovered that, as their opposition to the excesses of National Socialism proved ineffective, their alternative ideas and techniques became little more than additional weapons in the armory of the radical NS. The second type of organization active in *Volkstumspolitik* arose out of the official National Socialist movement itself. Relations with ethnic Germans provided yet another field of political activity for the ambitious newcomers which the movement brought into power. Many of these NS parvenus, especially the idealistic, perceived Germandom politics as an opportunity to put NS principles into practice and to extend the *Volksgemeinschaft* ("ethnic community") to Germans outside the Reich. Others, more personally ambitious, were merely trying to build careers and bailiwicks in an overcrowded and fiercely competitive political arena. Finally, a third type of Germandom group active in the Reich were small, "splinter" organizations close to the National Socialists, but much more openly radical than the official movement. These radical organizations were only on the fringes of power in Nazi Germany; however, the general atmosphere of competition in the area of Germandom work and the lack of clear competencies and ideological guidelines enabled such groups to exert influence and cause problems far out of proportion to their size and place in the power structure.

There is yet another organization involved in the problem of Germandom work and foreign policy formation that does not fall into any of these three categories. Ironically, it is the one organization in the Third Reich that theoretically had foreign policy as its exclusive domain: namely, the *Auswärtiges Amt* (AA). That the Foreign Office should come last in a discussion of groups working within the Reich in the formulation of foreign policy is some indication of how much the National Socialist system distorted traditional political structures and channels. The *official* foreign policy organization, the Foreign Office, actually played a subordinate role in identifying and shaping the relationship of ethnic Germans to the Reich.

Within this general framework—traditionalist, official NS, and radical "splinter" groups—there were many diverse Germandom organizations with their own unique interests and goals. Within the traditionalist-oriented Germandom camp, for example, a wide range of groups competed with one another, each hoping to impose its conception of ethnic politics on the makers of German foreign policy.

Some, such as the *Deutsch-österreichische Arbeitsgemeinschaft,* limited themselves geographically. Others concentrated on certain kinds of contact with ethnic Germans, *e.g.,* educational contacts in the case of the *Deutsche Akademie* in Munich and the *Deutsches Auslandsinstitut* (DAI) in Stuttgart. Still others were umbrella organizations like the *Deutscher Schutzbund,* founded in 1919 to take some of the workload from the *Verein für das Deutschtum im Ausland.* The *Verband Deutscher Volksgruppen in Europa* (founded in 1922) represented the interests of the various German ethnic groups at the League of Nations in Geneva. Economically, the OSSA and the *Vereinigte Finanzkontore,* semipublic companies closely linked to the German Foreign Office, pumped needed funds to the *Volksgruppen* outside the Reich.[2]

There is little value in elaborately detailing the structure, history, leadership, and goals of each of these organizations, for most of them were eclipsed in the Nazi regime and lost their importance. One of them, however, stands out quite clearly and warrants discussion in greater depth, for it was to play a critical role in the development of the Sudeten problem: the *Verein für das Deutschtum im Ausland* (VDA). This organization was the most powerful of the traditionalist *Volkstum* groups. Ultimately, it was the only one to maintain a degree of independence and integrity under the Nazi regime. Founded in 1881 as the *Deutscher Schulverein,* the VDA specialized for years—as its earlier name indicates—in developing German schools among the ethnic German communities abroad, but it did so within the larger context of a general cultural and social concern. The shock of 1918 added impetus and intensity to the VDA's activities and, during the 1920s, the group considerably expanded in size and in the range of its political and cultural involvement. By 1932 it had 27 *Landesverbände* (that is, it was organizationally represented and involved with German ethnic groups in twenty-seven countries). There were over 3,200 local branches (*Ostsgruppen*) and 5,500 school groups.[3] The VDA's yearly collections in all German towns plus a certain amount of subvention from the Foreign Office gave it considerable power and influence financially and politically.

The Nazi seizure of power in 1933 brought changes to the VDA just as to virtually every other organization in Germany. On April 29, Dr. Hans Steinacher, hero of the nationality struggle against the Yugoslavs in Carinthia, veteran of the *Ruhrkampf* in 1923, and vigorous supporter of German minorities everywhere, was elected *Bundesführer* of the VDA.[4] Shortly thereafter, the *Verein* was renamed *Volksbund*—a term more congenial to the ears of the *völkisch* Right. These were moves which looked suspiciously like the *Gleichschaltung* process by which groups were ostensibly "coordinated" into the new National Socialist order. Many observers, in fact, from this point on labelled the VDA as one of many useful tools of an imperialist Reich foreign policy, in the forefront of attempts to build fifth columns wherever large groups of Germans were settled.[5] But this view of VDA activities in the early 1930s is simply not tenable in light of the organization's orientation during this period.[6] True, Steinacher's takeover of the VDA did seem to represent the triumph of much that the Nazi movement itself stood for: it was the triumph of a younger generation over the old and, as such, represented the ascendancy of the militant front generation over their more comfortable *Verein*-oriented fathers who, according to the young, did not exhibit any real patriotism beyond sentimental talk at the *Stammtisch.* Young VDA members and the Nazis shared this rejection of *Verein*-ism. The young VDA rank and file had no desire to be members of a charitable organization devoted only to cultural pursuits. Rather they wanted above all to struggle, using the resources of the whole *Volk* to realize a political and spiritual new order (*Neugestaltung*) in the European sphere.[7] This kind of language was common currency to the NS movement as well. Both traditionalists and Nazis had borrowed it freely from the same source: the broad *völkisch* movement had provided them with a fund of ideas and terms. Thus, both groups spoke of renewal, of spiritual rebirth, of militant struggle to create a new world, and above all, of the *Volk.* But here similarities ended. For despite these elements in common, especially language, some fundamental differences separated the Nazis from traditionalists like Steinacher: underlying the common idiom were radically different goals.

The most critical distinction between the Nazi conception of what ethnic German relations should be and that of men like Steinacher lay in the fact that the interest of the Nazis in the Volk was at all times etatist in nature: that is, it emphasized the Reich or core state (*Kernstaat*), rather than the individual ethnic groups. In questions of policy, the Reich and its goals had priority; ethnic Germans were significant primarily in terms of their usefulness in the service of the core state. This etatist approach is radically different from the *volklich*—to use the term coined by the traditionalists to describe their orientation—emphasis of men like Steinacher.[8] Loyalty to the *Volk* as expressed by Steinacher arose out of the tradition of the Austrian *Schutzverbände* ("cultural, social, and economic 'protective' societies") and the war experience. The main concern of these traditionalists was for the welfare of the ethnic Germans, particularly for those living along cultural boundaries in Europe. This approach deemphasized the core state and its needs: the Reich, as the stronghold of Germandom, was important mainly in that it was in a position to serve German groups by lending its strength and influence to ethnic communities abroad which enjoyed a less secure position. Far from being useful tools of the Reich brought into line with discipline and conformity, the various German ethnic groups, by their very independence and self-reliance, would bring credit to the *Volk* as a whole. Thus, whatever the interests of the German state may have been, there had to be the necessary allowance for the unhampered, autonomous development of the various ethnic German groups.[9]

Steinacher's whole career is evidence of his belief in the local integrity of ethnic German groups, in direct conflict with the pan-German thinking of many National Socialists. His early practical experience, particularly in organizing the referendum in Carinthia in 1920, constantly reflected his deep-rooted faith in the resourcefulness of a *Volksgruppe* in solving its own problems at a time when the Reich was unwilling and unable to help. His political demise in 1937 came to a great extent as a result of his hard line stand in favor of autonomy, if not *Anschluss* with Austria, for the Germans of South Tirol, at a time when Hitler was more than willing to sacrifice a bit of ethnic Germandom on the altar of Greater German imperialism.[10] Steinacher's public statements regarding the work of the VDA in the months after the Nazi seizure of power reflect his *volklich* ideal, as do his diary entries. His second audience with Hitler, on November 15, 1933, caused him to despair about this very issue:

> Then Hitler made a half-hour speech on the significance of the German core state. This must be strong. Then everything else can also be gotten. But only by this means. I cannot get around this basic attitude [of Hitler]. . . . I cannot get past this argument on the primacy of the strong state. I am unhappy. Can't I talk with him?[11]

Steinacher once again met with Hitler a month later, but at no time did the dialogue which Steinacher hoped for on this subject come about. Already at this early date, the ideological lines were being clearly drawn.

In this context superficial similarities between the traditionalists and the Nazis had advantages as well as disadvantages. On the one hand, vagueness of language disguised the differences between the two groups and allowed the traditionalists to survive and even compete within Hitler's Germany; on the other hand, similarity of idiom made the traditionalists, particularly, blind to the nature and degree of the opposition against them. Precisely because the Nazis spoke the same kind of language, the traditionalists were too long in assessing the implications of the very different goals the NS had in mind. Perhaps the traditionalists thought that Hitler's Austrian background would eventually give him an understanding for their approach to ethnic German politics (Steinacher, too, was Austrian by birth). But they were soon to find out that the führer's racial notions had little in common with their conception of the *Volkstum* issue.

It was not only the superficial similarities, however, that caused the traditionalists to be fooled so long by the Nazis. Some basic inconsistencies in their own position contributed to the same end. Theoretically the *volklich* ideal credited other non-German peoples with the right to their own separate identity, their own *Volkstum*. Steinacher himself had proclaimed: "[the concept of] *Volkstum* does not countenance the renunciation of one's own national identity, but neither does it permit the denial of someone else's." [12] This would seem to be in direct contradiction to Nazi racism. Unfortunately, in practice, the traditionalist *Volkstum* organizations like the VDA only rarely got over a myopic concentration on the problems of German minorities, usually within the mentality of hostility to other ethnic groups. This preoccupation made the traditionalists blind to the danger of twisting such one-sided concern for the *Volk* into racial policies involving the suppression and possible extermination of non-German ethnic groups.

The traditionalists, then, made many mistakes. They welcomed Hitler rather uncritically;[13] they underestimated the power of the core state while at the same time overestimating the ability of German minorities to work without the support of the Reich; they insisted on couching their not unreasonable goals within the mentality of the

Heroic Struggle (*heroisch-kämpferisch*).[14] In doing so they invited their own exploitation. Albeit unwittingly, their activities ultimately worked against the best interests of the ethnic groups they sought to help, aiding instead future National Socialist policies of imperialistic expansion and militant racism. But this aid was inadvertent and must be balanced against the fact that many of these men, precisely because they spoke in the same idiom as the Nazis, were in a position to provide the basis for what little resistance did confront the regime and mitigate its activities. As one observer put it: "[Among those who spoke the *völkisch* language] a broad range of opinions resulted scarcely found anywhere else in Hitler's state, varying widely from independent interpretation of party jargon to hidden nonconformity all the way to clear resistance." [15] In short, the similarities represented a two edged sword. In the end it would spell the doom of the traditionalists; in the short run, however, it was a boon to them and gave them the opportunity to put their ideas into practice in the viciously competitive world of *Volkstumspolitik*.

Despite its conflicts with its National Socialist rivals over the nature of Germandom, then, the VDA was able to achieve a great deal of power in the field of ethnic German work. Several important factors tended to strengthen the traditionalists' hand at this point. National Socialist leaders were not unaware of the value of an organization involved in Germandom work apparently independent of any official connections. This lack of official ties would enable the VDA to continue its work of organizing ethnic Germans abroad without being compromised and would give the new regime the respectable image it desired. In a letter to Steinacher on the occasion of the Passau Congress of the VDA in June of 1933, Rudolf Hess stated: "the possibilities of effectiveness of the [VDA] would be that much greater to the extent that it is able as before to keep itself free of influence by the 'official' Germany, whether embodied in government or in party agencies. . . ." Hess assured Steinacher that the führer shared this opinion.[16] This letter was to be the Magna Carta of the VDA—the *carte blanche* which enabled it, under Steinacher's leadership, to pursue a quite independent course of action. Regular rallies, as well as street corner and school collections all over Germany, brought in considerable sums of money, which were then often supplemented by subsidies from the Foreign Office or the Interior Ministry.[17] Even with such financial and political support, however, the ideas advocated by the VDA's leadership could not have achieved the currency they did during the early 1930s if this organization had not been intimately connected to a relatively new, yet powerful group involved in *Volkstumspolitik:* namely, to the Ethnic German Council (*Volksdeutscher Rat* or VR).[18] Many VDA leaders actually served simultaneously on the VR and the two organizations were frequently linked by National Socialist critics in their attacks on the traditional approach to Germandom work.

The *Volksdeutscher Rat* was founded in 1933, partly as a result of the prodding of Steinacher and the VDA. Although it was a late-comer among organizations involved in Germandom work, the VR nonetheless enjoyed a more privileged position from the start than even the VDA. This advantage stemmed from the fact that the VR, through one of its leaders, General Karl Haushofer, and the patronage of Rudolf Hess, was closer to the center of political power in the Third Reich than any of the other traditionalist groups working with ethnic Germans. Although the VDA had a *carte blanche* from Hess to pursue its activities independently, Steinacher himself was never particularly close to Hitler's deputy. In the VR, Steinacher shared leadership with Haushofer, who was extremely close to Hess on a personal level. Thus, the VR, through the Haushofer family, was able to protect the VDA when conflicts with rival organizations arose.

The impetus for the establishment of an organization like the VR, which would end the confusion and competition in the work with ethnic Germans and centralize and rationalize these endeavors, came from many sides. Alfred Rosenberg, always on the lookout for influence in this area, proposed a *Kommissariat,* an "undersecretary-ship," to handle the problem of Germans abroad. He recommended an old party man, Otto von Kursell, for the job.[19] Nothing came of it, but Kursell would appear later to play a pivotal role in Germandom politics. Steinacher, too, pushed for such centralization. He approved the extension of the *Kulturabteilung* ("cultural department") of the Foreign Office and recommended that a second *Staatssekretariat* for Ethnic [German] and Germandom Questions (*Volkstums- und Deutschtumsfragen*) be organized in the Reich Chancellory.[20] But probably the most effective voices for the centralization of Germandom work came from General Karl Haushofer and his son Albrecht—primarily because of this family's great influence with Rudolf Hess. An almost father-son relationship had developed between General Haushofer, who had been Hess's commanding officer during the war, and Hess, who followed Haushofer to Munich after the war to study under him at the university.[21] After the Nazi takeover, Hess wrote *Schutzbriefe* for both of Haushofer's sons, whose mother was Jewish, and got Albrecht a position as *Dozent* in political geography at the Berlin *Hochschule für Politik.*[22] Albrecht, as it becomes clear from the correspondence with his father, was the real political force in the family. He provided much of the impetus and many of the ideas, particularly in connection with the formation of the VR, which the elder Haushofer passed on to Hess as advice. Although he never occupied an official position, Albrecht, as a kind of deputy for his father, was also an important political advisor to Hess.

Working under the imperative, "let's educate our masters," Albrecht hoped to exert influence on German foreign policy through his connections with Hess.[23] As representative of the new order in power Hess would of necessity be an exponent of etatist thinking. The elder Haushofer and Albrecht, on the other hand, like Steinacher, advocated the position that the important thing was the defense and consolidation of Germandom wherever it might be, not merely within the Reich. With Albrecht as mediator, it was possible for quite a long time to achieve a delicate balance between these two positions. Enjoying Hess's protection the traditionalists were actually able to carve out a sphere of influence in the area of foreign policy formulation to deal with ethnic Germans abroad. Eventually, with the rise of the *Schutzstaffel* (SS) and the official change to an overtly aggressive foreign policy, this influence would end. Meanwhile, people like Steinacher and the Haushofers asserted their position with all the force and conviction at their disposal.

Unfortunately, the Haushofers overestimated their chances of positively influencing foreign policy toward the ethnic Germans. Hess's power, despite his commission from Hitler to take charge of Germandom work, was more limited than they at first thought. Whatever the potential of his power position might have been, Hess proved himself too vacillating and unstable to exploit it effectively. The Haushofers were constantly forced to reckon with his inability to assert himself or to make a necessary decision when under pressure from several directions. Albrecht once wrote to his mother about Hess: "I have the impression of strong good will in every direction, but I don't have the feeling that it is enough."[24] But whatever weaknesses there may have been in Hess's character, he was one of the few if not the only man in the immediate proximity of the führer who was accessible to the traditionalists and their ideas. His high position and relationship with General Haushofer was ultimately the most important single factor that made it possible for the *volklich* approach to *Volkstumspolitik* to achieve any practical influence on the formation of foreign policy at all.

The VR began to take shape during a series of conversations between Steinacher, the two Haushofers, and Dr. Robert Ernst (an old wartime comrade of the elder Haushofer and, since early 1933, director of the *Deutscher Schutzbund*). All met in Stuttgart in early September of 1933 on the occasion of the reorganization of the *Deutsches Auslandsinstitut,* a traditionalist-oriented information agency and educational institution which fostered cultural contacts between the Reich and ethnic German groups.[25] Albrecht Haushofer offered to use his connections with Hess in the matter of the VR and wrote him on September 7, urging Hess to assume control in the sector of Germandom.[26] On September 18, at a meeting of the *Kleiner Rat* of the *Deutsche Akademie* in Munich, Hess met with Karl Haushofer and Steinacher to discuss the whole question. He approved of their conceptions of what had to be done: that centralization in the area of Germandom work was badly needed. Many of Albrecht's ideas played a decisive role in the plan for the VR which Steinacher and the elder Haushofer outlined to Hess at this time. On October 27, 1933, Hess issued a *Verfügung* ("decree") proclaiming the formation of the *Volksdeutscher Rat.*[27]

The VR held its first formal meeting on November 1, 1933 in Berlin. Chairman of the Council was General Haushofer; its managing director was Hans Steinacher. The rest of the members included various experts on the problems of German minorities, most of them individuals who had worked together in the past with basically the same traditional methods. Hess did not take part in the meetings, but kept himself informed of the proceedings through a liaison, Heinrich Kersken. From the beginning the VR asserted itself as the final authority in the area of *Volkstumspolitik.* It laid claim to the Germandom funds administered by the Foreign Office and the Finance Ministry. It claimed exclusive rights to advise and aid all ethnic Germans abroad and demanded that the NSDAP *Gaue,* the *Hitler Jugend,* and the NS *Studentenschaft* end all independent

activities in the area of Germandom work. The VR even tried to
subordinate an official NS agency operating in the *Volkstum* field,
Ernst Bohle's *Auslandsorganisation.*[28] Clearly, this kind of claim to
power was not going to remain unchallenged.

The VDA-VR leadership, then, gradually became the most
influential and active of the traditionally-oriented Germandom groups
working within the Reich. Despite the often vicious competition for
power among the various groups; despite a power struggle as the work
was centralized; and despite the fact that the thrust of VDA-VR work
differed ideologically from the Nazis, these two groups and the people
sympathetic to their ideas were able to assert themselves for a
surprisingly long period of time. They were the only traditional groups
able to do so. Especially after 1933, the plethora of former smaller
organizations in one way or another lost what independence and
influence they once had. Some, like the *Grenz- und Ostmarkenvereine*
(the organizations representing the border and eastern Marches),
disappeared into larger Germandom units—in this particular case, the
groups were absorbed by Rosenberg's agency, the *Bund Deutscher
Osten* (BDO). A few, like the *Deutscher Schutzbund* simply were
overshadowed by more dynamic organizations and gradually lost
their importance and effectiveness. Other groups were infiltrated and
reorganized from within along the lines of the *Führerprinzip,* usually
by ambitious National Socialists anxious to capture the foundations
of a power base.[29] But the Nazis, wont as they were to cast power
structures in their own image, also developed their own organizations.
With the formation of such outright NS Germandom agencies during
the 1930s, a whole new dimension of rivalry and jurisdictional
confusion was added to *Volkstum* work.

One such tenacious competitor in the NS Germandom camp was
Alfred Rosenberg who, through his *Aussenpolitisches Amt,* attempted
to establish a position of influence in the field of foreign policy
formulation vis-à-vis the ethnic groups. At various times he was
maneuvering to gain control of the VDA, as well as initiating drives
toward centralization of Germandom activities by formation of an
agency he could later manipulate. But Rosenberg's star, in the realm
of Germandom at least, was soon to wane.[30] Far more influential
among the National Socialist Germandom groups, particularly in
regard to the Sudeten question, was Ernst Bohle and the *Auslandsorganisation* (AO).[31] Bohle's savage personal struggle with Steinacher

came to symbolize the intense conflict between the traditionalist and the National Socialist approach to Germandom work. Until the rise of the SS, Bohle's AO remained the greatest single threat to the independent position of the VDA and the VR. Under Bohle's leadership, the *Auslandsorganisation* reacted in a manner typical of the Germandom groups with a National Socialist orientation. Bohle was an extremely ambitious young man, a convinced National Socialist, who aspired to create an organization that would take charge of the German community abroad and make it into a disciplined tool of Reich foreign policy. The VDA, with its emphasis on traditional cultural and welfare activity, would naturally seem contemptible to a man like Bohle. Despite the militant language of the young VDA leadership, Bohle reacted with open hostility toward "reactionaries" like Steinacher who did not understand or approve of the imperialist potential of the new movement.

Bohle's rise to a position enabling him to threaten the VDA—one of the most powerful, well known, and well financed traditionalist Germandom groups with thousands of connections in Germany and abroad—is characteristic of the kind of political entrepreneurship possible under National Socialism.[32] Born in Bradford, England, on July 28, 1903, Bohle spent his formative years in Capetown, South Africa, where his father was called as a professor in 1906. Young Bohle graduated from the English high school there in 1919. These years in South Africa brought him a mastery of English which was to stand him in good stead among the Nazi leadership with its relative paucity of foreign experience.[33] In 1920 Bohle came to Germany for the first time, where he studied *Staats- und Handelswissenschaften* at the universities of Cologne and Berlin, as well as at the *Handelshochschule* in Berlin. He passed the examination for *Diplomkaufmann* in 1923, and for the next six years he devoted himself to his business career, working in Hamburg and the Rhineland for a number of English and American export firms, including the Chrysler Corporation. In 1930 he struck out on his own, founding his own company to handle automobile equipment. Apparently dissatisfied with only a business career, he joined the NSDAP on November 27, 1931 and soon thereafter placed himself at the disposal (*ehrenamtlich*) of the newly founded *Auslandsabteilung* of the party.[34] He took over the desks for South Africa, England, and the United States until Dr. Hans Nieland, director of the *Abteilung*, made Bohle his adjutant and *Gau* inspector. Simultaneously Bohle was organizational director of the Friends of the Hitler Movement (*Bund der Freunde der Hitler-Bewegung* or BFHB).[35] He might have remained in these positions as a relatively insignificant party member were it not for his good connections with Rudolf Hess (Bohle was a friend of Hess's brother Alfred) and for the fact of rivalry and conflict within the party. On December 8, 1932 Gregor Strasser, on whose initiative the *Auslands-abteilung* had been organized, resigned all his party offices. With his political demise, the whole existence of the *Auslandsabteilung* itself was called into question and Nieland's position as director was shaken. An attempt by Alfred Rosenberg to absorb the *Abteilung* into his *Aussenpolitisches Amt* apparently nearly succeeded. Allegedly, it was only due to a conversation between Rudolf Hess and his brother Alfred that the department was able to retain its independent existence at all.[36]

On January 30, 1933 Hitler was appointed German chancellor. Along with the many other changes which accompanied this new allocation of power, the *Abteilung* was reorganized. On March 15, 1933 it was renamed *Abteilung für Deutsche im Ausland* and its headquarters was transferred to Munich.[37] That same day Nieland was named police president of Hamburg and a provisional director of the *Abteilung* was appointed. During this period of flux Bohle saw an opportunity to advance his career. On April 4 he inquired whether a position was open in the new Munich office, recommending himself as one who had previously handled all questions connected with the organization of Germans abroad on behalf of the *Abteilung* and extolling the future potential of the department.[38] On April 26 Bohle succeeded in being appointed provisional director and on May 8 director of the *Abteilung für Deutsche im Ausland.*[39]

Bohle brought with him into the *Abteilung* an aggressive ambition, a great deal of enthusiasm for National Socialism, and a good head for organization. Although he sometimes compromised in ideological matters, he could be a ruthless opponent in matters of competency and authority. Unlike the conspiratorial Himmler, Bohle was open and direct in his attacks on his rivals. Lacking Göring's inclination toward the trappings of power, he lived relatively unpretentiously and devoted himself quietly to the acquisition of power.[40] Bohle lost little time in building up his organization and asserting its competency. He defended himself successfully in brief encounters over competency with the NSBO (*Nationalsozialistische Betriebszellen-organisation*) and with Rosenberg, who tried to form an *Ortsgruppe Auswärtiges Amt der NSDAP* for party members abroad in the diplomatic and consular service. Bohle also contacted Franz Xaver Schwarz, the party treasurer, about lifting the ban on party membership abroad.[41] By the fall of 1933, his efforts to establish the authority of the *Abteilung* had met with significant success. On October 3 Hess elevated the organization to the position of a *Hauptabteilung der Reichsleitung* and placed it under his direct supervision.[42] The *Abteilung* was designated the only party office qualified to deal with all party organizations abroad (except those in Austria, Danzig, and Memel). All party travel and communication between the Reich and abroad was, without exception, to take place through the *Abteilung*. NS groups were forbidden to establish direct contact independently with groups abroad. All party members living abroad were placed under the authority of this department. In addition to all of this, Bohle could claim in a circular letter on October 10 to the *Leiter* of the NSDAP *Landesgruppen, Ortsgruppen,* and *Stützpunkte* abroad, that the party treasurer as of October 1 had finally lifted the ban on NSDAP membership for Reich Germans living abroad.[43]

These successes in themselves would have been enough to give Bohle the encouragement and confidence to expand the horizons of his *Abteilung* even further. The Law to Safeguard the Unity of the Party and State (*Gesetz zur Sicherstellung der Einheit von Partei und Staat*) passed on December 1, 1933 gave Bohle's ambitions the decisive push.[44] This law made the party the only legitimate political authority in Germany and thus the "trustee of the German state tradition" (*Träger des deutschen Staatsgedankens*). There was to be no divergency of interest between the party and the state. From this point on, the party would represent the interests of the new German National Socialist state. Bohle accepted the consequences of this law for his organization. Up until this time, the *Abteilung* represented only the party abroad; now, under the new rubric of *Auslandsorganisation der NSDAP* (AO), it was to represent the interests of the entire National Socialist state among Germandom abroad—a considerably larger task. With this in mind, Bohle set down in detail the goals of his organization—goals which were supposed to give the AO primacy in Germandom work in general, not only in party affairs abroad.[45] Bohle's claim to authority in matters involving both Reich and ethnic

Germans represented a direct challenge both to the principles and to the jurisdiction of Steinacher's VDA and the VR. The AO was a threat to the very nature of Germandom work as it had been traditionally defined.

Bohle acknowledged that the many *Deutschtumsverbände* and *Vereine* had performed well intentioned service in the area of Germandom problems since 1919. However, he stressed that in their cultural and charitable orientation, these groups had consciously resisted "political steering": they were useless in the area of power politics (*machtpolitisch*). Even the Foreign Office in its present form, Bohle maintained, was no guarantee that Germany would be represented properly abroad—i.e., *kraftvoll und positiv im nationalsozialist-ischen Sinn* ("effectively and positively in the NS sense"). In place of all these traditional organizations, Bohle proposed a Reich ministry for *Ausland-Deutschtum* to organize the more than thirty-five million Germans abroad into a power instrument (*Machtinstrument*) to serve the National Socialist state. This ministry, which would have the already existing 230 Nazi cell groups abroad as a base, would be a means "mit dem man draussen praktisch Politik treiben [könnte]." [46] This early conception of the AO and its activities corresponded very closely to the concept of a fifth column as it later developed and as it was used in the destruction of Czechoslovakia. It was typical of Nazi politics, however, that Bohle, who had originally articulated the idea, had little to do with its implementation in Czechoslovakia. In this sense he was a man slightly ahead of his time, as well as a bit naïve about how power politics in the Third Reich worked. There is no sign that the führer paid the slightest attention to the plan when Bohle originally formulated it; moreover, development of such a fifth column would come not as a result of action on the part of a centralized Germandom agency, but as a by-product of the friction between a wide range of competing organizations over a long period of time.

Despite Bohle's plans and claims to power, then, the AO never achieved anything remotely approaching a *Gleichschaltung* of Germandom work abroad; and as time went by, Bohle himself realized the naïveté of his concept and adjusted the goals of the AO correspondingly. Meanwhile, however, the struggle with the VDA was very real and critical: the etatist thinking inherent in Bohle's projected program for the AO represented a real danger to the traditionalist

Volkstum ideas of men like Steinacher—and both Bohle and the traditionalists recognized this. To men like Steinacher and the Haushofers, Bohle's Reich-oriented concept of the *Volk* and Germandom was completely unintelligible.[47]

In addition to these two major types of Reich-based organizations involved in Germandom work—the traditionalists as represented by Steinacher (VDA-VR) and the National Socialists as typified by Bohle (AO)—there was yet another kind of group involved in the field of ethnic German politics. These were the small, irredentist organizations outside the official Nazi party structure which advocated a more radical approach to work with ethnic Germans than the larger, official NS groups like the AO. Not all the members of these radical organizations were members of the NSDAP, although many were. An extraordinarily large percentage were émigrés, refugees from the various German ethnic groups who had been forced to flee their homeland, often because of their radical irredentist views. It was especially the presence of these émigrés that gave such a radical tone to the programs of this third type of Germandom organization. One reason for this radical influence was the fact that the refugees were concerned primarily with their home areas and the annexation of these areas to the Reich. They pursued these irredentist objectives, disregarding the temporary exigencies of official National Socialist policies. The fact they did not share in the responsibility of power within the Reich party structure also meant that the émigrés were in a position to be radical about Reich Germandom policies in a way which leaders of large, official Nazi organizations could not.

Because so many of them were living in close proximity to the Reich, the Sudeten Germans were especially strongly represented and active in the radical Germandom organizations. Their influence, moreover, was essential to the independent functioning of the smaller, relatively powerless, radical Germandom groups working within the Reich. The Sudeten Germans, in contrast to the Polish, Rumanian, and other German *Volksgruppen*, were the only ethnic German population which could boast of an indigenous National Socialist movement with a tradition separate from that of the Reich. After all, there had been a National Socialist movement in Bohemia long before Hitler organized his party in Germany.[48] Given the lack of clear ideological guidelines in Germandom work, the Sudeten Germans who were in the radical groups could advance ideas and pursue policies different from the official Reich line and still legitimately claim to be working for National Socialism. They added immeasurably to the already existent confusion in Germandom work by advocating "National Socialist" principles, which either had never been a part of the NSDAP program or had been so but were now conveniently sacrificed to the needs of tactical expediency. Despite the fact they were on the periphery of power in the Third Reich, these small, radical groups brought no end of trouble and embarrassment to the regime. Their ill-considered and amateurish ventures into irredentist politics threatened the peaceful image which the Hitler regime was initially presenting to the world and complicated the already complex rivalry between traditionalist Germandom groups and the official NS organizations.

It may seem incredible that such small groups could be capable of any degree of disruptive power, especially in a totalitarian society. When compared with the great empire builders of the Third Reich, these radicals and their organizations were quite minor. But even an obscure personality, if supposedly speaking or acting with the authorization of an important one, can exert considerable influence or cause a great deal of trouble. This was especially true in Nazi Germany, where men of comparatively low rank or office, but with good personal connections, were quite often given virtually unlimited power to carry out special assignments—sometimes in competition with other individuals or groups armed with similar authority. It frequently happened, then, in the area of Germandom politics as elsewhere, that comparatively minor figures would claim to have special powers from the führer or from some other Nazi leader. These claims were particularly important to the small, radical Germandom groups. Because they had no real power or normal legitimate authority to back them up, their claims to special sanctions were important weapons that enabled these radical groups to pursue their independent irredentist goals. Both in their method of competition and in their independent policies, these radical splinter organizations were an embarrassment to the National Socialist regime. Their loud claims of special authority from high places in the Reich, especially when combined with irredentist activity, often threatened to seriously compromise the NS regime, which officially denied any aspirations of annexing areas with German settlements and which tried to obscure any ties between official agencies and organizations cultivating contacts with ethnic German groups. Neither the claims nor the activities of the radical groups went unnoticed in countries with German minorities and the ensuing protests were an annoyance to the Hitler government.

One particular *Volkstum* group, the *Sudetendeutscher Heimatbund* (SHB), is representative of the small, radical organizations within the Reich that attempted to exert influence in Germandom work. Its leaders are typical of the political parvenus who could arise in the freewheeling atmosphere during the early years of the Third Reich; its irredentist activities are characteristic of the trouble such a radical organization could cause. The SHB had originally been formed in Germany soon after World War I, when it had become apparent that the three-and-a-half million Germans in the Historic Provinces and Slovakia were going permanently to become citizens of the new Czechoslovakian state.[49] Although ostensibly organized to provide relief care for the Sudeten German refugees who had fled from Czechoslovakia to Germany or Austria, the SHB soon revealed itself politically as a vocal irredentist organization. Its leaders frequently staged rallies at which they demanded the secession of German settlement areas from Czechoslovakia. These noisy calls for irredenta caused great embarrassment to the Weimar government, which tried again and again to counsel moderation.[50] Because many of the SHB leaders were former Sudeten Germans who had been politically active in Czechoslovakia, there was no lack of contacts between the SHB and the German speaking citizens of Czechoslovakia. Frequent trips across the border by SHB members for consultations with Sudeten Germans were bound to increase Czech suspicions and to exacerbate relations between the two countries.[51] The Czechoslovak government frequently protested the irredentist nature of the SHB and the "traitorous" activities of its members.[52]

After the Nazi seizure of power in Germany, the SHB finally appeared to have a chance to realize its irredentist goals. Hitler, after all, had spoken of a *Grossreich* of all Germans, which presumably meant that he would be in sympathy with the SHB's call for annexation of the Sudetenland to Germany. Hitler was soon to indicate that at this particular moment irredentism was the last sort of political action he wanted. Meanwhile, mistakenly anticipating his support, SHB leaders laid plans to expand the activities of their organization. Early in 1933 the SHB intensified its recruiting efforts by writing letters to the various *Polizeipräsidien* requesting lists of Czechoslovak citizens registered in each area of the Reich.[53] Neither the Foreign Office, nor the Gestapo objected.[54] The SHB also requested financial aid from the Interior Ministry. *Reichsminister* Wilhelm Frick replied that the money budgeted for 1932 had been exhausted; however, if he received sufficient funds for 1933, he would extend to the SHB a special *Reichsbeihilfe*, the sum of which he had yet to determine.[55]

The SHB really only began to achieve importance, however, after the appearance of Hans Krebs in Germany in October of 1933. Krebs, former leader of the National Socialist party in Czechoslovakia (DNSAP), had fled to Germany after the Prague government had threatened legal action to terminate the political activities of the DNSAP and to jail many of its members. Both the DNSAP and its conservative ally, the German National party (DNP), had been dissolved by their own members before the Czech government took action, and many of these groups' leaders fled the country.[56] Once in Germany, Krebs, using his National Socialist credentials and his contacts with Reich NSDAP people, found a position in Frick's Interior Ministry, which allowed him to exert great influence on the development of the Sudeten question. From his post in the ministry, Krebs was to have a base from which to launch attacks on the moderate, non-Nazi leaders of the Sudeten German party in subsequent years. Seeking to broaden his power base, Krebs also turned his attention to the *Sudetendeutscher Heimatbund.* Under his tutelage, the organization was strengthened and extended to the point where it was becoming the central agency for all Czechoslovak citizens of German background living in the Reich. It numbered among its tasks the creation of a net of confidantes within Czechoslovakia and the collection of funds to help Sudeten refugees. The organization also compiled a central directory of all Sudeten Germans living in the Reich as a prerequisite to issuing an identification card proving ethnic German origin (*Deutschstämmigkeitsausweis*).[57]

The SHB continued to expand its activities for the better part of a year after Hitler came to power. It might have continued to do so had not two developments shown the limitations that the Nazi regime put on the exercise of political free enterprise. First, the SHB leaders continued their irredentist policies to the point where they represented an increasing embarrassment to the National Socialist government which was stressing its acceptance of the status quo in Eastern and Central Europe. The Sudeten question was the furthest thing from Hitler's mind in 1933 and he wanted no difficulties that might earn the animosity of the Czechs. Secondly, in addition to this continued irredentist activity, one of the SHB leaders, Hanns Beer, overreached himself in the competition for power and influence in the field of Germandom. The official response to the SHB's excesses and the Beer's in-fighting showed how very far such a group or an individual could go before the NS leadership would put a halt to their independent activities.

The brief political career of Hanns Beer, *Treuhänder* ("trustee") of the *Sudetendeutscher Heimatbund*, is an outstanding example of the political career opportunities opened by the Nazi seizure of power and the limitations placed on how one could pursue that career. If one knew the right people; if one spoke the right ideological language and exhibited those attacks of energy typical of National Socialist leaders; if one were careful not to compromise the führer's public policy by ill-advised actions and public utterances, one could go far in Nazi leadership circles. But loyalty to the wrong people, a militant speech that received too much publicity, or incompetence combined with either of these things could put a quick end to a seemingly promising career. Hanns Beer did just enough of the right things well enough to rise meteorically in Germandom circles and, just as quickly, did enough of the wrong things to end that career precipitously.

Beer originally came from the NS circles around Rosenberg. In 1933 he appears in the leadership of the *Bund Deutscher Osten,* the umbrella organization created by Rosenberg to extend his influence over groups involved with East European Germandom.[58] In October of 1933, as part of Rosenberg's attempt to subordinate all of the smaller, specialized *Volkstum* organizations to the BDO, Beer was commissioned to take over the Reich trusteeship of the *Sudetendeutscher Heimatbund.*[59] Unlike many potential policy-makers, Beer was keen enough to realize that wherever its ultimate sympathies might lie, the Hitler regime needed a period of quiescence to consolidate its power and would look no more favorably on a vocal, irredentist organization than had the Weimar Republic. With this in mind, Beer set out to build a career. On November 4, 1933 he paid a visit to the Foreign Office, where he made a most favorable impression.[60] He agreed with officials that there were far too many "little men" (*kleine Geister*) in the Sudeten organization who thought they could make foreign policy. These people would have to be brought under control. Furthermore, there was far too much wild, purposeless journeying of all sorts on the part of Germans into Czechoslovakia; this would have to be stopped. Similarly, the flow of young Sudeten Germans into the Reich to join the SS or *Sturmabteilung* (SA) or to work in the labor camps would have to be stemmed. Keenly aware of the face of respectability that the new order was turning to the world, Beer cleverly pointed out that since *Gleichschaltung* had started, the Czech government was interpreting *all* connections between the Reich and the Czechoslovak state as official ones. This gave the Prague government ample opportunity to accuse the new regime in Germany of interference in the internal affairs of its neighbors. To avoid such a risk, Beer demanded that control of all relations with the Sudeten Germans be placed with an agency experienced in *Volkstumspolitik,* which would have the authority to decide dictatorially on measures to be or not to be taken. He left little doubt that this proposed organization should be his own, the SHB. When questioned about a formal Czech complaint about SHB irredentist activities, Beer responded that most of the incidents cited took place under the Weimar Republic. He, Beer, would move decisively against anyone who tried to interfere with Hitler's peaceful foreign policy.[61]

The very fact that such an interview could take place is some indication of the enormous changes that came with the National Socialist seizure of power. In another time, the spectacle of a man like Beer, totally unknown and with dubious credentials, discussing foreign policy with a senior member of the Foreign Office, much less making demands that a certain area of foreign policy formulation be put under his dictatorial control, would have been utterly inconceivable. As things were in 1933, Beer made a very favorable impression. But Beer was also astute enough to realize that this was far less than what it took to build an empire. Without an independent power base, the only way to get ahead was by cultivating still other people who did have one. Again he did not hesitate to turn to the very top. In an ingratiating letter to Willy Meerwald, departmental director in the Reich Chancellory and personal *Referent* to Hitler, Beer requested an audience with the führer himself. In the neofeudal world of National Socialist society, a position of trust with Hitler was a *carte blanche* to a potentially brilliant career. After all, the nearly absolute power of the *Gauleiter* in their own territory was based almost exclusively on their personal relationship with Hitler. An interview with the führer could be the beginning of such a relationship. Conceivably, then, Beer's big moment had come: he was informed that he could speak with Hitler on January 18, 1934.[62]

But Beer's interview, for some unknown reason, did not take place as scheduled. Perhaps it had come to Hitler's attention or the attention of someone close to him, what Beer had really been doing. For if it were not yet clear in January of 1934, by April there could be little doubt that Hanns Beer was overreaching himself. His attempt to see Hitler appears to have been only one in a series of steps to go over the head of his patron, Rosenberg, and achieve a power position of his own. Rosenberg may not have been one of the most powerful paladins in the Third Reich, but he was nonetheless someone to reckon with. Moreover, personal fealty and comradeship were highly prized qualities in the Nazi scale of values; one had to be extremely careful when changing loyalties. On April 28, Beer again directed a letter to Meerwald, this time reviewing the previous year's work.[63] He complained that after a whole year, Rosenberg's attempts to reach a "total solution" to the problem of "coordinating" Germandom work had failed. Although the *Bund Deutscher Osten* had long since absorbed the *Ostverbände,* the host of small organizations which concerned themselves with contacts between German ethnic groups in Eastern Europe and the Reich, these groups were still showing a great deal of political independence. Beer blamed unnamed, insubordinate figures within these organizations, "me-too-National Socialists," for turning the BDO into a meaningless little "borderlands club." Now, he claimed, these same people are working to undermine his control of the *Sudetendeutscher Heimatbund* and to cast aspersions on his good name.

It was perhaps not clear to Beer yet, but with the rise of the *Auslandsorganisation* and the *Volksdeutscher Rat* during these months, Rosenberg and his BDO were distinctly on the defensive. Beer would eventually be squeezed out in a battle for competencies where he could hardly hope to compete—even if he abandoned Rosenberg's tutelage.[64] Once again in May of 1934, Beer tried to gain access to Hitler and was denied it. Referred to Hess, he was also refused a hearing there.[65] On May 31, SA-*Oberführer* Kersken divested Beer of his office and replaced him with Dr. Triebel, SS-*Hauptsturmführer* and Hess's deputy for the *Ostverbände.* In the course of his appeals for reinstatement, it became clear that Beer had failed in his aspirations to power in the Third Reich largely because he had overreached himself, had allowed himself to be used by the wrong people for irredentist purposes, and had demonstrated general incompetence in the exercise of his office. In a letter to Meerwald, Kersken explained the reasons for Beer's dismissal.[66] Beer, Kersken stated, is a political swindler who, by claiming friendships and close connections with high officials, is only trying to satisfy his own ambition; he is unworthy to head any political group in the Third Reich. Although forbidden any kind of independence in foreign policy, he soon let himself be used by Hans Krebs, who was pursuing his own political goals. By allowing Krebs to speak at a rally in Dresden and by naming Dr. Karl Viererbl—a Sudeten German refugee well known to the Czechs as a pan-German and an irredentist—to the post of *Bundesführer* of the SHB, Beer was acting directly against Hess's orders. Moreover, Beer was guilty of the rankest sort of nepotism and mismanagement in office. In four-and-a-half months he ran up a deficit of 20,000 marks, which he tried to redeem by peddling bad pictures of leading Nazi personalities. He had not been, as he claimed, a party member since 1922, nor did he ever have a *carte blanche* from Rosenberg to make all sorts of political deals. His main motivation, Kersken concludes, seems to have been personal prestige and money.

The surprising thing about the long indictment against Beer is not the degree of incompetency, dishonesty, personal ambition, and greed exhibited by this incipient representative of National Socialism. These qualities seem to be present in many of the competitors for power during this period of political freewheeling, perhaps tempered from time to time by quantities of idealism and decency. The surprising thing is rather the degree of latitude allowed in the pursuit of high office and the failure of the system, totalitarian as it was, to impose the most basic standards on its aspirants to power. Within certain limits, the chief of which seemed to be the demand to pay lip service to the system, an astounding amount of political free enterprise could and did flourish. Once an individual had pledged allegiance to the system and had begun to be admitted to even the fringes of the political power center, it was possible to deviate quite a distance from the established norm—both in personal and policy matters—before feeling the disapprobation of that system. Whether Bohle's AO, Ribbentrop's *Büro*, Rosenberg's *Aussenpolitisches Amt*, or the various organizations under Hess's tutelage, all were characterized not by an insistence on experience or technical ability, but by the importance of chance personal acquaintance, political amateurism, lack of binding guidelines, and an intense competition for power and empire.[67] Beer may have been more dishonest than some and less competent than others, but he was by no means unique among the National Socialist leadership involved in Germandom work.

With Beer's departure from politics, the *Sudetendeutscher Heimatbund* continued to function as a power base for Hans Krebs. Its irredentist activities were toned down to a great extent, although it played a role through Krebs in the eventual victory of the more radical NS wing of the Sudeten German party over the more moderate traditionalist faction. Eventually, like so many other organizations, it was to be absorbed by an SS-directed organization, the *Volksdeutsche Mittelstelle*. In the meantime, the SHB, along with many similar organizations like the *Bund Deutscher Osten* and the *Bund der Auslandsdeutschen* (BdA), continued to exist with a kind of nuisance value.[68] Amid the greater competition of such agencies as the AO and the VDA-VR complex, the *Heimatbund* along with many equivalent groups served as independent outlets for the personal and political ambitions of a host of minor personalities and represented one of many independent variables in the complex problem of Germandom work.

By now it may seem less surprising that in a discussion of various *Volkstum* groups and their influence on foreign policy formation, the very institution that in most countries and at most times plays a dominant role in foreign policy questions, the Foreign Office, should be given only secondary importance. Among the Reich groups competing with one another to shape foreign policy toward the various German settlements abroad, the *Auswärtiges Amt* played a very ambivalent, vacillating role.[69] The Wilhelmstrasse was, from the first days of the new Reich, an institution on the defensive, not the offensive. As such, it became increasingly an object, rather than a driving force in the area of foreign policy formulation relating to the various ethnic groups. Until 1938, especially during the period in which Hitler stressed peaceful relations with the rest of the world, the officials in the Foreign Office did succeed to some extent in holding their own in the battle of competencies with aggressive up-and-coming organizations like the AO—but only because the long experience and expertise of the men in the Wilhelmstrasse were necessary to the new rulers of the Reich, who were themselves inexperienced in the niceties of keeping up good formal relationships with Germany's neighbors. Increasingly, however, the Foreign Office lost one area of competence after another to the more aggressive NS agencies. Goebbels's Propaganda Ministry took over press and information functions formerly controlled by the Foreign Office; interlopers like Ribbentrop and Göring interfered constantly in matters of diplomacy, often not even informing the appropriate Foreign Office official of their actions. The cultural department of the Foreign Office, which had once coordinated a great deal of Germandom work, was forced to give up more and more of its prerogatives to rivals like the AO and the VDA-VR. It was largely this defensiveness, the need constantly to be on guard against the loss of one area of competency after another, that put the AA into such an ambiguous position with regard to foreign policy in general and Germandom in particular.

When the Nazi regime first came to power, it was an open question whether the new leaders of Germany could or would work with the traditional *Auswärtiges Amt.* Militating against any cooperation was the fact that the National Socialists simply did not trust the civil servants of the Foreign Office. The officials in the Wilhelmstrasse were regarded as conservative, if not reactionary, representatives of another era, who should be allowed to have little influence on Germany's future revolutionary foreign policy. Hitler himself had nothing but contempt for foreign service officials. Among his associates he referred to them as bumbling, inept bureaucrats, no more talented than the caricatures of civil servants so popular in comic operas. It was no accident, he once said, that diplomats were depicted as "bumbling" in operettas; for if a father had several sons, he would let the "most capable take over the estate or do something otherwise useful." Only the one "who came out short on brains would be sent into the diplomatic service." [70] Such stereotyping and mistrust were further complicated by the generation gap that existed between the new leadership and the Foreign Office personnel. The average age of the AA officials was some years higher than that of the NS hierarchy. [71]

Despite these grounds for hostility, the antagonism between the Foreign Office and the Hitler government should not be overestimated as a cause of AA weakness. There were also many factors that actually furthered cooperation between the two groups. The Nazi leaders quickly recognized that if Germany were to pursue a peaceful foreign policy in order to relieve the anxieties of critics abroad, it would not be advisable to dispense with the services of the men in the Wilhelmstrasse. As long as any kind of normal relations existed between Germany and its neighbors, a condition that required the execution of many technical and legal procedures, the diplomats were useful. This willingness on the part of the Nazi leadership to tolerate a necessary evil was matched on the side of the civil servants by a large degree of conformity to the needs and demands of the new order. It was all too easy to ignore some of the more nefarious aspects of National Socialism and to conduct "business as usual." Gradually this reluctant tolerance on both sides was to evolve into actual cooperation between party officials and the staff of the Foreign Office.

Cooperation between the Foreign Office and the NS leadership eventually began to develop mainly because AA officials gradually became convinced that their own foreign policy goals were not so different after all from those which Hitler was publicly professing. Despite the aggressive image he had projected prior to assuming power, during the early period of his regime Hitler was making every effort to project a peaceful, moderate image in the area of foreign affairs. Moreover, his stand on important international issues seemed remarkably similar to that of the Foreign Office itself: both were anti-Marxist; both demanded the dismantlement of the Versailles system and an expanded German *Grossraum*.[72] With regard to Czechoslovakia, most of the diplomats saw this area as a part of the German sphere of influence, if not hegemony, and projected Germany's economic, if not political dominance of this part of the Danube basin.[73] Of course, the conservatives would have stopped short of war in the pursuit of these aims, and certainly would have shunned the gangster tactics later used by Hitler. The fact remains, however, that during the first several years of Hitler's rule, there were few occasions when Constantin von Neurath, the foreign minister, would have disagreed with Hitler's foreign policy.[74] Whatever doubts the Foreign Office might have had about Hitler's former aggressive demeanor, they were rapidly assuaged by his numerous peaceful speeches and public assurances. Eventually, most of the Foreign Office officials were able to swallow what scruples they may have had about the new regime and give their full professional cooperation to the NS leadership.

Although the Foreign Office gradually began to serve the Hitler regime, this does not alter the fact that in the field of Germandom policy, the AA continued to play a most ambiguous role. After all, Hitler himself was not initially concerned with this problem and allowed a large number of competing organizations to pursue their very different ideological goals. With no official guidelines to follow regarding the Germandom question, the Foreign Office vacillated considerably in its reactions to the various groups attempting to influence foreign policy regarding the ethnic Germans. This is particularly apparent in the way the Foreign Office responded to the rivalry between the VDA-VR and NS organizations like the AO. At times, the AA worked with one faction; at times, with the other. On the one hand, being predominantly conservative themselves, foreign service officials tended to sympathize more readily with men like Steinacher, speaking about preserving the cultural integrity of German ethnic groups, as opposed to those NS officials trying to "coordinate" and organize these groups to conform with National Socialist principles. For this reason the Foreign Office frequently cooperated with Steinacher and the Haushofers in their various Germandom programs, as they had done before the Nazis came to power.[75] On the other hand, the VDA-VR claim to complete dominance in the Germandom question represented a competency threat to the Foreign Office, particularly to the *Kulturabteilung* which was supposedly responsible for relations with German ethnic groups. This was clearly a challenge which the AA had to meet. Whatever its ideological stance, the Foreign Office was a bureaucracy and bureaucracies react to jurisdictional challenges as a bull to a red flag. When, for example, the VR showed an interest in funds used to underwrite ethnic German groups—funds which were jointly administered by the Foreign Office and the Finance Ministry—both of these agencies reacted strongly to this threat to their authority. Officials from the two ministries denied that the VR had any claim to the funds at all. Moreover, they also denied that the VR had any competency over their respective agencies either in Germandom work: the function of the VR should be nothing more than advisory.[76]

Because of Bohle's attempts to gain authority over Reich Germans abroad, relations between his AO and the Foreign Office were initially bad, but as time went on, they were to improve considerably. Bohle's position had grown too powerful to assail frontally and Bohle's notorious enmity against Steinacher and the VDA made him a natural ally of the Foreign Office when competency problems arose between the Wilhelmstrasse and the VDA-VR circle. It was to the advantage of AA officials to choose their priorities carefully and to cooperate with whatever agency offered the best alliance at any given moment: competency threats generally were treated as more dangerous than ideological differences. Despite all attempts to hold on to traditional rights and prerogatives, however, the Foreign Office found itself increasingly on the defensive. Although it kept its personnel more or less intact until 1938, its authority and functions in ethnic German questions were gradually challenged and usurped by the more dynamic Germandom organizations. It was only one of many Reich agencies involved in formulating foreign policy relating to ethnic Germans, and it was by no means the most important: eventually it functioned more and more as a tool at the disposal of other, more powerful Germandom groups within the Reich.

Thus, as the second year of the National Socialist regime began, the area of Germandom work was anything but "coordinated." A plethora of large and small organizations, with a wide spectrum of goals and functions, still competed with one another for the right to influence Reich foreign policy regarding ethnic German populations.

III

Sudeten Germandom Organizations

AT the end of the First World War, Germans in the Reich and in the Sudetenland turned to Germandom work for much the same reason—as an outlet for political frustration. Both Reich and Sudeten Germans were disillusioned that four years of enormous sacrifice during the war had produced nothing but defeat; moreover, both were faced with the loss of traditional monarchies and were forced to cope with new, alien political systems, which did not command their loyalties. But although Germany had been defeated in war, it was still a powerful nation. It had lost some territory, but it had not suffered the complete partition that would have destroyed its very identity as a state. Even if Reich Germans felt threatened to some degree by *Einkreisung* ("encirclement") on the part of their neighbors, they could, with a population of eighty million, still feel secure as a people. For the Sudeten Germans, however, the question of territorial and ethnic integrity was more immediate and urgent. Austria-Hungary had not merely lost territory in 1918, it had ceased to exist. As a consequence, Sudeten Germans suddenly had no territorial identity, not even in the watered down form of a provincial autonomy: they had become a scattered minority within the new Czechoslovak state. Not only had they lost their territorial identity, they also felt that their whole existence as an ethnic group was gravely threatened. From their perspective, it appeared that the Czechs could and would use their position of dominance in order eventually to "Czech-ify" the Germans living within the new Czechoslovak state.

This dual threat, territorial and ethnic, gave Sudeten German involvement in *Volkstum* work an entirely different thrust and intensity than Germandom work as it was pursued in the Reich.[1] Within the Reich Germandom work was just one means of expressing political dissatisfaction with the Weimar Republic, one way of showing that one's loyalties lay outside the System. Depending on the degree of radicalism an individual advocated, it was possible to use *Volkstum* work and the concept of a German *Volk* community either to strengthen cultural ties between ethnic Germans and the Reich, or to dream of an expanded Greater Germany, which would incorporate German ethnic groups abroad into the Reich itself. There were many other Reich organizations, however, that tackled the issue of political dissent more directly than the *Volkstum* groups with their utopian dreams and nebulous programs. Reich Germans had the real opportunity of altering, reforming, or even overthrowing the existing political system: by participating in orthodox opposition parties or by joining a wide variety of subversive groups like the *Freikorps, "Black" Reichswehr,* and the *Schutz- und Trutzbund.*[2] In the Sudetenland, many of these forms of dissent were simply not feasible. As a heavily outnumbered minority, the Sudeten Germans could scarcely join military or para-military organizations in the hope of capturing the state for their own purposes. For many Sudeten nationalists orthodox politics also seemed to be an unsatisfactory outlet for political dissent. While there was a spectrum of parties to choose from, at least one of them (DNP) officially rejecting the state, many Germans discarded the whole idea of poltiical action in the belief that a government dominated by the Czechs would condemn minority parties to a position of permanent, impotent opposition. It would not be until 1926 that any Sudeten party could bring itself to participate in government; no wonder, then, that so many individuals turned to unorthodox schemes outside the mainstream of official political life in order to express dissatisfaction with their lot. In the Sudetenland, then, Germandom work was not just one of many outlets for expressing political dissent. Many Sudeten Germans in the nationalist camp saw in ethnic unity their only means of survival as a people.

One such Germandom activity pursued over the years was the attempt to found a central "umbrella" organization which would represent all Sudeten Germans regardless of class or party affiliation.[3] It was hoped that if the social, economic, and political life of the Sudeten population could somehow find expression through such a central organization, then the Germans in Czechoslovakia would finally have the united front necessary for their survival as an ethnic group. From as early as the summer of 1919, when Rudolf Lodgman von Auen, Sudeten German delegate in Paris and *Landeshauptmann* of the short-lived province of *Deutschböhmen,* called for a *Nationalrat*

("National Council") to deliberate the fate of Germans in the new
Czechoslovak state, to as late as 1932, when Othmar Kallina, leader of
the Nationalist party, suggested a *Notparlament* ("Emergency Parliament"), Sudeten Germans in the nationalist camp tried again and
again to form a centralized organization to represent their whole
people. Invariably they had little success, mainly for the quite
understandable reason that the existing political parties on the Right,
although approving in principle of such a unity organization, were
unwilling to relinquish any of their political authority to such a body:
they had too high a stake in the existing political structure to
surrender their power and identity. The umbrella organizations also
lacked the kind of mass following which would have assured them any
real effectiveness. Particularly those of the young "front generation"
returning from the war were so completely disillusioned with politics
that they would not have thrown their support behind even such
utopian political schemes.

Still other Sudeten Germandom organizations were the so-called
protective associations, or *Schutzverbände,* originally developed during the nationality struggle at the turn of the century.[4] These
traditional nonparty organizations appealed primarily to the older,
prewar generation. But the main efforts in Germandom work after
1918 were not carried out by either political parties or these
traditional societies, but by the young Sudeten German population—
particularly the former frontline soldiers. Although initially apolitical,
these young men were actively searching for other ways to foster their
newly found folk nationalism. In doing so they both gave a new spirit
and ethos to familiar organizations and developed entirely new
organizational forms. Some turned to the familiar youth movement,
the *Wandervogel,* as an outlet (*see* Appendix C).[5] Before the war, the
Sudeten youth had used the *Wandervogel* in their adolescent revolt
against the strictures and hypocricies they had encountered in
bourgeois society: now, in the postwar years they gave new meaning
to the movement, seeing in it a framework within which to define and
build a national ethnic community. The *Jugendbewegung* (or *Böhmerlandbewegung,* as it was now rechristened) lent itself well to these
tasks, for in its positive aspects it had always been animated by the
same kind of drive for moral and spiritual renewal that young Sudeten
Germans were now positing as a prerequisite for ethnic unity and
survival. The language of the reborn youth movement was a peculiar

mixture, combining the terminology of the prewar *Wandervogel* with that of the frontline soldier—a reflection of the two formative experiences in these young men's lives. The moral stance within the context of a cultural renewal came from the earlier youth movement; but the strident tone was basically military. Youth was to be the "advance column for the renewal of life in the new era"; it would bring a "general spiritual-moral rearmament of the people." The *Böhmerland* movement was important because of the inspiration it gave to a large number of youth groups to make the idea of *Volksgemeinschaft* their guiding principle.[6] Among the academic youth, for example, the *Bund der böhmerländischen Freischaren* was formed in the university towns of Prague and Brünn (Brno) to replace the old style fraternities, which cared more about drinking and dueling than about spiritual renewal or the fate of the ethnic community.

The movement toward ethnic unity began to acquire institutional roots not only among urban, university youth, but also in the ranks of the rural, peasant youth. And not surprisingly so. For it was often in the rural areas, along the *Sprachgrenze,* where the nationality struggle was fought out day to day. Peasant Germandom organizations were formed in all of the Historic Provinces. In Moravia and Silesia, Franz Künzel—later to be an important figure in the Henlein movement—organized the *Landständische Jungmannschaft* which, as its name implies, advocated unity within the framework of a classless, preindustrial society of estates. Perhaps the most successful of the peasant young organizations was the *Bauernvolkshochschule* at Bad Ullersdorf in Moravia. This school, the best known of such educational experiments, combined practical courses in farming methods with the ethos of *Volk* unity and moral renewal. Friedrich Bürger, who would become Henlein's representative in Berlin, was one of the initiators of this institution. The *Bund der deutschen Landjugend* played a similar role among the young peasantry in Bohemia.[7]

Another Germandom movement—primarily literary and ethnographic—developed parallel to the youth movement: the so-called *Heimatbewegung,* centered in the north Bohemian town of Reichenberg.[8] Through research into the *Volk* institutions of the Sudeten homeland, a number of young scholars hoped to make their people aware and proud of their folk heritage. Once this pride and folk consciousness had been developed, it would be but a short step to proclaiming the necessity of unity as a means of preserving a threatened tradition. The *Heimat* movement gained momentum as more and more young Germans delved into local history and folklore, making the results of their work available to a fairly large reading public through cheap popular editions and through the establishment of local libraries. Adult education programs and vocational schools were further institutions through which this material was disseminated. Emil Lehmann and Erich Gierach, who had both come out of the *Wandervogel*, were prime movers in the program to use *Heimat* research to educate a broad base of the Sudeten Germans toward the idea of unity in the *Volksgemeinschaft*. In 1923 Gierach founded the *Bücherei der Deutschen* ("Library of the Germans") in Reichenberg, an institution which—in collaboration with a whole network of sympathetic publishers and book dealers—became the largest depository of *Heimat* literature in Czechoslovakia. Numerous other organizations, along the lines of the traditional *Vereine*, were founded during the early twenties, all devoted to furthering the idea of Sudeten German unity.

Taken separately these various organizations and movements were relatively small and unimportant, but together they formed an extensive network of agencies that educated the masses of Sudeten Germans to their role in the original settlement of the Historic Provinces and spread the ideas of unity and *Volksgemeinschaft* as a solution to the contemporary problems of the German people in the new Czechoslovakian state. By the time the larger, politically oriented protagonists in Sudeten Germandom work came to the fore in the late 1920s, these smaller organizations were functioning as catalysts, providing an ethos and serving as useful recruiting grounds for the more powerful groups struggling for influence among the Sudeten German population. The smaller organizations served one other purpose as well, although their supporters were quite possibly unaware of it: they had laid the groundwork for the overt politicization of Sudeten Germandom work, which took place later in the twenties. This may seem ironic in light of the fact that people like the young founders of the *Böhmerlandbewegung* had taken great pride in being apolitical; but as was the case in the Reich, *Volkstumsarbeit* was always by its very nature implicitly political. Ultimately, no less than their counterparts in Germany, Sudeten Germandom advocates found that in the course of their day-to-day activities, they were also being consciously drawn into the political arena. This pull toward the political reached its apogee in the Sudetenland by the early 1930s. By that time it is possible to speak of "Sudeten *Volkstumspolitik,*" characterized by much the same alignment that prevailed in the Reich during the same period. There were the National Socialists, initially organized into a political party, whose role corresponded roughly to that of the official Nazi *Volkstum* organizations in Germany like Bohle's AO; there were the traditionalists—men like Steinacher and the younger VDA generation in the Reich, "conservative revolution-aries" who hoped to use National Socialism in order to achieve their own brand of national regeneration; and, finally, there were a number of radical NS fringe groups analogous to the *Sudetendeutscher Heimatbund* in Germany. But for all the similarities there were significant differences, too, both in the nature of the protagonists and in the context in which they confronted each other.

Despite the increasing influence which the Reich NS exerted on the Sudeten Nazi movement over the years, the National Socialists in the Sudetenland are not to be unqualifiedly equated with those in the Hitler movement.[9] For most of its existence the DNSAP was not simply a branch of the Hitler party, but an independent party with its own longstanding traditions and with problems often quite unlike those faced by the Reich party.

The National Socialist party (DNSAP) in the Sudeten areas had its origins in the nationality conflicts of the closing decades of the nineteenth century. Accompanying the rapid industrialization of Bohemia, there was a large influx of Czech laborers who were used to a lower standard of living than the German population of the area and who were willing to accept far lower wages than the average Sudeten worker. Many Sudeten Germans, finding their jobs threat-ened by this cheap Czech labor force and witnessing the failure of orthodox social democracy to remedy the situation, left the Social Democratic party and formed their own nationalist trade unions. A number of these groups gradually coalesced into a larger organization, the *Mährisch-Trübauer Verband.* This new association, named after the town in which its headquarters was located, was headed by Ferdinand Burschofsky, a Moravian typesetter, and Hans Knirsch, a textile journeyman. By 1902 the organization had gained considerable strength, including more than 17,000 members organized into 136 branches.[10] Many of its leaders, however, especially Hans Knirsch, felt that a trade union association was too narrow a base from which effectively to implement this new combination of nationalist and socialist ideals. What was really needed, they concluded, was a political party. Thus, on August 15, 1904, a number of delegates met in the Bohemian town of Trautenau and proclaimed the founding of the *Deutsche Arbeiterpartei* ("German Workers' party").[11] During the remaining years of the monarchy, the DAP remained a small, but vocal political organization. In May of 1918, in a congress at Vienna, the party was reconstituted as the *Deutsche Nationalsozialistische Arbeiterpartei* (DNSAP, or "German National Socialist Workers' party"), and after the exclusion of the Sudeten areas from the postwar Austrian state, a Czechoslovakian branch of the party was formed as an independent entity.[12]

This whole development was pre–Hitlerian. The National Socialist movement in Bohemia was in existence fully twenty-eight years before Adolf Hitler entered politics—a seniority that later gave the Bohemian movement a degree of integrity vis-à-vis the Reich party that NS groups in other countries frequently did not enjoy. It was this integrity, for example, that prompted the DNSAP leader, Rudolf Jung, to challenge Hitler himself as premier ideologist of the movement. As Jung was fond of pointing out, his treatise *Der Nationale Sozialismus* had appeared years before Hitler's *Mein Kampf.*[13] Vestiges of this integrity and autonomy remained, even after the dissolution of the DNSAP in 1933 after Hitler had come to power in Germany. It meant that former DNSAP leaders who fled Czechoslovakia and subsequently tried to build power positions for themselves in the Reich in order to influence *Volkstumspolitik* had an extra power lever. After all, it was not entirely meaningless in the Third Reich to have fought for National Socialism during the dark years of the *Kampfzeit,* wherever the scene of that struggle might have been. Men like Hans Krebs and Rudolf Jung played this advantage for all it was worth.[14] As former high ranking members of the DNSAP, they laid claim to leadership positions in Germandom circles in the Reich and to special influence regarding Czechoslovakia, where they still had contacts.

The early development of the NS party in Bohemia not only gave it a certain degree of integrity vis-à-vis the Reich movement, it also meant that the Sudeten party would take a much different form than its Reich counterpart. This difference, too, would not be without importance in the development of the Germandom struggle. Hitler's movement, created as it was out of the war experience, fell—almost from the start—into a totalitarian-dictatorial mold. The DNSAP, on the other hand, kept a strong radical democratic cast, which reflected its development in the peaceful, prewar era.[15] If the Reich Nazis could claim descent from Georg von Schönerer, the Austrian pan-Germanist, then the Sudeten National Socialists could point to their origins in the revolt *against* Schönerer: a revolt which claimed, quite rightly, that Schönerer had forgotten his earlier democratic ideas and had come to concentrate more and more on a *völkisch* appeal to the middle class and on obscure Nordic cults.[16] This democratic heritage by no means made the DNSAP a liberal, democratic party during the twenties, but it did serve to militate against the same exalted führer mystique that gave Hitler such a relatively high degree of control over the NSDAP in Germany. Thus, whereas there was pluralism in the competition among Germandom groups in the Reich because of the phenomenon of political free enterprise, in Czechosolvakia pluralism arose both from the democratic structure of the state in which the competition was taking place and from the radical democratic tradition of the DNSAP itself. The DNSAP never had a tradition of one man rule; rather, collective rule by several leaders who reflected, to some degree, grass roots pressures exerted by the larger body of party members. With regard to *Volkstum* politics, this meant a diminishing of the control that the party leadership could exercise on its rank and file. As a result there was a great deal of independent action taken on a local level, often uncountenanced by the men at the top. Independent initiative was also apparent in the Reich, even after 1933, but for different reasons and never quite to the same degree. Such independent action on the part of the DNSAP members seriously compromised the party's existence. More important, particularly during the early phase of the Hitler regime, these independent activities—including thinly disguised demands for irredentism on the part of some groups—threatened to upset the international status quo the führer was being careful not to disturb. Thus, the DNSAP often unconsciously invited interference and "coordination" from the Reich to eliminate such independent action.

Another characteristic that tended to set the DNSAP off from the NSDAP was the strong proletarian element in the Sudeten party. Many observers have come to regard the Reich Nazi party as a movement *par excellence* of the lower middle classes. One could hardly make the same claim of the Sudeten party. The predecessor of the DNSAP, the *Deutsche Arbeiterpartei* (DAP) after all, had its very roots in a trade union movement. After the DAP reconstituted itself as the DNSAP in 1918, it continued to place strong emphasis on the problems of the working man. The party program of 1918 devoted a great deal of attention to working conditions and workers' demands, within a strongly nationalist context of course.[17] This proletarian cast to National Socialism in the Sudetenland would ultimately have serious consequences for the Germandom struggle, particularly after the DNSAP was dissolved in 1933.

These basic differences should not disguise the fact that from the earliest days of the Hitler party, there had been many congenial contacts between National Socialists in Czechoslovakia and those in the Reich, as members of both parties, especially on the local level, gave one another advice and encouragement. In 1920, the so-called Interstate Chancellory (*zwischenstaatliche Kanzlei*) was set up to facilitate communication among German, Austrian, and Bohemian National Socialists.[18] As the twenties wore on and the Hitler movement achieved greater prominence, such contacts increased. Delegations and speakers were exchanged across the borders and traffic among members of the Reich and Sudeten parties increased markedly on a local level.[19] Sudeten German Nazis availed themselves more and more of the opportunity to publish their books and brochures in the same Reich publishing houses which catered to Hitler's party. For example, Hans Krebs's inflammatory brochure *Paneuropa oder Mitteleuropa* appeared in the NS *Bibliothek Gottfried Feder* in 1931, a tactless blunder which the Czechs did not fail to exploit.[20] Later in the twenties, Hitler's party by its very size and dynamicism became very much the senior partner among the various National Socialist groups. What had been a relationship of cooperation among equals became increasingly one of deference toward the largest and most active branch of National Socialism. The DNSAP reflected this deference in several ways. Both organizationally and doctrinally it came to imitate the Hitler movement. Much of the early democratic character of the DNSAP was lost, as the idea of *Führerprinzip* became popular, although by no means dominant. In 1929 young Sudeten German National Socialists founded the *Volkssport* organization—a conscious imitation of the Reich German SA.[21]

During the latter half of 1931, Rudolf Jung, the DNSAP leader in parliament who had long laid claim to being the leading theoretician of National Socialism, patched up his quarrel with Hitler by recognizing the führer's position of primacy in the movement.[22]

As these influences from the Reich movement became stronger and more obvious, it was increasingly difficult for the DNSAP to maintain its position as a radical, but still ostensibly loyal, party vis-à-vis the Czech state. The symbiotic relationship between the Reich and Sudeten NS thus compounded a dilemma in which the DNSAP had found itself since the very beginning of its independent existence within the Czechoslovakian state. On the one hand, the DNSAP was—theoretically at least—a "negativist" party: its first program in 1918 called for the "unification of the whole German settlement area in Europe in a democratic, social German Reich." [23] Many of the party's members were and remained, in fact, irredentist. On the other hand, as the Czech republic became a going concern, the DNSAP could scarcely go on openly advocating *Anschluss,* still less actually working toward it. Such activities would have invited dissolution and punitive action from the Czech authorities. Confronted with this dilemma, the DNSAP leaders, though leaving the original program unchanged, spoke in public not of reunification but of autonomy and self-administration (*Selbstverwaltung*). Under the leadership of Rudolf Jung, a talented parliamentary tactician, the party emerged during the twenties as a radical, but well behaved political organization, careful not to overstep the bounds set by the Czechs.[24] In some respects, the DNSAP was in a position similar to that which had confronted Social Democracy in Germany before the First World War. It was the old question of reformism versus revolution. In a period of quiescence the German Social Democratic party (Sozialdemokratische Partei Deutschlands or SPD) could quietly go its schizoid way, preserving the idea of revolution in its theoretical program, but conforming to a spirit of reformism in its day-to-day practice. Only when it was confronted by the catastrophe of war was the SPD forced to give up its compartmentalized existence and to choose between the two very different alternatives. Similarly, during the stable years of the mid-twenties, the DNSAP could function from day to day as a parliamentary party within the framework of Czech democracy without being forced to come to terms with its original program. The rise of Hitler's movement to power made this expedient kind of existence increasingly untenable.

The world depression which broke out in 1929—itself a precondition for Hitler's success—was also a mixed blessing for the Sudeten NS. In the wake of the misery and dislocation of the great economic crisis, thousands of radicalized Sudeten Germans flocked to the DNSAP. Between 1930 and 1932 membership more than doubled, from 30,000 to over 61,000.[25] In the five months prior to June of 1932 alone, 14,000 new members were recruited and 110 *Ortsgruppen* founded.[26] This increase was also reflected in various municipal elections. In Gablonz, the 1931 elections put twelve DNSAP members on the forty-two-man city council. On March 19, 1933 in Eger, the National Socialists won seventeen of thirty-eight seats.[27] These new members were predominantly young people, very strongly under the influence of the Hitler movement, who had little truck with the parliamentary tactics of the older generation in the party: which meant that as the DNSAP expanded, it was at the same time forced increasingly toward the Right. The farther toward the Right it went in its program, however, the greater the danger of a Czech crackdown.[28] As early as 1931, DNSAP leaders were living in constant fear of imminent dissolution of the party. At a meeting of Reich and Sudeten Nazis on February 25 in Brünn, Jung pleaded for the termination of illegal aid from National Socialists in Germany on the grounds that the party was becoming much too compromised. The meeting was marked by an extreme nervousness on the part of Sudeten participants. A factional struggle developed, with the Brünn group opposing further contacts with the Reich, the Prague faction supporting further collaboration.[29] Despite Jung's plea, illegal contacts continued—even multiplied—especially on the local level, as more and more Sudeten Germans saw radical politics as the only way out of their economic dilemma.

The long expected crackdown came in 1932 when the Czech government opened the highly publicized *Volkssport* trial in which seven leaders of the DNSAP youth orgainzation were tried and convicted of violating the Law for the Protection of the Republic. During the trial, which went on for months, the DNSAP was subjected to intensified surveillance and harassment.[30] On November 4, the court in Prague submitted a request that the parliamentary immunity of leading DNSAP representatives be lifted because of their complicity in the *Volkssport* organization. Protests on the part of

National Socialist leaders went unheeded. The party leadership found itself in the impossibly difficult position of being carried to the Right by a radicalized rank and file, while at the same time needing more than ever to assure the Czechs of their basic loyalty to the state. After each protestation of loyalty, however, yet another incident would follow to compromise the party's position, necessitating yet another feat of verbal gymnastics.[31] Pulled in opposing directions, the DNSAP leaders saw their position becoming more and more precarious. On January 10, 1933, Rudolf Jung appeared before the Budgetary Committee of Parliament to proclaim one more time that his party really only wanted autonomy and not some greater Third Reich. "Every National Socialist knows," Jung said, "that the Third Reich is a state ideal which would not be realized by a long shot even if Hitler were chancellor, which he is not and is not likely to become very soon."[32] Twenty days later President Hindenberg appointed Hitler chancellor of the German Reich.

Hitler's accession to power only served to heighten the tension and to spur the Czechs to renewed vigilance, despite the peaceful reassurances of the new regime. The Nazi victory in Germany also served to bring new waves of Sudeten Germans into the DNSAP in Czechoslovakia.[33] The Czechs reacted accordingly. On February 23, 1933, the House of Deputies, acting on the judicial request of three months earlier, lifted the parliamentary immunity of the DNSAP delegates Hans Krebs, Leo Schubert, and Rudolf Kasper, by a vote of 120 to 44.[34] Throughout the spring and summer of 1933 DNSAP leaders again expected that at any moment their party would be forbidden and that they themselves would be jailed. When the Czech Supreme Court in Brünn upheld the verdict in the *Volkssport* trial, the National Socialists saw the handwriting on the wall. On September 28, 1933, at an extraordinary meeting, the DNSAP leaders voted to dissolve the party. DNP leaders followed suit. Soon thereafter, two of the most prominent party leaders, Hans Krebs and Karl Viererbl, fled to Germany.[35] Rudolf Jung followed some months later.

The NS party in the Sudetenland had been subjected to inner tension and outside pressure so strong that it could no longer survive. A radicalized membership and the influence of the larger Hitler movement had been pulling it increasingly to the Right, while at the same time the aroused and watchful Czech authorities poised to strike should the party go too far in that direction. The pressures of this situation proved too much for the DNSAP leaders and they chose to end the existence of their party. "Up to its dissolution," one Sudeten German wrote, "[the DNSAP] suffered from the unresolvable contradiction of having to favor ideologically the national dictator, but in Czechoslovakia, of course, having to deny it and to demand a pure democracy." [36] As the German envoy in Prague, Walter Koch, summarized it:

> The party leadership . . . fell into a tragic conflict. Having grown and developed in the old, liberal epoch, being averse to any violent action, it saw itself confronted by a stormily advancing youth, to whom languishing in prison for freedom did not matter. Such a movement, advanced beyond the old petit bourgeois form, lacked a leader who would have been in a position to determine, clearly and concisely, the party line. The assurances that the party was only striving for autonomy were not taken seriously by the Czech authorities, in light of the acitvities of the party members. [37]

On October 7, 1933, less than a week after the DNSAP and DNP dissolved themselves, the Czech government officially forbade both parties. [38]

With the official NS Sudeten organization removed from the political arena, it was inevitable that the Germandom struggle in Czechoslovakia would take on diffierent dimensions than in the Reich. Within Germany, the main thrust of the power struggle was between the official NS and the traditionalist *Volkstum* groups, with the radical Nazi splinter factions like the *Sudetendeutscher Heimatbund* playing a relatively tertiary role. In the Sudetenland, on the other hand, the struggle centered around the traditionalists, who dominated Germandom work organizationally, and the unofficial radical splinter groups. The ban on the DNSAP changed not only the form of NS involvement in the Germandom conflict in the Sudetenland, it also affected its nature: freewheeling NS splinter groups tended to be more militant at an earlier date and on a larger scale than in the Reich. This resulted in part from the frustration of having no official NS party within which to be politically active. Also the absence of an official NS party meant that there was less possibility of directing or controlling radical activity. Even before the ban on the DNSAP, of course, the Sudeten NS leaders were limited in the degree to which they could control the party's membership. Because the DNSAP was functioning in a democratic society that viewed its activities with hostility, NS leaders feared any kind of drastic measures as a way of bringing the more militant members to heel. After the DNSAP's dissolution, this problem of control and guidance got completely out of hand, with the result that after 1933 the radical NS splinter groups played havoc with the other Germandom organizations in Czechoslovakia and ultimately helped push the Sudeten crisis along in ways that no one could fully anticipate or direct. Finally, the ban on the DNSAP made the Germandom conflict more difficult for the Sudeten traditionalists, because many former NS members, left without a party of their own, went underground after 1933 and joined the main *Volkstum* organization dominated by the traditionalists themselves. In this way, the Germandon struggle became internalized within the traditionalist camp, making it difficult for the conservative revolutionaries to identify and come to grips with the "enemy" and to fight off encroachments from the radical side. Thus, the Sudeten traditionalists were compelled to combat a radicalized NS in two very different guises: as small, often vicious, organized splinter factions and as "subversive elements" within the traditionalist camp itself.

Typical of the small, organized radical National Socialist Germandom factions prior to 1933 was the *Bereitschaft* ("Preparedness") organization.[39] In its brief three year history this group functioned as a kind of unofficial bellwether for the orthodox DNSAP, testing the wind for the degree of official severity in dealing with radical German political organizations. It also tended to fight the DNSAP's battles for it against the more obscure opponents on the periphery of the political world: battles in which the official NS party, involved so much in the legitimate political sphere, hesitated to take part. Thus, the *Bereitschaft* bore the brunt of the rivalry with the traditionalist organization, the *Kameradschaftsbund* (KB) during the years 1930 to 1933, in the period prior to the KB's open involvement in national politics. Month after month, *Der Weg*, the organ of the *Bereitschaft* organization, would exchange broadsides with the KB's *Die junge Front*.[40] This stage of the rivalry between NS and traditionalist factions only came to an end when, in 1933, the *Bereitschaft* leader Dr. Patschneider was arrested and put on trial by the Czechs. The rivalry had been so heated that it was widely rumored the KB had somehow engineered Patschneider's arrest.[41]

After 1933 the *Bereitschaft* was supplanted by an even more militant radical splinter organization calling itself the *Aufbruch,* or "Awakening"—a vaguely emotive term popularized in the youth movement as a call to revolutionary renewal.[42] This circle was, for the most part, composed of former members of the DNSAP, but there were two distinct subgroups involved.[43] First, there were the younger, more radical individuals who had once stood in opposition to the older, more cautious DNSAP leadership. Leaders of this faction were Rudolf Haider, one of the seven men convicted in the *Volkssport* trial, and Ferdinand Fischer, copublisher with Haider of *Aufbruch,* the official organ of this new radical organization. The second faction within the *Aufbruchkreis* consisted of former orthodox DNSAP leaders who had not been imprisoned or forced to flee after the dissolution of the party. Among them were Rudolf Kasper, Dr. Anton Kreissl, and Otto Liebl—all men who, without any party organization left to lead, now made common cause with their erstwhile younger rivals. This faction also included a number of ambitious former lower echelon party secretaries, including Albert Smagon (Olmütz) and Friedrich Brehm (Eger). In its persistent and bitter attacks on the traditionalists, particularly the *Kameradschaftsbund,* the "Awakening" circle also had support from certain segments of the ethnic German press and from student groups. The *Rumburger Zeitung,* for example, an influential newspaper in the border town of Rumburg, often lent its voice to the sharp outcry against the traditionalists. At the German university in Prague, particularly the former members of the *National-sozialistischer Studentenbund* (NSSTB), but also students active in the *Bund der Böhmerländischen Freischaren,* gave active assistance to the *Aufbruch* faction.

SUDETEN TRADITIONALISTS: HENLEIN'S SHF

Almost immediately following the dissolution of the DNSAP and the DNP in September of 1933, another Germandom organization sprang into the position of leadership in the nationalist Sudeten camp: the *Sudetendeutsche Heimatfront* (SHF) of Konrad Henlein. Contacts between Henlein and the old NS leaders, the common political currency of the Right which both the DNSAP and the Home Front shared, and above all the very short time span between the dissolution of the NS party and the founding of the Henlein movement understandably led observers to conclude Henlein was merely offering a surrogate for the dissolved Sudeten Nazi organization. In a very limited sense there is perhaps some truth in this contention. With the national-minded sector of the Sudeten population so politicized, the void left by the dissolution of both radical parties on the Right logically had to be filled in some way, in all likelihood by another major political organization. But to view the *Heimatfront* merely as substitute for the DNSAP is to misunderstand the nature of *Volkstumspolitik* in the Sudetenland. In virtually every respect, Helein's SHF was the culmination of a traditionalist, rather than a radical NS, political heritage.

The SHF's base of support, its leadership, as well as its ideological rationale and political orientation were decidedly unlike those of the NS. Although the *Front* ultimately absorbed much of the rank and file of the old DNSAP membership, when it was formed in 1933 the Henlein movement initially based its support on the members of the hitherto apolitical *Turnvereine* or "gymnastic societies," organized in the Sudeten *Turnverband.*[44] Similarly, the leadership of the SHF was composed almost exclusively of men outside the DNSAP: members of the elitist *Kameradschaftsbund,* a secret society that was one of the strongest opponents of the NS. Because of this leadership core, the Henlein movement traced its ideological foundation not to the DNSAP party program, but rather to the antithetical teachings of the mentor of the KB, the Viennese sociologist and social theorist Othmar Spann. Finally, unlike the DNSAP—which for all its talk of unity within the Sudeten ethnic group always had its eye mainly on Germany, the Hitler movement, and *Anschluss*—the traditionalists were genuinely preoccupied with the unity of the Sudeten Germans within the context of the Czechoslovak state.

Since the time of *Turnvater* Jahn, who used his *Turngemeinden* to instil nationalism in German youth during the Napoleonic Wars, the gymnastic societies both in Germany and in the Crownlands of Bohemia and Moravia, had been important institutions in the development of German national feeling. In the course of the late nineteenth century, however, the groups had lost much of their early vitality, becoming little more than nonpolitical, provincial "clubs." [45] As a result, after 1918 the young folk nationalists regarded the *Turnvereine* with the same disdain as they did many of the other ethnic organizations. In Germany, where a wide variety of organizations were available for the expression of nationalist ideas, there was little motivation to rejuvenate the *Turnvereine,* so these groups never regained their former importance. In Czechoslovakia, however, where the formation of radical, militant German nationalist organizations was not feasible, the widespread network of gymnastic societies was too important an institutional form to ignore permanently. The *Turnverband,* or central organization of gymnastic societies, offered an ideal channel for disseminating the ideas of *Volk* nationalism. Renewed interest in the *Turnvereine* also came as a result of Czech participation in similar sport societies, the so-called *Sokol*—groups which had originally been formed in the 1860s after the Jahn model and which had played an important role in the Czech struggle for independence. After 1918 the *Sokol* continued to function as strongholds of Czech nationalism, encouraging the Germans in the Sudetenland to revive their own gymnastic societies in order to foster ethnic unity.

Two young conservative revolutionaries were instrumental in reforming the *Turner* movement in keeping with this new spirit of Sudeten nationalism: Heinz Rutha and Konrad Henlein.[46] Rutha, who had been one of the early postwar leaders in both the *Wandervogel* and *Böhmerland* movements, contributed many of the ideas for reforming the gymnastic societies. He envisioned infusing the *Turner* societies with the same spirit of moral and national renewal which had characterized the youth movement; but whereas the youth movement had split up into numerous splinter groups and factions, the *Turnvereine,* as affiliates of a larger centralized organization, offered a cohesive base for furthering Sudeten unity on a grand scale. While Rutha initiated many of the ideas for reforming the gymnastic societies, his close friend Konrad Henlein was the organizational specialist who undertook to change the personnel and the programs of the *Turner* movement to correspond with the ideas introduced by Rutha. From humble beginnings as a gymnastics teacher in Asch, traditionally a hotbed of radical German national feeling in western Bohemia, Henlein rose quickly in the hierarchy of the *Turner* movement.[47] With his rise, the spirit of reform and folk nationalism spread proportionately. By 1931 Henlein had reached the influential post of *Verbandsturnwart* and was in a position to transform the whole *Turnverband.* He soon introduced a number of reforms which he hoped would make the Sudeten gymnastic societies bastions of folk nationalism—including a stress on competitive, as well as mass, gymnastics as symbols of the preparedness and unity of the folk. All of this infused the rather prosaic exercises with the aura of moral and spiritual renewal.

Since many of those in the *Turner* movement (Henlein included) were veterans, it was natural that the whole ethos of the *Frontkämpfer,* or "front fighter," which had been so characteristic of the Sudeten youth organizations after 1918, would also be incorporated in the *Turner* mystique. Militarylike exercises were introduced, as were overland marching, outdoor gymnastics, and even map reading. In addition, the reformers tried to discourage "artificial" bourgeois customs which to them typified the *Verein* of the sentimental, self-satisfied burger; instead, genuine *Volk* mores were stressed. In *Turner* circles, for example, student drinking songs—considered artificial constructions of a self-indulgent upper class elite—gave way to traditional folk songs reflecting the roots and heritage of the broad segment of the Sudeten population.[48] According to a new constitution, which Henlein pushed through, the *Verband* was completely divested of any vestiges of the *Verein* mentality, with all the nineteenth century liberal implications of that term. The association was now defined as a *Gemeinschaft* or "community," organized according to the *Führerprinzip.* Thus, the *Turnverband* became, in microcosm, the *Volksgemeinschaft* which was to be the goal for all of Sudeten German society.[49] With time, the gymnastic costume was called the "uniform of the Sudeten Germans"; the gymnasts themselves, the "scouts and shock troops of the [folk] movement." [50] With its 1,100 local affiliates and 180,000 members schooled in the ideology of *Volksgemeinschaft,* the Gymnastic Association became an ideal political recruiting ground. In part, of course, Nazis drew on these cadres, but for the most part the *Turner* represented a power base for Henlein's entry into politics. It was the gymnastic gathering in the summer of 1933 at Saaz—where Henlein directed the largest display of mass gymnastics ever seen in the Sudeten German community—that brought Henlein himself into the national spotlight as a leader of the *Volk* movement.[51]

Just as the mass membership of the Henlein movement came from outside the DNSAP initially, the SHF's leadership also emerged from a non-Nazi background for the most part. Not surprisingly, many of the SHF leaders, like the rank and file, came over from the *Turner* movement. The outstanding example was Heinz Rutha,

Henlein's close friend and foreign policy advisor.[52] But the main source of leadership came from another, much smaller organization, the elitist *Kameradschaftsbund.*[53] Father and mentor of the KB, Othmar Spann, like so many conservative revolutionaries of his time, reacted strongly against both Marxism and Liberalism. In trying to find an alternative to both these doctrines, he (again like many of his contemporaries) looked to the past. As the social basis of a utopian state, he revived the concept of a preindustrial society of estates as a means of ending fractious class strife; politically, he took as his model the universal Catholic state of the medieval epoch. Combining these two traditions, Spann developed—in a number of books, the best known of which was *Der Wahre Staat*—his theory of a universalist society of estates (*Ständestaat*) as the prototype for a future new order in Central Europe.[54] In this new order, the Germans would dominate a great universal empire like that of the middle ages and the smaller Slavic peoples would be vassals to the German masters. "Today we can understand clearly, why Poland, Bohemia, Hungary, the South Slavs (even Greece) were once German vassals," Spann wrote. "It must be that way once again. When the German people find their leader, and things take their natural course, a glorious future awaits us, one like the old imperial days." [55] Divested of its jargon, Spann's theory amounts to a model for a clerical fascist state; in fact, Austria under Engelbert Dollfuss reflected many of Spann's ideas.[56]

To many young Sudeten Germans, returning in defeat to an alien polity, this vision was tremendously attractive. Hundreds of young men flocked to Spann's lectures in Vienna and steeped themselves in his philosophy. In light of this great appeal, it was only a matter of time until Spann's disciples would attempt actually to implement and institutionalize some of these ideas. In 1925, Walter Heinrich, Spann's chief disciple and assistant, formed the Workshop for the Social Sciences (*Arbeitskreis für Gesellschaftswissenschaften*).[57] This workshop sponsored a number of seminars that attracted a large circle of young men, for the most part from the youth movement. After several years of discussion and debate, a number of participants in the workshop, above all Heinz Rutha from the *Turner* movement, pressed for a more cohesive organization through which to implement Spann's theories.

In 1928 Spann's adherents were able to found such an organization, the *Kameradschaftsbund.* KB membership was in no way proportional to the influence that the group was able to exert. It never exceeded two hundred, but these two hundred were carefully chosen. Informally, the KB was divided into an "inner circle" (*engerer Kreis*) of about fifty older leaders and a larger group (*Jungmannschaft*) of younger men and boys.[58] The potential strength of the group was not in its tight organization—the structure was much too fluid for that—but rather in the close personal relationships that existed among the members, especially those in the inner circle. This net of personal contacts, held together by the peculiar friendships characteristic of the Central European *Männerbund,* enabled the membership to function within a scattered range of Sudeten German organizations without losing the coherent identity of the KB group. This technique of diversification was, in fact, the reason for much of the KB's success and influence ("technique" in the sense that, at least to some degree, KB members were consciously developing and employing methods of infiltrating Sudeten organizations with the goal of eventually using these organizations as a future political power base). One such deliberate tactic was the so-called second man (*zweiter Mann*) approach, by which the KB member would attempt to occupy the position of advisor, secretary, or adjutant to an organizational leader and eventually displace him.[59] In this manner, KB members moved into influential positions in both the *Kulturverband* and the *Bund der Deutschen,* to some extent replacing older, conservative leaders within these Germandom organizations.[60] The greatest success was with the *Turnverband,* which came completely under the influence of KB personnel.[61] Although Henlein, leader of the *Turnverband,* only considered himself a passive KB member, he was strongly influenced by his close friends Heinz Rutha and Walter Brand, both active KB members. After Henlein procalimed the founding of his movement, these two men became Henlein's chief advisors.

Thus both the mass base and the leadership of Henlein's *Heimatfront* would set it off from the Sudeten NS; but in ideology and orientation, there was a great difference as well. This became apparent in the intense quarrels between the traditionalists and the NS. Prior to 1933 the NS had been taking potshots at the traditionalists, especially at these in *Kameradschaftsbund.* The quarrels would only intensify after 1933 when the traditionalists entered politics via Henlein's movement. The German minister to Prague, Walter Koch, himself recognized this in a report to Berlin just a short time after Henlein proclaimed the formation of the SHF:

It is certain, that the KB emphasizes strongly the Sudeten German geographic position and its uniqueness. The National Socialists, who are looking toward a Greater Germany, accuse the *Kameradschaftsbund* people of wanting to create a "Sudeten German" analogous to an "Austrian": that is, that they are not striving toward the Reich, but away from it.[62]

Koch was only belatedly recognizing an ideological struggle which had been going on for a long time.

Although both the Sudeten NS and the *Kameradschaftsbund* shared a heightened German national feeling, on the most basic level their views of society were in opposition to each other.[63] The Spann disciples found their model for an ideal state in the universal Catholic empire of the middle ages; their inspiration came from Rome and from Vienna. All this had little to do with the racial Social Darwinism that underlay the National Socialist movement. Along with a strong contempt for the Catholic Church, National Socialism looked not to Austria but to Prussia and the Reich as the foundation for a great empire. The KB and NS factions also clashed in their conception of leadership. The KB opted for an intellectual, aristocratic elite along Neoplatonic lines to run society—an elite especially trained and groomed for leadership. National Socialists, on the other hand, were much more antiintellectual and plebeian in their view of leadership: the true leaders would arise spontaneously from among the ranks of the people, emerging triumphant from the exigencies of the day-to-day struggle for survival. There would be no effete philosopher-kings. In response to such slaps at traditionalist ideals, the KB retaliated as did conservative revolutionaries in Germany by calling the National Socialists *ideenlos* ("without ideas") and political adventurers.[64]

A third issue of contention was the problem of Sudeten unity. Although both groups advocated unity and community as essential for Sudeten ethnic survival, they were not at all in agreement as to the kind of unity this was to be. The National Socialists, parliamentary tactics notwithstanding, still thought basically in irredentist, Greater German terms.[65] The KB members, on the other hand, for all their dreams of a medieval German empire, were often associated with the idea of developing the Sudeten German *Stamm* (by analogy with the older tribal structure of Bavarians, Saxons, *etc.*)—a concept which, as Koch noted, led away from the modern Reich. Finally, the traditionalists and the National Socialists were separated from one another geographically: a factor which both isolated the groups physically from one another and, to some extent, exacerbated their other differences as well. The KB, to a great degree, was a northern Bohemian group; its headquarters was in Böhmisch-Leipa, home of both Walter Heinrich and Heinz Rutha, prominent KB members. The professional classes in this area had traditionally fostered close ties with the interior and Prague, both culturally and emotionally, and thus were more immune to a movement whose appeal emanated from the Reich. The National Socialists, on the other hand, received much of their strength from the western parts of Bohemia, especially from the region around Asch and Eger. This area was intensely nationalistic and for centuries had been oriented toward the Reich and Nuremburg, rather than toward the interior.[66] To the extent that the KB did have contacts in the Reich during the 1920s, these were not with National Socialist circles, but rather with such conservative groups as Hans Zehrer's *Tatkreis,* which enjoyed the patronage of General Kurt von Schleicher and advocated a kind of conservative socialism.[67]

There were, then, more than enough major differences, personal ones aside, to make for a serious conflict between traditionalists and National Socialists in the Sudeten areas. Prior to 1933, however, this struggle was not carried out directly between the DNSAP and the *Kameradschaftsbund.* The two organizations were, for one thing, operating on different levels. The DNSAP was a viable political party, carefully maneuvering in the mainstream of politics, while the KB was a private, ostensibly educational organization which existed on the fringes of political life. Also, given the precarious situation in which the DNSAP found itself during the late 1920s it would have been ill-advised to involve itself in any more altercations than absolutely necessary. For these reasons, the National Socialist rivalries with the traditionalists, particularly with the KB, were for the most part carried out by the small radical NS factions such as the *Bereitschaft,* which were themselves functioning on the fringes of politics. After the dissolution of the DNSAP in September of 1933, these small splinter groups became more important: in the absence of a National Socialist party, those radicals who could not or would not join the Henlein Front found the small splinter organizations, particularly the *Aufbruch* circle, a convenient place to coalesce and regroup for their attacks on the traditionalists around Henlein. Since both Henlein and the SHF were clearly too popular among the masses of Sudeten Germans at this point, *Aufbruch* initially avoided attacking either directly. The radicals, however, waged war furiously on the people around Henlein, complaining that they were influencing the new Sudeten leader in the direction of Spannist thought.

The *Sudetendeutsche Heimatfront* of Konrad Henlein must be regarded, then, as something very different and far larger in its inception and scope than simply a hasty step to place the old wine of the DNSAP into a new organizational bottle. Rather, it was the culmination of a totally different movement to achieve unity in the Sudeten German nationalist camp. Even the hasty, confused negotiations between Henlein and the leaders of the soon-to-be-defunct DNSAP and DNP in the weeks immediately preceding the organizational turnover in September of 1933—so often used as evidence for the ersatz-interpretation—indicate that the SHF was much more than simply a replacement for the NS party. Henlein was approached several times, both by Hans Krebs of the DNSAP and Othmar Kallina of the DNP, about assuming leadership of a *Volksfront* of all non-Marxist nationalist parties. He resisted all such proposals.[68] Unless the existing right-wing parties first surrendered their power, Henlein felt that any step he would take into politics appeared doomed from the start, just like the many other attempts to form a Sudeten unity organization. In Henlein's eyes, the self-dissolution of the DNSAP (and DNP) eliminated the problem of jealous rival political parties and it was this consideration rather than any desire to act as a trustee of National Socialism in Bohemia which impelled him to act when he did. Unfortunately, Henlein's move to proclaim the founding of the SHF, carried out in the enthusiasm of finally confronting a political *tabula rasa* on the Right, was ill-timed. Coming as it did so close on the heels of the disappearance of the other right-wing parties, the Czechs—just as later scholars—interpreted the formation of the SHF as an attempt to replace the DNSAP. The resulting suspicion, as understandable as it may be, hampered the traditionalists in the SHF in effectively combating the radicals. The former radical party leaders, meanwhile, regarded the Henlein movement in a very different light. Former DNSAP Deputy Hans Knirsch warned his people to stay away from the *Heimatfront*, "since this new organization can only be seen as a Spina filial" (a reference to Agrarian party [Bund der Landwirte] leader Franz Spina, German health minister in the Prague government).[69] Even a German diplomat in Prague noted: "Today Henlein is more loyal than Spina and nothing causes him more anxiety than when one or another member of the dissolved parties reports to join the *Heimatfront.*" [70]

With the founding of the *Heimatfront* in October of 1933, Germandom politics in the Sudetenland finally seemed to have been "coordinated" under the aegis of the traditionalists: ironically, in appearance at least, coordinated to a higher degree than in the Reich itself. But appearances were deceiving. Although the dissolution of the old right-wing parties had deprived their adherents of a political home, many of these people now flocked to the *Heimatfront* as the only remaining outlet at all for their political aspirations. As a result, long standing quarrels endemic between the traditionalists and the NS now became internalized in the new movement itself. It remained to be seen whether the SHF and its leader, Konrad Henlein, could withstand the conflicts and pressures which were bound to follow. Obviously Krebs and his colleagues, in approaching Henlein in the first place, thought to use him as a figurehead, as a puppet which they could control from behind the scenes—an ironic variation on what Reich conservatives had originally planned for Hitler and his Nazis.[71] Henlein, just as clearly, hoped that with the NS leaders out of the way he could proceed unchallenged with his own unity plans. His subsequent denunciation of Krebs as a deserter and Krebs's long time campaign to unseat Henlein scarcely point to any deal between the two men.

The key to the future of Germandom politics in the Sudetenland, then, lay to a large extent in what kind of a leader Konrad Henlein proved to be. It was he who had taken the step of proclaiming a political movement to encompass all Sudeten Germans; he, who by drawing his friends in the *Kameradschaftsbund* into positions of leadership in the SHF, gave the Sudeten Germans a viable, traditionalist-oriented political power base; and, it was he who would become the fulcrum in the rivalry between Sudeten traditionalists and NS Germandom factions. Yet, it is hard to imagine this man, Konrad Henlein, as the leader of any kind of mass movement—particularly one with such a difficult task as uniting a minority of three-and-a-half million people in the politically explosive atmosphere of Czechoslovakia of the 1930s. Anything but a power hungry autocrat capable of manipulating people and events, Henlein was basically a man who unwittingly stumbled into a position far more demanding than his abilities to cope with it. Although enormously popular among the masses of Sudeten Germans, he was never a strong leader within his own party; his simplicity and vacillation gradually made him a pawn in the bitter power struggle between the various Germandom factions in the SHF.

Henlein was born in Maffersdorf bei Reichenau on May 6, 1898, of a German father and a Czech mother. It is significant to note that at no time in his career did he make any statement regarding the Czech aspect of his ancestry—an admission which might have, any number of times, gone a long way toward assuaging official doubts as to his political intentions. Rather, Henlein took pains to hide this background: in 1941 he had the spelling of his mother's name, Hedwig Dvořáček, changed on his birth certificate to Dworaschek, the German version of the name.[72] There is nothing in Henlein's early life that betrays the kind of frustration and dislocation that formed and deformed personalities like Hitler. Rather, Henlein was an average boy, neither failing nor excelling, except that he showed some proficiency in gymnastics. During the war he served for two years, 1916 to 1918, as an officer at the front; then, he was captured by the Italians and spent the rest of the war in a prison camp. After his release, he moved to Gablonz, where he worked as a bank clerk in the local branch of the *Kreditanstalt der Deutschen* before devoting himself, after 1925, completely to the *Turner* movement.

Far from suffering the frustration and disillusionment so typical of his contemporaries, Henlein appears to have reverted to normalcy fairly easily after the war; there is no sign of that fierce "fire in the guts" one has come to associate with the leaders of mass movements. Even his official biographer, who took great pains to write a panegyric, had difficulty in finding anything unusual to report about this early period of Henlein's life.[73] His world-view was no more out of the ordinary than the early experiences which had formed it. Though he shared, with thousands of his contemporaries, an intense concern for Germandom and for the unity of his people, throughout his career in the *Turner* movement he never advanced philosophically beyond the provincial, philistine views of any small town, petit bourgeois German of that time.[74]

Even Henlein's contemporaries showed astonishment that a man of his qualities—or lack of them—should come to lead a mass political movement, which in so many ways resembled the Hitlerian movement across the borders. One writer observed:

> Truthfully, there is nothing about Henlein which would call attention to him. He is completely average. . . . How average this man is can be seen in the fact that even cartoonists, who, with a sharp glance, can find the characteristic features in any face, find nothing of the sort in Henlein's. It is clear that this is not their fault. If it were not for the glasses, which have already torn so many faces from the sea of anonymity, we would not have any cartoons of Henlein at all.[75]

Still another political observer commented:

> Konrad Henlein was, from his background, the prototype of an upright petty official and, by no means, a conspirator. Undoubtedly he had organizational capabilities and, supposedly, as an officer, made a good troop leader. He was not [however] politically gifted; as a speaker, he came across dryly and helpless. Indeed, he had nothing about him of that fascinating demagogic type which has arisen in the twentieth century.[76]

Given this very average character and ability, the question arises: how did Henlein organize and lead the Sudeten unity movement and achieve such enormous popularity as a political leader? Some observers attributed the phenomenon to the very provincial inexperience and isolation from the outside world so typical of the German Bohemian area. Only in a *kleinbürgerlich* milieu like that of the Sudetenland could such a pale, amateurish reflection of the "great leader" come into existence.[77] Others have pointed out that the cheers of the enthusiastic crowds at mass demonstrations of the SHF were not for Henlein at all. Initially, they represented approval of the idea of unity and of the breakdown of the old party politics; later, they echoed enthusiasm for the man who was ostensibly standing behind Henlein—Hitler himself.[78] There is some truth to both these statements, but neither adequately explains Henlein's phenomenal success.

In order to evaluate Henlein's role in the *Sudetendeutsche Heimatfront,* it is essential to separate Henlein as a political symbol from Henlein as a party leader. As a political symbol, Henlein enjoyed enormous popularity among the masses of Sudeten Germans. However, it was not just the idea of unity for which the people were shouting at the various meetings and rallies of the SHF; they were also acclaiming Henlein as a more personal kind of symbol. True,

Henlein and his movement did represent a culmination for many people of the long struggle toward achieving ethnic unity. But even more important, Henlein was someone with whom the ordinary Sudeten German, caught up in the disaster of economic and social crisis, could identify. The average Sudeten German did not see in Henlein, as many Reich Germans did in Hitler, the embodiment of the will of the nation. What he did see in Henlein was, in essence, a reflection of his own condition: economically deprived, politically disenfranchised, and ethnically threatened, yet determined to resist destruction. Thus, Henlein did not make his appeal with raging speeches or emotional tirades. Rather, he managed, in a simple, sincere, and undramatic way, to articulate the fears and hopes that many Sudeten Germans felt within themselves. It was this ability, to function as an Everyman in a time of great national stress, that was behind much of Henlein's success in attracting people to his movement. In later years, when some Sudeten Germans, of course, looked beyond Henlein to Hitler, those traditionalists who desired only some sort of autonomy within the Czechoslovakian state kept their faith in Henlein.

Henlein as a political leader, however, was another matter entirely. Despite his ability to capture and articulate what was on the average man's mind, he was not a charismatic leader. It was one thing efficiently to organize a gymnastic society, but quite a different matter to steer a political movement. In the rough and tumble of day-to-day politics, Henlein lacked the dynamic drive and decisive convictions of a forceful leader; rather, he became, at best, an arbitrator among various factions within the party. Even observers hostile to Henlein and his movement commented on the "lamb's patience with which he let himself be led around at demonstrations, where he played the role of an adornment."[79] The man was capable of that occasional stubborn intransigence peculiar to indecisive people, but for the most part he was shoved this way and that by various party factions, while outwardly symbolizing a unity that did not really exist. This vacillating indecision, among other things, served to heighten even more the intensity of the *Volkstum* rivalries between the *Kameradschaftsbund* members and the National Socialists working within the SHF. In this respect Germandom policy formation in the Reich and in the Sudetenland were superficially similar. Both Henlein and Hitler gave their subordinates maximum free play in doing their work for them.

But they did so for different reasons. With Hitler it was a matter of conscious policy: giving competitors the chance to best one another under the Darwinian assumption that the winner would *ipso facto* have the best solution. In Henlein's case, letting others do the work for him, although partly a matter of articulated policy, was largely a function of his lack of ability or determination to do more things himself. Once a favorable situation did arise, Hitler would act decisively and ruthlessly; when the time of ultimate decision came for Henlein, he would prove unable to do more than surrender his will once again. And it would be Adolf Hitler to whom he would capitulate.

IV

The Fronts Begin to Form

WHETHER motivated by his resentments from Habsburg days, by his racism toward the Slavs, his intention to dismantle Versailles, or his sense of strategic necessity, Hitler may have harbored the desire to one day "solve" the problem of Czechoslovakia's existence.[1] Whatever his long range intentions might have been, however, for the moment Hitler was far too concerned with consolidating his power at home to act upon them. The Roehm incident in June of 1934 was to testify to this. But even had Hitler wanted an immediate confrontation with Czechoslovakia, the moment was hardly propitious for a serious challenge to the international status quo. Obviously Hitler lacked the necessary military capability to back any revisionist moves. Perhaps just as important, Hitler did not as yet have the political tools to do so either. He had not, for example, gauged the will of the Western powers, as he was to do later with increasing success, to test the limits to which he could actually go. Nor had he as yet experimented with a whole range of techniques from outright intimidation to the sophisticated manipulation of German ethnic groups as a fifth column to undermine potential enemies from within. This latter "trick" existed at that point only in the mind of Ernst Bohle and he himself would never get to use it in his own right.

Here lay the real importance of Germandom politics: it was the conflict and rivalry among the various *Volkstum* groups over a period of years that would eventually give Hitler both the techniques and the concrete situations to exploit for German expansion. Through years of experience, often very painful experience—witness the abortive putsch of 1923—he had learned the requisite political gambits that put him in, and would now keep him in power in Germany. But foreign policy was very different from domestic policy (although later events would show the differences were perhaps not so great as one might expect), and it involved, by definition, contacts with other peoples and systems outside the führer's realm of experience. So, in the early years of the Third Reich, while there was still much work to be done domestically, Hitler gave the various people and organizations that had any interest and expertise at all in matters involving ethnic Germans free license to pursue their own philosophies with regard to these minorities, of course within the limits set by an officially quiescent foreign policy. In this way, the different agencies could competitively experiment with ideas and techniques related to foreign policy, while leaving Hitler in an uncompromising position. This approach was very much in keeping with Hitler's general predilection for the Social Darwinistic belief that the strongest and the best method would eventually win; it was also an excellent method to assure that no one man came to dominate or get too much influence in foreign policy. Finally, it enabled Hitler, through the experience of others, to accumulate effective tools for his later use, without himself risking the disapprobation of Germany's neighbors.

In the fall of 1933, then, Hitler showed little concern for the plight of the Germans in Czechoslovakia. Anxious to avoid international tension at this point on a critical section of Germany's frontier, Hitler was careful to take a peaceful stance in the Reich's foreign policy toward Czechoslovakia. Party and state agencies were to avoid any unauthorized interference in Sudeten German—*i.e.*, Czech internal—affairs. Eventually, unofficial feelers were even put out to test the possibility of negotiating a nonaggression pact with Czechoslovakia similar to that which Germany signed with Poland in January of 1934.[2] Another factor that in all likelihood restrained Hitler in his support of the Sudeten Germans was the dissolution of the Sudeten Nazi party. The DNSAP had compromised itself so much through its indiscreet contacts with NS agencies in the Reich that—in the face of Czech threats to outlaw the organization—the DNSAP leaders dissolved the party themselves in September of 1933. The whole incident reflected badly on Hitler's espoused peace policy and undoubtedly contributed to his wariness of any involvement in Sudeten German politics. The best way to prevent such occurrences in the future would be to enforce a strict hands off policy with regard to politics in countries where significant numbers of ethnic Germans were living. Considering the sensitive location and large numbers of the Sudeten Germans, this policy would be especially advisable with regard to Czechoslovakia.[3] Thus, although Hitler pretended a comradely sympathy for the disbanded, persecuted *Parteigenossen* in Czechoslovakia and even asked the foreign minister to render what aid and comfort was possible—of course with all due caution and discretion⁴—he expressed his real intentions most clearly in his words to Hans Knirsch, venerable leader of the DNSAP: the Sudeten Germans would have to solve their own problems; it would be a long time before the Reich could do anything to help them.⁵

As Hitler continued to turn his attention to the task of consolidating and strengthening National Socialist rule in Germany, he left the tangled problem of relations with ethnic Germans to his deputy, Rudolf Hess.⁶ It was at this point that the confused and fragmented competencies characteristic of the Nazi power structure developed in the realm of ethnic politics—particularly in politics related to the Sudeten Germans: Hess withdrew all authority or special powers that had been granted to the exiled leaders of the DNSAP and, on March 13, 1934, gave the *Volksdeutscher Rat* full control in handling Sudeten German affairs "insofar as these [problems] do not fall within the competency of the Reich government, in particular the Foreign Office."⁷ There were several good reasons for choosing the *Volksdeutscher Rat* to look after Sudeten German affairs. As an organization operating with as few ties as possible to official agencies, it ran little risk of compromising the regime through its activities. The traditionally autonomous status of the VDA, with which the VR would be working so closely, would be an added help in this respect. Moreover, the men involved were seasoned in *Volkstum* work and thus were unlikely to make the mistakes one could expect from younger, inexperienced enthusiasts such as Bohle. Even more important, the men in the group around Steinacher had, through years of experience, acquired an enormous range of contacts among almost all segments of the Sudeten German population. These contacts would be invaluable in handling delicate problems within the *Volksgruppe,* especially since they had existed prior to the Nazi regime and therefore, theoretically, should not engender undue suspicion on the part of the Czechs. Finally, it was clear to Hess that the traditionalists who formed the backbone of the VR-VDA were indeed concerned with promoting the unity and integrity of the ethnic groups, and not, as was the case with many of the more radical National Socialists like Bohle, with exporting National Socialism to Germans abroad. There is some question as to the degree of conviction with which Hess held to the traditionalist point of view or even if he understood it at all. This approach, however, did coincide nicely with the führer's injunction that there should be no interference in the affairs of neighboring states, and so Hess went along with it.[8] So, from the outset, the traditionalists—as the VR-VDA people for the most part were—seemed to enjoy a position of primacy with regard to at least one, indeed the largest, of the ethnic German groups. Appearances were to prove deceiving. In bestowing competency, Hess had given the Foreign Office a slice of the pie, too; moreover, it remained to be seen if the radical NS groups would be ready to let themselves be elbowed out of the picture, bestowed competency or not. All this notwithstanding, the traditionalists initially perceived their new status as an opportunity to show that the new Germany was truly aware of its responsibilities in protecting the heritage and integrity of Germans living outside the Reich. Perhaps more importantly, it represented a chance to make the traditionalist *volklich* approach one of the foundations of German foreign policy.[9]

Armed with the full backing of Hess, the VR—particularly through the driving leadership of its executive officer, Hans Steinacher—took charge of Sudeten German affairs in the spring of 1934. One of Steinacher's first moves was to initiate contact with the *Auswärtiges Amt,* the only other agency that, officially at least, was supposed to have anything to do with the Sudeten Germans. The grounds for this were, in part, financial. Although the policy was frequently debated, money to ethnic groups was still frequently dispensed through diplomatic channels. Since financial aid to Sudeten Germans would from time to time be funneled through the mission in Prague, close VR cooperation with the German minister there, Walter Koch, was both advisable and necessary. The VDA was to use this channel to make two deliveries in May and June of 1934: the funds, 29,385 and 41,300 Czech crowns respectively, were sent through the German embassy in Vienna to the *Sudetendeutsche Heimatfront.*[10] In addition to this financial consideration, the VR shared one of its most potentially valuable powers with Foreign Minister von Neurath—that of determining which ethnic German visitors to the Reich might gain access to Hitler.[11] This screening power would be of great importance in a dictatorship where specially designated authority and personal ties often meant so much politically.

Over a period of several months, Steinacher put out feelers to establish a basis of cooperation with various AA officials. Even before Hess gave the VR its special powers in March, Steinacher had already met with the Foreign Office official most intimately concerned with ethnic Germans, Friedrich Stieve, head of the *Kulturabteilung*.[12] On February 24, 1934, Stieve had agreed with Steinacher in regarding any actions which would interfere with the internal consolidation of the Sudeten Germans as something to be avoided—which included any attempt to renew the NS movement in Czechoslovakia.[13] On the same day that Hess issued his directive—March 13—Steinacher initiated a meeting with *Ministerialdirektor* Gerhard Köpke, director of *Abteilung II* of the AA (which included southeastern Europe), on the subject of the Sudeten problem. In the discussion Steinacher again emphasized the traditionalist viewpoint: under the present circumstances and for the forseeable future, it was not possible to think in terms of a National Socialist organization in Czechoslovakia. For the coming years, the Sudeten Germans would have to take care of themselves. It was not permissible, therefore, as was done in the case of Austria, to set up any kind of a National Socialist *Kampfstelle*, or "command post," for the Sudeten Germans.[14] Finally, on March 27 and 28, a series of conferences were held to clarify the new distribution of competencies. Steinacher represented the VR; from the AA offices in Berlin came Gerhard Köpke and Dr. Conrad Rödiger, from the cultural department, with several colleagues; Minister Koch returned from Prague for the occasion. The group agreed that the centralization of Sudeten German affairs in the hands of the VR would further the interests of a quiescent foreign policy and that, to this end, the VR and the *Auswärtiges Amt* should work closely together. There was also general agreement with Steinacher's statement that both German-Czech relations and the interests of Germandom would best be served if any interference from unauthorized circles would be prevented. Especially in light of the complete collapse of the National Socialist party in Czechoslovakia, the new national movement that was slowly crystallizing among the Sudeten Germans would have to develop independently without any perceivable influence from Reich German organizations. At the end of the meeting it was announced that the *Hilfsaktion* for former DNSAP members had been terminated. The operation had begun after the dissolution of the party and had placed a heavy political burden on the mission in Prague. Its termination now was further evidence of the emphasis on a cautious foreign policy.[15]

Once a basis for cooperation with the *Auswärtiges Amt* had been created, Steinacher turned his attention to the Sudeten Germans themselves, and here both his political persuasions and his earlier contacts soon led him to Konrad Henlein and the *Sudetendeutsche Heimatfront*. It was logical that Steinacher and Henlein would ultimately work together. Henlein, after all, was attempting something which Steinacher felt was the very root and essence of *Volkstum* activity: namely, the self-maintenance of an ethnic group vis-à-vis an alien people. For years, Steinacher had been in contact with men (including Hans Neuwirth and Othmar Spann) who had participated in the various organizations concerned with Sudeten unity. It was through one of these contacts, Friedrich Bürger, that Steinacher was to meet Henlein for the first time.[16] Bürger had been active for a time during the 1920s, along with his brother Ehrhardt, in the *Ullersdorfer Bauernschule* in Moravia. On the occasion of a VDA library conference in Flensburg, he had come to know Steinacher, who invited him to work with Hermann Ullmann, VDA member in charge of the Sudeten German desk. Bürger agreed and came to Berlin. At this point, his first job—as liaison between Steinacher and the Sudeten unity movement—was to bring Henlein and Steinacher together.

Bürger made very careful arrangements for this meeting. The two leaders were to come together surreptitiously on April 28, 1934, at Krummhübel at the foot of the Riesengebirge, near the border in order to minimize compromising risks to both parties. Steinacher has preserved a somewhat melodramatic account of the meeting in his diaries:

> We arrived at the site about a half hour before Henlein, carefully parked the car somewhere and went with Fritz [Friedrich] Bürger, who had awaited us, to an out-of-the-way forest path. In a secluded place, two young, inconspicuously clothed men came up to us out of a thicket. One was wearing glasses. It was Konrad Henlein!

The meeting lasted for some three hours. Henlein reported to the VR group on the situation in Czechoslovakia and showed himself receptive to advice. Steinacher, in turn, informed Henlein of the VR-VDA competence in Sudeten affairs. "I was able to make it clear to Henlein," Steinacher wrote, "that his political path led only

through the *Volksdeutscher Rat* and not in any other direction."
Steinacher emphasized that their connection be as confidential as
possible and be limited to a small circle directly involved. The two of
them should meet as little as possible, so Bürger would be the liaison
man between them. Steinacher made it clear, finally, that Henlein had
complete authority to act on his own, in the knowledge that he had
the confidence of the sole agency in the Reich with competence in
ethnic German affairs. When the meeting ended Henlein returned to
Asch assured that, with the apparent blessing of the new regime in
Germany, he would have a free hand in organizing the nationalist
camp in the Sudetenland and from there eventually the whole Sudeten
population. Steinacher returned to Berlin with a trump card in his
hand as well: for if Henlein were successful under his tutelage, the
Volksdeutscher Rat would be able to show that its conception of
Germandom was indeed the most viable.[17]

After this meeting concrete ties were built up between the
Henlein circle and the VR. To avoid being compromised by letters,
the VR people and Bürger set up a courier system to pass on messages
orally. A certain businessman, who had an office in Sebnitz (Germany) and in Asch (Czechoslovakia) and who could cross the border
daily without arousing suspicion, was the contact man. When a
message was to be delivered, he would inform Wilhelm Rümmler,
close colleague of Henlein and later chief of his private chancellory,
who would then go to Sednitz, memorize the message, and return.[18]
Bürger was active in other respects as well. The German AA
representative in Pressburg (Bratislava), Ernst von Druffel, who was
introduced to Bürger by Steinacher, in turn arranged a meeting
between Bürger and the secretaries of German organizations in
Vienna with the purpose of establishing a *Wirtschaftskanzlei* in
Pressburg to underwrite small Sudeten German businesses and
peasant holdings.[19] This "economic chancellory" was to be supported
in part by the VDA with 1,050 marks each quarter to be channeled
discreetly through the consulate in Pressburg.[20]

Despite these attempts to strengthen the traditionalist position,
both Henlein and Steinacher were soon challenged by other forces
working for influence in the Germandom field, both in Germany and
in Czechoslovakia. The first, and perhaps most serious challenge at
this point to Steinacher, the competence of the *Volksdeutscher Rat*,
and the traditionalist conception of *Volkstum* work came from Ernst

Bohle and his *Auslandsorganisation.* Bohle refused to accept the VR-VDA complex for several reasons. It represented a threat to the domain that he considered to be his by right—that of organizing the Germans living abroad. Moreover, as a radical National Socialist, Bohle rejected on principle the traditionalist distinction between *Reichsdeutsche* and *Auslandsdeutsche.* To him Germans were Germans, all suitable material to be organized as tools for the new movement. Finally, a personal note quite possibly entered into the picture. Steinacher was an extremely resolute, untactful man, used to imposing his will on others without particular regard for their feelings. This kind of behavior on the part of a traditionalist—men whom the new National Socialists liked to call reactionary "Santa Clauses" (*Weihnachtsmänner*)—must have been intolerable to Bohle. His personal struggle against Steinacher was to become one of the most bitter aspects of the VR-VDA-AO rivalry.

Bohle could, however, be quite ingratiating when it suited his purposes. Through Hess's brother, Alfred (who eventually became Bohle's deputy in the *Auslandsorganisation*), Bohle wormed his way into the good graces of Hess himself. On February 17, 1934, Hess officially elevated Bohle's *Abteilung* to *Auslandsorganisation der NSDAP*: Bohle was accorded the rank of *Gauleiter* and was appointed to Hess's staff.[21] Thus, the incredible situation arose in which one of the most protracted and bitter struggles in the Third Reich was fought out between two organizations that were under the patronage of the same man—Rudolf Hess. It was a veritable caricature of the kind of situation that came to be typical of politics in Nazi Germany. In this case, the situation resulted largely because of Hess's utter inability to make effective decisions when confronted by conflicting alternatives and points of view.

With his power base thus assured for the time being, Bohle proceeded to enforce his claim to predominance in *Volkstum* affairs. He first confronted the VDA with a *fait accompli* by arbitrarily subordinating all Germans teaching abroad under the *Gau Ausland* of the National Socialist Teachers Association (*Nationalsozialistischer Lehrerbund* or NSLB).[22] Extending his influence in other directions, Bohle also began to try to infiltrate the *Auswärtiges Amt.* In March, Hess permitted him to open an office in the Wilhelmstrasse, but—initially at least—Bohle's influence there amounted to little.[23] For the most part, his attacks centered on the circle involved in the VDA and the VR. By April of 1934 the threat was already approaching sufficient proportions that the VDA leadership felt constrained to issue a clarifying message. An Easter *Rundschreiben* emphasized that the VDA was the "only general, encompassing representative of the German *Volk* idea to reach out over the borders and embrace all Germans regardless of their citizenship in the cause of Germandom work." On the other hand, the *Gau Ausland der NSDAP* only had charge of Reich German party members abroad; its task was to bring National Socialism to Reich Germans living abroad. "By contrast, the VDA movement [*sic*] is international [*überstaatlich*], *volksdeutsch*, and independent."[24]

Of course such circular letters would really make little difference in the struggle. The only hope was, and remained, the personal support of Rudolf Hess. "[Hess] must understand quite clearly," Albrecht Haushofer wrote to his father on June 23, 1934, "what dangers are inherent in Herr B.'s [Bohle's] drive for expansion." He added that Bohle's recent behavior in cases involving Luxemburg and Switzerland had shown that Bohle "understands absolutely nothing about the deeper meaning of the distinction between *reichsdeutsch* and *volksdeutsch!*"[25] The best that Hess would do, however, was to offer a compromise solution on July 25. He determined a regional distribution whereby the AO could be competent in areas where Germans of Reich citizenship were in the majority; otherwise the VDA would have competence.[26] But trouble continued between the two factions, until finally, Albrecht Haushofer suggested to his father they ask Hess for an official ukase.[27] Two months later, on September 17, Hess was constrained to rebuke both sides: he forbade the AO to interfere in affairs concerning ethnic Germans who did not possess Reich citizenship; and, at the same time, he warned the VDA not to interfere in the organization of Reich Germans living abroad. The latter were the responsibility of the AO.[28]

Until this time the traditionalists had been able to hold out quite effectively against the encroachments of Bohle. This success was in part attributable to the fact that Bohle had a number of other enemies. For one thing, although Hess had given Bohle the rank of *Gauleiter,* the other "territorial" *Gauleiter* were very reluctant to accept the AO leader as an equal.[29] For another, *Reichsminister* Josef Goebbels, head of the Propaganda Ministry and one of the most powerful men in Germany, rejected entirely the AO and its activities abroad: the National Socialist revolution was something, he felt, which should limit itself exclusively to Germans in the Reich.[30] The traditionalists were also fortunate in having some friends of their own. Friedrich Stieve, director of the *Kulturabteilung* of the Foreign Office, was a supporter, although a weak one; so were the education minister, Bernhard Rust, and, until his seduction at the hands of the refugee Sudeten National Socialists, Interior Minister Wilhelm Frick. More importantly, perhaps, Hermann Göring, Vice-Chancellor Franz von Papen, and especially the senior generals—among them Werner von Blomberg, Walter von Reichenau, and Walther von Brauchitsch— were well disposed toward the VDA and its efforts. This was something Bohle had to take into account.[31]

Beyond doubt, though, it was the efforts of Heinrich Kersken, Hess's personal representative in the VR, that enabled the VR-VDA people to resist so successfully. This tough and combative SA man (He had earned the sobriquet *Raubein der SA vom Niederrhein*—"SA roughneck from the lower Rhein"—in earlier days) again and again succeeded in heading off challenges from Bohle. For example, when Bohle had hinted that the AO would eventually organize all Germans abroad, Reich citizens and otherwise, Kersken immediately refuted him, contending that the AO would have nothing to do with ethnic German politics—that was the job of the VDA. There is an abundance of evidence illustrating just how Kersken manipulated and fought to keep the VDA-VR circle from going under in the running battle for Hess's favor.[32]

The AO was not the only organization, however, which challenged the competence of the VR-VDA. The VDA, in particular, because of its large youth contingents, became the target of the *Hitlerjugend* (HJ). To Baldur von Schirach, anxious to see only *one* youth organization in Germany—that dressed in the brown of the Hitler Youth—the ubiquitous VDA boys, with their white shirts and blue pennants, were a provocation of the first magnitude. The fact that these boys also had collection cups in their hands into which were flowing millions of marks destined for VDA coffers may also have influenced Schirach's feelings. At first, the two organizations managed to reach an agreement of sorts.[33] While the HJ would handle the education of youth in the realms of military sport, politics, and *völkisch* ideas, the VDA could take the lead in training the youth in ethnic German thinking ("Schulung zum volksdeutschen Denken"), especially with regard to Germandom along the borders and abroad ("Fragen des Grenz- und Auslandsdeutschtums"). This differentiation, however, was much too fuzzy, and Schirach much too ambitious for the agreement to have any permanence. On December 18, 1933, under pressure from Schirach, Hess issued a *Verfügung* which changed the VDA-*Jugend* into the more harmless sounding VDA-*Schulgruppen* ("School Groups"), and provided at the same time that these groups should never comprise more than 20 percent of the pupils in any one school.[34] The VDA and *Reichsjugendführung* (RJF), had also agreed that in cases of double membership, the young people involved would appear at VDA affairs in their white shirts and at HJ proceedings in brown ones. Again, the Hitler Youth leader failed to live up to the agreement. Orders went out that on the occasion of the annual VDA-*Pfingsten* gathering (Whitsun), HJ members should appear in uniform without VDA pennants. Steinacher protested in vain against this ruling as well as against the other encroachments.[35]

Not only in the realm of domestic youth activities, but also in affairs relating to Germans abroad, the *Reichsjugendführung* represented a threat to the VDA. Like almost all agencies, especially party ones, in Nazi Germany, the RJF had offices which sought competence of one kind or another in almost every phase of life and political activity. It was no surprise, then, that the Reich Youth leadership also had a *Grenz- und Auslandsamt*. The head of this office was Karl Nabersberg, a particularly ambitious man whose activities in organizing excursions abroad brought him into constant friction with the VDA. He earned the animosity of the VDA leadership in 1934 when he organized special offices in thirteen German cities to "observe" events in the German ethnic groups just beyond the borders.[36] This cut into the competency of the VDA Department for Work with German Youth Abroad (*Abteilung für auslandsdeutsche Jugendarbeit*).[37]

The most serious gulf between the VDA and the HJ youth leadership developed during the course of 1934 as Schirach began to form an alliance with Bohle against the traditionalists. Schirach shared Bohle's ideas on Germandom abroad, seeing no distinction between Reich and ethnic Germans as far as National Socialism was concerned. So when Schirach's request that the VDA youth be dissolved entirely was denied—in June of 1934—he declared open war on the VDA.[38] The radical front against the traditionalists had grown significantly.

By the fall of 1934, then, the traditionalists were already very much on the defensive, attacked on at least two fronts by aspiring NS newcomers. A document labelled simply *Feststellungen* ("Ascertainments"), unsigned and undated, catalogued the frustrations which the AO and RJF had aroused in the course of 1934.[39] On the one hand, the document noted, the radicals were always on the offensive. During the VDA gathering in Königsberg, the ethnic German youth jamboree at Rossiten had been turned into a HJ-*Lager* by swarms of boys in brown. Attempts at educational work among the young people had been hindered time and again by derisive cries of "blue romantic"— linking the blue pennants of the VDA youth with the "blue flower" of the Romantic movement. On the other hand, however, whenever HJ people caused some kind of embarrassing political incident abroad, they were quick to garb themselves in the respectable colors of VDA blue. They encouraged youth groups abroad to go around singing "Today we own Germany, tomorrow the World!" and to call VDA gatherings "reactionary," or *bündisch,* or "civilian"—while at the same time foreign governments were labelling the VDA subversive. If the VDA tried to disguise its political activities abroad by emphasizing its harmlessness, party leaders at home took their cue and derided it as *really* harmless. The AO and RJF people conducted a whispering campaign against the VDA, taking advantage of the generation gap to call its leaders *Weihnachtsmänner* ("Santa Clauses"), but when the VDA tried to recruit younger people among the SA, SS, or Labor Front, it was accused of conducting secret intrigues (*bündische Umtriebe*). The list of grievances goes on and on, but this sampling is sufficient to characterize the situation in which the traditionalists found themselves. It represents the plaintive uncomprehending cries of men who were just beginning to realize the import of the new National Socialist regime. They were conservatives and revolutionaries at the same time: men whose nationalist slogans and romantic longings, whose unclear thinking and thoughtless acceptance helped to bring, or at least welcomed at its arrival, the National Socialist *Erhebung.* They had worked with National Socialism, hoping to guide its direction, only to find themselves slowly being swallowed up by it—gradually overtaken by the movement's dynamism and submerged under its relentless organizational drive.

While the traditionalists slowly lost ground in the Reich, Konrad Henlein returned home from the April meeting with Steinacher to find that his new movement was continuing to generate a great deal of enthusiasm. In less than six months, over three hundred *Ortsgruppen* had been founded and were continuing to appear at the rate of one hundred a month. Membership had jumped from ninety-five hundred in October of 1933 to thirteen thousand in January of 1934, then more than doubled in the next three months: by April it was an estimated thirty-two thousand.[40] Not content to confine its activities merely to Germans in the Sudetenland, the SHF sought organizational contact with Germans living in Slovakia. These so-called *Karpathendeutsche,* apart from the bourgeoisie in towns like Pressburg (Bratislava) and Kaschau (Košice), were for the most part poor peasants eking out a living on the Carpathian slopes, very much the poor country cousins of the Bohemian and Moravian Germans. But the spirit of unity had caught on there, too, so that many Germans in the Slovakian part of the country began to loosen their political ties with the Hungarian minority and to organize themselves as Germans. The SHF moved to exploit this new potential and tried to include these ethnic Germans in its broad front.[41]

The leaders of the SHF were careful to protect their fast growing organization. Despite the very unfavorable time and circumstances under which the new movement was founded, Henlein acted very circumspectly and carefully chose his words in a deliberate attempt to avoid anything which smacked of irredentism or treason. His proclamation founding the Front and his first news conference had both been calculated to reassure the suspicious authorities. On November 11, 1934, Henlein made a speech, pointing out that fate had made the Sudeten Germans a part of the Czechoslovakian state and that they would just have to make the best of it and reach some kind of understanding with the Czechs.[42] Assurances of loyalty, however, especially in light of the events of the past year, would in themselves have been scarcely enough to prevent the aroused Czech authorities from exercising restraints provided for under the Law for the Protection of the Republic had there not been some support for Henlein from the officialdom in Prague.

One man who was inclined to give Henlein a probationary period was Franz Spina, health minister, leader of the German Agrarian party (*Bund der Landwirte,* or BdL). Henlein, of course, had to pay a price for this protection in the form of promises to follow Spina's lead politically and to refrain from trying to organize German peasants in his new movement. The peasants were to remain the concern of the *Sudetendeutsche Landstand,* a close affiliate of the Farmers League. Other parties, too, notably the DAWG (*Deutsche Arbeits- und Wirtschaftsgemeinschaft* or German Labor and Economics Association) and the *Deutsche Demokratische Freiheitspartei* (German Democratic Freedom party), were also making overtures to the new movement.[43] Henlein seemed amenable to making peace with all these bourgeois Sudeten camps. Sometime in June, he asked one of the SHF leaders, Wilhelm Sebekowsky, to check with young Catholics in the Christian Social party about arranging some sort of truce, with the comment that if they were willing to stop fighting, so was the SHF. A month later, it appears that Henlein and the head of the Christian Social party, Senator Karl Hilgenreiner, had actually agreed to put an end to hostilities, at least for the time being.[44] Czech government circles apparently also decided that it was to their advantage to keep the new radical movement out in the open where it could be better controlled and perhaps even be drawn into the inevitable compromises that go into making up legitimate political activity. The alternative would have been to cope with a widely based, clandestine irredentism within an even more radicalized German nationalist camp.

All this Henlein had in his favor. On the other hand, the new unity movement still led a very tenuous existence. A wrong move, too much radical independent action on the local level, outside interference on the part of ambitious people across the border could still bring down the wrath of the government and destroy the SHF before it got off the ground politically. As for the Social Democratic and Communist parties, they had declared war to the death on the new movement, whose outward similarities they quite understandably took to be a carbon copy of German fascism. Not even the *Bund der Landwirte,* which stood solidly in the nationalist camp, fully trusted Henlein. As an internal BdL communique noted on December 4, 1933: "We must make . . . our members aware that joining the SHF means exclusion from our party. . . . The Henlein Front is no neutral club like the *Schutzverein* or the gymnastic [*Turner*] society. *It's a political movement.* Any other interpretation amounts to word play."[45]

However, the real threat, at least for the time being, did not come from outside the *Sudetendeutsche Heimatfront,* but from within. With the founding of the Sudeten German unity front, a number of antagonisms that had previously been fought out between different organizations suddenly became factional disputes within one large organization. The fact that the SHF aspired to political leadership of the entire German minority in Czechoslovakia gave these antagonisms a critical importance they otherwise might not have had. Initially, it appeared that the *Sudetendeutsche Heimatfront* was attempting to carry out the ideas of the Spann-oriented *Kameradschaftsbund,* for the top leadership of the SHF consisted for the most part of members of that *Bund.* If that had been the case, there was probably little likelihood that the new party would make common cause with National Socialism across the border; rather, it would have been more prone to orient itself toward some sort of clerical fascism of the Austrian variety. The KB people, however, did not remain unchallenged. A political movement, after all, involves by definition large masses of people, and the KB was a small elitist group, unused to the mobilization and control of large numbers of members. Although the cadres of Henlein's *Turner* movement did form a part of the new Home Front, the membership as a whole was also drawn from the dissolved DNSAP and DNP. Many of these former NS members were infinitely more experienced in handling the problems of mass politics than was the KB circle. A mass movement grows on the basis of a great deal of political free enterprise on the local level and it was the old National Socialists who had had experience in forming *Ortsgruppen* and neighborhood cells.

Thus, as the *Sudetendeutsche Heimatfront* took shape, it contained within itself the seeds of a schism between the top leadership—a closely knit group, emphasizing the elitist ideas of Othmar Spann— and the mass membership—a large, amorphous group looking more toward the successes of the new regime in Germany. The friction was not simply one of top against bottom, but actually spread with time into the upper leadership itself: at a critical point in the development of the SHF, the arrest of a number of the KB leaders enabled men of National Socialist persuasion to penetrate the higher echelons of the movement.[46] Perhaps the most important of these newcomers to the leadership circle around Henlein was the man who would eventually overshadow Henlein himself after the Sudetenland was annexed to the Reich: a man who, for the Czechs, came to symbolize the hated

German repression of the war years—Karl Hermann Frank.[47] Frank, whom one SdP leader has called "the most fateful of those from our ranks," was a petty book dealer from Karlsbad who had come to the SHF by way of the youth movement, the *Böhmerlandbewegung*, and the DNSAP. His career is a good example of that political free enterprise which characterizes any mass movement: he met Henlein personally for the first time in November of 1933 when he came to report the founding of the first SHF *Ortsgruppe* in Karlsbad. Frank was a "torn, ambitious man," a lone wolf who was imbued with a kind of mystical enthusiasm for things old-Germanic, an intellectually primitive man who harbored strong hatreds, especially for the Czechs whom he considered inferior, but also a man who had a strong bent for conspiracy. It was Frank who in later years came more and more to represent the radical National Socialist ideas in the top ranks of the party, and who, more than any other person, pulled Henlein in that direction. At the outset, however, there was no indication of the role Frank was to play. Initially, Frank seemed in every way to follow the lead established by Henlein; it was only gradually that he, along with many of his colleagues, would be drawn into the service of an aggressive NS Germany.[48]

Up until the first meeting between Henlein and Steinacher in April of 1934, and even in the ensuing months, both men had been fairly occupied with their separate problems. Steinacher struggled on in the Reich to establish the traditionalist concept of Germandom politics; Henlein fought meanwhile in Czechoslovakia to build a unified Sudeten German movement which could attract as many people as possible without incurring the risk of government intervention. Now, however, a factor came into play that tended to take these separate struggles and mold them into essentially one conflict straddling the border: the activity of a growing number of former Sudeten National Socialists who were strongly displeased with Henlein and the direction in which he seemed to be leading the SHF. Some of these radical Sudeten NS members had fled to Germany after 1933 and had gotten into positions of power there, from which they launched their attacks on the traditionalist camp; others were still living in Czechoslovakia. At first, both groups began to direct their attacks fairly exclusively on the KB circle around Henlein. As it became apparent, however, that Henlein's main source of support in the Reich came from Steinacher and the VR traditionalists, the radicals broadened their attacks to include these men as well. In doing so they struck natural alliances with Reich groups sharing this hostility toward the traditionalists—whether for personal or political reasons. In this way, broad, fluctuating fronts grew up on both sides of the border and the traditionalist-radical conflicts which had been fought separately in Germany and in Czechoslovakia now became increasingly one and the same battle. This situation really, in a sense, internationalized the Sudeten problem long before Henlein made his way to London and certainly long before Hitler took any interest in the question. Steinacher and Henlein would have had other reasons to collaborate, certainly, but it was this unified NS attack which really threw them together, made their separate struggles part of the larger Germandom question, and united the seemingly unrelated problems of political rivalry in Berlin and the movement for unity among the German ethnic group in Czechoslovakia.

One of the key figures in the radical NS camp was Hans Krebs, former DNSAP leader who had fled to the Reich in October of 1933.[49] Krebs already had good connections in the Reich—he had known Hitler since 1920. Also, he had access to Interior Minister Frick, whom he had come to know through Frick's political junkets to Czechoslovakia in the late twenties; moreover, for what that was worth, the wives of the two men were very close friends. The day he crossed the border, Krebs heard that Hitler would address a jurists' congress two days later in Schandow. Krebs attended the meeting and was invited to accompany Hitler back to Berlin. The führer promised to find something for him. As a result, some weeks later Krebs received the post of *Oberpräsident der Provinz Hannover,*[50] a position which seemed ideally conceived for Hitler to discharge himself of an obligation to an *Altkämpfer* without, at the same time, putting Krebs in a spot where he could cause embarrassing trouble. Krebs, however, was an ambitious man and with politics being what they were in Nazi Germany, it was no time until he had found a position in Berlin in the ministry of his old friend, Wilhelm Frick, where he assumed the rank of *Regierungsrat* in the press department. After the Reich and Prussian Interior ministries were combined, Krebs became press chief of the Interior Ministry and director of the Technical Library of the Combined Ministries (*Fachbücherei der vereinigten Ministerien*).[51] Thus safely ensconced and with the backing of a powerful figure in the new regime, Krebs proceeded to pursue his own brand of Germandom politics in the Sudeten question.

Krebs's motivations for beginning his long term campaign against Henlein and Steinacher were both political and personal. Politically, Krebs felt outdistanced and cheated by the direction which the *Heimatfront* took after its inception. Krebs apparently wanted to build an NS organization for Czechoslovakia similar to the one which already existed in Austria. He had, or thought he had, Henlein's guarantee to continue on in the old spirit of the DNSAP. He had fully expected to control Henlein through his own man in Czechoslovakia, Dr. Anton Kreissl, and when Henlein did not prove to be amenable to such direction, Krebs was most resentful. According to a report which Henlein gave to Kersken, Kreissl appeared at Henlein's home and arrogantly demanded that Henlein subordinate himself, whereupon Henlein showed him the door.[52] In a letter to Hans Neuwirth on May 13, 1934, Krebs insisted that Neuwirth recognize Kreissl as the only liaison man in Czechoslovakia and Krebs as the single authoritative figure in Germany on relations with Sudeten Germans—something Henlein had no intention of doing.[53] Krebs's resentment focussed on Steinacher, too, for it was the VR-VDA backing of Henlein which enabled the SHF leader to remain independent of Krebs and the other Sudeten National Socialists. Moreover, Krebs was a vain man, one who could not take criticism, and Steinacher, outspoken as he was, constantly found reason to criticize Krebs and his actions.[54] Thus, a problem of personalities complicated the already existing political differences between Krebs and the traditionalists.

Initially, Krebs used two weapons in his political battles against the traditionalists. By gathering material both on Steinacher's colleagues and on the various people around Henlein, he tried to incriminate these men in the eyes of the new regime in Germany as well as to get both groups in trouble with the Czechs. Moreover, he availed himself of allies among organizations already active in the Germandom rivalries. He centered his attack particularly, at first, on Hermann Ullmann, the *Volksdeutscher Rat* member responsible for Sudeten German affairs. Krebs pointed to Ullmann's earlier connections with the center party to show that he had been politically close to a camp that opposed National Socialism. On February 9, 1934,

Krebs wrote to Steinacher trying to drive a wedge between Ullmann and the VDA leadership.[55] Apparently failing in this, he began to take a new tack. In March Steinacher wrote in his diaries: "Continuing crisis in the NS's attacks against Ullmann. Against me, too."; "Ullmann is only working along on the periphery from time to time. Under heavy attack (Krebs in RIM [i.e. Interior Ministry])." By the fall of 1934 Krebs had succeeded in getting rid of Ullmann entirely as VR Sudeten *Referent.*[56]

The same sort of tactic served to cast aspersions on Friedrich Bürger and Hans Neuwirth, both Sudeten Germans who served as liaisons between Henlein and Steinacher. For example, on June 7, 1934, Krebs sent a memorandum to Hitler in which he tried to link both these men (and Ullmann as well) with Catholic-Conservative circles. On another occasion he wrote to Willy Meerwald in the Reich Chancellory, accusing the VDA of subsidizing Christian Social organizations in Czechoslovakia.[57]

Krebs also manipulated the radical splinter organization, the *Sudetendeutscher Heimatbund,* and its director, Hanns Beer. As early as March 16, 1934, in his opening discussions with Köpke of the *Auswärtiges Amt,* Steinacher had cause to complain about SHB ventures across the border.[58] Krebs succeeded in getting his old colleague, Karl Viererbl, who also had fled to Germany and who had found a job on the editorial staff of the *Völkischer Beobachter,* named to an influential position in the SHB.[59] Krebs then proceeded to use the organization, its official publication, and its rallies as his own propaganda platform. He also worked together with a SHB leader in Vienna, Anton Clement, to disseminate the inflammatory brochure "Die Sudetendeutschen in der Tschechoslowakei nicht unterdrückt?" all over Europe.[60] Krebs and Viererbl considered plans to set up a *Vertretung der Minderheiten aus der Tschechoslowakei* ("Representation of the Czechoslovakian Minorities") in Geneva, along with representatives of the Hungarian and Slovakian minorities in Czechoslovakia.[61]

Through these many activities Krebs never lost sight of any opportunity that might help him gain control of the unity movement in the Sudetenland in the name of the National Socialists. It was to this end that he pursued his continuing search for allies in the Germandom camp. Two contacts Krebs found very useful were Walter von Lierau (consul in Reichenberg and a protégé of Bohle and

Himmler) and Freiherr Sigismund von Bibra (who was attached to the
mission in Prague). These foreign service officers were in strong
sympathy with the radical Nazis and worked closely with Krebs, both
as sources of information and as liaisons for transmitting propaganda
material against the KB people around Henlein. Krebs would write to
Lierau at a special address in Zittau and a messenger would then
carry the message across the border.[62] For his part, Bibra was in close
contact with Anton Kreissl in Czechoslovakia.[63] Bibra, particularly,
harbored a strong resentment against Kersken and refused to refer to
him as *Oberführer,* claiming that he only knew of a *"Standartenführer
Kersken."* [64] Bibra also tried to associate Kersken's name with some
prominent Prague Jews and thus discredit him.[65] At an AA conference
in December of 1933, which dealt with help for Sudeten National
Socialists, Bibra again threw his support against the traditionalists.
Funds for this relief effort were to be administered jointly by the
Foreign Office and the Finance Ministry. These funds were not to be
sent through VDA channels, but were to be dispensed to trusted men
via the diplomatic mission in Prague. Bibra was probably responsible
for the remark that "In the choice of these agents we must be very
careful; the *Kameradschaftsbund* should be rejected as unreliable from
the outset." [66] With their combined influence, Bibra and Lierau were
able not only to work with Krebs directly, but also indirectly aided his
cause by clouding the whole relationship between the *Volksdeutscher
Rat* and the *Auswärtiges Amt.*

Perhaps the most serious blow which Krebs dealt to the VR was
his success in winning Interior Minister Wilhelm Frick over to his
side. Frick had originally been well disposed to Steinacher and the
work of the VDA: in fact, he had spoken at several VDA congresses.[67]
After the beginning of 1934, however, Krebs was gradually able to
turn him against the VDA-VR group and their goals. At first, Frick
urged Steinacher to work with Krebs; he even offered to let Steinacher
use the police to get rid of any embarrassing "friends" of Krebs who
might compromise the VDA leader.[68] Later, however, particularly
after he came into possession of an especially "incriminating"
Denkschrift which had been written by Hans Neuwirth, VDA
colleague of Steinacher, Frick changed his attitude completely and
gave Krebs a free hand.[69] Frick may not have been one of the most
powerful paladins in the Third Reich and he was ultimately to be
overshadowed by Himmler, but given the stage of rivalry between

conservatives and radicals in fields even beyond the Germandom question, he was an ally the traditionalists could not afford to lose. One other benefit for Krebs in working for Frick was his proximity to the police. In fact, with Frick's help, a so-called *Sudetendeutsche Kontrollstelle* was set up in Dresden with a Major Wilhelm Krichbaum in charge. Krebs came to work very closely with Krichbaum, part of whose duties was to screen all political refugees coming from Czechoslovakia. One thing Krebs did through the control office was to smuggle material across the border into Germany, including twenty years of back issues of the DNSAP newspaper *Der Tag*. Also, with the help of the consul in Reichenberg, he used the *Kontrollstelle* to arrange the escape of Emil Lehmann, a National Socialist professor, across the border to Germany.[70]

But if Krebs was skilled in using others to play his own particular political game, he also was used at times himself by even more powerful aspirants in the field of Germandom politics—not an uncommon situation in the Third Reich. In this case, it was Bohle who made use of Krebs's connections in Czechoslovakia to strike in his own way at Steinacher and the VR. With the cooperation of Krebs and through the agitation of Bibra in Prague, Bohle utilized the radical National Socialist student groups in Prague to bring discredit on the youth work of the traditionalists.[71]

As the different factions both cooperated with and manipulated one another on both sides of, and across, the border, out of shared principles and sheer convenience, the situation soon reached the point where one could almost say that "any enemy of yours is an enemy of mine." Krebs, whose guns were originally aimed at Henlein, soon found another target in Steinacher; Bohle, whose main goal was unseating Steinacher, found it convenient to fire his shots via Prague. As the fronts began to form, what had been two separate problem complexes—Steinacher versus Bohle in the Reich, and Henlein versus the sharpshooting of Krebs—rapidly became one: traditionalists in the Reich and in Czechoslovakia in competition with the radical National Socialists on both sides of the border.

However, it was not only the main protagonists in the Germandom field who contributed to a kind of internationalization of the Sudeten problem. The activities of the small radical splinter groups were also an important factor, perhaps at times even more important than the institutionalized machinations of men like Bohle or Krebs.

Having less at stake in the bureaucratic power struggle, the smaller radical factions could afford to engage in more extreme activities— sometimes even to the point of outright sabotage. Particularly Krebs often found himself being "aided" by such enthusiastic, embarrassingly imprudent former colleagues from the DNSAP. For example, one observer noted in a report to the AA: "In northern Bohemia (and supposedly in all other German areas) old DNSAP groups are still surviving which prefer to work illegally. These people conduct themselves in a colossally radical manner, prefer working with gunpowder, and still swear allegiance to Representatives Jung and Krebs." [72] Such radical elements, being closer to the day-to-day reality of Sudeten politics than the heads of the bureaucratic NS opposition, were able to gather information more effectively and act on it more impulsively than men like Bohle. For example, the KB people attributed the arrest of Walter Brand in December of 1933 to denunciation by such radical rivals. (The Patschneider trial against the radicals was, in turn, reputed to be counter-treachery on the part of the KB.) [73] In this way, the radicals could, and often did, deliver extremely compromising evidence to the Czech authorities, who were only too glad to have an excuse to crack down on Henlein. Another particularly nasty weapon was to send a rival a compromising letter in the knowledge that it would be intercepted by the Czech authorities. Henlein himself received a letter like this in the fall of 1934, in which the writer announced a forthcoming armed rebellion in which he urged Henlein to take part.[74] A variation on this technique was to send damaging articles to newspapers under the signature of a rival. Ernst Kundt, a KB man and a close associate of Henlein, complained that someone had signed his name to an article in the *Völkischer Beobachter* praising the Henlein Front.[75] The radicals in the Sudetenland were also useful sources of information to Reich authorities and quite often they would write reports putting their rivals in the SHF in a very damaging light. For example, on June 9, 1934, Minister Koch passed on to his superiors accusations from one Sudeten circle that Henlein was accepting aid from Prague Jews.[76]

Like the pre-1934 SA in Germany, the old DNSAP party activists, once having been politicized, were not so easily shut off again. They were impatient and angry that the National Socialization of the Sudeten Germans had apparently stopped for the time being and they did not hesitate to express their chagrin in the highest quarters. One such complaint, from a very minor former member of the DNSAP who had been active in the *Kreisleitung* at Turn-Teplitz, was directed to Adolf Hitler himself—eloquent witness to this highly combustible political frustration. The writer laments that it had been a year since Krebs left for the Reich and "nothing has been done yet." In Henlein the writer sees only a surrogate for the führer. Henlein's colleagues hadn't proven themselves reliable as yet: many of them had even made critical remarks about National Socialism or its leaders. One of them, Rudolf Sandner, had even been an SPD man up until 1930. By contrast, the writer emphasized his own unquestionable loyalty and reliability and that of his friends: "I, myself, and thousands of my comrades have joined the *Heimatfront* in the past months, following directives from above, and are seeing to it that our ideas are not watered down in the individual local and regional organizations." The letter concludes by mentioning the writer's contacts with the Dresden *Gauleitung*, his recruitment to work for the *Nachrichtendienst*, and a plan he has worked out for reorganizing the German intelligence network.[77] The whole letter could be dismissed as totally ludicrous had it not been so typical: the sort of independent political action of idealistic, ambitious men who, for the first time, had been caught up in a movement and "politicized." Many Sudeten Nazis liked to think of their movement as being genuinely democratic in contrast to the false "democracy" of Czechoslovakia and the West. Their democracy they defined as the utmost political mobilization of the little man—and when one considers the myriad independent activities of small, often radical groups on both sides of the border, the Sudetens were, within the framework of their own definition, correct.

The formation of these various fronts across the frontiers in the Germandom conflict posed a grave potential threat to the international status quo. In this light it is interesting to assess Hitler's role in the whole process. Surely a situation fraught with such diplomatic and military consequences would have elicited some action on the part of the führer and chancellor of the Reich. As one regards the apex of power in Nazi Germany, however, one gets the unnerving impression that, in contrast to the usual image of a totalitarian dictatorship, a great deal of activity seemed to be pointing toward the center of power, while precious little was emanating from that locus. On the part of the second and third echelons, there was feverish activity as rival contenders attempted both to secure a decision from the führer that would be favorable to them and to convince their opponents that it was indeed they who were acting in the führer's name. However, when one turns to the Reich Chancellory seeking a reaction to this plethora of stimuli, one is greeted by silence or ambiguity.

The most common method of approaching the führer, of course, was to ask for a personal audience. To have spoken recently with Hitler could be a powerful weapon with which to confront one's rivals, even if not much came of the audience (just as in the early days of the party to have Hitler visit a *Gau* personally and give a speech conferred considerable prestige on that *Gauleiter*).[78] Barring this alternative, one could put one's complaints, requests, and plans in writing and submit them to the Chancellory in the hope that the führer would take cognizance of them and act accordingly. Since, however, so many people were trying to see Hitler, and so few actually succeeded, the use of the written *Denkschrift* or "position paper" became a common tactic in Germandom struggles, as well as in other competency battles in the Third Reich. The interesting thing about these papers was that they seldom accomplished what the author set out to do. A few might have been read, but they were rarely acted upon directly. Most went into the files. Some were passed on to a rival and added fuel to an already raging conflict. They do have value, however, as a kind of mirror of the plans, ambitions, pretentions, and temerity of those involved in Germandom politics in the Third Reich. For example, the way in which these *Denkschriften* were often formulated is interesting and revealing, for they combined a tone of slavish obedience with a surprising bravado in telling Hitler what *his* intentions were—at least as perceived by the writer. If Hitler actually read them, he was, or would have been as the case may be, in the strange position of hearing his vassals tell him what he thought or was supposed to have been thinking. It was apparently a standard trick in the power struggles in the Third Reich to claim a special insight into Hitler's intentions, and to judge by the confused and contradictory claims put forth in the führer's name on the Germandom question, Hitler's intentions—as they were funneling down to his subordinates in 1934—were none too clear to the führer himself.

A "battle of the *Denkschriften*" was opened on May 27, 1934, by Hans Neuwirth, Henlein's liaison man to the Reich in financial affairs, whom Heinrich Kersken had asked to submit ideas for a reorganization of ethnic German politics.[79] In a ninety-one page, verbose document entitled *Südosten,* Neuwirth went into a drawn out discussion of *Volkstumspolitik,* decrying the rivalries and confused competencies which had developed. He pointed out, regretfully, that more people and agencies were making policy in this area now than before the NS seizure of power. He carefully distinguished the "real ethnic Germans" in Germandom work, who carried out their duties autonomously and parallel to the official leadership, and those opportunists, especially in party circles, who were causing confusion and antagonisms. His paper concluded with a series of recommendations, which, if carried out, would have put Steinacher and the VR in a position of absolute authority in ethnic German affairs and would have outlawed the small independent groups which were making so much trouble. Neuwirth drew special attention to the *Sudetendeutscher Heimatbund,* the organization through which Krebs was working, and advised that it be severely restricted in its activities. Indirectly, of course, by appealing for the strengthened authority of Steinacher and the VR, Neuwirth would be working for Henlein, too, since Steinacher was virtually the only mentor Henlein had in the Reich at the time.

Like so many recommendations put before the Reich leadership in these position papers, Neuwirth's suggestions found no echo in the Reich Chancellory; but they did represent a challenge which Hans Krebs was not long in answering. On June 7, 1934, Krebs submitted a seven page position paper to the Reich Chancellory.[80] In his paper Krebs claimed that *he* and *his* comrades were really the people best equipped to handle relations between the various Reich authorities and the Sudeten Germans. He maintained that in previous months Steinacher had deliberately kept the old National Socialists from exerting any influence whatsoever on relations with the German minority in Czechoslovakia. The whole Sudeten question, therefore, was being handled by people who had never been National Socialists, many of whom in fact had been in organizations hostile to National Socialism (here he was referring to Bürger, Ullmann, and Neuwirth). He claimed also that "Konrad Henlein has promised to lead his party in the spirit of National Socialism and to keep contact with the NSDAP in the Reich through Sudeten German National Socialists." Krebs referred to a meeting on May 11, 1934 with the führer, Krebs himself, and Kreissl, Krebs's representative in Czechoslovakia, after which "the necessary inclusion of the Sudeten German National Socialists [into Germandom work] was finally achieved." Soon thereafter, however, Henlein—acting on information from the VDA—absolutely refused to allow any interference on the part of the old National Socialists. The upshot, Krebs concluded, is that a thorough-going transformation of the VR-VDA complex is urgently needed. Naturally, his idea of transformation was diametrically opposed to that suggested by Neuwirth.

The plot was soon to thicken considerably. On June 19, Henrich Kersken, Hess's adjutant in ethnic German affairs and a protector of the VR-VDA, himself submitted a lengthy document for Hitler's consideration.[81] In his position paper, Kersken refuted point by point all the arguments offered by Krebs. He denied that Krebs was sent to the Reich as a plenipotentiary of the Sudeten Nazis; Krebs, in fact, just ran away. Any other interpretation, he asserted, represents *ex post facto* rationalization. In light of this Krebs's claim that only National Socialists in Czechoslovakia are entitled to influence in the German-dom question is not valid. Moreover, Kersken pointed to supposed instructions by Hitler which clearly forbade, for reasons of discretion, any control of Germandom work by former Sudeten National Socialists: "The months-long attempts by Herr Krebs to insinuate the Sudeten German National Socialists [into Germandom work] without laying claim to the führer's authority, represents basically—in light of the führer's clear decision—an undisciplined revolt against a decision of the führer." [82] What Krebs, in fact, is doing is trying to set up an organization similar to that operated by the Austrian NS. Henlein, on the other hand, despite Krebs's claims to the contrary, never intended to found an ersatz party for the old DNSAP: "Henlein himself has indicated time and again that he sticks by the fact that the Sudeten German Home Front was founded by him, on his own initiative, and under no outside influence, in order to fill the gap left by the failure of Krebs and the circle around him." In this connection Kersken adds, "Henlein has offered for a long time to subordinate himself to the führer."

Scholars have used this reference at face value in an attempt to support the claim that Henlein was working hand-in-hand with Hitler from the very beginning.[83] For a number of important reasons, however, such a literal assessment of the Kersken *Denkschrift* does not stand up under close scrutiny. First, the paper itself—although it systematically attacks Krebs's arguments—is itself not internally consistent. Kersken assures Hitler that the SHF is not a substitute for the disbanded DNSAP, yet what else would the Front be if it were founded merely to "fill the gap left by the failure of Krebs and the circle around him"? Several of Kersken's other remarks, among them that ethnic German work was "under absolute National Socialist control" or that the VR and VDA were under Hess's strict control, are also either demonstrably misleading or untrue. In light of this, it would be an error to take this position paper at face value and to hit upon the term "subordinate" literally without trying to put the statement and the *Denkschrift* as a whole into the larger context of the Germandom struggle at this point. The issue here is not what Kersken ostensibly reveals about any of Henlein's "secret" motives; rather, it is vital to view Kersken's claims in light of Henlein's specific problems at this stage of the Germandom conflict. What Henlein was looking for at this point was a way of consolidating and legitimizing his political position at home. He was having problems within the SHF and it was complicating things considerably that Krebs and other Sudeten emigrés were also agitating against him in Germany. Steinacher had offered to aid him; but Steinacher was only one figure in the second echelon of power in the new Reich. Krebs meanwhile was looking around for more powerful support for his claims of leadership, at the same time trying to discredit Henlein—even with Hitler himself. It made sense for Henlein to combat this threat as quickly and energetically as possible—and perhaps even win the imprimatur of the new government in the process. Hitler knew full well that Henlein was not a National Socialist: in that sense Krebs *did* have more in common with the führer. Kersken, then, does not dispute Henlein's "outsider" status. Rather, he tries in a variety of ways to assure Hitler that this non-NS status is an asset and a compelling reason to recognize Henlein's leadership claims in the Sudetenland. Hitler had encouraged quiescence—this was one thing in Henlein's favor. But Kersken also had to make clear that Henlein, although outside the NS fold, was not unwilling to cooperate with the new regime. Hence the word "subordination" to Hitler. For a man like Kersken, steeped in the rhetoric of the Third Reich, this was the only relationship possible with the führer. As far as Henlein was concerned, whether he personally used the word "subordination" or not, the question was what any such offer meant in concrete terms:

i.e., what would Henlein have been willing to offer in exchange for support? In this context, "subordinate" is ambiguous. It promises everything, but binds one to nothing. At the same time, in the jargon of the new Reich regime, it was a polite bow to the leadership of a large power.

One thing is certain, as the Germandom struggle from this point bears out, Henlein was not a fifth-columnist at this stage nor was he offering to be one. What he was doing was making noises for support—nothing more. As for Hitler, the führer did not react to any ostensible Henlein offer or request, much less did it occur to him to use Henlein as a fifth column. If there had been any indication of this whatsoever, Kersken would scarcely have neglected to emphasize it. In reality, like it or not, Henlein was on his own and would continue to be so for a long time to come. He did eventually, of course, become the agent for a Hitlerian fifth column, but the process took a long time: the story of how it came about is the story of the Germandom struggle from here on.

On the face of it, then, both Krebs and Kersken were making statements indicating that Hitler had already taken action—*i.e.,* had made a decision in their favor. Yet their claims are directly in opposition to one another. It is highly unlikely that either of the two men was lying. After all, it was one thing to "interpret" Hitler's will, as both men were undoubtedly doing to confound and discredit the other; but it is something else entirely to remind the führer to his face of a meeting which never took place or to confront him with a decision he never made. Both men, then, were probably "telling the truth." The most logical explanation for the discrepancy is that Hitler did actually tell each man what he claimed Hitler told him: he informed Kersken that he did not want the Sudeten emigrés involved in Germandom politics and he insinuated to Krebs that his sympathies lay with the old guard. Beyond saying this, to get both out of his hair, Hitler at this point did nothing more to help or hinder either man, the *Denkschriften* notwithstanding. In fact, there is some doubt whether he even bothered to read the papers at all. With regard to Krebs's *Denkschrift,* Meerwald in Hitler's Chancellory passed it on to Hess a week after its arrival—an action which, as it turns out, served to exacerbate the conflict (Kersken's paper was clearly a reaction against Krebs's note). Meerwald's only note to Hess about the paper was: "zur gefälligen Kenntnisnahme und mit dem Anheimstellen der weiteren Veranlassung" [note at your convenience; leaving further action to you].[84] What the further action might be was not specified. The Kersken paper appears, in turn, to have been relegated to the files of the Reich Chancellory without Hitler having taken any action on it either. Krebs, meanwhile, continued to forge his alliances under the cover of Frick's ministry and Kersken went on battling for the competency of the VR. What originally were attempts to sway Hitler into making a decision and to elicit a binding response from the source of power turned out in retrospect to be something very different: just another tactical weapon in the continuing rivalries, or as Meerwald showed by sending the Krebs paper to Hess, a tool to encourage still more rivalry.

The whole episode is just one more indication that Hitler was clearly not concerned with definitively settling the problem of competency in Germandom politics—at least not in 1934. He was content to let well enough alone and to turn his attention to domestic consolidation, leaving ethnic German politics in general and the Sudeten question in particular lie by the wayside. But Germandom politics contained far too much explosive potential to remain dormant. Broad political fronts continued to spring up across personal and ideological lines, competing to fill the power vacuum created by Hitler's disinterest. It remained to be seen which group, traditionalists or radicals, would succeed in imposing its political conception on Germandom politics and, by inference, help define the nature of German foreign policy toward Czechoslovakia.

V

The Situation in Flux

BY the fall of 1934 the combined attacks of Krebs, Bohle, and others were making themselves very much felt in the traditionalist Germandom camp. It was becoming more and more apparent to both Henlein and Steinacher that if either were to survive politically, they had to stick together. Steinacher, especially hard pressed by the radicals, needed the success of Henlein's movement to show both the viability of his idea of *Volkstum* and the efficacy of the VR in Germandom work.[1] Now, with the RJF and the AO cutting into the competency of both the VR and the VDA, Steinacher had to engineer some dramatic *coup* to stay alive politically. Henlein offered him this opportunity: if, with the help of the VDA, the Sudeten German party could make a good showing in the elections of 1935, then the credit would redound to Steinacher's benefit.

As for Henlein, he needed Steinacher by now just as much as the VDA leader needed him. Whereas the old NS emigrés seemed to have excellent contacts in the new Germany, Henlein still only had access to the sources of power in the Reich through Steinacher and the VR. In the course of 1934, however, the attacks on Henlein and his colleagues mounted so much in intensity, that Steinacher's assurances were no longer enough for Henlein. He needed a strong imprimatur from the new regime in order to hold his own; so, he asked Steinacher several times to get him more concrete legitimization from someone in high authority.[2] Steinacher agreed, realizing that if adequate preparations were going to be made for the elections, then Henlein must have protection from political sniping. Never being one to do something obliquely when he could confront the situation head-on, Steinacher resolved to go right to the top: he would bring Henlein to see Hess! It was a very propitious time to solicit Hess's backing for VR competence in Sudeten German affairs. The abortive Austrian Nazi coup in July of 1934 had shown what could happen if radicals were permitted to pursue their kind of international politics. Europe was still edgy about the Austrian venture and Mussolini, future alliance partner of Hitler, was furious at the apparent subterfuge. This situation, combined with the bad taste left by the bloody Roehm purge in June, militated against anything untoward happening with the Sudeten Germans. In all probability Hess would be only too glad to leave things in the hands of the traditionalists.

In the middle of September Steinacher heard from Albrecht Haushofer that Hess had taken one of his frequent recuperative holidays and was resting in a cottage near Wunsiedl in the Fichtelgebirge, not far from the Czech border. In a scene reminiscent of the April 1934 meeting between Henlein and Steinacher, the VDA leader brought Henlein directly to Hess—without Hess's prior knowledge of the plan. Although at first annoyed at the intrusion, Hess consented to talk with Henlein.[3] Steinacher recalls the meeting:

> The few words of agreement which Hess said to Henlein *tête-à-tête* gave him the desired clarification that his way was the right one at this time and that I and the VR were not standing alone. Until his election success in May of 1935, Henlein took reassurance from this meeting. And I had the impression that Rudolf Hess also got a definitely positive impression of Henlein.[4]

After this meeting with Hess, the two Germandom leaders separated again, each to return to his own political problems: Henlein with assurances that theoretically gave him more freedom and confidence to act; Steinacher with the hope that one crowning success would justify his position and that of the VR.

Although his meeting with Hess might have given him some degree of confidence in his leadership, Henlein returned to the Sudetenland to confront much the same unstable situation as before. On the one hand, like an omnipresent swarm of bees droning away in the background, the radicals continued to snipe at the traditionalists on all fronts for their "conservative" ideology; on the other, the SHF found itself compelled to convince its detractors in the Czechoslovakian government of its political respectability. Without a broad base of support—including the large number of former Sudeten NS members—the Sudeten German Home Front might well be unable to win any kind of mandate; without the toleration of the Czech government, the Front could find itself dissolved even before it had been given official permission to take part in the May elections. Henlein opted for pacifying the Czechs. At the risk of alienating the radicals even more, he issued all the correct assurances, entered into electoral negotiations with "respectable" German bourgeois parties, and even cultivated right-wing Czech politicians.

Throughout the final months of 1934, Henlein had been very careful indeed to assure his loyalty to the Czech state and to deny any ties to the Reich of a political nature. At an SHF *Hauptleitungssitzung* on September 9, 1934, under the influence of the KB faction, it had been decided that the Front should take a clear position "against fascism, including the fascism in National Socialism. Programmatic declaration for democracy, against imperialism and against fascism." [5] In an interview a few weeks later published in *Večer*, the organ of the Czech Agrarians, Henlein stated unequivocally:

> I say clearly, that I never have nor have had anything in common with National Socialism. German National Socialism ends for us at the border, just as the SHF ends there, too. We are not a continuation of the Krebs party; and it should finally be openly declared that we completely despise Krebs and similar leaders who deserted. When someone flees from his responsibility, then he's through as far as we're concerned. [6]

Henlein's greatest effort to assure his loyalty came in the largest rally of the SHF up until that date—the one at Böhmisch-Leipa on October 21, 1934. There, in front of nearly twenty thousand people, Henlein proclaimed in the strongest terms yet his fealty to democracy and to the Czechoslovakian Republic. He condemned both pan-Germanism and pan-Slavism as unsuitable for a Europe of the future: they could only lead to a war which would be disastrous for the Sudeten Germans. Most surprising was the passage in his speech contrasting his movement with National Socialism. *His* movement, he proclaimed, would never deny the fundamental human rights of the individual! [7] All in all, Henlein's speech was calculated to have the most ameliorating effect possible on the Czech government—much of what he said was obviously aimed directly at pacifying Beneš. However conciliatory his words might have been, they lost much of their effectiveness because of the form that the mass rally took. The disciplined columns, the waving banners, and the military music seemed frighteningly like the Nazi model—and did, in fact, underline the fact that a good portion of the rank and file membership and grass roots organizers in the SHF were former DNSAP members who had long been accustomed to emulating the political style of the regime across the border.[8]

Henlein's second tactic at this point, negotiating with the other German parties, offered the chance to edge into the glow of respectability enjoyed by the "activist" parties. Initially, Henlein negotiated an agreement with the small *Gewerbepartei* headed by Alfred Rosche, by which that party would be absorbed into the SHF.[9] Henlein also began what was to be long, drawn out negotiations with the German Agrarian party (*Bund der Landwirte*) on the possibility of a common election list. This turned out to be a very clever move, for Franz Spina, the head of the BdL, was a government minister and Henlein's only protector in official circles: by negotiating with him, Henlein not only contributed to his acceptance as a legitimate politician, but also weakened the position of the Agrarians, who appeared to be putting their own loyalty in question by "collaborating" with the SHF.[10] It is probable that Henlein was not negotiating in good faith. Although the talks did not end until March of 1935, when the SHF broke them off, Henlein remarked to Steinacher as early as January that he would go into the elections alone.[11]

Henlein's other trump card in the fight to assure the survival of his movement was the possibility of support from right-wing Czechs. A number of Czech Agrarians had Henlein in mind as an ally against the Left. In late 1933 and early 1934 Henlein had conferred with and received sums of money from Viktor Stoupal, leader of the conservative wing of the Czech Agrarian party.[12] Now Henlein was ready to play on the right-wing Czech desire for an alliance in order to secure his own political survival. This policy was summarized in the SHF *Hauptleitungssitzung* of November 5, 1934: "Collaboration with the Czech Agrarians. Henlein is ready to assure that there are no ties of any kind to the Left, but then they [the Agrarians] have to really make an effort." [13]

In the end these various maneuvers did pay off: the Henlein party was finally granted permission in April of 1935 to take part in the elections scheduled for May. It was a close call, however, for the government had very nearly not agreed to allow the SHF to participate. When the question came up in the cabinet, the political committee voted, by a four vote margin, not to allow the Henlein organization to go into the elections at all. It was agreed, however, to refer the final decision to President Masaryk. The aging leader then chose to give Henlein a chance to work within the political framework of the state.[14] One condition attached to this permission was that the *Sudetendeutsche Heimatfront* had to agree to change its name to *Sudetendeutsche Partei* (SdP).[15] The Czechs pointed out that the term "Front" was a bit too military sounding for an organization involved in parliamentary elections.

Henlein, however, had to pay a stiff price for these guarantees of his survival. His assurances of loyalty, his very careful behavior in all his political actions, and his contacts with the Czechs and other German parties earned him the reprobation of large numbers of the radical National Socialists who formed the backbone of his movement. These actions also furnished men like Krebs in the Reich with ammunition for their attacks. Especially the speech at Böhmisch-Leipa struck a very disharmonious chord among the old National Socialists. Graf Pfeil reported from the consulate in Reichenberg that the general mood of the former DNSAP membership was "much put out" (*stark verschnupft*).[16] Although the NS faction understood the necessity of making some sort of declaration of loyalty, Pfeil explained, it also thought that Henlein should have made his remarks against National Socialism shorter and not as vivid. One member of the radical *Aufbruch* circle told Minister Koch:

> We expected something completely different from Henlein. He has not projected any ideas at all. He, who was out to fight liberalism and to put universalism in its place, has wound up with the artificial construction of "liberty" which he accepts to make the Czechs happy. Here he's beginning to get wound up in contradictions.[17]

This whole furor over Henlein's speech reflects not only grass roots discontent, but also the growing split in the party leadership itself, between the NS and KB factions. The passages in Henlein's speech which expressed strong rejection of National Socialism only came to be included after a hard struggle. It was only through the influence of the *Kameradschaftsbund* led by Walter Brand, Hans Neuwirth, Ernst Kundt, and Wilhelm Sebekowsky, that the controversial sections were included at all—over the strenuous objections of Karl Hermann Frank.[18] In the ensuing months criticism from the radicals increased. Particularly the *Aufbruch* members, the most articulate and powerful radical opponents of Henlein in the Sudetenland, stepped up their infiltration of the SHF at lower levels of the party. At the main leadership meetings Walter Brand demanded immediate and effective action against these people. There was very little agreement in the SHF *Hauptleitung,* however, as to how this was to be done, or even if it should be done. This disagreement at the very highest party levels, even among the moderates, reflects how deep the factionalism in the SHF had grown.[19]

Meanwhile in the Reich, Steinacher was beset by problems every bit as complicated as those confronting Henlein: not only did the meeting with Hess fail to produce any immediate improvement in the traditionalist position, barely a month later Steinacher and his colleagues suddenly found themselves facing a major setback—perhaps the worst they had experienced to date. In October of 1934, one of the strongest defenders of the traditionalists, Heinrich Kersken, was dropped from his position as Hess's *Volkspolitischer Adjutant.*[20] On October 15, to replace Kersken, Hess appointed Ernst Bohle to be his "official [staff] expert on all questions of Germans living abroad." At the same time, Hess made Bohle—as well as Joachim von Ribbentrop, who had recently been appointed *Beauftragte für aussenpolitische Fragen im Stab des Stellvertreters des Führers* ("Plenipotentiary for Foreign Policy Questions on the Staff of the Führer's Deputy") —full members of the *Volksdeutscher Rat.*[21] Both men immediately selected deputies to represent them on the VR: Bohle chose his colleague Wolfgang Graf Yorck von Wartenburg; Ribbentrop designated one of his younger assistants, Hermann Kügler. With this, the radicals had succeeded in breaching the walls of the traditionalist stronghold. Even more important, it was a sign that Hess, despite his assurances to Henlein, was apparently quite susceptible to the increasingly heavy pressure from the radical side.

As far as the traditionalists were concerned, the events of October 14 and 15 could only be termed a disaster. More than any other individual, the tough Kersken had succeeded in mediating disputes between the VDA-VR and rival party agencies, as well as protecting Steinacher and the VR against the encroachments of more radical Germandom groups. In all fairness, a number of excesses—not the least of which had been drink and critical remarks about Hess himself—had left Kersken open to dismissal. But Bohle's quick rise would seem to indicate that these were not the only grounds for

Kersken's change in fortune. Already on October 9, Bohle had reiterated his philosophy of Germandom work, without receiving Kersken's usual rebuke. "Germandom abroad," Bohle had proclaimed, "must as a whole . . . become more and more a reliable instrument in the hands of the state." [22] Now, with Kersken gone and Bohle represented on the VR, the AO leader seemed to be in a position to put his ideas into action. Steinacher recorded the traditionalists' despair in his diary:

> Catastrophe in Munich. . . . We meet the elder Haushofer at the Brown House, visibly shaken. Bohle has won! . . . Kersken has fallen. In total disgrace. We've only been asked to come to hear the verdict which Hess will pronounce. . . . [Overseas] is supposed to be the political domain of the AO. Bohle will be taking over, so to speak, the chairmanship of the VR. An impossible construction.

Distraught, but powerless, Steinacher could do little but warn Hess about the dangers posed by AO activity in border questions, emphasizing especially the delicate situation in South Tirol and in the Sudetenland.[23]

But to everyone's surprise, the immediate effect of the change was not as dramatic as feared. Apparently although the need for caution in foreign affairs did not deter the radicals as far as infiltrating the VR was concerned, it seems to have cautioned them against exploiting their successes too fast. In any case, despite Steinacher's pessimism, Kersken's replacement did not bring a sudden collapse of the VR. The next meeting, held on October 22 with Bohle attending, proceeded without incident. Steinacher gave a general situation report and, so as not to irritate Bohle, he carefully refrained from mentioning the VDA. The AO leader, for his part, did not say a word. "Those who were looking forward to a fight have been disappointed," Steinacher wrote. "However I have the freedom to proceed along the lines of my presentation." [24] The next day Hess wrote to Haushofer, thanking him for not jumping to hasty conclusions about the new situation and assuring him that he would soon change his opinion of Bohle as the AO leader began to cooperate.[25] But all this was just the calm before the storm. By the beginning of 1935 the radicals were attacking with new intensity, perhaps because as the events of the summer of 1934 receded into the past the need for caution was no longer so keenly felt. Conceivably, too, the dramatic results of the Saar referendum at the beginning of 1935 gave the radical initiative new impetus. Through intrigues and interruptions, Bohle's representative on the VR, Wartenburg, soon made all sober discussion impossible.[26] Albrecht Haushofer, in desperation, wrote to his father, warning him that he must resist Bohle: cooperation, he maintained, is all right, but Bohle must not be allowed to interfere or give orders.[27]

The crisis came at the VR meeting on February 1, 1935—a meeting that would for all purposes mark the end of the VR as an organization.[28] At this session, Wartenburg demanded that in future aid to German organizations in Poland the VR should support not only the *Deutsche Vereinigung,* the older German unity organization which had been recognized by the Polish government, but also the *Jungdeutschen,* a group of radicals closer to the National Socialists in orientation. This course of action was clearly counter to everything the VR and the traditionalists had stood for: by catering to two rival Germandom organizations within the same country, the basic philosophy that underlay the traditionalist approach—namely, encouraging the integrity and unity of each ethnic group—would have been undermined. "We need a counterattack," Steinacher wrote, "or we shall abandon the VR." [29] The following day Karl Haushofer wrote to Hess, tendering his resignation as head of the VR, pointing out that it was impossible to work with Bohle and Wartenburg:

> If you want the ethnic German task to be fulfilled and if you want to avoid a general dog fight between half a dozen ministries over the carcass of the VR, then the forms will have to be created in which work can be done without constant sniping! The experience of the last months has shown me that Bohle will only recognize a sharp dividing line—perhaps! He ought not give orders in the realm of ethnic German affairs.[30]

Again confronted with the necessity of some tough decision-making, Hess responded in his usual way: he temporized. The most he would do was to get his adjutant, Alfred Leitgen, to mediate between the two factions.[31]

With the collapse of the VR in early 1935, the whole burden of traditionalist Germandom work in the Sudetenland fell heavily on Steinacher's shoulders and on the VDA. Above all, the scheduled May 19 elections in Czechoslovakia had to go well for Henlein and the SHF: it was Steinacher's only real hope that he could salvage his power base and vindicate his concept of Germandom work. As early as December 13, 1934, he had met with Hans Krebs and the latter's representative in the Sudetenland, Anton Kreissl, to try to assure lack of interference with the SHF plans for the coming elections.[32] Steinacher had insisted once more that only he, as far as the Reich was concerned, had the responsibility of contact with Henlein; he had even gained the impression that Krebs and Kreissl were impressed by the success of the SHF and would be conciliatory. It would soon become quite clear that Steinacher had been mistaken. Krebs and Bohle, acting together and separately, were going to make any election plans of Steinacher or Henlein difficult to implement.

With the defeat of the VR under his belt, Bohle continued his sniping not only against Steinacher and the VDA, but also against Henlein and his circle. On February 23, 1935, he launched an attack on Hans Neuwirth, liaison man in financial matters between Steinacher and Henlein. In a letter to the AA, Bohle tried to draw the diplomats into his camp by pointing out that in recent visits to Vienna and Prague he had discovered that neither embassy was "correctly informed" on VDA activities: they were not, for example, aware that Neuwirth was not a "reliable" man for handling money shipments to Czechoslovakia.[33] Bohle also succeeded in raising suspicions about the VDA in Hess's mind. In a note to all *Gauleiter,* Hess asked for confidential reports on the personnel and activities of local VDA branches.[34] Perhaps the worst threat to Steinacher was the attempt by Bohle and Krebs, acting together, either to stop the annual VDA collections or to get a significant portion of this money channeled off to the AO. Since much of the money was earmarked for the Sudetenland, the interference on the part of the two radicals posed an indirect threat to Henlein as well. On December 19, 1934, Bohle had set the dangerous precedent of demanding that the VDA turn over 6,000 marks to him: Hess backed him and Steinacher had to pay.[35] Partly as a result of Krebs's intrigues, the *Reichsleiter* for *Winterhilfswerk,* Erich Hilgenfeldt, at the last moment threatened to cancel the annual VDA street collection set for March 9, 1935, because he had been informed of the "dark role" of the VDA in foreign policy. Steinacher engineered a confrontation with Krebs, who couldn't prove his charges, and the permission was given to carry out the collection after all.[36] Bohle was somewhat more successful. He demanded that 50 percent of all money collected abroad for the VDA be channelled to the AO, and here, Steinacher was forced to give in.[37]

This financial harassment was an especially lethal threat in light of the fact that with the VR rendered ineffectual, Steinacher's only power base was the VDA.

By this time the opposition to the traditionalists had become so brazen that attacks on Henlein were appearing in Reich newspapers. Once again Hess was called upon to intervene. On March 11, 1935, Ribbentrop—acting on behalf of Hess—was compelled to issue orders forbidding attacks on the Sudeten German leader by the German press.[38] It remained to be seen how effective this high level intervention would be.

On March 16, 1935, Hitler announced to the world the reintroduction of general military conscription in Germany. It was the first major radical step he had taken since withdrawing Germany from the disarmament conference and the League of Nations in October of 1933. It was also a violation of the Versailles settlement and, as such, represented a testing of both the international situation and the will of the Western powers to restrain Germany's breakout from the restrictions imposed upon it in 1918. At first glance, Hitler's announcement would appear both to vindicate and encourage the radicals in their activities. That same day the AO organized a rally in Argentina in which over twelve thousand Reich Germans proclaimed their loyalty to Adolf Hitler.[39] However, Hitler's calculated risk was quickly followed by a period of retrenchment: just as he had done after leaving the League, Hitler once again assured the world of his peaceful intentions.[40] After all, although he had made a bold step which brought with it important foreign policy implications, Hitler could maintain that he had not embarked on a program to alter swiftly the international balance of power. Hitler was an astute enough statesman to realize that Germany was not yet in a position to challenge the West with too much temerity: a decisive move could only be followed at this point by a quiescent period, in which the wind of policy could be tested. In contrast to the announcement of conscription itself, then, the signal for retrenchment could potentially be propitious to the traditionalists and their activities. Hess's order through Ribbentrop, muzzling the German press, might possibly have betrayed an awareness of Hitler's imminent move and the desire to facilitate the inevitable period of assurances which would follow.

Regardless of the motivation behind Hess's instructions, once again as so often in the past, the radicals ignored attempts to curtail their activities. Despite Ribbentrop's orders to the contrary, press attacks against the leadership of the Sudeten German party not only continued, but intensified. One article from the radical Sudeten German publication *Aufbruch*, entitled "Sudetendeutsche Entschei-dungen" ("Sudeten German Decisions"), printed on April 4, even found its way by April 9 into the pages of the chief organ of the Nazi party in Germany, the *Völkischer Beobachter*.[41] Here entitled "The Christian Society of Estates and its Augures," the article made the same old allegations linking the SHF leadership with Othmar Spann and his ideas. The difference, of course, was that this time the attack was not being launched through some obscure provincial weekly, but—thanks to the position of the radical Sudeten emigré Karl Viererbl on the *Beobachter* staff—in the pages of the official organ of the new Germany itself. Again, as so often before, the *Denkschrift* was also used to cast aspersions on both the traditionalists in Germany and on the KB circle in the Sudetenland, to link the activities of both to some Catholic political conspiracy, and to undermine the support of the two factions in higher Reich circles. In a report on May 8, 1935, Minister Walter Koch passed on one such document which appar-ently originated with the AO, with instructions not to let it get into the hands of the VDA. The position paper pictured Henlein as a "puppet" in the hands of men like Walter Brand and blamed Steinacher for the whole situation.[42] Wilhelm Krichbaum, director of the Sudeten German Control Office and ally of Hans Krebs, was also busy collecting incriminating evidence on the men around Steinacher and Henlein, which he then passed on to the Interior Ministry.[43]

To make matters even worse for the traditionalists, Bohle's personal star apparently continued to rise. In March of 1935 he had moved his offices to Berlin and on April 15 Hess made the AO an official *Gau*, corresponding to the other territorial *Gaue*.[44] Now Bohle finally had an organizational base to give substance to his title of *Gauleiter*. Moreover, on April 29 he was given competence over Reich German party members in Austria, an area hitherto closed to him.[45]

But if the radicals were not allowing themselves to be muzzled or their activities to be severely circumscribed, the traditionalists were not yet beaten either. Radical attacks notwithstanding, Henlein and Steinacher continued preparations for what they hoped would be their most successful joint effort: funding the Henlein party for the May 1935 national elections. In this endeavor success was anything but a foregone conclusion. Not only did the traditionalists have to reckon with radical attacks, they also had difficulties with men who had a great deal in common with them ideologically and whose interests would seem to coincide with theirs. The problem of financing Henlein's political endeavors reflects just how tenuous alliances were in the Germandom camp: in this case, the parties in question were Henlein and Steinacher and the *Auswärtiges Amt,* whose help would be necessary in the transference of funds for the campaign. Given the fact that both Steinacher's organization and the AA were targets of NS attack and infiltration, and that both could be regarded generally as being in the traditionalist camp, mutual cooperation would have seemed natural and easy. After all, as Steinacher noted later, the AA needed help so that it would not come under Bohle's influence.[46] Yet, cooperation between Steinacher and AA officials was at best a tricky and spasmodic affair, characterized by an admixture of caution and jealousy on the part of the AA and stubbornness and assertiveness on the part of Steinacher himself. The reluctance of the AA stemmed partly from the fact that since January of 1933, the Foreign Office had for the most part played a very cautious, defensive role amid the competency struggles in the Germandom question. When, for example, Kersken had asked the AA for its position on Krebs and his activities, the Foreign Office replied in deliberately vague terms—no doubt somewhat confused as to who really did have competency in ethnic German affairs.[47] Partly, too, AA reluctance to work closely with Steinacher may have resulted from an awareness that the Foreign Office was itself on shaky ground at this point. There were clear signs that the AA was being ignored in decisions relating to Germandom work: Hess, for example, had not even bothered officially to inform the AA that Kersken had been dismissed until four months later.[48] Then, too, there was the element of what Albrecht Haushofer termed *Ressortabsolutismus* ("agency egotism"): a desire to preserve what prerogatives remained in the relentless struggle for political competency.[49] Finally, Steinacher's personality itself must have made AA officials wary of working with him too closely. Basically a strong-willed man to whom collaboration came hard, Steinacher simply could not muster either the tact or deviousness so important in the personal intrigues in Hitler's court.

As early as March of 1934, Steinacher had met with AA officials involved in the Sudeten question, attempting to establish a basis for cooperation. Even at this first conference, he had tried to take some of the leverage away from Walter Koch and the legation in Prague by emphasizing that it was too compromising politically to help the Sudeten Germans centrally from the Czech capital: rather, it would be advisable to provide aid and cover from those areas in the Reich closest to the Sudeten territory in question (Bavaria, Saxony, *etc.*).[50] Koch responded with the counterproposal that the VR use the legation as an "informational center" on various tendencies within the Sudeten camp; the mission, in turn, should be kept informed about the projected programs of the VR. Several months later, however, Koch lamented that Steinacher apparently did not intend to respond to the offer: "As of today, the mission is *without any information* on the political direction which the *Volksrat* [sic] is supposed to be pursuing toward Sudeten German politics; indeed, it is not even certain whether [the VR] is the actual representative of such policies." [51] Koch concluded that while there were no basic contradictions in the policies of the AA and the VR, neither was there much real cooperation.

With this kind of gap opening between the AA and the VDA, it is not surprising that the Foreign Office dragged its feet on the question of financing Henlein's election campaign. Steinacher had met with Henlein on December 16 and 17, 1934—just three days after the deceptively peaceful discussion about the elections with Krebs—to go over tactics for the campaign, even though at this point it was not at all certain whether the Czechs would even permit the SHF to participate in the elections.[52] A short time later Steinacher came to the AA with his proposals.[53] At a meeting in the Foreign Office on February 28, 1935, Constantin von Neurath, the foreign minister; Schwerin von Krosigk, the finance minister; Dr. Hjalmar Schacht, president of the Reichsbank; and General Walter von Reichenau discussed the problem of funding the campaign. They felt that the sum of 300,000 marks, which the VDA had suggested as sufficient, was far too high. Half that figure should do. Neurath especially was very nervous about supplying the funds from Reich money: this, he felt, was politically objectionable. He suggested that perhaps financing through the party, possibly in the disguised form of goods, would be a better idea. Krosigk undertook to discuss the problem with Hess.

Steinacher reports that he spoke with Neurath in April about the problem of transferring currency and the difficulty of monetary exchange.[54] Neurath again expressed fears that the deliveries could not be kept secret. Steinacher offered to guarantee secrecy, but Neurath stalled and referred him to Krosigk. Ten days later, Steinacher called the AA and was told that Neurath would not release the funds. It seems that Koch had had occasion to speak to Lany, chief of Czech security, and was told that the Czechs knew all the details of money being given to Henlein from the Reich. Whether this was true or not, the report served to panic the AA.[55] With the Foreign Office refusing its support, the whole question of financing became critical. The Czech government had by this time agreed to let the SHF take part in the elections, but it had made participation contingent upon the Front's changing its name. This change, of course, involved the complete redoing of all campaign literature, posters, and everything in print which carried the old name of the organization—an enormously costly undertaking which would in all likelihood exhaust the funds which the Henlein movement had available in Czechoslovakia.

With Reich channels closed to him, Steinacher now turned to his liaison man for financial questions in Czechoslovakia, Hans Neuwirth, to see what could be accomplished from the Sudeten side.[56] Neuwirth, in turn, approached Anton Kiesewetter, director of the *Kreditanstalt der Deutschen* (KdD), the largest cooperative bank in Czechoslovakia: perhaps a loan of some kind could be arranged. Kiesewetter, who had already been implicated in the Patschneider trials and had even been confined for a time under suspicion of subversive contacts with irredentist groups in Germany, was reluctant to lend the money without adequate collateral. Neuwirth then turned to the big Sudeten industrialists—men like Kreibig, the textiles magnate, and Theodor Liebig—to request backing. They, too, demanded some kind of collateral. At this point, the complicated negotiations came around again full circle to the VDA. With the possibility of handling the transaction in a very indirect manner assured, Steinacher secured funds from the Reich (he mentions the name of Schacht in this connection—although as late as May 7, Schacht was still refusing to agree to release currency for Henlein).[57] With the VDA thus able to function as the ultimate financial backer, the industrialists provided collateral and the KdD came through with 800,000 crowns (300,000 marks) for Henlein's campaign fund. The traditionalists could congratulate themselves on their success: at least they would now have enough funds to put up a good fight in the coming elections.

As events leading up to the elections of 1935 indicate, then, the period from the middle of 1934 to the spring of 1935 was clearly a time of flux, both in the Reich and in the Sudetenland. In Reich foreign policy, periods of adventurism and retrenchment had followed one another in succession. In the Germandom struggle, there was a similar kind of fluctuation during these months. Just as Reich foreign policy blew now hot, now cold, so did the fortunes of the traditionalists and the radicals: the battle over ethnic German politics was turning into a game of seesaw—with first one side up, then the other.

There is a link between Reich foreign policy and the Germandom struggle at this point, but as yet only a tenuous one. True, both radicals and traditionalists had to take cognizance, to some extent at least, of the foreign policy climate in which they were working. Periods of quiescence might work somewhat to the benefit of the traditionalists, while a sudden exploratory move on Hitler's part might signal encouragement to the radicals. But, for the most part, foreign policy formulation and the struggle over Germandom questions were carried out on very different planes. One clear example of this is the fact that radical activity persisted so often in the face of orders to the contrary: periods of quiescence were by no means strictly enforced or honored. Hitler's obvious disinterest in ethnic Germans in general and Sudeten Germans in particular, as well as his willingness to tolerate rivalries which led to one embarrassing gaffe after another—or threatened momentarily to do so—also attest to the fact that his foreign policy interests were still far from touching upon Germandom abroad as a pressing question. By implication, this means also that in this period there can be no talk of *Gleichschaltung*, either of groups in the Reich interested in ethnic German politics or of Henlein's Sudeten German movement. The attempt to fund Henlein's party in early 1935 is just one case in point: the complicated process by which Steinacher appropriated funds for Henlein looks like anything but the smooth, well oiled machinations that have come to be associated with Nazi "synchronization." The entire maneuver was a classic example of improvisation, which could just as easily have failed at any number of points.

The fact that such large sums of money were passed on to

Henlein from the Reich to finance the election campaign—in fact, the ample evidence that various amounts were transferred regularly to one Sudeten organization or other—has been cited as proof of *Gleichschaltung* within the Sudeten German camp: unless Henlein and his colleagues were loyal tools of Hitler from the very beginning, such magnanimity on the part of Reich agencies would have been unthinkable.[58] True, these revelations, well documented, have laid to rest many of the myths which some postwar apologists have used in order to whitewash the events of the thirties. Former Sudeten Germans can no longer deny that they had regular and varied contacts, including financial support, leading to the Reich at an early date. To insist, however, that because of such financial aid these men were loyal National Socialists from the very beginning, working with Reich Nazis from the outset to destroy Czechoslovakia, is a distortion which contributes nothing either to an understanding of the intricate workings of the Nazi state, or to a clarification of how people of various conservative hues get drawn to a radical movement. The fact is that the Reich was giving money—at times in impressive amounts— to all kinds of Germandom agencies that could not possibly have been working hand-in-glove with National Socialism at the time. Moreover, it was not uncommon for the same Reich agency to be financing several organizations at once that were working at cross-purposes. Minister Koch, for one, complained about the constant requests for funds to be used as defense money in political trials—the most recent one being a request for 50,000 marks for use in the Patschneider appeals. Recommending that the requests be denied, Koch argued that in light of the scarcity of exchange monies, the Reich could scarcely afford to spend money for every political trial that came along as a result of naïveté, carelessness, or denunciations on the part of the various Sudeten factions. The only people who profited from all of this, he added, were the lawyers! [59] Yet, despite such complaints, the money kept on flowing.[60]

Through all the financial maneuvering, it is clear how little in touch the Berlin agencies—official and nonofficial—were, both with each other and with the situation in Czechoslovakia. As one observer noted, all any two-bit organization in Czechoslovakia had to do was scream "Germandom," and the money immediately started pouring in from Berlin with no questions asked.[61] This situation was a far cry from anything approaching a financial *Gleichschaltung* from the

Reich. True, many of the recipients of these funds did eventually fall into the grip of National Socialism and became deliberate tools of the Reich regime—and their financial dependence on the Reich must be regarded as one factor in this development. But financial involvement, in light of the very real ideological struggles going on at this time both among Sudeten Germandom factions and factions within the Reich itself, cannot be regarded as proof positive of complicity and sympathy with National Socialism; nor can such involvement be cited as the only reason for the fact that many Sudeten Germans eventually did come to collaborate with the more radical NS Germandom groups.

Just as it would be mistaken to attribute "coordination" to Reich support of the SHF at this point, it would be an error to see in Henlein a loyal tool of Hitler, leading the Sudetenland surreptitiously down the road toward *Anschluss*. Konrad Henlein's whole political approach during this period is not that of a man confidently treading in Hitler's shadow, but rather of one anxiously confronting a dilemma which he cannot seem to solve alone—and which Hitler refuses to solve for him. Nothing illustrates this situation better than Henlein's various interviews and speeches during these months and the contexts in which they were given. In December of 1934, just a few months after Henlein had publicly proclaimed his loathing for the radical emigré Hans Krebs, Steinacher was trying to win that same gentleman's support for Henlein's 1935 election plans. At first glance the incident smacks of duplicity and has been interpreted as a prime example of Henlein's perfidy as a secret supporter of Hitler. Yet, on closer examination, this explanation fails to take into consideration the very nature of the Germandom struggle in which Henlein was embroiled. In view of the whole spectrum of the *Volkstum* conflict in the Reich and in the Sudetenland, it seems most unlikely that Henlein was secretly and consciously allowing himself to be used by Hitler at this point. First of all, there were substantial differences between what Henlein and the traditionalists were trying to accomplish and the goals of men like Krebs and Bohle: the very ferocity of the feud going on between these factions must certainly be seen as some gauge of these differences. It is also apparent that Hitler was not behaving at this point like a single-minded dictator, steering the actions of the VDA and SHF—or even the radical NS Germandom advocates, for that matter—toward some concrete, predetermined foreign policy goals. Finally, the halting steps Henlein took in the direction of Berlin lent little credibility to theories of "master plans" and conscious control from the Reich Chancellory. It was not Hitler who thought of setting up Henlein, but rather Henlein who was attempting to approach the Reich for support—support which came through the very precarious connections via Steinacher to Hess.

Conceivably, one could maintain that Henlein did not really need to have contact with Hitler at all: he knew very well what Hitler wanted in 1933, namely quiescence in his foreign relations, and so Henlein pursued his parallel game of professing loyalty to the Czechs on the one hand, while waiting for Hitler's plans to mature on the other. Given the international situation in 1933 and 1934, however, no one—not even Hitler himself, and certainly not Henlein—could have predicted the approximate path that world events would take in the next five years. The prospect of England and France standing by, even taking part, while Germany proceeded to carve up Czechoslovakia, adding the three-and-a-half million Germans of that unfortunate country to the Greater German Reich, was utterly inconceivable in 1933, even to the most fanatical Nazi, and *Anschluss* under any other imaginable conditions would have meant a war ultimately disastrous to the whole Sudeten German community, over whose lands most of the fighting would have taken place.

The fundamental error behind such interpretations of Henlein as a crypto-Nazi from the outset lies in the failure to recognize the political variety in Germany during the thirties and in the tendency to view Nazi Germany instead as a "totalitarian" monolith. The entire development of the Germandom struggle points to a very different kind of power structure in Hitler's Reich. There were Nazis, of course, both in the Reich and in the Sudetenland; but there were also German nationalists, fuzzy-minded conservative revolutionaries, and reactionaries who were taken in by the dazzling imagery of the *nationale Erhebung*—men and organizations across a whole spectrum of political persuasions, all to one degree or another captured by the intense ideologies of the day. In view of this, Henlein—indeed, the whole movement for Sudeten unity—must be assessed in a somewhat different light. The image of "conspiracy" gives way to a more variegated, but even more tragic, picture: of amateur politicians who, with the best interests of their people supposedly at heart, set a mighty movement into action without the hard, sober thinking which could anticipate and guide where that movement was to go; of nationalists who, so enchanted with the *Romantik* of their new found politics, with the heady success of "politics across the border," emulated, courted, and used the similar movement in Germany, only to be used themselves and eventually to be swallowed up by those forces they had never really understood.

As the SHF moved more and more into the political limelight during the latter part of 1934 and the months leading to the election in 1935, it became increasingly difficult for Henlein to maintain any kind of integrity and still survive politically. Frightened by the dissent within his own party, pressured by the radicals from within the Reich as well as the Sudetenland, worried that the Czechs might at any time intervene to force the dissolution of his movement, Henlein began to temporize, particularly in his public speeches. But far from solving his problems, his attempts to reassure and pacify both Czechs and radicals only added to the maelstrom in which he found himself. He was, indeed, beginning to get wound up in contradictions! Ultimately, neither the Czechs, nor the radicals ever really trusted him.

All Henlein's statements affirming his belief in Czech democracy cannot merely be chalked up to tactical expediency, however—just as they dare not be interpreted as proof of any duplicitous commitment on his part to National Socialism. Henlein did not wholly lie in his protestations of loyalty: rather, he told a half truth (or a half lie, as the case may be). If one took his words to mean that his heart lay with the Czech republic, then he was lying. Fealty to the German *Volksgemeinschaft,* as many national-minded Germans in the Sudetenland were to discover, ultimately would not square with loyalty to the republic. If one took Henlein's words to mean, however, that he accepted the existence of the republic because there was nothing he could do to make it go away and thus would obey its laws and pursue his course of unifying the Sudeten Germans within the framework of the existing state, then he was telling the truth. When Henlein tried publicly to convince the Czechs that his movement had no political connections with Reich agencies, he was again telling a lie. But if by "political" connections his critics in the Czech government understood "subversive," then Henlein was being truthful in denying such an allegation. Henlein did have contacts, but then so did everyone else in his organization, down to the lowest levels. This, in short, was the problem: too many people were grinding their own political axes.

Some of these contacts were harmless cultural ones, others were downright subversive in nature; some were of a long standing nature, others like those between Henlein and Steinacher were relatively new. At least up until this point, there was no systematic network of fifth columnists, not even among the more subversive factions. To explain all of this at a mass rally such as the one at Böhmisch-Leipa, with members of the international press at hand, would have been ludicrous. The Czechs, many of whom erroneously assumed that *all* the organizations with which Henlein was dealing were radical National Socialist in nature, would not have believed such a story anyway. So Henlein lied, and his lies reflect the tenuous position he was in: neither a completely loyal citizen of Czechoslovakia nor, as yet, a conscious agent of Nazi expansion.

Concerned more with unity and the maintenance of his own position than with principle or the fine points of ethnic politics, Henlein continued to place his hopes in the traditionalists, though he never had either the character or convictions of Steinacher. Radical attacks from both sides of the border forced the men even closer together and soon made Henlein—principles or no principles—at least seem to be a traditionalist. But Henlein always remained the weak link in the traditionalist chain, as his fluctuating policies and ultimate capitulation would show. Under the extreme attacks of the radicals, even Steinacher gradually began to violate one of his own major tenets: that subsumed under the rubric of *volklich* thinking. The *volklich* approach to Germandom politics had, after all, always put the main emphasis on the German ethnic group itself—on its integrity, staying power, and ability to survive with a minimum of aid from the central German state (even though, somewhat contradictorily, Germandom workers had always complained about lack of interest in their activities on the part of the Reich government). Now, in a desperate effort to come up with some kind of success, Steinacher had gone all out to aid Henlein, financially and in every other way possible—an act which could only make the Sudeten German ethnic group increasingly dependent on a Reich organization and less and less capable of going it on its own. To be sure, the VR and VDA were not the official German government, but they were quasi-official in a regime where such lines tended to be fuzzy anyway. Should different people get control of the many links which were beginning to tie the Sudeten German unity movement to the Reich, the results might be far different than those envisioned by the traditionalists. Little aware of it, in their very struggle to survive and wield influence, the traditionalists were creating options and possibilities for men with a far more radical conception of what Germandom work and what German foreign policy should be.

VI

The Traditionalists under Siege

THE Sudeten German party emerged from the general elections of May 19, 1935 with a stunning victory. Over 60 percent of the Sudeten German electorate opted for the Henlein party, which—with 1,249,350 votes—was now the strongest vote-getter in the republic. Not even the two most powerful Czech parties managed to muster so much support: the Agrarians received only 1,116,593 votes; the Social Democrats, 1,034,774.[1] The "activist" German parties, *i.e.*, those participating in the government, lost up to half of their support.

The question arises as to what this tremendous mandate for the Henlein party really meant. Was this, as some have maintained, a sign that the majority of Sudeten Germans had fallen victim to National Socialism? Did the Sudeten Germans really see Henlein as the temporary stand-in for Hitler? Many contemporaries thought so. Wenzel Jaksch, leader of the Social Democrats in parliament, cried out to the newly elected SdP representatives: "The greater part of your constituents has given you the task of working for union with Germany." [2] Yet to make that assertion is an oversimplification which fails to take into account both the disunity and the great variety of political motives at play in the Sudeten camp. Not even in the Henlein movement itself was there a unity of purpose, as the KB-NS feud only too clearly demonstrated. As the German minister in Prague, Walter Koch, himself pointed out after the elections, the new SdP deputies who took their places in the Czech parliament formed a conglomeration of "practically all [political] shades . . . ranging from implicit loyalty to absolute rejection" in regard to the Czech state.[3] If this range of differences existed within the Sudeten leadership itself, it is only logical to ascribe at least as high a degree of differentiation to the masses of people who voted for the SdP.

Jaksch's claims of a mandate for irredentism, then, were distortions of both the political intentions of the Sudeten Germans and the significance of the 1935 election results. It is probable that many, if not most, Sudeten nationalists were not happy about belonging to the Czech state, but this does not mean that they were actively pursuing *Anschluss*. Many businessmen, particularly, would actually have had much to lose if the Sudetenland were united with Germany.[4] But even if large numbers of those who voted for the SdP in 1935 might theoretically have agreed to *Anschluss*—witness the outcome of the Saar referendum that same year—the point is, union with Germany was scarcely a real alternative at that time. Germany was still isolated; the Austrian coup of the previous summer had been a miserable fiasco. As the Stresa front indicated, Italy and the other Western powers were united in their resistance to Germany's encroachments on the sovereignty of neighboring countries. Moreover, just three days before the elections, the Czechoslovak government signed a mutual assistance treaty with the Soviet Union. Thus, the average Sudeten German in 1935, like his counterpart in the Reich, could not possibly have envisaged a situation in which *Anschluss* could be brought about without a war and the bulk of the Sudetenland population was not endorsing a war—to be fought over *their* lands.

What the Sudeten Germans *were* voting for in May of 1935 was the party which best represented their radical nationalism. Certainly, Hitler's successes up to that time, including the introduction of general conscription, played a role in that strong national feeling. If left-wing German emigrés did spread "scare stories" about concentration camps, it was the full employment, the well fed and well paid German workers on *Kraft durch Freude* tours, the miles of spanking new *Autobahn* that most Sudeten Germans saw and they took pride in the accomplishments of the mother country under the auspices of the new "national awakening." Even to those wary of National Socialism, these triumphs and signs of economic progress under the NS regime were seen as *German* triumphs—and this enthusiasm made itself felt at the ballot box. To assert this interpretation is not to divest the Sudeten Germans of their "culpability" in politics, but merely to explain these politics. While it is a rank distortion to maintain that most Sudeten Germans were democrats who merely sought a federal republic, it is also a distortion to see them all as National Socialists. For every voter who did cast his ballot with a conscious loyalty to Hitler and National Socialism, there were certainly many others who voted with regional autonomy in mind or simply out of protest; or because they were caught up in the rallies and the stirring renditions of the "Hohenfriedberger"; or because newly politicized neighbors urged them to get out and vote, whereas the local Agrarian party people had not sent anyone around for months. To maintain anything else would be to misread or overlook the very real power struggles that men like Henlein and Steinacher, and those of the Krebs variety as well, had been engaging in over the past months and years.

After 1936, certainly, once Hitler had "coordinated" Germany to the extent that German nationalism meant only National Socialism and once he had—with the help of the West—succeeded in proving his political genius in 1938, then the patriotic feelings which had long characterized the political consciousness of large numbers of Sudeten Germans, in very different forms, became channeled into the all-encompassing dynamic of National Socialist expansion. But that long series of bloodless, intoxicating triumphs which Hitler would enjoy at the expense of the befuddled West had not yet taken place, and it would be a distortion arising from hindsight to maintain that Hitler himself—to say nothing of the Sudeten Germans voting in the election of 1935—could have foreseen them. If the majority of Sudeten Germans must bear the brunt of an accusation, they must share with other Germans elsewhere the culpability of abandoning themselves to the romantic excesses of an all-pervading nationalism, to a vague but all-encompassing political spirit, to the fateful *Ganzheitstendenzen* ("totality tendencies") which made them blind to the uses that ruthless men make of such feelings.[5]

Initially, and for some time afterward, the outcome of the Czechoslovakian elections seemed to usher in a period of grace for the traditionalist concept of *Volkstum* politics—at least in the Reich. The victory of the SdP seemed to vindicate Steinacher's idea that *Volkstum* on its own was *Volkstum* at its best. By actually achieving their long sought unity, on the surface at least, the Sudeten Germans had made their political organization the largest in the Czech state. Having aided Henlein, Steinacher could take a great deal of credit for the triumph. It was a success that shored up, at least psychologically, his crumbling position in the Germandom struggle. Even people the National Socialist regime would normally consider not particularly radical or even reliable could hold onto powerful and influential positions if they came up with a success now and then. One example was Ernst Vollert in the Interior Ministry. He had only gotten around to joining the party in May of 1933, yet he had been promoted because of his surprising success in organizing the Saar plebiscite.[6] Steinacher, hoping that his political fortunes, too, would now be on the rise once again, wrote elatedly in his diary:

> Gigantic success in Bohemia. What perspectives? . . . I will call up K. Haushofer and congratulate him in any case, even if he bore little responsibility and let the reins drop in the last months. Now we have success for the VR—100% alone and independently. Now back to the old principles. The VR will have to be highly credited in some way. . . . I am celebrating for myself. Since October, I've not only represented the VR alone, but protected and preserved it, too.[7]

It should be noted here that Steinacher was most probably referring to the VDA rather than the VR, since the *Volksdeutscher Rat* had virtually ceased to function by this time; or, he may have been thinking in terms of a vindication of his idea of the VR and its role in Germandom work.[8] In any case, it was the VDA that aided Henlein throughout the preparations for the election and Steinacher's feelings of optimism as a result are unmistakable. The Germandom traditionalists seemed further vindicated when the führer himself included a passage formulated by Albrecht Haushofer in his "peace" speech of May 21, 1935: Germany would not assimilate any foreign *Volkstum*, Hitler assured.[9]

Perhaps the most favorable development of all for the traditionalists in the course of 1935 was the eclipse of their old enemy, Ernst Bohle. During the first months of 1935, it had seemed that the AO leader had succeeded in permanently paralyzing the *Volksdeutscher Rat* and in pushing through his conception of Germandom work. The VR had not met at all after February 1 and was languishing in a state of "permanent adjournment." However, Bohle's very successes were leading to his downfall. On his way to the top of the NS leadership hierarchy, he had made at least two fatal mistakes: he had trod on too many toes without the necessary contacts and power base to back him; and he had been a little too far ahead of his time with his ideas and their implementation. His interference in the affairs of the German ethnic group in Poland had brought the Foreign Minister Constantin von Neurath complaining to Hess. Many other complaints were coming in, too, dealing with Bohle's intrigues, arbitrary actions, and excesses.[10] Steinacher noted with satisfaction on June 20: "Now it's really hit the fan. Bohle's managed to get everybody up against him. So, I'm not alone any more. Bohle's strongest opponent is Ribbentrop. The coming man. A. Haushofer is supposed to be his political mentor." [11] Here, then, was another—perhaps the most important—reason for Bohle's slide from favor: he himself had been outrivaled by a competitor. As Steinacher's remarks indicate, a new man had entered the battlefield of Germandom politics—Joachim von Ribbentrop.

Ribbentrop, whom Hitler would name as foreign minister four years later, in fall of 1934, had been appointed by Hess as plenipotentiary for foreign policy questions on the staff of the führer's deputy, which had given him a foot in the door of foreign policy questions. [12] Ribbentrop had also founded his own organization, the *Büro Ribbentrop*, which he was rapidly expanding, but which did not really offer him a strong enough power base. His forays into foreign policy matters were putting him on a potential collision course both with his nominal superior, Foreign Minister von Neurath, and with Alfred Rosenberg, the party's original foreign affairs expert, who was still a force to contend with in 1935. [13] To secure his position Ribbentrop needed allies. He proceeded to get them, first by insinuating himself into Hess's good graces (in part by attaching Albrecht Haushofer to his staff); then, when the führer's deputy showed himself to be indecisive, by forging an alliance with Heinrich Himmler, chief of the SS. [14]

These alliances came in very handy in the hard scramble of organizational rivalry and they were a great help to the ambitious former champagne salesman. But the really decisive factor in Ribbentrop's rise was his relationship to Hitler—a relationship characterized by a combination of blind, abject fealty and the ability to discern what the führer really wanted in advance and then to feed this back to Hitler in the form of advice. [15] It was this ability that had gotten Ribbentrop the chance of his life in the spring of 1935: the negotiation of the Anglo-German Naval Agreement which, due to a fortunate conjuncture of circumstances, Ribbentrop managed to realize successfully on June 18. [16]

As Steinacher had observed, Ribbentrop's fortunes were definitely on the rise. The traditionalists now had a potential ally in their struggles against Bohle, and in fact, with Ribbentrop's help, they did win an encouraging victory over Bohle in the summer of 1935. The crisis came on July 16 at a stormy meeting in Hess's office.[17] The immediate reason for the meeting had been a flurry of requests coming in through a number of ministries demanding the dissolution of the VDA. These requests all came from National Socialist youth groups in Prague (most likely, the *Aufbruch* circle). The tactic had been engineered by Bohle and was part and parcel of the radical tactics on both sides of the border to discredit the Steinacher-Henlein alliance. Hess passed on the complaints to Ribbentrop to give his new foreign policy advisor something to do; Ribbentrop, in turn, assigned his assistant, Hermann Kügler, the task of handling the problem. The result was the showdown in Hess's office, with Alfred Leitgen (Hess's adjutant), Ribbentrop, General Karl Haushofer, and Bohle and his aides, as well as Kügler in attendance. Bohle demanded that the AO be given competency over all ethnic Germans. Ribbentrop, speaking through Kügler, pointed out the inexpediency of such a move and Hess agreed. In a rage Bohle threatened to resign all his offices. As always the temporizer, Hess offered him the consolation prize of responsibility for all Germans in South America, bestowing competency with the remark: "There we won't get into a war so fast." Steinacher, who had apparently been told of the events by Haushofer, wrote that same evening in his diary that Ribbentrop had been decisive in getting such a favorable outcome.[18]

Steinacher successfully faced one other challenge in 1935, thus giving himself and his concept of *Volkstum* work new impetus. This time the threat came not from a rival organization moving up on the political horizon, but from within his own secure domain, the VDA itself. For some time, several of Steinacher's coworkers in the VDA-VR believed that only by "coordinating" itself—*i.e.,* building on the basis of the Nazi party rather than working as an independent entity—could the VDA preserve any degree of autonomy. The same had been true of the VR, they maintained: if the VR had been closer to the party and not so bound up with the VDA, it could have been much more effective as a coordinating organization with real authority in Germandom work. On June 19, Robert Ernst, speaker for the dissident group within the VDA, resigned his offices, and at a meeting of top VDA leaders in Lübeck on August 3, tried to engineer a coup. Along with Dr. Theodor Oberländer, VDA executive and later the director of the *Bund Deutscher Osten* working with Rosenberg, and Ernst Zörner, VDA-*Landesführer* in Saxony and mayor of Dresden,

Ernst demanded that the VDA give up its youth organization to the HJ, that Steinacher appoint him (Ernst) as his deputy, and then take a long trip overseas.[19] Steinacher maintains that already at the *Königsberger VDA Tagung* early in 1935, Ernst had felt compelled to be "active in the NSDAP sense." In this spirit, Ernst had disobeyed Steinacher's directions that a sharp dividing line be drawn between the VDA and the HJ at gatherings. When Steinacher arrived to speak at the VDA youth camp near Rossiten, where Ernst was to be the VDA representative, he found the area surrounded by HJ pennants. This, in Steinacher's eyes, was a serious breach of faith on Ernst's part.[20]

Steinacher met this challenge from within his own camp with his customary gusto. Two days before Ernst's showdown, Steinacher wrote: "Dr. Ernst practically wants the VDA to be a party formation. That's complete *Gleichschaltung*"; and on the next day, "Ernst has lost his balance completely. . . . 150% Nazi! Whoever doesn't go along is a reactionary and a party enemy. That's the language of our erstwhile foes in the party." [21] At the crucial meeting on August 3, Steinacher carried the majority along with him, getting thirty-two of thirty-eight votes, with two abstentions.[22] The coup had been effectively aborted and Steinacher had won again, but the fact that the challenge came this time from within his own organization showed the enormous pressures to conform which could be exerted in the Third Reich.

Meanwhile, another of Steinacher's rivals, Baldur von Schirach, was not idle either. On the occasion of the same Königsberg gathering at which Ernst had begun his party activity against Steinacher, Schirach, too, struck at the authority of the VDA leader. The attack was instigated as the result of a supposed indiscretion by a VDA agent in South Tirol: allegedly, the agent had telephoned the names of the South Tirolean VDA representatives who would be attending a meeting at Innsbruck. Schirach heard of the incident and used it to accuse Steinacher and his associates of endangering the lives of the Tirolean comrades by such carelessness. Schirach telegraphed Steinacher: ". . . any further endangerment of our ethnic German comrades by you and your crazy subordinates will not be tolerated." [23] Steinacher, furious at Schirach's allegations, retaliated with a few well chosen words of his own. A flurry of accusations and counteraccusations resulted which finally led to appeals to Hitler himself. Characteristically, the führer did nothing.[24] Steinacher finally struck back at

Schirach by firing *Oberbannführer* Teichmann, HJ liaison man to the VDA youth department by virtue of an earlier agreement between the two organizations. Teichmann and a friend by the name of Poller had become involved with the *Aufbruch* circle in Prague and had been sending *Aufbruch* printed material attacking both the VDA and Henlein to various Reich offices.[25] Incidentally, this same ill-fated gathering at Königsberg provided yet another enemy of Steinacher, Karl Viererbl, with an opportunity to "vent his anger on the VDA." [26]

Despite all these skirmishes and holding actions, the main problem in Germandom politics in 1935, as far as both the National Socialists and the traditionalists were concerned, continued unresolved: after the demise of the VR, there was still no organization which could claim total competence in handling the question of Germans living abroad. During the summer of 1935, the Haushofers had decided in conversations with Hess that if they could find someone with the necessary party credentials to act as a reliable replacement for the former adjutant Kersken, they could forego rebuilding the VR.[27] Steinacher pretty much went along with these considerations. Despite his temporary victories, he was still operating on very exposed ground. "I'm acting now without the VR and without direct connection to Hess's staff," he wrote. "That cannot last. The NS formations are shooting to kill. Preventing permission for VDA collections. . . . A[dolf] H[itler] cannot be reached! Only through Hess." [28] For his own part, Steinacher was thinking in terms of getting support through several sympathetic *Gauleiter*. Something had to be done. If the various factions ever isolated Steinacher completely from the sources of power, then despite temporary victories, he would be through.

Out of the conversations between the Haushofers and Hess came the new ersatz-VR: the *Büro Kursell.* Otto von Kursell had ideal credentials to fulfill the function of liaison man between the traditionalists and Hess, basically the same role played by Kersken before his dismissal in the fall of 1934—a link to power so badly missed and needed by the traditionalists. On the one hand, Kursell was an old party man, an *Altkämpfer,* who had taken part in the November 9, 1923 putsch attempt, and by now had reached the rank of *Sturmbannführer* in the SS. On the other hand, he was not a fanatical Nazi of the crude variety. He was an artist and a gentleman *par excellence,* professor at the Berlin *Hochschule für Bildende Künste,* and since 1934 departmental director in Bernhard Rust's Education Ministry. He was an *Auslandsdeutscher* himself, having come from the Baltic area, and had some experience in Germandom work through the *Baltische Brüderschaft*.[29] As early as 1933, his name had come up—recommended by Rosenberg and others—as a possible undersecretary for a proposed *Auslandsdeutsches Ministerium*. Nothing came of that idea, but Hess evidently remembered the name, for sometime in 1934 he called Kursell to his villa to discuss the ethnic German problem.[30] During the latter part of 1935, Hess again called in Kursell and informed the surprised man that he would be the head of a new Germandom office. Hess gave him a new, even lower party number, ninety-three, a commonly used trick in the Third Reich to bestow instant seniority, and by the middle of October Kursell was in business. His office was known officially as the *Büro Kursell*, but gradually, because of its extensive work with German ethnic minorities, it became known as *Volksdeutsche Mittelstelle* or VOMI ("Liaison Office for Ethnic Germans").[31]

So it seemed during 1935 that the traditionalist position still had some viability. Steinacher and his allies had managed to strike new alliances; to beat down challenges both from within and without; to achieve the creation of a new liaison organization to the sources of power; and apparently, to exert some small influence on the führer himself. Above all, the traditionalists could contrast their immense success in the Czechoslovakian elections with the dismal failure of the radical Nazi putsch the previous year in Austria. But such hopeful appearances were deceiving. In the constantly shifting kaleidoscope of Nazi politics, solid victories could crumble like sand castles, alliance partners could switch sides and loyalties overnight, and precipitate reverses in official policy could leave one high and dry with yesterday's principles intact. Even if one survived frontal attack by a given enemy, there was always the back door of conspiracy. Nor should it be forgotten that the Third Reich, with its inherent revolutionary dynamic, posed other threats as well in the form of subtle pressures and cooption.

Thus, the Reich traditionalists were to find their positions slowly being undermined after the great victories of mid-year: not yet by a consciously pursued policy of *Gleichschaltung*, but through the natural mechanics of power in Nazi Germany and, ironically, partly through the very activities of the traditionalists themselves. Each of the apparent successes harbored beneath the surface the seeds of defeat, as was the case with the new Germandom liaison office. Taken at face value, with the creation of the Kursell office, the traditionalists in the Reich appeared to have come out of the rivalries of 1934 and 1935 virtually unscathed. There seemed to be every indication that Kursell would fill the liaison role at least as well, if not better, than Kersken had done. The close relationship between the Haushofers and Hess remained not only intact, but apparently was now strengthened and protected by the new, more diplomatic equivalent of Kersken. Steinacher, too, seemed to have achieved the cover he needed to continue, for in fact, Kursell did work to the best of his ability to back Steinacher and the autonomy of the VDA.[32] These rosy appearances, however, were deceiving. However sympathetic its director might have been, the *Büro Kursell* was no longer the autonomous, nonparty traditionalist organization that the VR had been. It was a special *party* office, nominally under the control of Ribbentrop (as Hess's plenipotentiary in foreign affairs questions).[33] This meant that the traditionalists no longer had any institutional independence; now they had to operate within the structure of the party. The situation was advantageous in that it gave them badly needed protection at this point; but it was also extremely risky, for it left their circle open to infiltration and compromise, which it could not in the long run afford.

Another sign of trouble to come lay in the fact that with the formation of the new office, a whole younger generation had come into its own. The VR members, for the most part, had been older, experienced Germandom fighters who had been working in the field long before the Nazis had come to power. Even more important, seven out of eight of the VR circle had never been members of the party at all.[34] The staff of the Kursell office, on the other hand, consisted entirely of party members, most of whom were in the SS as well.[35] True, at least one of them, Franz Wehofsich, a close friend of the Haushofers, was an experienced Germandom man in the traditionalist sense, but most of the other members of the staff were far more oriented to the needs of the new Reich than those of the different ethnic German groups. The presence of these new people in the Kursell office represented a subtle process of ideological erosion going on in Germandom work at this point. These younger men had matured politically not in the earlier years of the Germandom struggle, but rather in the later phases, during the National Socialist

Erhebung. To this younger generation, Germandom work—regardless of the organization with which they would associate themselves—would almost invariably mean service to the core state, rather than to the *volklich* ideal of the independent ethnic community. The distinction would not go unnoticed.

The defeat of Bohle was another *Scheinerfolg* for the traditionalists. It came about not really as a result of their efforts, but by way of a lucky conjuncture in the competition of Nazi politics which provided them an ally in Ribbentrop. Moreover, Ribbentrop's eclipse of Bohle was not so much a positive victory for Steinacher and Henlein as a negative one: it only provided the traditionalists with a new lease on life because Ribbentrop had no interest in Germandom work—which temporarily left the field clear. Most important, however, although the traditionalists did not yet realize it, Ribbentrop was a walking time bomb. His slavish anticipation of Hitler's changing moods and intentions would eventually make him one of the most radical of the top Nazis once Hitler started to turn toward an aggressive foreign policy. When the cries for war were raised, Ribbentrop was to be in the forefront. As far as the Germandom struggle itself is concerned, he was also a threat in another respect. His alliance with the SS would provide the Himmler-Heydrich team with an important entrée when these men turned their attention to ethnic German politics. Thus, a highly questionable alliance, struck by exigency in the midst of a heated rivalry with Bohle, would eventually help open the way for the traditionalists' defeat.

The traditionalists had on the surface, then, been successful in heading off defections within their own camp and attacks from other rivals. Yet the very attempt of men like Ernst to seize power in the VDA, especially in the face of Steinacher's strong leadership, illustrates what enormous pressures and erosive forces were at work in Nazi political life. Even those men with years of non-NS experience in Germandom work, men of integrity and principle, found themselves being drawn into the National Socialist maelstrom. No one came marching in one fine day and turned things inside out in a NS coup of "synchronization." That tactic had not worked for the Nazis in 1923 in attempting to seize power, and even in consolidating power after 1933 it was preferable to use other methods. As the circle of men around Steinacher, and eventually Steinacher himself, would find out, defeat was to come so gradually that it would be difficult ever to pinpoint just where everything went wrong: the slow day-to-day grinding in the grist mill of personal competition and ideological rivalry, the reluctant abandonment of a principle here, and the acceptance of a questionable tactic there to gain a temporary ally or to win a tactical victory all did not actually turn the nationalist into a Nazi—but these things were eventually to make collaboration so close that the meaningful differences for all practical purposes disappeared.

From this point on, then, despite the successes of mid-1935, the traditionalists in the Reich would find themselves increasingly on the defensive, as radical attacks accelerated and the competitive mechanisms of National Socialist politics went into high gear. Now even temporary lulls and retrenchments had to be bought at the expense of alliances and methods which exposed the traditionalists to the dangers of compromise and cooption. In the Sudetenland the situation was even less encouraging. Although the Czechoslovakian election victory won by the Sudeten German party seemed to buy time for the traditionalists in the Reich, the same cannot—ironically—be said for Henlein and his closest colleagues. Like his collaborator, Hans Steinacher, Konrad Henlein was elated by the electoral success in May of 1935. The landslide in favor of his party had shown that the effrontery of naming a political organization "Sudeten German" party, with the claim of totality that the name implied, was not such effrontery after all. The taste of victory was made all the sweeter the following month, when the government banned the very journal which had been causing Henlein and his aides so much trouble, the *Aufbruch*.[36] Henlein, it would appear, should now have been in an unassailable power position, free to pursue an independent policy. One would have expected, given the magnitude of the SdP victory, that Henlein would now take a commensurate position of power and responsibility in the government. This, however, was not the case. After a short interval, Henlein and his party moved away from any kind of substantial responsibility and participation in government and, eventually, toward radicalization and even closer proximity to the Reich.

Initially, it looked as if Henlein were going to take his mandate seriously and participate in government. Those senators and representatives elected from his party took their seats in parliament. On May 20, immediately after the election results had become known, Henlein sent a telegram to President Masaryk and Prime Minister

Malypetr, emphasizing that only SdP participation in the cabinet would mean true representation for the Germans in Czechoslovakia; the continued presence of other German parties there meant a distortion of the election results.[37] Having taken this step to reassert the exclusiveness of his party as representative of all Sudeten Germans and to undermine the position of the other German parties, Henlein then dangled the lure of cooperation in front of these very parties. On May 28, at the SdP *Hauptleitungssitzung,* the decision was made to send letters both to the German Agrarians and to the Christian Socialists, exorting them to join in building a united national front and in taking common stands on all important questions involving Sudeten Germans.[38] This gesture was probably made primarily in the hope of using the leverage of the SdP victory to draw as much support as possible away from the other German parties and toward the Henlein movement.

Henlein also turned to the non-German camp, ostensibly looking for allies: here lay a real possibility of sharing power. If an alliance could be worked out with the Czech Agrarians and Hlinka's Peoples party in Slovakia, the so-called Hrad group around Beneš could conceivably be overthrown in favor of a conservative, right-wing government. As a price for such an alliance, substantial concessions might be made to the Sudeten Germans in the direction of autonomy and self-government in domestic policy, while closer ties with Germany might follow in foreign policy. It was precisely this line that Henlein pursued. He had already opened channels to the Czech Agrarians through Viktor Stoupal, who had played such an important role just prior to the elections in preventing the dissolution of Henlein's organization.[39] In the end, however, all the grandiose talk of a conservative coalition came to nothing. The failure to achieve such a coalition stemmed largely from intense nationalism on both sides, as well as from the antidemocratic conservative-revolutionary ideology which underlay the Sudeten German movement. There were, to be sure, factions in the right-wing of both the Czech Agrarian and the Slovak parties which were amenable to collaboration with Henlein in building a strong conservative front against the leftists and middle-of-the-road factions dominant in Prague. However, under intense pressure from their own nationalists of the Kramář variety and from the political Left, the Czech Agrarians particularly began to distance themselves gradually from the Germans.[40] By mid-August of 1935, relations between the two camps had already cooled considerably. Chauvinistic speeches by both Viktor Stoupal and the Agrarian representative Jan Dubitzky on August 21 elicited a sharp reaction from the Sudeten German party press: the SdP would not enter any coalition which practiced "domestic imperialism." [41] A German diplomat in Prague noted on August 28 that the "result of this polemic is a regrettable estrangement between the Sudeten German party and the Czech Agrarian party. The outlook for parliamentary effectiveness this fall, toward an improvement in the state of emergency of the Sudeten Germans, has thereby diminished considerably." [42] Several days later, the same observer reported a still grayer picture: ". . . one gets the impression that the fronts between the Czech and German camps are solidifying. . . . The question of SdP entrance into the government appears farther away than ever." [43]

From this point on, the SdP never again came close to sharing power in the Czechoslovakian Republic. However, those who assess this development as a lost chance, because of Czech chauvinism and arrogance, to involve the Sudeten Germans in the democratic process are in error: for an even more important factor in the failure to form a cross-national conservative coalition was the romantic, antidemocratic ideology which lay behind the whole Sudeten drive for unity.[44] The danger inherent in this particular ideology was that it pinpointed quite definitely and concretely what it did not want, but was very vague and imprecise—albeit wildly enthusiastic—about what it did want. This attitude was clearly reflected in Henlein's original proclamation in 1933, announcing the formation of the *Heimatfront:* "I am no party man and won't become one! I don't want any congressional mandate either; instead, I'll remain what I always was, the simple man of the people." [45] It was precisely this antidemocratic ethos which militated most strongly against any inclination, even on the part of moderates in the SdP, to become involved more deeply in the politics of the republic.[46] Some participation in the political process was, of course, unavoidable. Any modern movement which purports to speak in the interests of large numbers of people will perforce be drawn into the political arena—and Henlein's Sudeten unity movement was no exception. Since the republic represented the only feasible political arena in sight and one which was not about to oblige the Sudeten Germans by collapsing, the only political action possible for the Sudeten Germans was that which conformed, however minimally, to the exigencies of the existing polity. Moreover, for sheer reasons of survival, Henlein's party had to show some political activity: election victory notwithstanding, the SdP could not simply assume that its further existence was assured. Henlein's offers, both to the other bourgeois German parties and to the conservative Czech and Slovak parties, represent more than anything else survival tactics.

But for all their necessary legitimate political activity (the SdP representatives did take their seats in parliament), the conservative revolutionaries in the Sudeten movement were determined to avoid becoming "just another party" embroiled in the parliamentary politics of *das System*—politics which they despised and which, in their opinion, had kept the Sudeten Germans divided and weak. It was to avoid this that Henlein, apparently taking an example from Hitler's tactics during the twenties, had refused to run as a candidate at all, preferring not to sully his political purity by getting involved in Prague politics. He would remain instead a "simple man of the people": in itself a vague role for any political leader to play.

This line of thought on the part of the conservative revolutionaries and the tactics which followed from it were to have even greater repercussions than the failure of the SdP to become involved in the Czech polity: in the end, it was to prove fatal to the entire traditionalist approach to the ethnic German problem. Knowing what they did not want, but not precisely what they *did* want left the Sudeten leaders in the same bind as their like-minded contemporaries in Germany before 1933. As with conservative revolutionaries in the Weimar Republic, knowing what they did not want alienated the Sudeten Germans from the existing polity; but not knowing clearly what they wanted—and approaching the problem of the political future with uncritical enthusiasm rather than with sober thought—left the Sudeten Germans in a kind of no-man's-land, incapable of linking vague aspirations with concrete political action. In both cases, National Socialism was more than willing to bridge the gap. Rejection of the Czech polity would also lead the Sudeten Germans into betrayal of their whole identity as "ethnic Germans"—*i.e.*, people of German stock in a country ruled or at least populated by a majority of different ethnic stock. By denying their place within the Czech state, conservative revolutionaries were paving the way ultimately for the radicals in Germandom work who felt all along that ethnic Germans belonged in the Reich. This betrayal of "ethnicity" by Sudeten Germans after the 1935 elections dovetailed with the compromise of *volklich* thinking in the Reich by men like Steinacher—something which had happened already during the financing of those elections. The actions of both groups against principles that had once motivated them were mutually reinforcing and tended to work in tandem. Steinacher's massive aid to Henlein weakened what ties the SdP did have to the Czechoslovak state and drew the party closer to Germany; Henlein's move away from Czechoslovakia and toward Germany, in turn, undermined Steinacher's *raison d'être*, which always stressed integral, somewhat self-sufficient ethnic German communities and downplayed the role of the German core state. The Czechs, by their attitude, contributed to the process. By neither welcoming Henlein with open arms nor crushing his movement completely, they helped to create the most favorable conditions for the flowering of charismatic movements, whether political or religious: intermittent persecution. By falling between the two stools of complete acceptance and complete rejection, the government in Prague also assured maximum free play for those forces drawing Henlein slowly toward the radical National Socialist camp.[47]

Another factor that helped to pull the SdP into the arms of radical political elements in the Reich was the serious split within the Sudeten German party. Although inherent in the "unity" movement from the very beginning, the entire problem was to worsen dramatically after the 1935 election. On the surface, this split centered around the rivalry between the dominant factions in the leadership of the party: the *Kameradschaftsbund* members versus the mass of lower level functionaries who had come over to the *Heimatfront* from the dissolved DNSAP. Because the rivalry usually took the form of personal antagonisms and petty intrigues, many observers have mistakenly interpreted the quarrels as merely superficial ones—a question of personality clashes, or at most, tactical differences. In reality, however, the division in the SdP had far deeper roots than this. For when a movement as large as Henlein's brings a considerable portion of the population under its banner, as the SdP did in the May elections, it must also come to grips with the social antagonisms and divisions already inherent in that population. Great success, moreover, unlike strong persecution, tends to relax vigilance and allow inherent antagonisms, subdued to that point by the exigencies of defense, to come to the fore; this is precisely what happened to the Henlein movement after May of 1935.

In its election victory, the Henlein party not only won the overwhelming endorsement of the bourgeois German nationalist camp, but also cut deeply into the ranks of the German handicraft and small factory wage earners.[48] The party had already absorbed the *Deutsche Arbeits- und Wirtschaftsgemeinschaft* (DAWG), the political organization of Sudeten big business, and along with it had brought men like Dr. Alfred Rosche and Gustav Peters into the leadership of the party. Henlein had also accepted the collateral of big industrialists to finance his election campaign and made use of aristocratic landowners like the Hohenlohes and the Kinskys to make the new movement more respectable.[49] Now, having already drawn a goodly proportion of the old handicraft-oriented DNSAP into its ranks, the SdP added a host of unemployed factory workers as well. With these two disparate elements, business and labor, under the wing of the same movement and without the power of the state which would be necessary to enforce a fascist "resolution" of these class antagonisms, the SdP was subject to some intense internal pressures indeed! [50] When the overwhelming victory of the SdP at the polls did not pay off in the form of better economic conditions in the course of 1935, this internal pressure grew steadily worse. It is no accident that Rudolf Haider, one of Henlein's main antagonists in the power struggle within the party at this point, had his base of support among the dissatisfied workers in the old *Deutsch-Böhmisch* National Socialist unions.

The other stream of dissent, the "intellectual" opposition—characterized by the rubric *Aufbruch*—fed on the social antagonisms and grew. From its original National Socialist base the *Aufbruch* circle expanded to include a goodly portion of the radical German student organizations in Prague; a number of dissident, independent newspapers (particularly the *Rumburger Zeitung*); and political malcontents across the German nationalist spectrum.[51] As the case of Haider and his unions illustrates, social discontent added fuel to the fire of "intellectual" opposition to produce quite a potent force for radicalism in and close to the SdP. The radical opposition was strengthened even more by its contacts with radical NS circles in the Reich and by NS diplomats in Czechoslovakia: above all, Krebs's contacts—Bibra in Prague and Lierau in Reichenberg. Using political rumor and betrayal as their chief weapons, tactics from which official Czech government circles and organs were more than happy to benefit, the radicals grew increasingly bolder. Soon they did not hesitate to direct their attacks at Henlein himself, the very embodiment of the Sudeten German unity movement.

Thus, far from being bagatelles, the schisms in the Henlein movement threatened to split the party wide open and destroy it. The threat was made even more serious by the fact that Henlein and many of his colleagues themselves underestimated the extent of the dissidence until it was almost too late; when they did realize the danger, they then acted hesitantly and ineffectually. On July 4, 1935, a conference of *Kreisleiter* of the SdP on the question of the *Aufbruch* circle showed that no basic agreement existed on what measures should be taken.[52] Some were for strong and immediate action; others hesitated and recommended negotiations with the dissenters; still others preferred to ignore the whole question. Several of the top leaders of the party present at the conference, including Karl Hermann Frank and Henlein himself, took a strong position against the *Aufbruch* people, but they made no decision on what action to take. The indecision probably resulted partly from the fact that many of the *Kreisleiter* themselves were in sympathy with the opposition. As for Henlein and his colleagues, perhaps the fact that the chief publication of the dissidents, the *Aufbruch,* had been forbidden by the Czechs had lulled the SdP leadership into a false sense of security. In reality, the attacks—coming from underground now—were more difficult to deal with than before. Betrayal, for example, could be a more lethal and insidious weapon than a few newspaper articles. Moreover, since the election victory, when the political stakes had gone up considerably, the attacks had increased sharply in number, particularly from organizations based in the Reich.

One important aspect of the schisms in the party was the myriad of contacts that had grown up over the years between the lower levels of both the NSDAP and the SdP in the border areas—contacts that only encouraged radicalization of Sudeten German politics and increased interference from the Reich. Although in a sense these "grass roots" ties were merely part of a long-standing collaboration on the part of radicals on both sides of the border, they do deserve separate mention, particularly because, in many respects, they kept the Sudeten pot boiling. This network of political contacts, much of which went undocumented, is very difficult to sketch in any detail. Like an iceberg, however, there are enough references to peaks here and there so that one can surmise a great mass beneath the surface. Even if the contacts had been perfectly harmless, as some of them undoubtedly were in the strict sense of the word, they would have worked against a quiescent status quo simply by drawing the Sudeten Germans in the border areas emotionally and organizationally closer to the Reich. All too often, however, the activities were deliberately and overtly radical, aimed at exacerbating frictions already present along the long border with Czechoslovakia.

There are countless references, especially in 1935 and in the years following, to uncountenanced activities of local party as well as SA and SS units;[53] to inflammatory and compromising materials being sent across the border;[54] to the establishment of wildcat guerrilla camps;[55] and to interference in the municipal politics of border towns. The following incident shows the degree of interference that took place in even the most minor affairs of border communities.[56] One Reich official suggested sending an architectural expert from the Reich to a Sudeten German town in order to discourage the construction of a new hospital there. The proposal for building the hospital, it was claimed, had only been made by the outgoing liberal majority on the city council because the incoming SdP would have to raise new taxes to pay for it and thus lose popularity. Similarly, at somewhat higher levels, a number of private agreements were made between various SdP offices and NSDAP offices in the Reich for guidance and material aid.[57]

Exacerbating the entire problem was the constant stream of political refugees who crossed the border into Germany only to continue their small scale activities in cooperation with some local, ambitious NSDAP leader. The activities of such refugees served to accelerate already growing international tension over the Sudeten situation. A warning to this effect went out on April 2, 1936 from the *Staatsminister des Innern* in Munich to all police, border police, district offices, mayors, and city commissars. Only those Sudeten refugees with a pass from the *Kontrollstelle* in Dresden were to be allowed to settle in the Reich, but not within fifteen kilometers of the border; even then, some of these emigrés were not automatically to be trusted.[58] The *Oberpräsident* of Silesia, among others, warned of the dangers of these independent contacts: "Only through the direct exertion of influence by the Reich on the Sudeten Germans can the danger of reckless action be averted." [59] All this is not to imply that the entire high level leadership in Nazi Germany was a force for quiescence, while local agencies exerted pressure for radicalization. It has been made abundantly clear that there were many prominent men in Berlin on both sides of the issue. It is fair to suggest, however, that more often than not, local party politicians independently exerted pressure for radical change. In part this was the result of the fact that no one, not even in Berlin—to say nothing of the provinces—knew exactly what Hitler really wanted. As Anton Kreissl, Krebs's representative in the Sudetenland, would complain even a year later: "[It is] extraordinarily difficult for SdP speakers to take account of the needs of Reich foreign policy in their speeches in [the Czechoslovak] parliament and on other occasions, since they have no indication whatsoever about it." [60] Each local paladin could then do pretty much as he pleased, convincing himself all the while that he was doing the führer's bidding.

The sociology of politics in the Third Reich itself and in the Sudetenland also contributed to such radicalization on a local level.[61] Because the NS revolution in Germany had not succeeded in transforming the traditional class structure, the result was that although the petty local party officials in the Reich had political power, they failed to command the social status commensurate with their political authority. An immense reservoir of frustration and resentment had accumulated during the early years of the regime, precisely among the lower ranks of the party. The temptation was, then, to push the revolution along by increasingly risky political activity in the hope of eventually closing the gap between political power and social position. When we combine this potential for radicalization in the Reich with the fact that right across the border in every local SdP unit there were large numbers of rank and file people who had been former DNSAP members—now also in a very real sense a frustrated and disinherited group—we can see the enormous force for radicalization that could be mustered when the two groups began working together. The apparent failure of the government to make rapid enough strides in alleviating the economic crisis which still beset the Sudetenland served to accelerate the process.[62] There was, to be sure, no well organized, coordinated activity all along the border; but large numbers of independent contacts on all levels could eventually reach a critical political mass, without any central guidance.[63]

Henlein's complete inability to cope with the schism in the SdP exacerbated the whole situation. With regard to running his own party, Henlein tended to permit a great deal of autonomy to SdP plenipotentiaries—which made independent local action all the easier. Even in 1936, when quarreling nearly destroyed the party entirely, Henlein still stuck to this policy, a reflection of his inability to provide dynamic leadership. As he stated in one *Hauptleitungssitzung:* "I repeat again: every *Hauptleitung* member is independent in his own realm, personally responsible, and is to show initiative in his work." [64] Unfortunately, initiative often meant radical initiative and an intensification of the warring within the party, both of which Henlein appeared to be powerless to prevent.

By late fall of 1935, the combination of party schisms and increasingly vehement radical activity had once again sent Henlein looking to the Reich for help. At the beginning of November he met with Steinacher to commiserate about the dangerous situation. Together, on November 4, they went to Kursell.[65] Henlein sketched the situation and spoke seriously of resigning, warning that then the party would fall apart. On November 22, a now quite angry Henlein met again with Steinacher, this time in Leipzig.[66] For fifteen years nobody concerned themselves with the Sudetenland at all, Henlein complained bitterly, and now "fronts" were growing up against him all over the place. He ticked off a list of all the forces in the opposition: the students in Prague were almost completely on the side of the *Aufbruch,* encouraged by the Hitler Youth and the Gestapo; the *Rumburger Zeitung* was writing openly against him, using information which could only come from Berlin.[67] Here he mentioned for the first time his suspicions about Heydrich and the SS. Henlein then played his trump card and threatened resignation if a final decision were not made in his favor.

It was obviously a situation which cried out for one of Hitler's "binding decisions." After all, the whole political unity of the Sudeten Germans was at stake; the fate of a potentially very useful political organization, the SdP, which commanded the loyalty of a high percentage of the Germans living in Czechoslovakia, lay in the balance. If Hitler had definite plans regarding the eventual disposal of Czechoslovakia, this was the time to guarantee the security of a most useful political tool. On November 23 Friedrich Bürger, Henlein's liaison man with Steinacher, went to the Reich Chancellory to arrange a meeting with the führer. Hitler declined to see him. The most the representative of a Sudeten German party which claimed to speak for three-and-a-half million Germans in Czechoslovakia could get from the *Reichskanzlei* were some more vague assurances that Krebs would be reined in. And this was not even from Hitler personally.[68] How binding these assurances against Krebs really were became clear a short time later, when he was promoted to *Oberregierungsrat* in the Interior Ministry and was also named a *Reichstag* delegate.[69]

The situation was clear, then. Hitler did not want to be bothered with Czechoslovakia and the Sudeten Germans at the moment. Although someone in the Reich Chancellory seems to have been supporting Krebs at this point, Hitler himself once again avoided the nasty chore of deciding definitely for one side and against the other. Instead, he let the rules of Social Darwinism come into play: if the factions fought it out among themselves, the strongest or the "better" man in that sense, the one with the most allies, would win. Henlein was thus left to resolve the split in his party on his own. Incapable of doing so he had little choice but to turn to other Reich agencies for aid in mediating the quarrels besetting his party. Ironically, far from consciously and surreptitiously leading the Sudeten Germans down the garden path into Hitler's waiting arms, Henlein—because of his failure to exert a modicum of leadership necessary to hold his own party together and his need to find someone to bring together the Sudeten German "unity" movement for him—was, to no small degree, gradually and indirectly drawn into Berlin's orbit.

Thus, 1935, which had seemed to be such a propitious year for the traditionalists, ended on an ominous note. The relentless mechanics of Nazi competitive power politics were beginning to take their toll. But even more portentous was the dramatic change in Hitler's approach to foreign policy at about this time. Until now, Hitler's ventures into the international arena had been relatively scattered and cautious. The withdrawal from the League (October of 1933) and the introduction of rearmament (March of 1935)—radical enough moves in themselves at the time—came nearly two years apart and both actions were followed by extensive periods of quiescence and retrenchment. The Austrian coup of July 1934, although staged with Hitler's knowledge, did not follow from any direct initiative on his part.[70] Now, after the middle of 1935, Hitler's forays in the foreign policy field increased dramatically, which exacerbated the already difficult situation in which the traditionalists found themselves. For just as it appeared to men like Steinacher—operating as they were within the framework of an isolated, quiescent Reich—that their conception of Germandom politics might have some viability, Germany entered upon a period of growing assertiveness which threatened to cut the ground away from beneath their feet. The Anglo-German Naval Agreement of June in itself already represented a first step for Germany out of isolation: it broke the Stresa front formed by France, Britain, and Italy in reaction to the Austrian coup and drove a wedge between Britain and France.[71] Even more importantly, from mid-year on, relations improved steadily between Germany and Italy—a direct result of Italy's actions in Ethiopia, as well as Britain and France's hostile reaction to those moves. Hitler assumed a stance of benevolent neutrality and sat back to reap the benefits. Especially after October of 1935, when active hostilities began in Ethiopia, Italo-German relations improved markedly.[72] Germany's emergence from isolation only served to give new impetus and elbow room to the radicals in Germandom politics. If the traditionalists had derived advantage from Germany's need to preserve correct relations with its neighbors, the radicals now gained leverage from the fact that Germany's growing strength permitted at least restrained hostilities in the Germandom rivalries.

But changing German foreign policy did not only affect the traditionalists and their position; the converse was also true. By bringing the Sudeten problem gradually into the sphere of international politics and by allowing the Sudeten German party to come into near dependency on the Reich because of the need for mediation, the traditionalists were creating situations to which German foreign policy might respond and options on which that response might be based. Should Hitler decide to radicalize German foreign policy toward Czechoslovakia, he would find that the traditionalists had inadvertently saved him considerable effort. In the meantime the radicals in Germandom politics continued in their own efforts and kept the Sudeten problem simmering just below the surface of international politics.

VII

The Sudeten Problem Internationalized

NINETEEN THIRTY-SIX was a decisive year in the development of German foreign policy.[1] Having already begun to register successes against token resistance and to lead Germany out of the isolation that had bound it in the past, Hitler now felt confident enough to venture even more frequently into the international arena and to take increasing risks in his foreign policy decisions. On March 7, 1936, he sent troops into the Rhineland in bold opposition to his international treaty obligations. Britain and France responded with verbal objections, but otherwise undertook nothing that could be construed as a direct challenge to Hitler's actions. In the wake of this *tour de force*, Hitler committed Germany to still further involvement internationally. In July he intervened in the Spanish civil war—the first time since the abortive Austrian coup of 1934 that he undertook or countenanced adventures outside the Reich. That same month, on July 11, 1936, Hitler was also able to reach an agreement with Austria. Germany would recognize Austrian independence in exchange for which Austria would follow Germany's lead in international affairs.

Hitler's conduct of foreign policy had clearly entered a new confident phase: a phase that signalled a major shift in the balance of power in Europe to Germany's favor. The occupation of the Rhineland had been a step toward altering the strategic military balance; even more so, it altered the psychological balance. By showing only token resistance to Hitler's bold initiative, the Western powers clearly put themselves on the defensive and left open to serious question the degree to which they would honor their treaty obligations. In diplomacy, the shift was even more apparent. The Austrian agreement meant that German influence, not Italian, predominated in Vienna; southeastern Europe was open to German penetration.[2] Mussolini's acceptance of that agreement—along with

Italo-German cooperation in Spain—also indicated that the original Stresa front [Italy, France, Britain] was a dead letter.

As surrounding countries were forced to take cognizance of these altered power relationships in Europe, the tenor of relations between Germany and its neighbors would also change perceptibly. Official diplomatic relations might for the moment continue on the surface as before, but the assumptions underlying those relationships had to change: no one could go on blithely accepting the postwar status quo as inviolable. It is not surprising, then, that Germany's relations with Czechoslovakia during 1936 were undergoing a subtle transition. On the one hand, Hitler slowly grew more assertive toward this southeastern neighbor. The Reich had reacted to the 1935 mutual assistance pact between Czechoslovakia and the Soviet Union with an official propaganda barrage: in 1936 the campaign intensified. Goebbels's propaganda machine now portrayed Czechoslovakia as a Bolshevik "aircraft carrier," poised to strike in the heart of Europe.[3] But although Hitler felt confident and irritated enough to issue propaganda warnings to Czechoslovakia, his hostility confined itself to that level. Formal relations between the two countries remained cool, but correct. Hitler apparently had no immediate intentions toward Czechoslovakia beyond serving notice that Germany would have to be reckoned with. Still, Hitler had officially and publicly taken cognizance of Czechoslovakia as a problem in international affairs.

Czechoslovakia's leaders were well aware that the tenor of relations between the two countries had changed. It is no accident that after the Rhineland occupation, President Beneš took the initiative in trying to reach some kind of accord with Germany. Characteristically, however, Hitler showed no interest in reaching an agreement with the Czechs on any outstanding issue: a binding settlement at this point might tie his hands and narrow his future options.[4]

Hitler's new aggressiveness and Germany's emergence from isolation during the course of 1936 had important ramifications for the Germandom struggle, too, for they posed both a threat and a promise. A quiescent foreign policy had been the foundation upon which the traditionalists had based their activity and survival. If the need for peaceful relations had not prevented the radicals from attacking them, then at least it had precluded being eliminated as a factor in ethnic German politics. As this foreign policy now became less quiescent and increasingly aggressive, would not the radicals be encouraged to carry the struggle on to the finish? This was the threat which now mobilized the traditionalists anew in 1936. However, the new trend in Reich foreign policy also offered a glimmer of hope as the traditionalists tried desperately to shore up their position. If, after all, Hitler was able to register successes in the international arena, why could not the traditionalists do the same? Both frightened and encouraged by the shift in German foreign policy, they embarked on a new course of action during 1936: consciously bringing the Sudeten question into the international arena. By winning support for their cause abroad, the traditionalists hoped both to improve the lot of the Sudeten Germans and to secure their own crumbling position in Germandom politics.

In one sense, a kind of internationalization of the Sudeten problem had been going on long before 1936. Already during the early 1930s, the evolution of the ideological and factional struggles in ethnic German politics had gradually tended to internationalize what might otherwise have remained a domestic problem involving only the Sudeten Germans and the Czech government. Radical National Socialism within the Reich and in the Sudetenland had gradually formed alliances that extended over the frontier. By attacking Henlein and Steinacher as part of the same traditionalist movement, the radicals had tended to push these two men and their otherwise separate concerns together as well, again forcing a cross-frontier collaboration. As radical Sudeten Nazis fled to Germany and continued, with the aid of various Reich agencies, to interfere in Sudeten politics, the internationalization process took on still more complex dimensions. Until this point, internationalization of the Sudeten German question had been, for the most part, unintentional and random—largely a by-product of the various Germandom rivalries. By 1936, however, this situation was to change dramatically. Now, desperately looking for some device to prop up their sagging position, the traditionalists deliberately and systematically brought the Sudeten German issue into the international arena.

Beginning in 1935, the leaders of the Sudeten German party actively attempted to solicit the interest of influential foreign circles, particularly in England, in the plight of the Sudeten Germans.[5] The impetus for this course of action most probably came from the moderates in the party—particularly Walter Brand and Heinz Rutha

—who at this time saw as much reason to look to England as to the Reich for sympathetic action on their behalf. "We recognized with complete clarity," Brand subsequently wrote, "that the key to aid from abroad lay in England. For that reason we cultivated relations there carefully." [6] In July of 1935, Henlein—spurred on by his foreign policy advisor, Heinz Rutha—consulted with his friend Steinacher about a proposed visit to England. This move seems to have been made independently by the Sudeten leaders and not engineered from Berlin, though Berlin certainly was kept informed of the developments. One indication of this is the fact that not all of the NS party agencies approved of the plan: Ribbentrop, with whom Henlein discussed the idea on July 8, disapproved, probably because he considered London his bailiwick. In any case Ribbentrop tried to discourage Henlein from undertaking the venture.[7]

Despite Ribbentrop's opposition, Henlein had Heinz Rutha make arrangements for a trip to London. The contact in England was Colonel Graham Christie, former British air attaché in Berlin. Christie and Henlein had been introduced some time earlier by an aristocratic landowner from Bohemia, Count Kuehn-Luetzow.[8] Christie, often erroneously believed to have been in the British Secret Service, in turn informed his friend Sir Robert Vansittart, permanent undersecretary in the Foreign Office, about the visit and was encouraged to pursue the contact with Henlein.[9] On December 9, 1935, Henlein journeyed to London, where he addressed a gathering sponsored by the Institute of International Affairs at Chatham House. He assured his sympathetic listeners that all his party really wanted was a reconciliation with the Czechs; he denied any interest in irredenta, and condemned pan-Germanism as being just as dangerous as pan-Slavism.[10] This kind of language was music to the ears of a number of Englishmen who either felt guilty about Versailles or harbored sympathies for what appeared to be an authoritarian, anticommunist regime in Germany. The group included such people as Lady Astor; the publisher, Alexander Henderson; and influential journalists like Ward Price and J. L. Garvin.[11]

The purpose behind this move of the Sudeten leaders was to bring their problem outside the framework of Czech domestic policy and perhaps out of Reich politics as well into the international spotlight. As Karl Hermann Frank put it later in his own convoluted way:

[The conversations with the English] followed the purpose of broaching the Sudeten German problem and thereby broadening the minorities problem onto the international level, in order to solve the Sudeten German problem as an international problem: that is, to make of the Sudeten Germans an international question.[12]

As one German diplomat realized, the talks would also be one way in which the SdP could protect itself from being dissolved by the Czechs. "The connection with these circles," he reported to Berlin, "can be of great value in case the idea of an elimination or even a ban on the Sudeten German party by the Czechoslovakian government should be implemented—something which Beneš in particular has not yet given up."[13]

Henlein visited England once again in July of 1936. By this time, however, Reich agencies had a great deal more to do with the affair than the year before, an involvement which reflected the renewed interest of official Germany in Czechoslovakia as well as Henlein's increased dependence on Reich agencies for sustenance. Perhaps it also indicated that at least some German officials saw the possibilities represented by the interest of prominent British citizens in the Sudeten German situation. This was the case, apparently, with the new agency in charge of ethnic Germans. In June of 1936 the Kursell Office, which thus far had limited itself to settling quarrels in ethnic German circles, took up the question of ties with the English. During the middle of June, the *Büro Kursell* tried to arrange a meeting between Henlein and Ward Price, who would be returning from Budapest to England via Czechoslovakia.[14] On July 15, however, a sudden invitation arrived from London for Henlein, who immediately sent Karl Hermann Frank to the German mission to inform the AA and Ribbentrop. Then, accompanied by Heinz Rutha, Henlein flew off to London.[15] Again he lectured at Chatham House, this time playing on the theme of communism, describing Czechoslovakia as a state "tainted" with that particular bacillus, bolshevism.[16] His reference to the Czech alliance with the Soviet Union and the dangers of that relationship struck a responsive chord among conservative Englishmen. This time, the cultivation of English contacts paid off in dividends. Anthony Eden, the foreign secretary, urged Jan Masaryk, Czechoslovak ambassador in London, to support the necessary measures to improve relations between Germans and Czechs. In a meeting with Kamil Krofta, Czech foreign minister, at Geneva in September, Eden again emphasized the importance of the Sudeten problem.[17]

Henlein's most successful conversations, however, were with Robert Vansittart. Vansittart, who spoke fluent German and prided himself on a thorough grasp of the German problem in Czechoslovakia, was very impressed with the uprightness of the young Sudeten leader.[18] As Henlein reported on his two-and-a-half hour conversation with Vansittart, the undersecretary had promised to take up the Sudeten question in the League of Nations, to give the English press instructions to take up the Sudeten problem (!), and in general to advise and help the Sudeten Germans.[19] It has been quite correctly pointed out, that it was unthinkable for a high British official to make binding commitments like this; to do so would not only have been a flagrant indiscretion, but a veritable revolution in British foreign policy.[20] Most likely Henlein, in order to enhance his own position, blew way out of proportion any assurances the sympathetic Vansittart may have made. At this period in 1936, Henlein and his colleagues were under severe fire from the radicals and needed every bit of prestige they could garner. It is not surprising, then, that he would have tried to put himself in the most favorable light possible by exaggerating Vansittart's statements. At any rate, whatever the accuracy of Henlein's report, Vansittart did discuss Henlein's demands with Hess and AA officials during his visit to Berlin on August 13, 1936.[21] Henlein's need to make himself appear more important and secure than he actually was also most probably lay behind his peculiar behavior in Berlin in August: when Henlein met with the German foreign minister during the Olympics, he both asked for aid against the radicals and felt compelled to minimize the trouble he was having. In short, he was not at all sure of his position.[22]

It is instructive to view Henlein's various visits to London in light of the constant information gathering which was going on in Berlin at this point. There is little doubt that Hitler, and others as well, tucked away for future reference this apparent British willingness to act in favor of the Sudeten Germans. Henlein had only limited contacts in London, partly official and partly private, but English officials were now discussing Sudeten affairs with Reich and Czechoslovak officials —which did represent the beginnings of a new kind of internationalization of the Sudeten problem. Even this token British involvement in

the whole question could not but give encouragement and maneuvera-
bility both to traditionalists and to radicals. To the traditionalists it
meant the possibility of improving their power position domestically
as well as the general condition of the Sudeten Germans in Czechoslovakia. To the radicals, otherwise bound to some extent by the führer's
warning against interference in the internal affairs of other countries,
English involvement and the precedent of outside intervention it set
now opened the door a crack to further action.

By October 9, 1936, Henlein could report to Dr. Günther
Altenburg in the AA that he was very satisfied about the interest
which the English public was showing in the Sudeten question.[23]
Among the more conservative members of the AA, the idea of gaining
English understanding on the Sudeten issue appears to have won an
enthusiastic response. By early 1937, a three way informal mechanism
seems to have been functioning between the German diplomatic
representation, the SdP, and English circles—all aimed at "clarification" of the Sudeten problem. In February of 1937, Friedrich Stieve of
the AA *Kulturabteilung* wrote to Ernst Eisenlohr, the new minister in
Prague, asking him to urge Henlein "that he use the good connections
that he made in England to arrange for a group of English
parliamentarians to make a junket to the areas in question. A
[venture] of this kind could, if correctly carried out, be of definite
use." [24] Eisenlohr passed the suggestion on to Henlein's deputy, Karl
Hermann Frank, and reported back that the SdP was already losing
no opportunity to acquaint every English journalist and parliamentar-
ian who happened to come to Czechoslovakia with the details of the
Sudeten question. He added confidentially that "the British embassy
here is doing everything to bring visiting English citizens of importance into contact with representatives of the SdP." [25] Conservative
Britons were wined and dined; trout fishing expeditions to the estates
of Bohemian nobles lent an air of respectability to the SdP, while trips
through the depressed Sudeten German industrial areas generated the
desired degree of sympathy. In England itself, Sudeten leaders
attempted to make their contacts firmer by setting up a permanent
press bureau in London under the direction of Walter Brand.[26]

During 1936, the traditionalists made a second conscious attempt
to internationalize the Sudeten problem: this time by way of direct
negotiations between Germany and Czechoslovakia. Although the
secret German-Czech negotiations of the fall and winter of 1936 did

not produce anything concrete, they do offer insight into Hitler's outlook toward Czechoslovakia and the Sudeten Germans at this time. They also are, in retrospect, an instructive example of how the traditionalists unwittingly forged potential tools of aggression for Hitler and the radicals.[27] The idea for a German-Czech treaty came originally from Albrecht Haushofer, a traditionalist who had figured importantly in the formation of the *Volksdeutscher Rat,* had been a personal liaison between that body and Hess, and had acted as one of the main traditionalist spokesmen at "court." He also worked from time to time as an unofficial member of the *Dienststelle Ribbentrop,* especially when the traditionalists were still looking to Ribbentrop as an ally against Bohle. In April of 1936, in a position paper entitled "Political Possibilities in the Southeast"—a report which he discussed in detail with Ribbentrop—Haushofer suggested a ten year nonagression pact with Czechoslovakia, the price for which would be complete cultural autonomy and economic equality for the Sudeten Germans.[28] The long range effect of such a treaty, Haushofer felt, would be to loosen Czechoslovakia's ties with the Soviet Union and France, while at the same time strengthening German influence in Central Europe. The entire plan was traditionalist in nature: it envisioned a peaceful, rather than violent, expansion of German influence and exhibited a concern for ethnic Germans for their own sake, not as tools to be manipulated in the interest of power politics.

Nothing came immediately of Haushofer's idea: like so many other *Denkschriften,* his paper also apparently disappeared into the files. In the fall of 1936, however, five months after Haushofer had submitted his paper to Ribbentrop, the question of Czech-German negotiations once again came up. Obviously with the sanction of the top German leadership—most probably with the approval of Hitler himself—Haushofer suddenly broached the subject of negotiations with Vojtěch Mastný, Czech ambassador to Berlin, and received a favorable response.[29] In the ensuing talks, Haushofer collaborated with Dr. Maximilian Karl Graf zu Trauttmansdorff, an official in the Labor Ministry and a self-styled expert on Czechoslovakian affairs. Although not a traditionalist in the strict sense of the word, Trauttmansdorff was a moderate. In September of 1936, probably under the auspices of the *Büro Kursell,* Trauttmansdorff had helped to adjudicate the quarrels in the SdP. He was interested in the Sudeten Germans, not so much for their own sake as in the interest of a peaceful expansion. of German influence.[30] To this end he advocated that the Sudeten Germans become an "instrument of the foreign policy of the Reich"—a phrase which would appear again a year later in a completely different and more fateful context.[31]

On November 13 and 14, 1936, Haushofer and Trauttmansdorff met with Czechoslovak President Eduard Beneš and Foreign Minister Kamil Krofta in Prague.[32] The two Czech leaders confirmed their interest in some kind of accommodation with Germany; the unofficial German emissaries hoped also to reach an agreement of some sort. Both sides were to be disappointed. The talks, in the end, produced no results because Hitler lost interest and allowed them to fail. It is puzzling why he permitted the mission in the first place, and then, just as quickly, aborted any real potential agreement which could have come from the negotiations. The real issue here, however, is not just Hitler's reason for permitting, then abandoning the Haushofer-Trauttmansdorff talks. In order to adequately assess the mission it is essential to come to grips with the more important problem of just what Hitler's intentions toward Czechoslovakia were at this time. The most revealing evidence regarding Hitler's state of mind during this period is the report on the Czech-German talks which Haushofer submitted and Hitler's marginal comments on them.[33] In a report dated November 25, 1936, Haushofer had listed six points which Hitler proceeded to reorder and alter, indicating what his priorities were. As Haushofer had listed them, the points included:

1. a ten-year nonaggression pact
2. neutralization of Czechoslovakia in case of Russian attack
3. Habsburg issue
4. restriction of émigrés' activities
5. trade agreement
6. improve lot of Sudeten Germans

Hitler's marginal notes indicate, above all, that his plans for "handling" the Czech situation were vague and had not, as yet, coalesced. He did not want a nonaggression pact (this suggestion on Haushofer's list was crossed out). The Reich had reached a high enough level of strength by this time that Hitler probably thought such a treaty unnecessary; it would only reduce the available options. Haushofer's second point, the neutralization of Czechoslovakia, was Hitler's second point as well. Obviously, a Czechoslovakia torn loose from its moorings with France and the Soviet Union would fall more easily under German influence or domination: yet, Hitler rejected the most obvious step toward neutralization, a nonaggression pact, because he would have had to make concessions to get it which might bind his hands in the future. He knew full well that Germany was not in any serious danger of being attacked, so he was unwilling to do anything which might have limited his options.

Haushofer's fourth and fifth points, restriction of emigrés' activity and a trade agreement, Hitler raised to three and one, respectively, on his priority scale: even if unwilling to tie himself down in the long run, he was willing to work on the more immediate, peripheral issues between the two countries. This, in turn, indicated that Hitler apparently had no urgent intentions to "solve" the Czechoslovakian situation by radical means. Although he rejected a pact that would limit his foreign policy options, he did not have any "blueprint for aggression" either at this point. Perhaps most interesting of all, Haushofer's final point, that of improving the lot of the Sudeten Germans, did not interest Hitler enough even to merit a comment. If Czechoslovakia was only of peripheral interest to Hitler, then the Sudeten Germans and their fate were at the moment at least seemingly of no interest whatsoever.

Even this fleeting concern with Czechoslovakia soon passed. Although Hitler did authorize Haushofer to return to Prague, when Haushofer appeared in Berlin again in January of 1937 to present Hitler with a proposed treaty draft, the führer was totally disinterested. Haushofer was merely instructed to drag out the negotiations— which of course meant that they would eventually be dropped.[34] This purely temporary concern on Hitler's part is the key to why he permitted the mission in the first place. Always willing to let others carry out his experiments for him, Hitler had apparently allowed the traditionalists to pursue a course that might conceivably have gained him something with no effort or sacrifice on his part. Had the Haushofer mission been able to induce Czechoslovakia to abandon its alliance system for a more close relationship with Germany—a highly unlikely proposition—then well and good; if not, then Hitler had nothing to lose by simply dropping the demarche, which is precisely what happened.

Although the Haushofer-Trauttmansdorff mission did nothing to alter German-Czech relations, it was not completely without benefit to

Hitler: in the long run, it had taught him something. Haushofer had written after his first visit to Prague: "Should for whatever reasons, concluding [a nonaggression treaty] not be expedient, then it would be best to initially draw out the talks, and if necessary, render them purposeless by tightening the screws of the Sudeten German demands."[35] Hitler was to follow this advice. Interestingly enough, almost two years later as he was seeking a pretext to smash Czechoslovakia, these were precisely the instructions that Hitler was also to give to Henlein. To use Haushofer's own terminology, this was truly "educating our masters"—but it was not the kind of education which Haushofer had intended.[36]

At the same time the traditionalists were *intentionally* internationalizing the Sudeten problem by bringing it to public attention abroad and by proposing direct negotiations between Germany and Czechoslovakia, the schism in the Sudeten German party, by drawing in Reich agencies to mediate factional quarrels, was *incidentally* leading to the same end. If one views the internationalization process in its broadest sense—making of the Sudeten Germans a problem outside the borders of the state in which they were living—then the split in the SdP contributed significantly to the entire process. The same quarrels and tensions that had plagued the SdP all during the previous years and that had nearly caused Henlein's resignation in December of 1935 continued undiminished into 1936. By May a crisis was imminent. Radical forces both within the party and outside it were concentrating their attacks on the KB circle around Henlein: particularly on Henlein's right-hand man, Walter Brand, whom the radicals hoped to replace with one of their own number. On May 7, Rudolf Kasper, already a dissident, came out openly on the side of *Aufbruch* and at a *Hauptratssitzung* of the party demanded a vote of no-confidence in Brand.[37] The campaign against Brand continued until several weeks later he was actually threatened with a pistol in the town of Haida.[38]

In the provinces the general struggle between radical and KB factions had become especially bitter. At Olmütz in Kreis Mährisch-Schönberg, a furious battle developed between the *Kreisleiter,* a KB man named Skomorowsky, and the Kreis *Arbeiterstandesführer,* a radical named Matis. At a district meeting on May 19, fifteen dissidents broke into the hall and assaulted Skomorowsky physically.[39] At an *Amtswaltertagung* in Teplitz-Schönau on May 24, a workers' delegation, reflecting the close collaboration between the

Aufbruch circle and dissident labor, declared: "We are loyal to Konrad Henlein. But we are also behind Kasper and Leibl [*sic*]. When they go [out of the SdP], we do too." [40] Alluding to the bloody Night of the Long Knives two years before in Germany, rumors persisted that a second June 30 was not far away—only this time it would be the SdP which would be purged.[41]

To add to Henlein's difficulties, May of 1936 was scarcely a propitious time for an internal crisis to come in the SdP. On May 13 the Czech parliament passed the Law for the Defense of the State under the terms of which restrictions were placed on unreliable political elements.[42] Since even many of the moderate Sudeten Germans had cultivated risky contacts, the new law could potentially become a weapon in the hands of the radicals, who did not hesitate to use denunciation and betrayal in their efforts to discredit their opponents. It was apparent that if something were not undertaken soon, the Sudeten German "unity" party would fall apart at the seams. Henlein finally roused himself to action and called a *Hauptratssitzung* on May 28, admitting his failure in not reacting in time to the gathering storm of opposition:

> After the unprecedented electoral campaign leading up to our victory, we really entered a period of satiated complaisance. We always glossed over and covered up tensions which arose, and so it got to the point where I was forced to recognize that the final hour for action had arrived. The defamation campaign which has doubled and tripled [in intensity] recently made me realize a few things, so that I was convinced that this is a matter of disloyalty. I saw myself forced to take measures to exclude one or another from the movement.

Rudolf Kasper, he said, had refused to part with his radical friends, so he had broken with Kasper the day before.[43]

Henlein's colleagues pointed out that the problem was not just with several dissidents in the SdP leadership, but rather that the discontent had widespread support. Rudolf Sandner, chairman of the SdP parliamentary *Fraktion*, noted that there appeared to be a system to the radicals' actions:

> To the day, almost to the exact hour in Moravia, in Aussig, Komotau, Eger, everywhere, the demand appears that Brand's head has to roll. And then Sebekowsky, Rutha, Sandner, Frank. . . . One thing is clear, though: when it's the same thing as with

the [Prague] students, Mährisch-Schönberg, and 100 other cases out there in the counties, that the groundwork for a rebellion is being systematically created, then it's high time that we acted, decisively and ruthlessly.

Sandner's reference to the Prague students concerned a specific, and typical, incident in the labyrinthine politics of the Sudeten German unity movement. The SdP had picked its own candidate for the leadership of the German students in Prague and had assigned Rudolf Meckel, the SdP liaison man with student organizations, to see to it that this candidate got elected. But Meckel, a former DNSAP member and radical student leader, had his own ideas. First, he formed an alliance with *Ramphold Gorenz*, the fraternity of a fellow radical, Rudolf Haider, one of the chief *Aufbruch* people. Meckel then proceeded to block any SdP infiltration of student groups at all, and even more dramatically deviating from his assigned tasks, he actually formed his own clandestine radical NS organization, the *Deutsche Hochschülerschaft*, with the hope of recruiting as many students as possible. Eventually, Henlein heard of all this and dismissed Meckel. It is some indication of the bizarre, treacherous nature of Sudeten right-wing politics that Meckel then went to the government itself for help against the SdP. Failing to mention anything about his own more radical activities, Meckel approached both Beneš and the Sudeten German minister, Franz Spina, with a colossal lie about his reasons for opposing the SdP: he was attempting, he maintained, to keep the SdP out of student affairs in order to prevent "politicization" of the fraternities! [44]

In light of these many examples of growing dissension, Henlein asked the men of his immediate leadership circle to get at the sources of dissidence, working through the *Kreisleiter*, and to remove anyone from the movement who could not prove loyalty. To underline the point, Frank announced the expulsion from the party of the most important radicals, including Anton Kreissl, who was Hans Krebs's agent in Czechoslovakia. In ordering the dissidents expelled, Henlein had chosen to side with his *Kameradschaftsbund* comrades at the top of the SdP leadership. It was highly questionable, however, if he could control dissent at the grass roots level of the party simply by eliminating radicals from positions of leadership: the lower SdP echelons were far too heavily manned by former DNSAP people for that. Thus, Henlein's colleagues continued to report trouble in many areas. Large numbers of dissatisfied *Ortsleiter* or *Bezirksleiter* were undermining the unity of the party. In some cases, as in the communities of Brüx, Sauerstein, Görken, and Tetschen, the party organization as a whole was on the side of the radicals. Kasper and Haider, the *Aufbruch* leaders, had constructed a widespread net of agents and sympathizers to exploit the unrest further.[45]

With his party dissolving before his eyes, Henlein once again felt he had no choice but to turn to his contacts in the Reich, a decision which made the quarrels besetting the SdP the common property of official Reich agencies. But although Henlein was coming hat in hand as the supplicant seeking official mediation to heal the rift in his party, the German agencies themselves had a stake in settling the disputes: for a full blown split in the SdP would have resulted in a wave of denunciations and betrayals, the cumulative effect of which would have been to blow the cover off practically all of the clandestine contacts between the Reich and Sudeten organizations, seriously compromising the Reich's official policy toward Czechoslovakia. As the German minister in Prague, Ernst Eisenlohr, put it: "We must reckon with the possibility that a struggle of all against all is beginning in the SdP, and that in this case, we can forget about any degree of discretion, including in contacts with Reich agencies." [46] So, from whatever direction the impetus came—whether as a result of Henlein's supplications, or from the *Büro Kursell* (anxious to assert its prerogatives in ethnic German politics), or from AA officials themselves (concerned about embarrassing incidents)—concrete action was finally taken. On June 9, 1936, a meeting was held in Berlin at the home of Günther Altenburg of the AA, a man with whom Steinacher had worked successfully in the past.[47] Karl Hermann Frank, Rudolf Sandner, and Fritz Zippelius represented the Sudeten German party; Adolf Metzner, who had temporarily replaced Friedrich Bürger as Henlein's permanent representative in Berlin, and the former German minister in Prague, Walter Koch, were also there. Most importantly, Franz Wehofsich, who had been assigned by the Kursell Office to mediate in the Sudeten quarrel, also was present. In the course of the meeting a compromise settlement was reached. Rudolf Kasper and Anton Kreissl, Krebs's man in Czechoslovakia, would be reinstated in the party on the condition that they stop attacking Brand; Brand himself would continue to be in the leadership of the party, but would be sent elsewhere, perhaps to Switzerland or London on assignment until things cooled down. Kasper and Rudolf Haider, the two *Aufbruch* people who had caused the most trouble, would be directed to come to Berlin and be reminded that Henlein had the full support of officials there. Two days later, on June 11, Henlein was able to announce at a meeting of the *Hauptrat* of the party in Eger: "In the past week, different people whom I know and regard have made an effort to try once again to end the quarrels somehow." [48]

The compromise struck in Berlin showed that the traditionalists were still in a relatively strong position in the SdP: the radicals were not, as yet, powerful enough to overthrow the KB faction represented by Brand. At the same time, it reflected the stage of development that the Germandom rivalries had reached in the Reich. The *Volksdeutsche Mittelstelle,* as the *Büro Kursell* was increasingly called, still was in no position to give binding orders to German ethnic groups.[49] Moreover, its composition was not yet such that anyone would have thought of giving such orders: mediation was as effective and as strong a role as it could play. The person who was chosen to represent the *Büro Kursell* at the Berlin talks is living proof of the fact that Germandom politics was very much in a transitional stage at this point. Earlier, the mediation would probably have been handled by the *Volksdeutscher Rat,* a traditionalist organization under the direction of an old *Volkstum* worker, Steinacher; soon this task would be left to a radical SS agency, VOMI, under an imperialist-minded director, Werner Lorenz. During this transitional period, however, the man chosen to handle the problem was Franz Wehofsich. A member of the SS since 1934, although not an officer, Wehofsich had had a decade or more of experience in ethnic German affairs; an intellectual, he was a friend of both Karl Haushofer and Steinacher. He was, therefore, a man with credentials acceptable to radicals, yet with a respectability and experience which linked him to the traditionalists as well. This situation, as Wehofsich himself, would change: as it became more and more apparent that radicals would win out in the Germandom struggle, Wehofsich—as pressure mounted—would tend to lean increasingly toward solutions favorable to the radical wing in the party. He proved to be, as many transitional figures are, rather flexible.[50]

As it was, the compromise solution adopted in Berlin was only temporarily honored by either faction. Henlein soon broke off negotiations with Kasper and the feud continued.[51] On July 25 Berlin intervened again. At a meeting in the Kursell Office, Karl Hermann Frank was told that it was the wish of all concerned that "Herr Henlein find a solution very soon that would restore peace in the Sudeten German camp." [52] It was also strongly urged that an end be made to the constant publication of explanations and counterexplanations in the Sudeten German press—exchanges which were not contributing to the relaxation of tensions. Frank was to consult Henlein and report back a week later on Henlein's intentions. Wehofsich himself was dispatched to Prague to do what he could from there. In the meantime, the radicals, who wanted nothing more than Berlin's intervention in their favor, were busy emphasizing how bad the split really was and that it could only be ended through binding intervention.[53] At the meeting in Kursell's office, the participants had emphasized that it was imperative to heal the rupture in the party right away because Henlein was to be an invited guest of the Reich at the Olympic games in Berlin during August. Nothing of the sort happened: when Henlein arrived in Berlin the split in the SdP was wider than ever. An issue of the *Rumburger Zeitung* published on August 8 listed still more communities in which the local SdP leadership had gone over to the radical opposition, including Plan, Hohenelbe, Wildstein, Elbogen, and Reichenberg. In Teplitz the district party leaders passed a resolution reflecting the grass roots nature of the rebellion: "In the interest of unity and uniformity and to reinforce trust in the party, the district leadership of Tetschen demands the resignation of the whole [*Hauptleitung*] directorship and the election of same from the bottom up on the broadest basis." [54] The radical journal, *Die junge Front*, hailed a similar demand on the part of the Böhmerwald *Kreisleitung*, but added: "Yes, indeed, but first all of the members who have resigned or been expelled must be brought in again, and this for the simple reason: the rebels were right!" [55]

Henlein's conversations with Reich leaders during his visit to Berlin in August appear to be anything but those of a self-assured paladin, confidently leading the Sudeten Germans into Hitler's waiting arms. Rather, he was a man desperately in need of help from the Reich to do a job which he was incapable of doing alone: namely, holding the Sudeten German party together. This was his big chance. He had availed himself of help from minor agencies with rather questionable results. Now, perhaps he could convince the highest Reich officials—even the führer himself—to back him ostentatiously and solidly. Henlein was to be disappointed once again. Although he talked to a number of Reich officials, he received no really binding committments. As for the führer, in the course of the games Hitler barely spoke to Henlein at all. Henlein managed only to meet briefly with several AA officials, who offered him little encouragement. On August 14, he consulted with Reich Foreign Minister von Neurath, dwelling for the most part on the difficulties he was having with the extremist elements in his party.[56] He gave assurances that he was going to get them under control, but he then turned around and asked if Neurath could not perhaps do something about the *Rumburger Zeitung* which was causing him so much trouble—such as forbidding the paper's import into the Reich. The foreign minister promised only that he would look into the matter; moreover, he also indicated that *he* was concerned that Sudeten radicals were not under strict enough control. Rumors persisted among the Sudeten Germans brought over for the Olympics that Germany was soon about to settle the Sudeten problem with the sword. Henlein assured the foreign minister that he knew this was nonsense—such rumors were mostly being manufactured at lower party levels in the Reich. He again promised to take steps to counter this new difficulty. Neurath urged him to do so most energetically: "For it is out of the question that we let ourselves get involved militarily in the foreseeable future because of the Sudeten Germans." For the time being, the Sudetens would have to rely on themselves in their struggle, although the Reich would help as much as possible financially. Pushed again to take charge of his own party without any real hope of help doing so, Henlein feebly tried to save face by assuring the foreign minister that he was happy to have met Hitler personally, even if the führer had only said a few words to him. It would do him a lot of good at home, he hoped, that the führer had spoken to him and had expressed regards. When Henlein met with Altenburg at the AA on the following day, he seemed even more desperate to rescue some dignity despite his precarious position: he now tried to minimize the disputes within his party as mere "bagatelles," even though he again attempted to get some help in fighting the *Rumburger Zeitung*.[57]

Disputes within the SdP continued during the fall until early in October of 1936, when—partly due to the activities of Wehofsich in Prague—the differences were temporarily papered over. Kasper and Kreissl were readmitted to the leadership circle of the SdP and Brand, on Henlein's instructions, was hustled off to London to try and interest influential Englishmen in the Sudeten question.[58] The truce did not last long. The important thing about it, however, was that it had come about entirely through the mediation of official Reich agencies. More than ever Henlein was falling into a fateful dependence on the Reich, a process which *nolens volens* made the whole Sudeten German question less and less an exclusively Czechoslovakian internal problem and increasingly a potential concern in all the chancelleries of Europe.

Henlein's growing dependence on the Reich was not only a result of the need for political mediation in the internal quarrels of the SdP, however. It stemmed also from his habit of turning to various Reich offices for financial aid. In early 1935, when the Sudeten German party faced the prospect of waging an expensive electoral campaign, practically the only significant source of money came through Steinacher and the VDA. Henlein's final bill for the elections had been over 330,000 marks.[59] In the following months of 1935 and into 1936, as Henlein's Reich connections multiplied and as the SdP expanded its organization and activities, more and more Reich agencies began increasingly funneling money across the border. The AA set up a regular, quite munificent program of subsidies for the SdP, channeling over fifteen thousand marks per month to the party in Czechoslovakia and three thousand to Henlein's liaison in Berlin, Friedrich Bürger.[60] In addition, the Foreign Office honored a series of special requests for aid: such as funds to support a petition on behalf of the SdP in the League of Nations and money for defense lawyers in the many political trials which came up after passage of the Law for the Defense of the State.[61] The VDA also continued to funnel money in varying amounts through the legation and various consulates in Czechoslovakia.[62]

It should not be construed that the official Reich agencies represented an inexhaustable source of income which Henlein could tap at will. Once in a while, on the principle that ethnic groups, if they were worth their salt, really ought to be able to look after themselves, one Reich agency or other would actually announce the intention of stopping the flow of funds. The AA, for example, informed the Finance Ministry of just such a plan in March of 1936.[63] Such intentions, however, were not usually honored: especially if money could be had somewhere and if the political need were pressing (which, if the word of the supplicants was any indication, it always was). The following is a typical case in point. In January of 1936, the Propaganda Ministry approached the Foreign Ministry for 230,000 marks needed to finance the SdP newspaper, *Die Zeit*. The Finance Ministry declined the request and suggested that PROMI take an advance on the money from next year's budget. PROMI refused. To save matters, Hess himself approached the Finance Ministry, which then agreed to go along if the Foreign Ministry thought it was necessary. As it turned out, it did: if the newspaper were to be discontinued for lack of funds, the Czechs would audit the books, discover the illegal funds that had already been given, and then have an excuse to dissolve the Sudeten German party.[64] The politics of helping illegally to finance a political movement abroad were complex indeed and the complicity such financing demanded led more and more to a mutual interdependence between Henlein and the Reich. This mutuality sustained Henlein despite his personal limitations as a leader.

By late 1936 and early 1937, Henlein had discovered newer and more lucrative sources of income. He now not only had good credit with the AA and with the people around Hess, but he had also begun successfully to knock on the doors of other party greats. By October of 1936 he was successfully negotiating for aid to the tune of 5 to 6 million marks from Dr. Robert Ley, the Reich labor czar.[65] Four months later, SdP requests were coming into Göring's Four Year Plan office for 100,000 marks: the first installment of what was hoped to be an eventual total of 1,000,000 marks.[66] This largess certainly must have been welcome after the desperate scrambling for funds in 1935, but where financial dependence went, political dependence could not be far behind, as Henlein was soon most painfully to discover.

It is significant that the whole pattern of financial aid followed by political complicity and then more aid to underwrite the investment already made was started by the traditionalists—the very people who preached that the cardinal law of *Volkstum* work was self-help on the part of the ethnic groups. If this principle had been honored, the Sudeten German leaders might have seen their way clear to seek some accommodation with the Czech state, thus depriving Hitler of at least this tool for expansion. However, it was not honored. On the contrary, men like Steinacher, in order to gain a better position for themselves in the political rivalries in Nazi Germany, had deeply involved themselves and the agencies they represented in Sudeten German politics. They thus linked their fate inextricably with the success or failure of the Henlein movement to which they had committed themselves. Conversely, when the piecemeal corruption of the traditionalist VR-VDA group began in the Reich and then accelerated during 1936, Henlein—through his very dependence on these people —found himself drawn into the maelstrom. With his earlier contacts endangered, Henlein sought other, more powerful ones in the ever changing kaleidoscope of Germandom politics. Just as with the traditionalists in Germany who had struck questionable alliances in order to survive, Henlein's search for allies brought him into contact with, and eventually dependence on, increasingly more radical men.

Henlein's speeches at this time reflected his increasing proximity to and dependence on the Reich. In Prague on February 23, 1936, Henlein—who had been assuring the world for years that his movement had nothing in the least to do with National Socialism and who had been trying to downplay any contacts his people had with the Reich—suddenly began to emphasize that his people did indeed belong to a larger German cultural entity. In this, his famous "culture" address, he still assiduously avoided any hint of political commonality with Germany; but even stressing cultural commonality was a step beyond anything he had publicly proclaimed before.[67] In a speech at Eger on June 21, he went even farther when he professed: "I would rather be hated with Germany than gain advantage from the hatred of Germany." [68] These remarks have often been used to illustrate the contention that Henlein was already a creature of the Reich, a sycophant uttering phrases put into his mouth by Berlin. In reality the opposite is the case. True, the speeches do reflect his growing militancy and identification with the Reich, but Henlein's words are not the result of planned complicity. Rather, they are the words of a man trying to catch up with developments that are threatening to bypass him: for Henlein was not only being drawn to the Reich through bureaucratic, financial, and personal ties; he was also being pushed in that direction by the radicalization of his own party. Regardless of Hitler's relative disinterest in Czechoslovakia and the Sudeten Germans at this time, his successful attempts at steering Germany out of isolation in no small way helped to mobilize and radicalize the grass roots Sudeten Germans and to draw them in spirit at least closer to Germany. The apparent failure of the Czech government to make rapid enough strides in combatting the economic dislocation that still prevailed in the Sudetenland also tended to radicalize the Sudeten rank and file, at the same time turning their hopes for relief toward Germany, where Hitler had apparently succeeded in achieving something close to full employment.[69] It is in light of all this that Henlein's rapidly changing attitudes must be interpreted.

Henlein was still not in command of his own movement; he was becoming increasingly dependent on the mediation of official agencies in the Reich at a time when great changes—the outcomes of which no one could foretell—were taking place in the central Reich Germandom agencies, such as VOMI.[70] Perhaps worst of all, he still did not know either where he stood with Hitler or what the führer's intentions were. Although he honored Henlein in Berlin with an Olympic medal, Hitler had not engaged in any political discussions with him. On the other hand, the führer had nominated three leading radical Sudeten emigrés, Hans Krebs, Rudolf Jung, and Leo Schubert, to the German *Reichstag*, sticking by the decision in the face of Czech protests.[71] It was no surprise, then, that on August 20, just after his return from Berlin, Henlein made another speech in which he proclaimed: "The Sudeten problem will be solved in its whole depth and breadth with us [meaning his party] or it will not be solved." [72] These words were meant not so much as a warning to the Czechs, but as a reminder to Berlin, and perhaps to himself, that he and his party counted for something. Although Henlein had a number of contacts in high places in Germany, the high attrition rate of political competition in the Third Reich would also not have escaped him. Unless he proved himself capable of gaining new ground for his Sudeten unity movement, he might well lose what backing he had. Yet, increasingly, he needed all the support he could get in order to hold his movement together at all. As 1937 approached, then, Henlein and his colleagues found themselves caught up in a vicious circle of ideological, bureaucratic, financial, and personal involvement with Reich agencies, from which they could scarcely extricate themselves without giving up their hard won positions in the Sudeten political arena entirely. Through it all, an even greater threat—one partly of the traditionalists' own making—loomed in the background: the internationalization of the whole Sudeten German issue, which tended to take events even more out of Henlein's control.

In the final analysis, the internationalization of the Sudeten question which Henlein and his colleagues had fostered—directly and indirectly—during this period was to have important implications for the Germandom struggle as well as for German foreign policy. In terms of *Volkstumspolitik,* internationalization ultimately played into the hands of the radicals in several different ways. By bringing outside forces, particularly the British, into the Sudeten question, the traditionalists were abetting and encouraging, albeit unwittingly, further radical interference. After all, if Great Britain, a foreign power, could become involved in problems on Germany's borders, then surely there was no further reason for the radicals to limit their own activities. Thus while trying to strengthen their own position, the traditionalists ironically undermined and watered down the very exclusive competency, once officially bestowed, which had been one of their chief arguments against radical encroachment. More subtle, yet just as deadly, was the implicit abandonment on the part of the traditionalists of yet another weapon against radical activity: the ideological issue involved. The *volklich* approach to ethnic German politics, in theory at least, had set up a barrier, however flimsy, between Reich German interests and those of ethnic Germans. It had been a line that was drawn from time to time as a rationale to curb radicals who were pushing for militant Reich intervention in ethnic German affairs. To be ethnic Germans, the traditionalists would maintain, meant preserving integrity and independence against all outside encroachment. Now however, the traditionalists themselves were violating this principle: Steinacher did so by using his quasi-official status as a spearhead for massive aid to Henlein and his party; Henlein, in turn, did so by accepting this aid, then going on to solicit more. But Henlein did more than just violate the *volklich* principle: he betrayed the whole concept of ethnicity itself. For what the two men were doing in their mutual cooperation, in their melting of each of their separate problems into one larger one, was removing the Sudeten German issue out of the sphere of a strictly Czechoslovak domestic question and opening it up to outside interference. This indeed was the essence of internationalization: a betrayal which would open the way almost certainly to massive Reich intervention and which, in turn, would bring the Sudeten Germans into the Reich and end their status as "ethnic" Germans. In breaking down this last, ideological barrier, the traditionalists were unwittingly opening the door to men whose drive for unlimited power left no room for the interests of the Sudeten Germans.

VIII

The SS and SD Enter Volkstumspolitik

THE traditionalists had initiated internationalization of the Sudeten problem, partly out of genuine concern for the welfare of the Sudeten Germans, partly in order to shore up their own positions. Although they did not realize it initially, this action—like so many others they had taken—would redound to the benefit of their enemies, the radicals. But ironically, the enemies in question would not be Bohle's *Auslandsorganisation*, Rosenberg's *Aussenpolitisches Amt*, the circle of former Sudeten NS members around Krebs, or any of the other factions against which the traditionalists had so long been struggling. Late in 1936, yet another radical organization—one which the traditionalists had only recently come to suspect and fear—suddenly broke openly and triumphantly into the field of ethnic German politics: the SS and SD, under Heinrich Himmler and Reinhard Heydrich. It is not surprising that it took the traditionalists so long to recognize their most dangerous rival. Like the slow evolution of the Germandom struggle itself, SS participation in that struggle proceeded by gradual, often clandestine steps. Moreover, the mechanics of SS involvement were such that it was most difficult at that time, and even now, to assess just how deeply embroiled in the struggle the organization really was at any given point.

SS involvement in the Germandom struggle had diverse roots. One was the tendency on the part of Hitler's paladins to construct bureaucratic empires as tools in the vicious rivalries of the Nazi "war games." The more bureaucratic machinery one controlled, the less likely it became that an enemy could undermine one's position and cut one off from the center of power. Himmler, who understood the workings of the National Socialist state as perhaps no other politician of the day (witness the singular efficiency with which he built his police network from 1933 to 1936), must certainly have seen in Germandom politics an opportunity to "capture" yet another valuable complex, the *Volksdeutsche Mittelstelle,* to be used in the internal NS power struggle. But political exigencies alone do not explain why the Germandom field was singled out as a target for SS expansion: involvement in this area was also an ideological matter.[1] To collect organizations in the Third Reich meant to collect "competencies" as well, and to Himmler, competency in Germandom politics gave him an outlet for achieving his long term racial and cultural goals. His personal fascination for the *völkisch* ideology and ethos was to become one of the main motivating forces behind the entire SS organization. He—and a great many of his subordinates—dreamed of resettlement in the East, of a new peasant aristocracy of race tilling the soil in a restoration of the golden days of the *Altgermanen.* The harsh political reality of trying to achieve such a myth involved, of necessity, a reshuffling of Germans all over Eastern Europe at the expense of "inferior" peoples already living there. Such an endeavor brought Himmler and the SS directly to the problem of ethnic Germans living side by side with other peoples—a problem which men like Steinacher had been confronting for decades from an altogether different standpoint. In short, it brought the SS into *Volkstumsarbeit.*

The SS racial ideology not only helped lead Himmler's elite into Germandom politics, it also predetermined that that involvement would be of a radical nature. Relocating Germans all over Europe was hardly conducive to tranquility in international politics. It was no accident that Himmler and Heydrich found themselves among the territorial imperialists in 1938 to 1939, advocating a violent solution to Germany's foreign policy problems. As curious as it may seem, the traditionalists apparently seriously underestimated, until it was too late, the threat posed by this, the most lethal of all their rivals.[2] In part, they seem to have misjudged the nature and motives of men like Himmler (recall that Haushofer did not hesitate to pass on information about his mission to Prague through Himmler). In part, too, it may simply have been the inability of the traditionalists to recognize the danger to themselves that lay behind the tendency in Nazi politics to collect unrelated competencies. After all, the traditionalists were completely involved in Germandom work, and only in Germandom work, as were most of their early enemies like Bohle. Thus they felt comfortable in choosing as allies men—like Ribbentrop, for example —who seemed to have no aspirations in that area. The SS, as primarily a domestic police power, might also have seemed to be innocuous in ethnic German politics. The gradualness with which the SS did penetrate *Volkstumspolitik* must only have strengthened this misapprehension—until it was too late.

Initially, the main vehicle for SS involvement in the Sudeten German problem was the *Sicherheitsdienst* (SD)-Gestapo complex.[3] The *Sicherheitsdienst* had started out as one of several party intelligence agencies. However, using his unique administrative talents and Himmler's support, Reinhard Heydrich managed quickly to enlarge the SD out of all proportion to the size of its rivals, including the "Schumann office" in the *Aussenpolitisches Amt der NSDAP* or Robert Ley's intelligence office in the Labor Service.[4] By the fall of 1933, at about the same time the *Volksdeutscher Rat* was organized, the SD had achieved sufficient importance that Himmler raised it to the status of a *Hauptamt* in his growing empire; Heydrich was rewarded with a promotion to SS-*Brigadeführer* and was given the title *Chef des Sicherheitsamtes des Reichsführers*-SS.[5] The Third Reich was full of men with such titles, most of which no one took very seriously (Göring, for example, liked to refer to Himmler himself as "Reichsheini"), but Heydrich would soon earn a reputation which made his title feared and respected. By 1934 the SD had so completely outdistanced its rivals that on June 9, by order of the führer's Deputy Rudolf Hess, the SD was proclaimed the sole intelligence agency of the Nazi party.[6] In the meantime Himmler was building up the other side of his dual empire—the police. Again starting from small beginnings, the Bavarian Political Police, Himmler moved on to larger stakes. Here he confronted Interior Minister Wilhelm Frick, who aspired to unite the German police, and Hermann Göring, who ran the powerful Prussian Secret State Police. In both cases, Himmler avoided a direct challenge.[7] He gradually outmaneuvered Frick in Berlin by going out into the *Länder* and capturing control of the state police one by one. With Göring he used another tack. In April of 1934, a deal was arranged that made Himmler Göring's "deputy" in charge of the Prussian Gestapo, at the same time that Heydrich was infiltrating the organization with his SD men. It was a technique that would be used again and again with increasing effectiveness. The result was, that although nominally Göring's deputy, Himmler was soon actual head of the Gestapo: an organization which he then ran through Heydrich. These developments meant that by late 1934 or early 1935, Himmler's _Schutzstaffel_ controlled a powerful police network, as well as the Nazi party's only official intelligence agency.

Even prior to 1934, at a time when Himmler and Heydrich were still consolidating their empires, both the Gestapo and SD—sometimes working together, sometimes independently—became involved in activities affecting Germany's relations with other countries, especially with Czechoslovakia.[8] With the Czech ban on the Sudeten Nazi party in 1933, Sudeten Germans began fleeing across the border to Germany. This influx of refugees brought with it the danger of infiltration by spies working for the Czechoslovak government, as well as the problem of coping with the embarrassing influx of politically ambitious former Sudeten Nazis. At this point both the SD and the Gestapo became involved. On December 7, 1933, to counter the dangers arising from an uncontrolled flow of Sudeten refugees into the Reich, Hess ordered the creation of a so-called _Sudetendeutsche Kontrollstelle_ in Dresden.[9] Director of the agency would be Major Wilhelm Krichbaum, director of the _Hauptabteilung III_ of the Gestapo in Dresden and, since October 7, 1933, assigned to the SD _Hauptamt_.[10] Thus, the _Kontrollstelle_—probably without Hess's knowledge—became an information gatherer for the SD. All Sudeten German refugees had to undergo the scrutiny of the _Kontrollstelle_ and receive a pass from it before they could settle down anywhere in the Reich. At the same time the _Kontrollstelle_ would glean as much information from these refugees as possible. That Krichbaum's activities would be invaluable to the SD with regard to Sudeten German affairs is clear from his Gestapo questionnaire dated four years later. In it he requests an assignment on the Czech-German border and remarks about himself: "Very knowledgeable on conditions in Czechoslovakia—politically, militarily, and with regard to intelligence." [11]

Krichbaum's activities with the Control Center illustrate not only the growing SS-SD involvement in the Sudeten question _per se_, but also indicate the direction that this involvement would take—for Krichbaum was deeply committed to the side of the radicals in the Germandom rivalries. Whether this commitment to the radical side was the direct result of orders from Berlin or whether Krichbaum was acting independently is difficult to determine. Himmler seemed to encourage the same kind of competition and independent action within the SS as Hitler did between the SS and other rivals in the

Third Reich.[12] This meant that men like Krichbaum, SD and Gestapo people on all levels, imitating the behavior of their superiors, would show political initiative, interpret obscure orders or contradictory ones as they wished, and actually attempt to affect the outcome of the situation about which they were supposedly merely reporting. Thus, Himmler and Heydrich were not only guided by the kind of information that they received from below, but often by the independent actions of their subordinates as well.

In any case, it is clear that Krichbaum *was* actively aiding and abetting the Sudeten Nazis, though Hess's instructions in creating the Control Center contain no directives to this effect and though there is no evidence that Himmler specified that Krichbaum was to engage in such activities. Krichbaum's closest collaborator was none other than the most aggressive of the DNSAP emigrés—Hans Krebs.[13] Krebs used the information that Krichbaum accumulated from refugees for his own purposes. Krichbaum also cooperated by writing intelligence reports for his superiors that were highly critical of the traditionalists and their colleagues in the Sudeten unity movement.[14] Moreover, the two also worked together within the framework of Krebs's puppet organization—the *Sudetendeutscher Heimatbund*—which was notorious for its rallies urging irredentism. Hanns Beer, the short-lived director of the SHB under Krebs's tutelage, had even planned to commission Krichbaum with organizing the SHB in Germany.[15] Hans Neuwirth, a favorite target of both Krebs and Krichbaum, claimed that Krebs had actually gained Himmler's support after 1934.[16] Conceivably, Krichbaum could have introduced Krebs to Himmler; but whether or not Neuwirth's assertion is correct, the fact that Krichbaum did strike alliances outside the framework of his own organization and did serve his superiors with such biased reports would seem to indicate that he did show some degree of political initiative in his Control Center activities. One should add that what cooperation existed between Krebs and the SS was not always smooth. In 1935 the Gestapo complained about SHB excesses on the border; three years later Heydrich warned about Krebs's attempts to infiltrate the SD with his own people.[17]

There is further evidence from 1934 that SS interest in Germandom politics and in the Sudeten question was not limited to Krichbaum's activities. During the summer of 1934, SD information gathering, independent of the *Kontrollstelle*, was going on along the

German-Czech border. A letter from a minor former DNSAP functionary, written to Hitler in the summer of 1934, cites Himmler and his intelligence organization by name, indicating that the SD had already gained notoriety of sorts in Czechoslovakia, at least among the old guard Nazis.[18] By 1935 reports from Czechoslovakia were coming in regularly to both SD and Gestapo headquarters on such diverse subjects as SdP emigrés, border crossings, arrests by Czech border police, and similar problems.[19] The top SD leadership also seemed by now to be taking quite an interest in the Czech situation: at a meeting between Steinacher and Kursell in September of 1935, during which the whole Sudeten problem was reviewed and the role of the Sudeten German party discussed, Dr. Werner Best, Heydrich's assistant and second in command of the Gestapo, was present.[20] Such gathering of information, as well as the contacts made in doing so, laid a kind of groundwork for more aggressive involvement in the realm of Germandom work and in questions of foreign policy regarding Czechoslovakia.

SS-SD activity in Czechoslovakia was not only limited to information gathering; often somewhat more lurid preoccupations took Himmler's men across the border. Frequently one of the SS agencies, the SD or Gestapo, would receive a *Sonderauftrag* or "special assignment" from Himmler: assignments which eventually became linked with preparations for SS involvement in the occupation of Austria and Czechoslovakia.[21] In the early stages, however, these "special assignments" were affairs like the murder of the engineer Rudolf Formis near Prague in 1935.[22] Formis, an expert on radio transmission, had fled to Czechoslovakia after the Nazi takeover of Germany and had become involved with Gregor Strasser and his clandestine underground radio broadcasts. Since these transmissions were an embarrassment to the Nazi regime, it was decided to eliminate Formis. The man chosen for the job was Alfred Naujocks, SD hatchet man and a companion of Heydrich. In an episode reminiscent of Hollywood gangster films, Naujocks and several companions, including Werner Göttsch, another SD man, crossed into Czechoslovakia; then, on the night of January 23, 1935, they murdered Formis in his room at the Hotel Zahoři, a short distance from Prague. Aside from the human tragedy, the incident was a minor one, but it did set a pattern for a certain kind of involvement in relations with other countries, in this case with the German emigrés in

Czechoslovakia. It was no doubt because of the expertise which the SD gained in incidents like this that it was picked to engineer the Gleiwitz affair in 1939 as a pretext for the war with Poland.[23]

But there were deeper, institutional and ideological reasons for direct SS-SD involvement in ethnic German affairs and the Sudeten problem: reasons which can best be characterized as a "search for a mission" on the part of the SD. Originally, Heydrich had ambitions for his SD to play the role of state security police; in fact, he had competed furiously for that position after the *Machtergreifung* of 1933. It gradually became apparent, however, that the SD personnel was not large enough, nor did it have the training to accomplish this goal. When Himmler succeeded in capturing control of the political police in the various German *Länder*, the SD was actually in danger of becoming superfluous. Heydrich did not have far to look, however, for new outlets for SD activity.[24] During the *Kampfzeit*, the SD had begun to keep a watchful eye on various rightist and leftist groups within the Reich; now, it could concentrate on this kind of intelligence work, styling itself as a kind of ideological watchdog for the party. When the party's ideological enemies disappeared into concentration camps, emigrated, or let themselves be coopted—threatening to leave the SD once again without targets—Heydrich could simply encourage his organization to extend its surveillance activities beyond Germany's borders, especially to Czechoslovakia where so many German political refugees had chosen to settle. At first this intelligence gathering was limited mainly to the political Left, to the Communists and Social Democrats, but gradually the SD broadened its investigations to observe the antagonisms within the Sudeten nationalist camp as well.[25] After all, reaction was also a threat to the National Socialist revolution, whether at home or abroad.

If any conservative group provided an ideal target for SD investigation and attack it was the *Kameradschaftsbund* so close to Henlein. Spann's clerical fascist model advocated by the KB conflicted on almost every point with the racial, revolutionary elitism of Himmler and the SS. Like many Nazis of their generation, both Himmler and Heydrich were extremely anti-Catholic. Heydrich's newspaper, the *Schwarze Korps*, which he founded in 1935 and himself edited for the next three or four years, exhibited in its articles a vehement anti-Catholicism which put even its anti-Semitism in the shade.[26] To men of this persuasion, the Austrian orientation of Spann and his circle was equally repugnant.

This ideological antagonism toward Spann and the KB led the SS-SD into an early alliance with both radical Sudeten emigrés and the *Aufbruch* circle within the Sudetenland. The *Aufbruch* faction, many of whom had been members of the Sudeten National Socialist party, had long resented and fought the "academic snobs" in the *Kameradschaftsbund*, who, for their part, had tended to look down on the Nazis as "plebeian." [27] The *Aufbruch* circle also emphasized the KB's Catholic orientation in many of its attacks. Phrases like "actio catholica," "connections with Rome," and "the "Habsburgs" stood out in the radical propaganda—including that coming from emigré circles in the Reich.[28] Karl Viererbl, former DNSAP leader who insinuated himself onto the editorial staff of the *Völkischer Beobachter*, frequently took this tack in his articles in the NS-*Monatshefte*.[29] A similar tone pervaded the long document *Der Spannkreis, Gefahren und Auswirkungen* ("The Spann Circle. Dangers and Implications"), prepared by the *Sicherheitshauptamt* in May of 1936.[30] This paper levelled a vehement blast against Spann's teachings and against the KB for trying to put these ideas into practice. Criticism was particularly sharp against Walter Heinrich and Walter Brand, the KB representatives in the SdP. Brand was singled out as the leading force in the Sudeten German party working against the radicals. The article summarized:

> Sudeten Germandom has been from time immemorial an intellectual battlefield between German and Roman thought. Until the World War it was completely under the influence of the Roman Catholic tendencies coming from Vienna. After the war, the Sudeten Germans increasingly got away from this on the basis of DNSAP influence and found connections to the intellectual tendencies in Germany. This happy development, which was in the interest of all Germans, was interrupted by the successful activities of the Spann circle, which influenced Sudeten Germandom in the direction of Roman universalism and alienated it from National Socialist Germany.[31]

This document was labelled top secret (*Geheim-Kommandosache*) and thus cannot have reached a very large circle of readers.[32] But it was very important in two respects. It reflected the temper and orientation in top SD circles toward the KB-*Aufbruch* conflict in Czechoslovakia;

it also explained the ideological background of the SS-SD support for the radicals in the Sudetenland. The timing of the article is significant, for it appeared in May of 1936, precisely when the crisis very nearly tore the Sudeten German party apart. This would seem to indicate that the SD certainly supported the radicals in the quarrels which beset the SdP, if indeed it did not foment the crisis itself.

There is explicit evidence that Heydrich himself took an active part in the Germandom struggles. Walter Schellenberg, who as second in command of the SD was close enough to Heydrich to know, remarked:

> Heydrich was kept informed by a special department on the position both of the Sudeten German party and of Konrad Henlein. The National Socialist wing of this party, the so-called *Aufbruch* circle pursued, under Karl Hermann Frank, . . . [a policy of] the quickest possible destruction of all Czechoslovakia. Henlein meanwhile was only interested in the accomplishment of the autonomy of the 3,500,000 Sudeten Germans. Heydrich then tried all means possible to discredit the less radical Henlein in Hitler's eyes—among other things by charging duplicitously that Henlein had connections with the English Secret Service.[33]

Further confirmation of the fact that Heydrich actively assisted the radicals in their dispute with the moderates in the Sudeten German party comes from Heydrich himself. In a note rejecting Karl Viererbl's request to join the SD—and Viererbl was by no means the least radical of the Sudeten emigrés—Heydrich wrote:

> In the ideological altercation in Sudeten Germany between the National Socialists and the KB clique, Viererbl has not always taken a clear position. At first he stood clearly on the side of the National Socialists, and then, apparently at the moment when he believed the Reich was going to decide in favor of the opposing side, he swung conspicuously over to it.[34]

It is clear that not only Heydrich, but Himmler, too, actively supported the radicals in *Volkstumspolitik* and that both men reckoned with the violent expansion of German power. As early as 1936, Walter von Lierau, Himmler's man (and Bohle's) at the consulate in Reichenberg, betrayed the lines along which his bosses in the SS were thinking: "We need the Germans in Czechoslovakia. They have to hold the area in occupation! You know of course . . . that a lot of things are going to change here in not too long a time. Then it would be totally wrong to want to aid in this flight [of Germans out of Czechoslovakia]."[35] The changes to which he referred were to be in conformity with the grandiose plans of *völkische Schicksalsgemein-schaft* and resettlement which Himmler was concocting. In the long run Himmler was prepared to shrink from nothing, including war, to bring his vision to reality. As one future resistance leader noted at the time of the Munich crisis in 1938: ". . . an excellent chance has been missed [to overthrow Hitler]. The German people did not want war; the army would have done everything to avoid it. Only Hitler, Himmler, and Ribbentrop were for war."[36]

Heydrich and the SD did not only intend to support the radicals in the Sudetenland, they also had the organizational capability to do so. By 1936 the SD connections with the *Aufbruch* opposition were so solid and extensive that it seems in retrospect that the *Aufbruch* circle was little more than an extension of Heydrich's long arm. Any number of old DNSAP stalwarts in or close to the SdP, some of them in high positions, were agents in the service of the SD. Perhaps the most important of Heydrich's agents in the Sudetenland was Friedrich Brehm. An *Egerländer,* Brehm had been active for years in the National Socialist movement on both sides of the border. He had been in the DNSAP in Czechoslovakia since 1923, and by the time of its dissolution in 1933, he had advanced to the position of *Kreisleiter.* During this period he had from time to time rendered valuable service to the Nazi party in the Reich. As early as 1923 he had collected money for the NSDAP and the SA. In the elections of 1924 and 1930 he had served as a campaign speaker, first for the former wartime commander, Erich Ludendorff, later for Hitler. In the general political crackdown following the dissolution of the right-wing German parties in Czechoslovakia during 1933, Brehm served a seven month jail term for his complicity in contacts with Reich organizations. After Henlein formed the Sudeten German Home Front in October of 1933, Brehm—like so many of the second echelon Sudeten Nazis—found a new political home in the movement. He managed to serve the Henlein organization in a fairly important capacity (*hauptamtlich*) without actually becoming an official member of the Front: a display of political gymnastics which might have reflected his desire to let his DNSAP background compromise the Henlein movement as little as possible. By the summer of 1936, however, Brehm had become involved in the KB-*Aufbruch* struggle and, in an acrimonious exchange with Henlein, had resigned his SHF position entirely. By 1937 he had gathered a number of disenchanted comrades around him and had become a principal figure in the publication of the anti-Henlein publication, the *Aufbruch.*[37]

It was probably his identification with the radical wing of Henlein's movement which initially brought Brehm to Heydrich's attention. It is not known whether the SD director first approached Brehm or if the initiative came from the Sudeten Nazi; at any rate, by late 1935 or early 1936, Brehm was actively working in the service of the *Sicherheitsdienst.* He seems to have played a quite important organizational role in the Sudetenland, claiming to have "laid the basis for the future organization of the SD in the Sudetenland."[38] At one point he wrote to Hess:

> I had created a net of agents which spread out over the whole Sudeten German language area, one which was composed exclusively of old National Socialists. . . . Nearly all the members of my circle stood either in the service of the *Sicherheitsdienst* of the *Reichsführer*-SS or in the *Wehrmacht* Intelligence Service.[39]

Brehm may have exaggerated his role somewhat in the formation of a net of SD agents in Czechoslovakia, but Heydrich at least considered the man's work important enough to receive him personally for a report on the Sudeten situation on December 3, 1936.[40]

One of Brehm's closest collaborators was Otto Liebl. A party member since 1922 and a DNSAP *Kreisleiter,* Liebl's career followed the familiar pattern of so many other radicals. He first joined the Henlein movement, advanced to a fairly important position (in this case to party representative in the Prague parliament), and then became embroiled in the *Aufbruch*-KB rivalry. As a result, he was expelled from the SdP in July of 1936. Brehm later praised him as "one of my best colleagues in organizing the very difficult northern Bohemian coal area." Like Brehm, Liebl was taken into the SD *Hauptamt* after the Sudeten *Anschluss* in October of 1938.[41]

One of the most prominent *Aufbruch* radicals and opponents of Henlein to have contacts with the SS was Rudolf Kasper. Kasper's connections with the SS were somewhat indirect, but in many ways just as important as Brehm's. Kasper was a long time activist in the Sudeten Nazi movement. As early as 1922 he had played a major role in building up the DNSAP in eastern Bohemia. Even more significantly, Kasper was one of the top leaders in the National Socialist labor union association in Czechoslovakia, the *Gewerkschaftsverband deutscher Arbeiter* and exerted strong influence among the unions comprising the association. Especially after the dissolution of the DNSAP in 1933, these unions were an important power base for the radical National Socialists in the Sudetenland in their partisan struggle against the overwhelmingly middle class leadership of the *Kameradschaftsbund*. Again, as in the case of Brehm, Kasper gravitated toward the Henlein movement after 1933, and by 1936, he had insinuated himself into a leadership position as the party's plenipotentiary for labor and white collar affairs. It was not long, however, until he also became embroiled in the factional warring within the Henlein party. After a long series of altercations with Henlein, Kasper was expelled from the movement in 1936. He promptly returned to his leadership position in the union association, where he continued the battle against what he regarded as the reactionary, non-NS leadership of the SdP.[42] It soon became apparent that the union movement was not the only political backstop which Kasper had. Sometime before the annexation of the Sudetenland, Kasper had made contact with the Reich labor plenipotentiary, Robert Ley, with whom he concluded a written pact, the nature of which remains unknown, but which quite probably involved financial assistance.[43] Even more important were Kasper's ties with the SS—so important in fact that his activities as labor leader seemed to be overshadowed by his work for Himmler: "I was [the German labor unions'] real representative and leader, but above all I was its liaison man to the Reich." [44] The man to whom Kasper was responsible in the Reich was SS-*Obergruppenführer* Fritz Tittmann, Himmler's representative in the *Reichsorganisationsleitung* and the ethnic German plenipotentiary for that office. Tittmann himself revealed the extent of Kasper's activities: "After the seizure of power—in particular, however, since the year 1934—*Parteigenosse* Rudolf Kasper has been active as a confidant for the SS, above all in connection with the forwarding of intelligence and SS preparatory work in the National Socialist Sudeten German union." [45] In August of 1938, on the personal invitation of SS-*Obergruppenführer* Werner Lorenz, Himmler's chief of ethnic German affairs, Kasper crossed the border into the Reich to continue his activities there.

In addition to these more or less prominent members of the

radical camp of the Sudeten German party who were actively in the service of the SD, there was a host of other figures, including several *Bürgermeister,* who were part of the SD intelligence net in the Sudetenland. Even Rudolf Meckel, the dissident who refused to infiltrate the Prague German students for the SdP, choosing instead to organize them himself, was an SD informant.[46] It is no longer possible to reconstruct the exact number of SD agents in Sudeten German politics, but at least sixty-five persons were officially taken into the *Sicherheitsdienst* after the annexation of the Sudetenland, ostensibly for important services rendered.[47] This number, presumably, was merely the tip of the iceberg.

Indirectly, of course, SS-SD involvement in the *Volkstum* question and support for the radical opposition in the Sudetenland had grave foreign policy implications. The SS also became directly embroiled in the realm of foreign policy formation, largely through the alliance Himmler formed with Ribbentrop after 1933. This association began merely as a function of the internal power rivalries in the NS regime; however, it was eventually to give the *Reichsführer* entree into further Germandom activities and foreign policy influence in general. Ribbentrop, whose field of activity had been foreign policy from the outset, found himself in tight competition with both Ernst Bohle and Alfred Rosenberg, and later with Hermann Göring as well. To counter these adversaries, he tried to make common cause with Himmler at a time when Himmler himself was working his way out from under Göring's mastery of the police in Prussia. The relationship between the two paladins was one which was to typify those between the SS and any organization that chose to work with it: what started out as a collaboration between roughly equal allies gradually turned into domination by the SS. The technique that Himmler used to accost a rival organization was a subtle one. He would seldom confront an organization head-on and destroy it; rather he would infiltrate it, either by insinuating SS (including SD) men into it or by spreading SS honors and titles among the people already there. In this fashion he would hollow out an organization until only its form remained the same. In this case, Himmler began by bringing Ribbentrop—who was only too eager at this point to win Himmler's backing—into the SS in May of 1933, with the rank of *Standartenführer.*[48] Himmler also liberally distributed SS ranks among Ribbentrop's colleagues or sent his own men into Ribbentrop's office as "liaisons." By 1936, eighteen of the forty-nine top people in Ribbentrop's *Dienststelle* were in the SS. At least three of them (Rudolf Likus, Lothar Kühne, and Rolf von Humann-Hainhofer) were SD men! As for Ribbentrop himself, Himmler used the occasion of the Party Day in Nuremburg in September of 1936 to promote him to *Gruppenführer.*[49]

Ribbentrop's *Dienststelle* was not among the organizations Himmler destroyed from within: he did not have to, for Ribbentrop himself practically abandoned the office after being appointed foreign minister in 1938. Nevertheless the somewhat shadowy collaboration between the *Dienststelle* and the SS-SD did indicate what success infiltration and conspiracy could engender.[50] One confidential memorandum, prepared in December of 1936 by Rudolf Likus, exemplifies the subtle but insistent way in which the SD, searching for a mission, was insinuating its way into foreign policy matters:

> In a conversation with SS-*Standartenführer* Albert from the *Sicherheitshauptampt,* I was informed in my capacity as an SD man [SD-*dienstlich*] that the work of the SD of the *Reichsführung* SS was leading it of necessity into the realm of foreign policy; that, however, at the point where the interest of the SD itself stopped, certain possibilities for the continuation of work along foreign policy lines were going unexploited. The *Sicherheitsdienst* as such did not concern itself with foreign policy. Still, in practice there often appeared opportunities that could be useful to those agencies that were entrusted with the conduct of foreign policy. As far as the *Sicherheitsdienst der RFSS* was concerned, the only possibility which came into question here, for ideological reasons, was the *Dienststelle Ribbentrop,* especially since the SD did not have any trust in the foreign policy machinations of the *Auswärtiges Amt.*[51]

Here utmost care is taken to keep Ribbentrop from suspecting any overly ambitious designs on his personal bailiwick. Although the report admits Heydrich's interest in working with Ribbentrop (Likus was commissioned with arranging a meeting between the two men), it strongly asserts that the SD has no interest in making foreign policy as such: that is the business of the Ribbentrop office. Moreover, by rejecting the *Auswärtiges Amt*—which, after all, was still the agency that officially handled Reich foreign policy—the note both flatters Ribbentrop's *Dienststelle* and suggests that the realm of foreign policy formulation is open to the same kind of competition which characterized every other political endeavor in the Third Reich.

Despite SS caution, Ribbentrop was not totally oblivious to what was happening within his organization. One report on *Dienststelle* personnel written by Lothar Kühne to the SD in September of 1937, linked many of Ribbentrop's colleagues with a number of agencies and people, including Othmar Spann, out of favor in SS circles at this point. The report leaked back to Ribbentrop, who was furious about such spying in his own organization.[52] Yet, cooperation between the *Dienststelle* and the SS continued, serving as a bridge to foreign policy matters for the SS-SD. Four years later, Likus sketched out what had become of SD interest in foreign policy in a report which was a veritable catalogue of the techniques and operations of the SD abroad:

> The operations of the SD abroad have the exclusive purposes of serving the foreign policy of the Greater German Reich. This happens:
>
> 1. through a technically perfect intelligence service;
> 2. through the preparation and execution of operations which the diplomatic representatives of the Reich abroad can neither arrange nor bear the responsibility for.
>
> There are unofficial agents active in most European countries as well as in North and South America whose job is to compile, to observe, and to report everything that is of interest and importance to the Reich. This task encompasses all areas of public life with the exception of military affairs as well as the diplomatic representation of the Reich. . . . The communication of intelligence ensues via the quickest means to the *Reichssicherheitshauptamt.* . . .
>
> a. through our own wireless transmission;
> b. through the courier service of the *Auswärtiges Amt,* according to the regulations in force;
> c. through our own courier;
> d. through customs and police officials or other suitable border crossers;
> e. via telegraph. . . .
>
> In addition to the SD agents constantly active abroad, through whose observing and reporting all the political events of recent years were prepared in the form stipulated by the foreign minister, the SD also has special operations forces [*Einsatzkräfte*] at its disposal for the execution of illegal operations. For example, SD agents were commissioned to take part in the following political measures, partly in preparation, partly in execution:

Preparation of the Austrian *Anschluss.*
Dissolution of Czechoslovakia.
Preparation of the war against Poland.[53]

As Likus's notes show, the SD was in a position not only to serve the needs of foreign policy, but was able to exert no small degree of influence on foreign policy formation itself. As an agency which provided critical intelligence information, it could actually shape the decision-making process in foreign affairs, regulating the kind and degree of information which Ribbentrop, Hitler, and even the SD's own chief, Heydrich, received on any given problem. At the same time, the way in which the SD as an executive tool performed its tasks—the degree of openness or discretion it used, whether it interpreted orders strictly or loosely, and the degree of initiative it showed—could have an impact on the way delicate situations related to foreign policy developed.

Himmler and Heydrich did not only have an "in" to foreign policy through contact with the Ribbentrop agency, they also had their people infiltrate the regular diplomatic service itself, the *Auswärtiges Amt.* Despite the SS's assurances to Ribbentrop that it rejected the AA, it did not hesitate to use the official foreign policy agency when convenient. Walter von Lierau, for example, the consul in Reichenberg was one of Himmler's men. A veteran party member, he could claim to have been active for the NS cause since 1921. He had been an SS member since July of 1932, and during his diplomatic activities in Czechoslovakia, he was assigned to Himmler for "special duty" (*zur besonderen Verwendung*).[54] Lierau made no secret of his sympathy with the radicals in the Sudeten movement, nor of his contempt for Henlein as a "weakling." His reports frequently contained pessimistic assessments of the SdP and pointed to the activities of the KB clique as the cause of the troubles. In the course of the traditionalist-radical struggle, Lierau also worked closely with Bohle and the AO in its attacks on Steinacher. In mid-1935, in fact, he actually asked for a transfer as an SS man to the AO, noting that he had worked for over a year and a half with Bohle anyway.[55] Himmler evidently decided that Lierau was more valuable in Reichenberg, for the transfer never came through. The fact that Lierau himself asked for the transfer and appeared to be working rather independently in Reichenberg illustrates once again that at least to some degree the impetus for SS-SD Germandom activity came from below as well as from above. There is still further indication of Lierau's independent activities, none of which were attendent upon his activity as a German diplomat. In 1936 he was discharged from the SS, a casualty of the power struggle between the SD and the military *Abwehr.* Apparently, he had been working for both organizations and could not decide where his loyalty lay.[56]

The SD apparently also had its men at the mission in Prague. Fritz von Chamier, *Pressebeirat,* and Sigismund von Bibra, *Gesandschaftsrat* and protégé of Bohle, were allegedly working in league with Heydrich, if indeed they were not officially SD members.[57] Bibra, whose reports on the unity of the Sudeten German party were every bit as pessimistic as were Lierau's, worked hand-in-hand with Bohle and Krebs. In 1936, he was finally transferred to Berne, Switzerland, where as AO *Landesgruppenleiter,* he played the dual role of diplomat and Nazi official, much to Foreign Minister von Neurath's chagrin. In Prague, Chamier corresponded so blatantly with the radicals that Henlein was finally forced to ask that the man be removed from his post.[58]

As the activity and orientation of men like Chamier, Bibra, and Lierau indicate, by 1936 the SS-SD was already deep into foreign policy matters relating to the Sudeten question. There are signs that during that year this involvement was getting both deeper and broader in scope. For example, when Albrecht Haushofer reported the progress of negotiations with Beneš in November of 1936, he contacted neither his nominal chief, Ribbentrop; nor the foreign minister, Neurath; nor, until his return to Germany, the führer himself; but rather Himmler, through the *Reichsführer*'s personal adjutant, Karl Wolff! [59] Haushofer may have been compelled, against his better judgment, to report to Himmler. If this was not the case, then Haushofer—who, as a *volklich* moderate stood at opposite poles from the radical *Volkstumspolitik* of the SS—was apparently unaware of Himmler's real opinions or he was an excessively bad judge of character, an assessment which is borne out by his first impression of Ribbentrop (of whom Haushofer said, "he makes a quiet, collected impression"). The fact that Haushofer was reporting to Himmler at all during this very sensitive diplomatic mission, in any case, indicated that the *Reichsführer* was achieving an increasingly powerful position vis-à-vis his "alliance partner," Ribbentrop.[60]

As the SD grew more deeply committed in the traditionalist-radical struggle on both sides of the border, its activities became more varied and the first massive signs of its participation in the free-for-all of Nazi "war games" in the Germandom question became apparent. A dramatic illustration of this was the bizarre series of incidents involving the *Rumburger Zeitung*. Traditionalists had noted for some time that the newspaper of the northern Bohemian town of Rumburg, once a mouthpiece for the German Nationalist party, had been writing increasingly biting articles against the Sudeten German party, especially against its moderate KB leaders. Quite often the information contained in these attacks could only have been gleaned from very high places in the Reich.[61] At the same time the newspaper was very thorough in its coverage of events in the Reich; frequently it carried the entire text of speeches made by important NS leaders.[62] By the middle of 1936, the attacks against the SdP had grown in intensity and scope. The newspaper's editor, Heinz Pfeiffer, appeared at public meetings to denounce the top leadership of the SdP.[63] Even more ominously, the attacks in the newspaper began to be directed against not only KB people in Czechoslovakia but also traditionalists in the Reich—particularly Steinacher. It became apparent that the SD was not limiting itself to the gathering of information, but had joined the game of disseminating it as propaganda: for there is substantial reason to believe that by this point, the *Rumburger Zeitung* had become a mouthpiece for the *Sicherheitsdienst*.[64] Apparently Heinz Pfeiffer, whom one former SdP leader labelled as an *eitler Querkopf* ("vain crank"), had looked around for aid in his attacks on the SdP and had found it in the SD. Acting as a source of information for the SD, Pfeiffer seemingly also let the SD make use of his newspaper to direct attacks on the traditionalists involved in Reich and Sudeten Germandom work.[65] The newspaper, at any rate, wrote warningly and authoritatively on events which, as it turns out, were to transpire in the not too distant future. Steinacher, for example, read in advance about his dismissal as head of the VDA.[66] Similarly, in November of 1936, the newspaper linked Steinacher and the *Baltische Bruderschaft*, an organization formerly led by Kursell, in a particularly vicious attack. It was an omen which boded nothing but ill for Kursell, who, at this point, as director of the agency which had replaced the VR as *the* mediating organization in ethnic German affairs, was the main ally of the traditionalists in the Germandom struggle. In just a very few weeks, Kursell would be forced out of his post by Himmler and Heydrich, even though he was a high ranking SS officer. The pretext for Kursell's dismissal was his association with the *Bruderschaft!* As the *Rumburger Zeitung* had put it in linking Kursell's activities with those of Steinacher:

> Folkish Sudeten Germandom has not the slightest interest in the preservation of Herr Prof. Steinacher's position. The only ones who are interested in it are the evil political wreckers in the *Kameradschaftsbund* and the intellectually related gentlemen of the "Baltic Brotherhood" in Berlin. One hand washes the other.
>
> Herr Prof. Steinacher's activity in the VDA bears full measure of responsibility for the difficult internal differences in folkish circles of all the German minorities. The folkish ethnic Germans from Bessarabia to North Schleswig and Memel to South Tirol will definitely not shed any tears if they should hear about the hopefully imminent resignation of Herr Steinacher.
>
> We would certainly hope that his further activity does not force us to be yet more explicit.[67]

Such scarcely veiled threats, which soon turned out to be predictive, made the newspaper into somewhat of a sensation; it was read not only in Prague but in Germany as well. Most of its circulation was actually in the Reich itself—a fact which made possible a counterattack on the part of the traditionalists.[68] There was some question, however, as to who would launch the offensive. Steinacher was scarcely in a position by this time to take on the SS; he had already been arrested and detained briefly by the Gestapo in October of 1936.[69] Ribbentrop's *Dienststelle* and the Kursell Office had been too thoroughly infiltrated by the SS to be of any use.[70] The Haushofer-Hess connection would scarcely be of value either: if Hess had only resisted Bohle reluctantly and with some difficulty, then he was hardly up to an encounter with the Himmler and Heydrich team. Henlein's attempts at getting the *Zeitung* attacks stopped while he was visiting Berlin for the Olympic games were also unsuccessful.[71]

Fortunately for the traditionalists at this point they found an ally—the only one really in a position effectively to challenge the growing power of the SD—the military intelligence organization under Admiral Wilhelm Canaris. The military *Abwehr*, in fact, had existed for some time in a tense symbiotic relationship with the expanding SD.[72] On occasion the two intelligence agencies did cooperate to some extent—for example, in the pursuit of Czech spies.

In 1936 the *Abwehr* also concluded a kind of working arrangement with the Gestapo, the so-called Ten Commandments, in which the competencies of the two agencies were roughly spelled out. The agreement represented a kind of tenuous personal rapprochement between the two rivals, Heydrich and Canaris.[73] However, the pact was none too explicit and neither man fully lived up to it. The philosophies of Heydrich and Canaris were so diametrically opposed, that conflict was certain to come to the surface eventually. Heydrich, the ruthless and driven revolutionary, represented—almost embodied —the restless imperialism inherent in the thinking of National Socialism's new elite. Canaris was much more the extremely patriotic, old line nationalist, glad to see Germany extending her sphere of influence, yet opposed to a violent European conflict as a means of achieving this end.[74]

One area of friction between the two organizations, brought about by these differences in philosophy, was the Sudeten problem. For while Heydrich leaned toward the radical NS faction in the Germandom struggle, Canaris—who did not want a war over Czechoslovakia—supported the more moderate faction around Henlein.[75] Heydrich was spinning his web of contacts in the Sudetenland through the SD and police network, but Canaris also had his own connections. For a time at least, Canaris was aided by Consul von Lierau, who—though he was an SS man and supported the radical faction in the SdP—was apparently playing a double game, delivering information to military intelligence as well.[76] Canaris also worked well with Ernst von Weizsäcker, the moderate *Staatssekretär* in the AA.[77] Most important, however, Canaris had connections with the traditionalist in Czechoslovakia, through his assistant in the *Abwehr,* Major Helmut Groscurth, whose office *Untergruppe IS* (later *Abteilung II*), was in charge of minorities as well as war sabotage.[78] In the years after 1935, Groscurth played the role of liaison between Canaris and the Sudeten moderates and helped considerably to strengthen their position.[79] On the side of the traditionalists, two men upheld the contacts with the *Abwehr*. One was Friedrich Bürger, Henlein's man in Berlin, who was apparently commissioned by Steinacher to liaison work with the military; the other was Hans Neuwirth, another intimate colleague of both Steinacher and Henlein, who knew the war minister, Field Marshall Werner von Blomberg, personally and who as early as 1933 had passed on information to the military in connection with the *Volkssport* trials.[80] It was from these connections, then, that initiative finally came to help solve the *Rumburger Zeitung* problem.

As the attacks from Rumburg grew more vehement in the course of 1936, the traditionalists invoked their connections with the War Ministry to have some action taken. The War Ministry, in turn, intervened with the Propaganda Ministry, with the result that Goebbels actually banned the *Rumburger Zeitung* in Germany.[81] The newspaper immediately struck back violently, denying that any ban had been imposed, and threatened to file suit against the SdP newspaper, *Die Zeit*, for saying so—an action which could have been highly embarrassing for the Sudeten German party. The *Zeitung*'s position was strengthened by the fact that the German police were not enforcing the ban on distribution in the Reich: another indication that the SS had a hand in the whole affair.[82] The situation got even hotter as Fritz von Chamier accosted one of the *Zeit* editors on the street in Prague and demanded a retraction of the story on the ban.[83] It was finally saved for the SdP newspaper when Hans Fritzsche in the Reich Propaganda Ministry came up with the idea of broadcasting news of the ban repeatedly on the Leipzig radio station, an action which at least stopped any potential lawsuit. The *Rumburger Zeitung*, however, continued to publish while its editor, Heinz Pfeiffer, sought further aid in the Reich: this time from Alfred Rosenberg, through the mediation of another old Sudeten radical, Karl Viererbl.[84]

The rivalry between the *Abwehr* and the SD was to continue, with Germandom work as the battlefield. At each opportunity, Canaris and Groscurth attempted to strengthen the more moderate faction of the SdP, especially Henlein's position vis-à-vis the radicals. The struggle was to be a losing one, however. Up until late 1936 and early 1937, the SS position in the Germandom struggle had still been sufficiently insecure that its activities on behalf of the radicals were carried out underground. From time to time, as with the *Rumburger Zeitung* incident, signs would point to probable SS involvement to one degree or another. Gradually, as SS men won more and more positions of influence in the various Germandom organizations, such secrecy was no longer necessary. Otto von Kursell, although friendly to the traditionalists, was nonetheless a member of the SS. Many of his colleagues, also SS members, were from the start far less sympathetic than he to the ideas of Steinacher and Henlein. Franz

Wehofsich, an old *Volkstum* fighter and personal friend of both Steinacher and General Haushofer, was also a member of the SS; and as time went by, Steinacher began to express doubts as to whether even this close friend could stay firm and loyal.[85] On a higher level, the Himmler-Ribbentrop alliance was becoming a more and more one-sided affair, as Ribbentrop—isolated in London—tried desperately to keep the führer's ear.[86] Even Hess's immediate environment was moving increasingly from "brown" to "black" as the SS infiltrated Nazi party headquarters. (Most SD party members were assigned to that office, the *Braunes Haus,* as their *Ortsgruppe.*)[87] By late 1936, then, the time was ripe for bringing the SS-SD interest in *Volksgruppenpolitik* out into the open.

Typical of politics in the Third Reich, the open breakthrough of the SS into the Germandom field was not initiated by Himmler or Heydrich, but came as a reaction on Himmler's part to the activities of someone else—in this case a subordinate. Otto von Kursell had accidently found out that Himmler and Heydrich were financing the *Rumburger Zeitung* and on December 17, 1936, he lodged a complaint with the Reich Chancellory that the articles against Henlein were destroying the unity of the ethnic German groups.[88] He also complained to Göring, who issued orders that from that point on all exchange currency related to ethnic German political affairs could only be dispensed under Kursell's countersignature.[89] This was, of course, an intolerable situation for Himmler. So, he made his move before the month was out. Kursell's challenge had apparently convinced him that the time was ripe for open SS involvement in Germandom affairs and that the opportunity was now there to "handle" both Steinacher and Henlein. Using Kursell's connections with the Baltic Brotherhood as a pretext, Himmler accused him of being active in a reactionary antistate organization. By January 7, 1937, Kursell was put on leave and forbidden to indulge in any political activity; he had already been compelled to resign from the SS. Wehofsich was commissioned to run the Kursell Office (VOMI) until Kursell's successor, already picked by Himmler, could take over.[90]

The traditionalists immediately recognized the tragic and far reaching implications of this change in personnel in the main Germandom agency. When General Haushofer found out about the impending change, he immediately wrote to Hess, his former protégé.

Actually, Haushofer wrote ironically, it was tempting to think of putting a high SS officer in charge of Germandom work. Haushofer felt he could then put his whole political responsibility back into Hess's hands, return to his estate, and plant cabbage "in the quiet hope of going to [my] grave before the next European catastrophe." Before he did so, however, it was necessary to point something out:

> The substitution of the previous organization in V.A. [*sic:* he must have meant VR] and V.D.A. work by openly engaging a very high SS officer in Steinacher's place and by giving Kursell's position to a trusted representative of the *Geheime Staatspolizei* means a complete change of system in [our] whole work. This can only be defended if our international political and military situation were so favorable, that the unavoidable and severe political and foreign policy setbacks from such a change could be put aside in favor of the doubtless, domestic political advantages. Above and beyond anything personal, this involves such a great *political* decision, that I ask you, in cooperation with Ribbentrop, . . . to solicit a *basic* decision from the führer.[91]

But once again, as so often before, Hitler was not to be available for any far reaching, definitive decision. The most he would do was to put his imprimatur on a situation that had already been brought about by someone else. In this case, he recognized the powerful position that the SS had carved out for itself and acquiesced in naming Himmler's man to head the *Volksdeutsche Mittelstelle,* which Kursell's Germandom office was not officially to be called. As to the VDA, although it was to be under the competency of VOMI, its leader, Steinacher, was left in his position, despite Haushofer's ominous reference to replacing him with a high ranking SS officer.[92] Thus the Germandom struggle had become more chaotic than ever. Steinacher still hung on as head of the VDA, however now the VDA was responsible to VOMI; VOMI, in turn, was responsible to Hess but through Ribbentrop; meanwhile Himmler prepared to move in and pull the real strings.

As director of VOMI, Himmler chose SS-*Obergruppenführer* Werner Lorenz, a dashing cavalry officer with a great deal of drawing room charm.[93] Lorenz knew very little about the Germandom question at all and he seemed to care even less. Kursell had the impression that he had little enthusiasm for his new task. The SS officer was, however, a splendid front man, whose charm and *bonhommie* disguised the challenge that VOMI really represented under SS control. The real driving force in the organization was, typically enough, the man second in command: Lorenz's chief of staff, Hermann Behrends. An SS-*Standartenführer* with a legal background, Behrends had likewise been nominated by Himmler. He was, as one observer put it, "the prototype of the rigorous, hardnosed SS leader," imbued with the revolutionary ideology of the SS as the avant-garde in the building of a Greater German Reich in Central Europe.[94] Behrends also was a leader in the SD, a personal friend of Heydrich, who had been active from the beginning in building up the *Sicherheitsdienst.* All records, especially Behrends' promotion record, indicate that he was one of those deeply involved in the Night of the Long Knives on June 30, 1934. He has been called, by one in a position to know, one of the "main thugs of the day." [95] It would be to Behrends, then, and behind him to Heydrich, that one would look for the dynamism in VOMI: indeed, Behrends' role of *eminence grise* to Lorenz is in some way reminiscent of the similar relationship between Heydrich and Himmler, although obviously Himmler was not the passive person Lorenz was.

Radical SS control of VOMI boded ill for the traditionalists in Germandom work. Although Lorenz gave assurances of cooperation and protection, particularly against Bohle and the AO, he seemed to have very little understanding of, or sympathy for, Steinacher's ideas.[96] He profusely praised Steinacher for his years of service in behalf of Germandom, but failed to convince him that he even realized what *Volkstum* really was.[97] Steinacher's talks with Behrends, the real power in VOMI, went smoothly enough initially, but here too Steinacher noticed "something sinister" about the man—and well he might: for Behrends, the radical, had some ideas of his own about what to do with the ethnic Germans, ideas which in no way coincided with Steinacher's.[98] Steinacher's skepticism, as it turned out, was more than warranted. His whole future and the fate of the VDA now depended on the whim of men he could not trust at all and who very soon would divest themselves of his services. With the beginning of open SS control of the most important agency in Germandom politics, it was only a matter of time until the traditionalists were forced out of Germandom work entirely and until Hitler would have a viable instrument should he wish to utilize the ethnic Germans for the goals of Reich foreign policy.

IX

Defeat for the Traditionalists

NINETEEN THIRTY-SEVEN was a year of triumph for the radicals in Germandom politics. Gradually, but inexorably, the SS consolidated its hold on ethnic German politics in the Reich, while the radical wing of the SdP proved dominant in the Sudetenland. For the traditionalists there were only two choices: elimination or cooption. Hans Steinacher faced the former; Konrad Henlein chose the latter course. But again, just as the Germandom rivalries had run erratically and in stages, final defeat for the traditionalists came not suddenly, but over a period of time. By the beginning of 1937, Steinacher's freedom of action was already severely circumscribed. He had only barely resisted an attempt on the part of the NSDAP *Reichsleitung* to "coordinate" his VDA through a "commissar," Rolf Brockhausen.[1] Moreover, although Werner Lorenz was giving him assurances, Steinacher could scarcely hope for help from the very people he was fighting—the radical SS now in charge of VOMI. Nevertheless, Steinacher was prepared to make one last ditch effort to shore up his position: he would try to convince the Czechs to allow the VDA to operate freely in their country.

For years, the Czechs had lumped the VDA together with all the other organizations in Nazi Germany, as imperialist and irredentist. The VDA's claim to be involved only in cultural affairs was rejected by the Czechs and labelled as a pretext for illicit activity. In one respect the Czechs had been right, of course: the VDA activities went far beyond the realm of the cultural, into the political. But in another respect, unfortunately, they had been wrong. In tossing all Reich organizations into one pot, they failed to recognize and exploit the basically different approaches to Germandom work which were vying for supremacy. Had they done so, they might have attempted to resist the Nazis under the principle of divide-and-conquer. This miscalculation on the part of the Czechs, although understandable, caused

Steinacher no end of difficulties as he fought to maintain his position. When one of his people was exposed and arrested, then his enemies in the Reich could self-righteously point out how VDA carelessness was endangering the führer's peace policy. When, however, the VDA emphasized its role as a purely cultural organization, then its foes could label it as a reactionary agency run by creaky old men.

Steinacher had tried for years, unsuccessfully, to convince the Prague government to recognize and sanction VDA activities in the Sudetenland. In 1936 Henlein recommended that he again attempt to get in touch with high Czech officials. Working over a period of months with the Sudeten Germans, Steinacher managed in January of 1937 to arrange an introduction to Vojtěch Mastný, the Czech ambassador to Berlin. After some maneuvering, the two men met again briefly at the Czechoslovakian embassy on April 28, 1937. Steinacher had secured permission for such a meeting from both the AA and from the newly installed director of the *Volksdeutsche Mittelstelle,* Werner Lorenz. Predictably, Steinacher tried to make the traditionalist concept of *Volkstum* and the work of the VDA sound as harmless as possible. Emphasizing his debt to Herder's ideas on the nature of the *Volk,* he reminded Mastný of that philosopher's significance for the development of Slavic consciousness as well. He also pointed to the decade-long success of German *Volkstum* in preserving its identity against Italian encroachments, arguing that this very effort "prevented foreign imperialism from being crowned with success . . . ." It was a point he obviously hoped would not be lost on Mastný. Steinacher went on to draw attention to the unfairness of persecuting Germans in Czechoslovakia for working with the VDA. He intimated that all the activities that the VDA pursued—collecting money for the *Sudeten Volkshilfe,* paying for vacation trips of Sudeten children to Germany, and providing stipends for needy and promising artists—were really innocuous. After all, both *The Times* of London and the *New York Times* admitted to the purely social and cultural activities of the VDA. (Of course, Steinacher failed to mention underwriting Henlein's election campaign.) Other European peoples, including the Poles, permitted the VDA to work within their borders; hopefully the Czechs would agree to do the same.[2]

As Steinacher related it, Mastný was surprisingly sympathetic. He gave the assurances of his understanding and promised to speak personally with the president and prime minister during his next stay in Prague. Although Steinacher may have exaggerated the degree of Mastný's sympathy in his report, it is true that the Czech ambassador did mention the VDA favorably in high circles in his own country. As a result, the VDA was allowed for the first time to work freely and openly in Czechoslovakia.[3] However, Steinacher's victory turned out to be a pyrrhic one. He had gained too little and too late for his official acceptance by the Czechs to be anything but a rear guard action. Ironically, even this modest success would play into the hands of the radicals once the SS fully captured the VDA.

The traditionalists' most recent ally, the *Abwehr*, continued to support both Henlein and Steinacher, but in the long run Canaris could not fend off the SS. With no one left, then, to effectively prevent it, the SS-SD began to close in on the VDA: as Steinacher had feared, VOMI's "helping" the VDA boded ill for his whole conception of Germandom work. On April 23, 1937—without Steinacher's knowledge and barely five days before his encouraging conversation with Mastný—both Lorenz and Behrends had privately revealed how things really stood. At a confidential meeting in the *Deutsche Auslandsinstitut*, Behrends disclosed that Lorenz had given Steinacher one more chance to bring the VDA to heel: meaning, of course, to "coordinate" it into the NS movement.[4] Steinacher had already taken some tentative steps in this direction by concluding agreements with the *Reichsjugendführung*, the *Nährstand*, and several other organizations.[5] But this was not enough. Nothing less than a thorough organizational overhaul of the VDA would do. Behrends made a portentous analogy: they had given Steinacher a shovel; he could use it either to construct a new edifice or to dig his own grave. Lorenz also made his position clear. He was completely willing to protect the VDA from the AO, and make no concessions whatsoever to Bohle's organization, but he regarded the VDA as his executive tool ("Organ der Durchführung, dessen Bundesleiter auf seine Anweisungen hört"). Clearly, VOMI was well on its way to becoming an ethnic German command post which would far surpass the functions of its predecessors—either the *Volksdeutscher Rat* or the Kursell Office.

Even before Lorenz's warning, the net was closing on Steinacher gradually and imperceptibly. The VDA itself was systematically cut off from the political mainstream. A ruling dated February 1, 1937, outlawed VDA speakers at any function of the party, its auxiliary, or related organizations.[6] The VDA also lost its financial independence,

Steinacher's most important weapon in the struggle against the AO and the Hitler Youth: Karl Janovsky, a confidante of Party Treasurer Franz Schwarz, became *Bundesschatzmeister* of the VDA, giving the party complete control of the organization's finances.[7] Rumors of Steinacher's impending dismissal tended to isolate him personally as well. He wrote on February 13: "Ribbentrop is supposed to have decided against me with Hess and Himmler. The bomb can go off any day." [8] But the end did not come as suddenly as Steinacher might have thought. Lorenz, always the *bon vivant,* apparently did not have the stomach to have it out with Steinacher. He preferred to smile and offer encouragement, while his assistant Behrends worked behind the scenes. In a meeting with Steinacher on June 23, Lorenz listened to Steinacher's complaints that Behrends was issuing orders to the VDA, then denied that any orders had been issued. "But B[ehrends] is still very caustic," Steinacher noted in his diary. "Is working for the fall of Schöneich [one of the top members of the VDA]. Looking for further victims." [9] Behrends was indeed looking for new victims. On July 31, 1937, he removed one of Steinacher's appointees, Theodor Oberländer, from his post as director of the *Bund Deutscher Osten* and took over the post himself.[10] One by one Steinacher lost still other trusted colleagues. From the old VR, Hermann Ullmann was gone; Robert Ernst had opted for the party. Most of the regional VDA leaders were now younger party men.[11] On September 2 the VDA was ordered to align its organization geographically with the party structure.[12]

Finally it was all over. In Cologne on September 27, Steinacher presided for the last time over a major gathering of the VDA. Compared to rallies in the past, it was not a very large or impressive affair. Party and state officials assiduously avoided it, knowing that Steinacher by now no longer mattered. One observer characterized Steinacher's last appearance:

> Steinacher gives the impression of being completely unchanged in any way. Above all, his nerves do not appear to have given in the least. Perhaps he has become somewhat more conciliatory, more careful, and amiable, although people have pointed out to me "admiringly" his absolute stubbornness in many things. . . . In any case, the self-assuredness and sovereignty of his appearance is remarkable, as is the effect which almost every one of his words makes, although he is really no overpowering orator.

Steinacher took the opportunity to speak once again about his concept of Germandom. He reasserted the need for keeping the VDA in its present form, "even if this is not understood inside the Reich, because of the pure statist thinking." [13] Once more he clearly drew the line between the kind of thinking which lay behind the VDA and that which motivated the AO. Tragically, even on the brink of total political defeat, Steinacher could not, or would not, see that as the power of the Reich grew internationally and as the radicals' influence continued to increase, the distinctions that he had been so careful to make over the years were gradually being eradicated. To men bent on imperialist expansion as well as domestic empire building, the differences between Reich German and ethnic German, and all the political connotations which those differences implied, were really not very important at all. Someone else—ironically, someone who was not a German at all, ethnic or otherwise—had clearly recognized what was really at stake here. In a conversation with Steinacher on August 13, Colonel Christie, the English officer who had been instrumental in bringing Henlein to England in 1935, remarked:

> Either there will be a condition of pacification and VDA success: when this way is assured, England will stand at Germany's side and with its power help to remove the mistakes of Versailles with English initiative. Or, however, Germany will reach out over the national boundaries into Bohemia: then England will resist in any case, and it would come unavoidably to war.[14]

But there was to be no VDA success. Steinacher's stock continued to fall in the coming weeks, until, in October of 1937, he was relieved of his post as VDA director and retired entirely from Germandom work. With him went the last vestiges of traditionalist influence in Reich *Volkstum* politics.

The rapid decline of the traditionalist position in Germany during the course of 1937 inevitably undermined Henlein's position within the Sudeten German camp as well. With the defeat of Steinacher, his original contacts to the Reich were becoming very weak indeed. Moreover, the SdP still was ideologically bankrupt and without effective leadership; it was still racked by internal quarrels and attacks from radicals in the Reich, and it had become increasingly dependent on German agencies to mediate those quarrels. Early in 1937 observers noted a resurgence of quarrels within the SdP, divisions that had supposedly been settled during the summer of 1936.

M. K. von Trauttmansdorff, at the conclusion of his mission to Beneš, described conditions within the SdP:

> The situation can be described as not very gratifying. While the solidity of the SdP structure in the countryside cannot be doubted, the leadership leaves a lot to be desired. The sharp schism between the old National Socialists and the camarilla [*i.e.,* the *Kameradschaftsbund!*] is making itself strongly felt in the leadership council [*Führerrat*]. One cannot avoid the impression that a total absence of goals and plans reigns in the council. . . . K[onrad] H[enlein] as before can claim great popularity, [but] seldom makes a decision, appears not to be the absolute master in his party, and is under the unhealthy influence of Neuwirth and his comrades.[15]

From the provinces, Consul Walter von Lierau also assessed the situation, though his report was really more a factor in the dissension than a description of it:

> The SdP must be blamed for the mistake of neither being able to find a correct solution to the inner conflicts nor having the means and sufficient strength to really eliminate the opposition. Because of this, the schism of national Sudeten Germandom into two fronts threatens once more with heightened intensity. . . . I have had the opportunity to hear the different complaints about the SdP leadership. They must unfortunately be characterized as, in part, basically justified. . . . One can observe increasingly that even in the ranks of the common folk, people are beginning to question the party leadership, something that before was only the case in certain intellectual circles.[16]

With the split in the SdP threatening again to destroy the movement, Henlein felt compelled once more to seek the aid of Reich Germandom agencies to mediate the disputes. This time, however, the *Volksdeutsche Mittelstelle* was ready and waiting.

Early in 1937, at the same time it had begun its program to "coordinate" the VDA, VOMI had been trying its wings in "handling" the perennial quarrels between rival German groups in Poland and Rumania. In the Polish quarrels VOMI continued to operate under the theory that it was a mediatory agency: when VOMI failed to achieve any reconciliation between the older Germandom people and the *Jungdeutschen* in April of 1937, Lorenz declined to make any binding decision. In this respect, his behavior was not really much different from that of his predecessor, Otto von Kursell.[17] The situation was similar in the wrangling between the Bonfort and Fabritius groups in Rumania. From April 19 to 23 negotiations to unite the two groups were undertaken at the VOMI offices in Berlin. Again, mediation failed.[18] But Behrends, especially, learned much from the experience, with the result that after the middle of 1937, VOMI evolved increasingly in the direction of a command post rather than a mediatory agency. This evolution became clear as the organization expanded its activities and contacts. To strengthen its position financially, it moved into the realm of economic development of the ethnic groups, elbowing its way into the *Vereinigte Finanzkontore* which channelled large amounts of state funds through the AA to the various German minority groups.[19] In July of 1937 VOMI also took over the work that had been done by the party *Gaugrenzlandsämter* and these offices were dissolved. By August, Lorenz or Behrends were to be present at all receptions which Hitler had with *Volksdeutsche*.[20] In the meantime, VOMI widened its field of contacts, working with Wilhelm Keppler, Göring's plenipotentiary for the Four Year Plan, and availing itself of the AA courier system.[21] As 1937 wore on the directives flowing from VOMI became clearer and sharper.[22] Perhaps its most important task now would be to bring the Sudeten German party to heel.

The quarrels in the SdP continued to center around the disputes between the radical National Socialists and the moderate KB wing of the party. As part of an earlier settlement during the quarrels in 1936, a group of radicals—including Herbert David; Anton Kreissl (Hans Krebs's representative in Czechoslovakia); Rudolf Kasper, the trade union leader; and Dr. Gustav Jonak—entered the leadership circle of the party. As Karl Hermann Frank described the resulting situation:

> In the meetings of the *Hauptleitung* after Kasper was admitted, there were very sharp attacks against the leadership. Kasper met with me after the meetings, since any discussion in his presence was impossible at the *Hauptleitung* meetings. It finally had gone so far that Henlein wouldn't even receive him any more, after Kasper had published a leaflet attacking Henlein [in which he maintained that Henlein was a tippler].[23]

By June and July of 1937, the quarrels reached an intensity bordering on that of the 1936 split which had almost destroyed the party. With Henlein on such bad personal terms with the radicals (most probably he was no longer able at this point to act decisively anyway), Frank took over the task of bringing VOMI in to mediate. On June 17 VOMI requested that Rudolf Haider, leader of the dissident youth in Prague, and Otto Liebl, SdP deputy who had been considering founding another party, come to Berlin for negotiations.[24] On June 30 VOMI stated that "authoritative for the representation of the ethnic groups vis-à-vis the Reich are Konrad Henlein and those official experts [*Sachbearbeiter*] named by him. Any contact with the opposition is to be broken off." [25] Apparently Frank, too, must have been active in the negotiations. Another VOMI notice of the same day asked again that Haider appear in Berlin and that Liebl resign from his deputy's position "in agreement with Frank's last letter." [26]

These directives, however, did nothing to resolve the split. Minister Eisenlohr reported several weeks later:

> . . . the mood in the Sudeten German party is again extraordinarily tense. Representative Kasper is supposed to be very embittered about the attitude of the leading members of the Sudeten German party. He declared that he was going to lay down his office in the leadership council, since he and the old National Socialists . . . could see no possibility of being effective. The organizational direction was doing everything to prevent the activity of the earlier National Socialist leaders. . . . My contact raised the question of why Konrad Henlein, who after all in the past wished to have unity in collaboration, was not bringing his influence to bear. Whereupon the unanimous response was that Konrad Henlein, as in many other cases, unfortunately could not make a decision, that things are dragged out again and again, and that a circle of party leaders [*Amtswalter*] was trying to elbow everyone else, in particular the National Socialists, out of the work.[27]

On July 15 a meeting was held in the offices of VOMI to decide what to do about the quarrels in the SdP.[28] Dr. Franz Wehofsich, Hans Krebs, and Günther Altenburg from the AA were present, as well as two agents who reported on the Sudeten situation. The participants established that the antagonisms in the party had indeed reached another high point and that something would have to be done. They decided that Henlein and members of the opposition, in particular Kasper and Haider, should come to Lorenz in Berlin at the beginning of August to resolve their differences. Meanwhile, a truce should be declared. Krebs, for his part, undertook to mediate between the two camps. The radicals in the Sudetenland responded to the VOMI suggestion with a counterproposal: Lorenz himself should come to Prague, where the negotiations could be held on the spot.[29]

In light of the fact that VOMI had apparently already given its blessing to Henlein and his colleagues in June, it is puzzling that the radicals within the Sudeten camp were behaving in such a cavalier manner toward Lorenz. Their confidence becomes understandable, however, in light of Henlein's other activities and VOMI's reactions to them: it was soon no secret that not everything Henlein was doing met with approval in Berlin. In 1936 Henlein had been elected president of the *Verband der deutschen Volksgruppen in Europa*, a regional organization representing the interests of German ethnic groups all over Europe. Now Werner Hasselblatt, Henlein's predecessor as head of the organization, reported to the AA that Henlein was in the process of "politicizing" the *Verband*. The *Verband* was funded entirely by the AA and its only purpose had been to deal with legal questions concerning German minorities. It was never intended to be overtly political, and if it were politicized, there was danger that the various leaders of German ethnic groups, who had been able to meet freely in most countries within the framework of the uncompromised *Verband*, would now be prevented from doing so. "Above all," Fritz von Twardowski of the AA cultural department stated, "Konrad Henlein's main idea appears to me to be completely wrong. [He] supposedly has the intention of forming a central office of *Volksgruppen* within the *Verband* . . . as an opposite pole to the command post [*Befehlstelle*] for minority questions vis-à-vis the party in the form of the *Volksdeutsche Mittelstelle*." [30]

Henlein, it appeared, had ambitions himself to be a kind of spokesman for the other ethnic German groups, probably yet another attempt to strengthen his sagging prestige.[31] VOMI soon made it clear, however, that it saw things in a different light. On August 23 Behrends informed an AA official that Lorenz had given Henlein detailed instructions several months previously as to the policy to be pursued with the *Verband*. In these instructions, he had foreseen no political activation of that organization: on the contrary, it was to continue its work as before. As the AA official reported:

> In the course of the conversation *Obergruppenführer* [sic] Behrends informed me that the *Volksdeutsche Mittelstelle* in no way approves of Conrad [sic] Henlein's activities lately, and that *Obergruppenführer* Lorenz would receive Herr H.[enlein] tomor-

row and notify him that his excursions into the realm of
international politics are undesired, that he stop his all too
frequent trips and in the future devote himself more to his real
task—*i.e.,* the Sudeten German party." [32]

As if to underscore its disapproval of Henlein's activities and at the
same time create the impression that its mediation was successful,
VOMI arranged that not only Henlein and his immediate entourage
were invited officially to the Nuremberg Party Day, but that two
dissident radicals in the SdP, Kreissl and Kasper, come as well.[33]

The radicals could continue to act independently, not only
because Henlein's relationship with VOMI did not improve, but also
because they had powerful connections of their own—among them
the close links between the *Aufbruch* circle and the SD. Karl Hermann
Frank, especially, seems to have acquired a direct line to Himmler,
which had not always been the case. In early 1936, Frank had been
among those members of the *Hauptleitung* pushing hardest to eject the
Aufbruch dissidents from the party. In May of 1936, however—particularly during the negotiations with Rudolf Kasper which he led—
Frank apparently did come over to a position of at least compromise
with the radicals. He and Kasper tentatively agreed, subject to
Henlein's approval (which Henlein did not give), that Walter Brand
might be sacrificed on the altar of unity.[34] An ambitious man, Frank
must have sensed in what direction the wind was blowing, for by early
1937 there is no doubt that he was wholly in the radical camp. Just
when he decided that his future lay with Himmler and the SS is not
certain—it must have been sometime between mid-1936 and early
1937. At any rate, in March of 1937, Frank told one AA official that
he had been "ordered" to see Himmler on a matter, indicating what
the relationship was between the two men by this time.[35] Possibly
under Himmler's influence, Frank began to speak increasingly about
a violent settlement of the Sudeten question. When Frank objected to
Göring's plan to bring sixty-five thousand young Sudeten laborers to
the Reich in connection with Four Year Plan work, Himmler
informed him that the measure was unavoidable and that the Sudeten
Germans were "coming into the Reich in the not too distant future
anyway." [36] A remark by Ernst Eisenlohr, the German minister in
Prague at the time, has documented this change of attitude on Frank's
part: "[He] is completely trustworthy and reasonable, but leans
occasionally toward the all too simple view that the Sudeten German

question will be solved in . . . the near future by German intervention." [37] It was most likely that Frank could make such a "simple"
prognosis because of his ties with Himmler and the SS. For Henlein,
this was a desertion of personnel parallel to and just as serious as that
which Steinacher was experiencing in the Reich.

Frank's growing leadership role in the SdP was symptomatic of a
dilemma facing VOMI at this point. As part of Himmler's SS empire,
VOMI logically had an interest in "coordinating" the Sudeten
German community to function in the best interests of a radical Reich
foreign policy—which meant that unity and discipline had to be
established within the SdP. Logically, then, VOMI should have
thrown its weight behind the radicals in the SdP with whom it had a
closer ideological affinity. Henlein's obvious shortcomings as a party
leader would have made this course of action a natural one. However,
Konrad Henlein was still—to the Sudeten German public, at least—
the very symbol of Sudeten unity and as such could not simply be
written off. Thus, although VOMI officials privately leaned toward
radicals like Frank, they could not come out openly in their favor.
Despite a vested interest in settling the traditionalist and radical
quarrels, VOMI did not at this point bring all its weight to bear to
achieve unity in the SdP at the expense of one side or the other.
Instead it vacillated, until in November of 1937, Henlein himself
solved the problem by coming over to the radical camp. Once free of
this bind, VOMI was able to develop its full potential as a command
post on the Sudeten German front, while simultaneously Frank was
gradually able to overshadow Henlein as the decisive voice within the
SdP.

As the fall of 1937 approached, Henlein found himself in a bad
situation. He had accomplished nothing toward unifying his party. On
the contrary, he had wound up expelling Rudolf Kasper from the
party entirely, whereupon another radical leader, Dr. Gustav Jonak,
resigned and two other radical deputies, Otto Liebl and Ludwig
Wagner, left the party caucus and took seats in parliament apart from
the other SdP representatives.[38] To make things even less encouraging,
there was still no sign from the führer as to whether Henlein stood on
solid ground as leader of the Sudeten German unity movement.
Rumors were spreading that some kind of shake-up in the leadership
of the SdP was imminent.[39]

It was against this background that three decisive events occurred in rapid succession in the fall of 1937: Steinacher's dismissal on October 19; Heinz Rutha's arrest on October 4 and his subsequent suicide on November 5; and the incident at Teplitz-Schönau on October 18. Two of these incidents marked the end of traditionalist influence in Germandom politics, both in the Reich and in the Sudetenland. The third marked the beginning of blatant activity on the part of radicals in the Sudeten German Party—activity which would turn the Sudeten problem into the Sudeten crisis. It was in the wake of these three events that Henlein finally capitulated completely to National Socialism.

On October 19, 1937, Hans Steinacher was relieved of his duties as director of the *Volksbund für das Deutschtum im Ausland.*[40] The reason given for dismissal was Lorenz's complaint that Steinacher had not lived up to certain agreements and the fact that the VDA "despite all objections and warnings" had pursued a course in South Tirol in opposition to the führer's foreign policy, which was to leave the South Tirolese to the mercy of Italy in exchange for Mussolini's good will.[41] Although Hitler as yet had showed no indication that he would pursue a radical policy of expansion, his willingness to sacrifice the Germans in South Tirol on the altar of Great Power politics did indicate that the fate of German minorities was not his chief concern. In contrast to Steinacher's constant emphasis on the *volklich,* ethnic-centered approach to Germandom work, Hitler was thinking in statist terms. For him, the Reich and its power interests came first. Until 1937 Steinacher had been able to continue his aid to the South Tirolese, as long as it remained discreet and as long as Hitler was too preoccupied with other things to take notice. But during the course of 1937, partly as a result of their cooperation in the Spanish civil war and England's behavior concerning that conflict, Germany and Italy moved closer toward rapprochement. All during 1937, Nazi leaders courted Mussolini, and finally won him for the Anti-Comintern pact in November.[42] In this situation, Steinacher, with his stubborn concern for all the German ethnic groups, and especially for the Germans in South Tirol, could no longer be allowed to continue as before. He was a stumbling block to the Italian alliance and had to be removed.

Steinacher had been aware of his impending dismissal. As early as the fall of 1936, Himmler and Heydrich had been pushing for the "quick replacement" of VDA leadership.[43] Their mouthpiece, the *Rumburger Zeitung,* had openly been predicting Steinacher's fall. It seems almost astonishing that Steinacher was able to hold out for a full year in the face of such pressure against him. Apparently, despite their growing strength, Himmler and Heydrich were not yet in such a strong position in the Germandom field to completely edge out the traditionalists. On October 9, 1937, however, Henlein told his friend Steinacher about a conversation with Göring. Mussolini, Göring had said, made it clear during his visit to Berlin in September, that he would welcome Steinacher's dismissal.[44] Ten days later, the axe fell and Wilhelm Luig of the *Volksdeutsche Mittelstelle* took over as provisional director of the VDA. Steinacher telegraphed in vain for Hitler's intercession.[45] Back from the *Reichskanzlei* came the message: "The führer has cognizance. He does not intend to decide in the matter. Therefore, he declines to receive Steinacher and the [other] person suggested by him." [46] Any chance Steinacher might still have had to alter the decision through his tie with Hess through the Haushofers was ruled out by the fact that Albrecht Haushofer was off on a world cruise at the time.[47] The only remnant Steinacher managed to save from the old VDA was his successful insistence that Hess commission Dr. Behagel, one of the few old colleagues left, as managing director of the VDA. Steinacher argued that Luig, as an SS man, would compromise the VDA's image abroad.[48] There was no doubt, however, that Steinacher's victory was only a face-saving one: through Behrends the SD was the real power behind VOMI, and VOMI now ran the VDA.

Steinacher's dismissal came as a severe blow to Henlein, both because the traditionalists in the Reich had been soundly defeated and because Steinacher had been Henlein's only source of moderate support in the Reich. With Steinacher gone, Henlein's position in his own party would be threatened even more than it already was. As Friedrich Bürger, speaking for Henlein, said in an appeal to Major Groscurth in the *Abwehr*: Henlein could only keep discipline among the masses if his authority was not impugned; the dismissal of the man who had been Henlein's strongest supporter in the Reich would now be seen by the opposition as a step against Henlein himself. "The measure against Dr. Steinacher comes at the most unfortunate time. It is not conceivable that the führer's deputy, who was always favorably inclined toward Henlein, would have ordered this measure at this time, if he had been aware of the consequences of the step for this side, too." [49] Bürger also directed letters of protest in Henlein's name to other top Reich leaders including Göring, Heinrich Lammers in the Reich Chancellory, Lorenz, Hess, Foreign Minister von Neurath, and War Minister Werner von Blomberg.[50] The protests, however, were of no avail. No one was left to influence Hess in the direction of traditional *Volkstum* politics. Now with VOMI virtually unchallenged in the Germandom field, men like Behrends, who were concerned with the Sudeten Germans only insofar as they could be a tool for Reich expansion, would either push Hess in their direction or bypass him completely. And although Hitler did not as yet give VOMI full powers in ethnic German affairs, experience had shown that the führer usually backed the winner of any confrontation. Henlein was scarcely unaware of the implications of that fact for him and his movement.

On a more personal level, Henlein was deeply shaken at this point by the arrest and suicide of his closest colleague, Heinz Rutha. Rutha, active in Germandom work since the youth movement days right after the war, had been—along with Walter Brand—the strongest force for moderation in the Sudeten German party.[51] As a KB leader, he had incurred the wrath of the radicals for years. Although he did not really hold any high rank in the party—he was the expert on nationalities questions in the *Hauptleitung*—Rutha was virtually in charge of all foreign policy considerations.[52] It had been he who pressed for settlement of many Sudeten problems in the League of Nations; he was active in many international organizations concerned with minority problems. Most importantly, it had been Rutha who had convinced Henlein to go to England to seek aid in 1935. The radicals were well aware of Henlein's dependence on Rutha and had sought for years to separate him from Henlein. Although ultimately any pretext might have been used for this purpose, Rutha had one serious personal problem which offered the radicals the chance they needed: he was a homosexual. On October 4, 1937, as Rutha and Henlein were about to board a plane for London, Czech police arrested Rutha on charges of homosexuality. Barely a month later, on November 5, Rutha was found hanged in his cell: in order to save embarrassment to the party, he had taken his own life.[53] Coming less than a month after Steinacher's dismissal, Rutha's death was a severe blow to Henlein. First he had lost his moderate contacts in the Reich; now with Rutha gone and with Brand isolated in London and Paris, Henlein also had no one within the Sudeten party with sufficient influence to keep him on a moderate track. Rumors that Rutha had been betrayed to the Czechs by the Haider-Kasper circle certainly would not have allayed Henlein's feelings of insecurity.

With traditionalist influence obviously at an end and with Henlein as isolated as Steinacher had been, the radicals seized upon an unfortunate incident in order to precipitate a crisis. On October 17, in the town of Teplitz-Schönau, several SdP leaders—among them Karl Hermann Frank—were leaving a political meeting in the presence of an enthusiastic crowd. One of the Czech security police, apparently unaware that the men were parliament members, hit Frank with his truncheon, whereupon Frank lost his temper, grabbed a truncheon from another officer, and struck back. More policemen arrived and escorted Frank and his companions to jail.[54] Almost before the incident had become known in Prague, the Reich German press was howling its disapproval of Czech brutality. The *Völkischer Beobachter* wrote: "Lies and hate, murder and terror stood beside the cradle of the Czechoslovak state and have never left it during its brief existence." [55] Forced into action by the radicals' stance and by the wave of public sympathy because of the incident, Henlein addressed a letter of protest to Beneš, demanding that steps be taken toward Sudeten German autonomy. At this point, the myriad connections between Sudeten and Reich offices paid off—but too well. The SdP Press Office got the text of the letter to the Reich News Office (*Deutsches Nachrichtenbüro*, or DNB), so quickly that it was announced on German radio while the letter itself was still on its way from Leitmeritz to Prague.[56]

The Czech reaction was swift and firm. The government postponed local elections and banned all political meetings.[57] The German radicals had obviously not counted on such resolute action on the part of the Czechs. Just as quickly as they had gone on the offensive, they now retreated—leaving Henlein holding the bag. The German minister in Prague, Ernst Eisenlohr, noted on October 22:

> Obviously Konrad Henlein has come to the realization that the time for the decisive struggle for power has not yet come, and that a too strongly emphasized aggressiveness patterned on the Reich might expose the party, and particularly its leadership, to dangers which they feel unable to cope with at present.[58]

In reality, Henlein was in an intolerable position. The split in his party

was unresolved. The radicals were coming more and more to the fore.
The incident at Teplitz-Schönau and the accompanying offensive,
which could have unified the party, came to nothing in the face of a
determined Czech reaction. Now Henlein was back where he started
—backpedalling from the advanced position of the party. He had had
an encouraging conversation with the Czech premier, Milan Hodža,
on September 16, but the Teplitz incident had wiped out any
advantage that this leverage might have given Henlein.[59] In the Reich,
VOMI was again showing dissatisfaction with Henlein's policy;
Lorenz was angry about the whole Rutha affair.[60]

Backed to the wall, Henlein took what he thought to be the only
step left to rescue his own position and the unity of his movement: he
wrote a letter to Adolf Hitler.[61] It becomes apparent from the content
of this message, that Henlein was a frightened man—afraid of losing
his position, on the one hand, and of Czech repression on the other.
He complained that the radicals both within and outside his own
party were using their connections with various Reich agencies to help
foment crises, while claiming at the same time—supposedly on best
authority—that a military solution to the Czech problem was at hand.
Henlein felt unable to control growing activism and could not fight it
"because considering the delicate and confidential character of the
matter" any public counterarguments would give the "Czech government the opportunity to get its hands on all those involved."
Moreover, the Sudeten masses were also becoming radicalized at a
grass roots level, as the plethora of contacts across the borders on a
local level began to bear their fruit. Henlein could not cope with this
development either, especially not when the Sudeten Germans saw
"every petty border official or SA or SS man as the representative of
the Reich and of the führer's will."

Meanwhile, the incident at Teplitz-Schönau had raised the
specter of Czech reprisals. Nor was it only the incident itself which
might bring repressive action in its wake. Henlein felt concern that the
violent Reich press and radio campaign that followed might turn the
situation into an international crisis. "Both in form and in content,"
the Reich propaganda was not in tune with the SdP line: the SdP had
been pressing for autonomy, but not so hard as to provoke crackdowns by the Czechs. Although the tremendous cry set up by the
Reich press might well have resulted in just such a crackdown, the
Reich had not followed with any action to rescue the Sudeten

Germans. Then, just as quickly as it had begun, the propaganda barrage itself ended. Henlein complained:

> The sudden termination of the press campaign rendered the action useless on the one hand and, on the other hand, made the Czech argument appear correct that Sudeten Germandom is only an occasional object of National Socialist propaganda with which serious Reich foreign policy has nothing to do.[62]

In short, if the Reich were going to intervene like that in the first place—with a propaganda war which was not in tune with current SdP policy and one which would certainly carry radicalization even further—then why didn't the Reich follow through with some kind of action as well? Caught in the middle of a situation over which he had no effective control, Henlein had to come up with a solution that might still save his movement and his own hide. Under tremendous pressure from radicals and Czechs alike, he opted for the most drastic solution possible: he asked Hitler to annex the whole Bohemian-Moravian-Silesian area to the Reich. As for himself and his party, these he offered to Hitler as a "factor in National Socialist Reich policy."

The question arises why Henlein—who obviously did not know earlier what Hitler wanted and who was desperately asking for a "basic consultation" on what SdP policy should be—would propose to Hitler, out of the blue, the most radical approach for solving his difficulties. With the passing of Steinacher and Rutha, Henlein had lost the last of his connections to moderates with authority in the Reich. At the same time, Henlein could not help but see that people who leaned toward the radical side seemed to have acquired the best contacts with the NS regime. Karl Hermann Frank, after all, seemed much more in the know about what was supposedly going to happen than Henlein himself: Frank was confidently predicting that it would not be long before the Sudeten Germans became part of the Reich. If it was dawning on Henlein that an eventual radical solution to the Sudeten problem was likely, then he had to offer Hitler something radical if he was going to survive politically.

Whether Henlein made this move to outflank Frank or whether he threw in the towel and merely went along with Frank is difficult to say. In later months the two leaders worked together to the exclusion of many of the others in the SdP leadership circle. At this stage, however, it seems more likely that Henlein was acting in the hope of still overtaking Frank. Frank had excellent connections to the SS and Himmler. If Henlein wanted to go over Himmler's head, Hitler was the only one left. By sending his pledge of support directly to Hitler through the Reich Chancellory, with a carbon copy to the foreign minister, and by deliberately bypassing Lorenz and Behrends through whom he was supposed to work, Henlein was apparently trying to outmaneuver Frank by forging even stronger connections with the Reich. Whether Henlein realized it, his decision was basically an admission of his total personal defeat as the leader of his own movement. With this secret commitment to Hitler, Henlein now consciously embarked on a *doppelgleisige Politik,* as one of his former colleagues called it: outwardly professing loyalty to the Czechoslovak state in the name of Sudeten autonomy, having inwardly surrendered his political fate to the will of Adolf Hitler.[63] This dual policy was already implicit in the deeply rooted split in the Sudeten German unity movement, but only now was Henlein forced to recognize and pursue it personally.

As so often before, Hitler reacted to this urgent appeal from one of his paladins by doing nothing (it was not until March of 1938, four months later, that he even agreed to see Henlein at all). This time, however—something Henlein could not have known—Hitler *was* thinking about Czechoslovakia. Two weeks before Henlein's fateful letter, Hitler had for the first time expressed his resolve to settle scores with the Czechs. On November 5, 1937, the foreign minister, Constantin von Neurath; the war minister, Werner von Blomberg; the commander-in-chief of the army, Werner von Fritsch; the commander of the navy, Erich Raeder; Hitler's *Wehrmacht* adjutant, Colonel Friedrich Hossbach; and Hermann Göring attended a secret conference with the führer. The meeting was so secret that no protocol was kept; however, several days later, Hossbach committed to paper from memory what Hitler had said.[64] Hitler projected that, in principle, force would be needed to expand German *Lebensraum* and to extend the German racial community, despite the risks entailed in such a course of action. It was in this context that he proclaimed the need to eliminate Czechoslovakia. In any future conflict between Germany and the West, Czechoslovakia posed a serious threat to Germany's flank. If, to counter such a potential threat, Czechoslovakia (and Austria) could be annexed, several problems would be solved at once. Germany would have shorter and more easily defensible frontiers; large numbers of German troops would be freed for other purposes; and in addition, the annexed areas could provide the manpower for up to twelve divisions as well as foodstuffs for five to six million people.

Although expressing such hostile designs on Czechoslovakia, Hitler continued to be the improviser: there is no detailed blueprint here for the destruction of Czechoslovakia. Rather, Hitler outlined certain contingencies which might possibly induce him to launch an attack. First, given a basically unchanged political situation in Europe, he looked vaguely ahead to the years 1943 to 1945. By this time, he felt, Germany would have to strike, for in those years Germany's strength would be greatest relative to that of its potential enemies. To wait longer would be to put the Reich into an increasingly disadvantageous position: the other powers would have rearmed, Germany's military equipment would have become obsolete, and the NS movement itself would be showing signs of age. Although he was not contemplating immediate moves against Czechoslovakia, Hitler did detail two other contingencies which might lead to precipitate action. If there were civil war in France or if Britain and France were to get into a war with Italy in the Mediterranean, then Hitler would seize the opportunity to act suddenly and smash Austria and Czechoslovakia together. Under these circumstances Germany would not in all probability have to reckon with a threat from the Western powers, which would be preoccupied and which would have probably written off the Czechs in any event.

Hitler's remarks on November 5 did reflect some change in his thinking: a shift of emphasis from west to east in military strategy and a somewhat greater sense of urgency in beginning his historic task of expansion. This change—further evidence of Hitler the improviser— became apparent in the alteration of military contingency plans which followed. German military projections prior to this point had been largely hypothetical and routine in nature and had assumed that a French attack on Germany (so-called Operation Red) was just as likely as a preventive war against Czechoslovakia (Operation Green). In the wake of Hitler's conference, however, military projections altered somewhat. The addenda (*Nachtrag*) of December 7, 1937, envisioned Operation Green as far more likely than Operation Red: Hitler was rather certain now that the Western powers would not intervene militarily. Moreover, the addenda, though making no exact

projections, did not rule out the possibility of an attack on Czechoslovakia in 1938.[65] But more than this it did not do: it was still too
nebulous to be labelled a "blueprint for aggression."

Perhaps even more interesting than what Hitler said at this point
was what he omitted. He made no mention whatsoever of the Sudeten
Germans as a fifth column to destroy Czechoslovakia from within.
Rather, he remained within the context of a traditional pattern of
aggression: waiting until the international power situation was
favorable and then striking militarily. Even after having received
Henlein's letter several weeks later offering the Sudeten German party
as a "factor in National Socialist Reich policy," Hitler still gave no
indication that he was seriously considering the use of a fifth column
as an aggressive tool of Reich foreign policy. In fact, Hitler did not
react in any way to Henlein's letter, not even to acknowledge its
receipt. At a time when radicals like Frank seemed to be getting all
kinds of hints and assurances from Reich radicals, Hitler did nothing
to take Henlein into his confidence. Hitler's lack of initial reaction
and the four-month silence until he saw Henlein again indicate that
the führer probably had little intention of using Henlein; or if he did,
he did not betray the fact. Yet he was not ready to dismiss Henlein's
offer either—which would have closed that option, however remotely
the führer may have been considering the prospect.

On balance, Hitler's remarks at the November 5 meeting
did not exhibit dynamic, aggressive leadership, but rather his passive,
patient, wait-and-see approach to political decision-making. He had,
to be sure, articulated his intentions toward Czechoslovakia, but in
doing so he still left his options open. Far from developing a schedule,
he plainly showed that he was willing to wait until opportunity—or
the actions or blunders of others—gave him an opening to act. As the
events of 1938 would show, Hitler was wrong in his projections at this
point. None of the contingencies he mentioned ever became reality.
When the Sudeten problem, which had been simmering for years close
to the surface of international politics, boiled into a crisis in 1938,
opportunities arose that Hitler had not previously envisioned: the key
to this development, ironically, lay in the Germandom struggle that
the führer had so long ignored. By maintaining a flexible stance
toward foreign-policy formulation, Hitler was able to compensate for
his faulty assessment of future political developments.

X

Volkstumspolitik *to* Aussenpolitik

BY the end of 1937, the long period of Germandom rivalry had presented Hitler, without any effort at all on his part, with a considerable array of potential weapons: a compliant political organization, the Sudeten German party, representing the largest German ethnic group in Europe outside the Reich and Austria; a powerful command agency in the Reich, VOMI, available for steering the German minorities; various groups of Reich and Sudeten Germans whose activities could push foreign policy in the direction of a radical solution to the Czech situation; an internationalization of the Sudeten problem which virtually invited intervention on the part of the Reich; and finally, a bag of political "tricks" developed through years of experimentation which could be used to handle the ethnic German problem. As the Sudeten crisis gradually evolved in 1938, Hitler availed himself of these various tools and situations to some extent. But certain elements arising from the battle over *Volkstumspolitik* were more than just passive tools which he could use at will: they had a dynamic of their own and kept the crisis moving with a minimum of manipulation on Hitler's part—all the more so since Hitler still continued to improvise and let other people create his opportunities for him. As much as Hitler took the reins of foreign policy into his own hands during 1938, several dynamic forces were usually ahead of him, actually shaping his plans and creating situations to which he then had to react. In short, factors outside his direct control were making his timetable for him. Hitler, to be sure, exploited these situations with aplomb and finesse, but the fact remains that he was at most points reacting to events more often than actually initiating them.

The two most important factors that tended to shape and precipitate the Czech crisis much sooner than Hitler had anticipated were the accelerating internationalization of the Sudeten problem and

the grass roots radicalization both in the Reich and in the Sudetenland. These two forces worked in tandem. Radicalization kept the pot
boiling, kept the Sudeten crisis from becoming just the old Sudeten
"problem" again; it also created the conditions for growing internationalization—for the most part English, but also French, interest and
initiative in cooling off tensions. Such increased international concern,
ironically, merely tended to generate still more pressure toward
resolving the situation, which also kept the crisis alive. Sometimes this
radicalization and internationalization pushed Hitler along; at other
times, he actually encouraged them. The cumulative effect was an
increasing momentum during 1938 toward a "final solution" of the
problem of Czechoslovakia's existence.

One of the fruits of traditionalist efforts to improve the condition
of the Sudeten German minority in Czechoslovakia had been
increased English interest in the problem. This interest was a
reflection of general British willingness to tolerate, and even encourage, revision of the Versailles settlement—provided that revision came
about peacefully. Unlike the French, who tended to regard the treaty
of Versailles as sacrosanct, the British, almost from the day it was
signed in 1919, had been ready to recognize the inadequacies and
injustices of the settlement and to acquiesce in its alteration. It was
this receptiveness that had provided the occasion for Henlein to
broach the Sudeten problem in 1935.[1] As a result, on several
occasions, owing to the efforts of Henlein and his representatives in
London, highly placed Britons had inquired solicitously in Prague as
to what was being done to improve relations with the German-speak-
ing populace. This was only the beginning of a British involvement
that would play a decisive role in the development of the Sudeten
crisis during 1938. Far more important than occasional inquiries in
Prague, however, was the Berlin visit of Lord Halifax, lord president
of the Council in Neville Chamberlain's government and occasional
hunting companion of Hermann Göring, on November 19, 1937—the
same day that Hitler received Henlein's letter of submission. It was
the first of many official English initiatives concerning the Sudeten
problem, and in a sense, marked the beginning of the "Sudeten crisis."
In a three hour audience with Hitler, Halifax made it clear that
England would not oppose changes in Central Europe as long as they
did not come about by force. He mentioned specifically Danzig,
Austria, and Czechoslovakia.[2] In a nonrevolutionary international

situation, Halifax's remarks made complete sense. They indicated clearly what England would and would not accept, creating a framework in which a defined and circumscribed problem could be resolved. Unfortunately, Europe in 1937 represented anything but a stable international situation: the common understandings that bind nations together in more normal times were not there. As Hitler's disclosures on November 5, 1937 indicated, he had no interest in solving limited problems within the existing international framework. Thus, Halifax's assurance that England would accept change in Central Europe was a dangerous admission to make. Hitler now knew, if he did not before, that he had room to push for territorial revision without necessarily starting a war: change could conceivably come through negotiations. Moreover, since the English were so determined to avoid a military conflict, there were still other alternatives available which lay between force and negotiations—Hitler also knew that he could still possibly use the *threat* of force to steer negotiations toward a successful conclusion. Henlein's letter of submission brought into the open the possibility of undermining the Czech state through exploitation of a fifth column. Here again, Halifax's statements were tragically mistimed. While the British continued to think and talk in "traditionalist" terms, the Germandom traditionalists both in the Reich and in the Sudetenland were capitulating. At the very time when the British were beginning to push for a "moderate" solution to the Sudeten problem, those people in the Reich who might have supported such a solution were losing out in the struggle for power and influence. Halifax's words not only presented alternatives to Hitler, they also offered encouragement to the radicals to push for expansion—and it was not long until the radicals made themselves heard. The year 1938 was scarcely two days old when Joachim von Ribbentrop laid out his view of the future in a *Notiz für den Führer,* projecting a violent expansion of German power to the east, conceivably involving Germany in a war with Britain and France.[3]

Hitler's policy of watching and waiting was beginning to bear fruit. By early 1938 he had been advised on several approaches to change in Central Europe. The Halifax approach meant peaceful change with regard to Czechoslovakia. It was a point of view shared to some extent by conservatives in the *Auswärtiges Amt:* "chemical dissolution" was to be a phrase used by State Secretary Ernst Weizsäcker.[4] Another point of view, that advanced by Ribbentrop, contained the seeds of war. Still another, that proffered by Henlein, made the Sudeten Germans an object of Reich foreign policy and might entail either peaceful or military change depending on how the proposal was exploited. It remained to be seen which course Hitler would choose.

Apparently encouraged by the possibilities opening to him during late 1937 and early 1938, Hitler began to take more direct control of the military as well as the foreign policy apparatus. After a long series of intrigues from the radical side and inopportune blunders by their conservative enemies, Hitler ridded himself of most conservatives remaining in high office, took personal charge of the military, and through Ribbentrop assumed direct control of official foreign policy making as well. Hjalmar Schacht, president of the Reichsbank, resigned in December of 1937 in a dispute over the economy. Then, in a single day, Hitler purged both the War Ministry and the Foreign Office. On February 4, 1938, Field Marshal Werner von Blomberg, the war minister, was fired—ostensibly as a result of the scandal stirred up by his marriage to a woman alleged to be a former prostitute. With him went Werner von Fritsch, the commander-in-chief of the army and heir apparent to Blomberg, an anti-Nazi whom Himmler and Heydrich framed on a homosexual charge. Also on February 4, Hitler dismissed the foreign minister, Constantin von Neurath, as well. Neurath was kicked upstairs to the chairmanship of a council which never met and was succeeded by the ambassador to London, Joachim von Ribbentrop.[5]

There is no doubt that these far ranging changes in personnel meant both a strengthening of the radical position and an expression of Hitler's intention to embark upon a policy of revision and expansion. Hitler was, in a sense, clearing the decks for action and it was not long until the first action came. On March 12, after a crisis the details of which do not concern us here, Austria joined the Third Reich.[6] What is important about the Austrian *Anschluss* at this point is its implications for the Sudeten Germans and for the further existence of Czechoslovakia—and these implications were immense. For one thing, Hitler's easy success in Austria made it appear as though the German chancellor were operating on the basis of a carefully thought-out plan. If this were the case, which it was not, then it probably would not be long before he moved on to the next step. This impression put Germany's potential opponents under a great psychological strain. The annexation of Austria to Germany also meant that the chain of border fortifications which protected Czechoslovakia were now completely outflanked. The Czechs had built their fortress wall facing the Reich, not Austria. Most important, however, the *Anschluss* set off a near hysterical reaction among the Sudeten German population, already enflamed with nationalist passions.[7] Rumors circulated among the Sudeten Germans that they were next on the list, that Hitler would soon bring them into the Reich along with their Austrian brothers, and that this would probably occur on April 20 in honor of the führer's birthday.[8] The general radicalization process, which had been taking place in the SdP as well as among the population at large, gained momentum and in doing so exerted tremendous pressure for imminent action on the Sudeten problem. After Austria, Czechoslovakia was the next logical step anyway; but the radicalization of the Sudeten German population literally placed the Sudeten problem on Hitler's agenda.

Henlein was under even greater pressure, for he found himself in the same tenuous position from which he had sent his report to Hitler the previous November. He still had not received any reply from the führer to his note; he was still trying to pursue the same old balancing act with the Czechs and his own party, but found it increasingly difficult to manage. The rift in the SdP, although temporarily papered over the previous fall, broke out once again, exacerbated by the radicalization process. Henlein was forced once again to turn to Reich agencies for help. Already in December, for the second time, he had expelled the leading dissidents from his party.[9] On December 9, he had asked both Günther Altenburg of the AA, whose competency was Czechoslovakia, and Foreign Minister von Neurath himself to remove Fritz von Chamier, the press attaché at the mission in Prague who had been working with Henlein's opposition and ruining his relations with the mission. Henlein also asked that the *Aufbruch* journal, which again was polemicizing vociferously against his colleagues, be forbidden in the Reich.[10] Both problems were referred to Lorenz in VOMI. However, VOMI was not pushing very hard in its support of Henlein either. Although in January of 1938, VOMI had once more formally proclaimed Henlein head of the Sudeten German movement and had ordered all Reich contact with the Sudeten radicals broken off, it had not taken further steps to enforce these orders: not surprisingly, many agencies simply ignored the instructions.[11]

To complicate things even more, radicals in the Reich were clamoring for action. Bohle and Himmler—despite opposition from Ernst Eisenlohr, the German minister in Prague—had successfully persuaded Hitler to threaten reprisals against Czechoslovak citizens living in Germany because of actions allegedly taken by the Czech government to dismiss Reich Germans in the Jägerndorfer area from their jobs.[12] An increasingly violent press campaign against the Czechs was also beginning once again in the Reich, similar to the propaganda barrage of the previous October. The result was still more confusion in the SdP ranks as well as rancorous misunderstandings between the SdP and the German mission in Prague.[13] Perhaps more ominously, Henlein's deputy, Karl Hermann Frank, was still confidently predicting a radical solution to the Sudeten problem. In fact, at the very time when the Austrian crisis had reached its peak, an incident occurred involving Frank which must have reminded Henlein how precarious his own position was and how indeterminate Reich policy toward the Sudeten problem really remained.

On March 11, Minister Eisenlohr angrily cabled the AA in Berlin.[14] He had been forced to take Frank to task that very day, "because the faction in the SdP led by Frank is becoming noticeable. It would like to thwart any settlement and relaxation of tension in order finally to bring about armed conflict with the Reich." Frank had assured Eisenlohr that he would go along fully with Reich policies, but was no sooner outside the mission than he threatened to "check out" Eisenlohr's remarks in Berlin. Eisenlohr asked that neither Frank nor Henlein be received by the AA or any other ministry, but instead be referred to VOMI and there be told "what it was all about." Frank travelled to Berlin only to be refused an audience both at the AA and at VOMI.[15] Nevertheless he managed to discredit Eisenlohr by telling certain officials in Berlin that the minister had demanded that the SdP do an about-face, become parliamentarily active, and join the Czech government: if the SdP did not go along with these demands, then the Reich would disavow it entirely.[16] There was no truth to these remarks, but they evidently caused enough doubt that Eisenlohr was compelled to clarify his statements to Berlin. Although he did so, the minister protested that he was sick and tired of the SdP people playing off the different agencies in Berlin against one another, thereby bringing his authority as representative of the Reich into question.[17] On March 16, 1938, Eisenlohr could report that Frank had apparently been chastened by his rejection in Berlin. Frank had now agreed to follow Eisenlohr's instructions explicitly and to clear foreign policy speeches with the mission; Henlein also promised to meet once a week with Eisenlohr to coordinate policy.[18] But Frank's assurances soon proved to be worthless. With contacts in the Reich which were much closer to the center of power than Eisenlohr's, Frank continued to go his own way, ignoring Eisenlohr's instructions.

Henlein, on the other hand, lacking such personal connections, could not be so confident. In a conversation with the German minister to Prague, probably at the beginning of February, Henlein betrayed his lack of confidence. In direct contrast to the arrogant Frank, Henlein, according to Eisenlohr, was not clear in his own mind on any of the great issues—on whether to remain in intransigent opposition or to enter into negotiations with the government in Prague. All Henlein really knew was that he needed "support in the rear from the Reich." [19] Several weeks later, on February 23, Henlein was in Berlin, again trying apparently without success to secure more aid from VOMI.[20] By mid-March it was imperative that Henlein do something drastic on his own behalf. Two events undoubtedly impelled him to act. One was Hitler's speech of February 20 in which he spoke of the ten million Germans outside the Reich: "To these interests of the German Reich belongs also the protection of those German peoples along our frontiers who are not in a position to secure their political and spiritual freedom by their own efforts." [21] This must have sounded to the eager Henlein like an invitation to collaboration. The other much more important event was, of course, the Austrian *Anschluss:* for the excitement that the union of Austria with Germany generated made it imperative for Henlein to secure Hitler's support and to find out exactly what the Reich was going to do regarding Czechoslovakia. Once again, Henlein decided on a bold step. Last time he had written both Hitler and the foreign minister without success, or so he believed. Now, with a new man as head of the Foreign Office, perhaps he would have better luck. Accordingly, on March 17, Henlein addressed himself to Ribbentrop.[22] He lavished praise on the führer for the Austrian *Anschluss* and promised redoubled efforts in the service of a Greater German policy. This new situation, he wrote, demanded a new look at Sudeten German policy. For this purpose, he suggested scheduling a meeting with Ribbentrop very soon (anticipating this, he had already postponed for a period of

four weeks a Party Day scheduled for March 26 and 27). Henlein
added he would be grateful if two of his closest collaborators and
Eisenlohr could also be included in any conference that might take
place. This time Henlein had more success than he had dared to
expect: the führer himself agreed to speak with him.

On March 28, Henlein and Frank met for three hours with Hitler
in Berlin to ascertain what sort of action they might anticipate from
the Reich. Hess, Ribbentrop, and Lorenz were present. Eisenlohr,
significantly, was not.[23] This time, Henlein and Frank were working
together. It was, after all, in the interests of both men now to
encourage Reich intervention: Frank, because he was a radical
anyway; Henlein, because he thought that such a move was the only
thing which could save him politically. At the meeting, they both
attempted to induce Hitler to intervene massively in Czechoslovakia,
along the lines of the Austrian coup. Frank had even come equipped
with scare stories about Communist plots, arming of the Czech
auxiliary organizations, an impending coup by the Czech army, and
similar nonsense. Hitler, however, would have none of it. He did say
that he intended "to solve the Czechoslovakian problem in the not all
too distant future," but more than that he would not say. Instead, he
tried to console Henlein with flattering remarks. He stated that he
knew how beloved Henlein was and that he was the rightful leader of
the Sudeten Germans; on the basis of Henlein's popularity and
Volkstümlichkeit, he also expressed confidence that Henlein could
master the political situation. When Henlein protested that he was,
after all, only a surrogate for Hitler, Hitler replied evasively: "I'll
stand by you. Tomorrow you'll be my viceroy. I won't tolerate any
agency in the Reich making trouble for you." Here was something
encouraging at last. Hitler had ostensibly given Henlein his personal
imprimatur as leader of the Sudeten Germans. But this assurance only
solved half of Henlein's problem: he was still in the dark about any
long range intentions Hitler might have, and he had been given no
hope for any immediate intervention from the Reich. The führer had
strongly emphasized that Henlein was still responsible for events. The
balancing act was to continue with no more assistance than before.
Hitler did give Henlein a few general instructions, however, and his
words betrayed how well the traditionalist policy of "educating our
masters" had worked. Borrowing from Haushofer's proposals submitted during the secret negotiations over a year before, Hitler instructed

Henlein to make demands on the Czechs which they could not accept. Henlein blinked and repeated his instructions: "We must therefore always demand so much that we cannot be satisfied." The führer nodded assent. Hitler had borrowed yet another technique from the traditionalists as well. He expressed approval of Henlein's success in England and encouraged him to return there as soon as possible, particularly to work toward nonintervention in the Czechoslovak question. As for France, Hitler admitted that he reckoned on internal upheaval there anyway.

As the Hitler-Henlein conversation reveals, the führer's plans for Czechoslovakia had not concretized much beyond his general statements of the previous November. He was clearly not, as yet, ready to act on his own. What he was ready to do, however, was something he had been doing all along: allow someone else to test out a line of action for him, at no risk to himself and without any commitments which might tie his hands. This is the essence of his statement that Henlein was "responsible for events." He would let Henlein take the risks and then see what evolved, all the while holding out the promise of eventual action as a kind of carrot. In doing so, whether consciously or unconsciously, Hitler was choosing, however tentatively, one of the many alternatives that had been presented to him since November: he was beginning to use Henlein as a personal fifth column. On the day after the conference, Ribbentrop met again with the Sudeten leaders in the *Auswärtiges Amt* to repeat essentially what Hitler had said on the previous day. Erich Kordt, AA liaison man in Ribbentrop's *Dienststelle,* described the meeting: "Ribbentrop apparently had exact instructions from Hitler, for he expressed himself with greater definitiveness than usual or than his expertise would have permitted. Before this he had not bothered in the slightest with minority questions." [24] Kordt, who was familiar with Henlein's struggle against the radicals (Rutha had kept him informed during his stay in London), noted that Ribbentrop cast a sideways glance at several of the Sudeten leaders present when he emphasized that Henlein was the leader of the party. "I had the impression now," Kordt stated, "that despite Hitler's investing Henlein with ring and staff, the radicals—above all Karl Hermann Frank—did not have all too much respect for their 'Sudeten leader.' "

There is some doubt as to what Henlein really gained from his long awaited visit with Hitler. He had Hitler's assurance that he was leader of the Sudeten Germans, but what did that mean to the radicals in the SdP—men who swore loyalty but then went their own way? He had some instructions, to be sure; but they went little beyond putting the official stamp of approval on a "dual track" policy which entailed being outwardly sincere, while inwardly pursuing other goals. This was little more than what Henlein had been doing all along anyway, walking the tightrope between the Czechs and the radicals in his own party. Besides, how could he pursue Hitler's goals without some knowledge of the führer's plans? The Ribbentrop meeting merely served to underline Henlein's difficulties, and though Henlein was apparently unaware of it, the session cast serious shadows over the whole trip to Berlin. Henlein had ostensibly won recognition as leader of the Sudeten Germans, but Ribbentrop apparently had doubts about this. Even if sincere, Hitler's assurances would do Henlein precious little public good. In the absence of German intervention, he obviously could not publicize this support. Henlein returned to Czechoslovakia, then, with his work cut out for him. Without specific instructions from Berlin, he had to negotiate with the Czechs in such a way as to propose a maximal, yet credible program toward Sudeten German autonomy, while at the same time being careful not to blunder into a settlement. Simultaneously, despite growing pressure for radicalization throughout the SdP and the Sudetenland itself, he had to try to keep his people in line. Henlein was barely in Prague again before he was made rudely aware of how difficult all of this would be.

It was becoming evident that the Sudeten crisis had a momentum all its own, far beyond any control or steering from Berlin. Excitement among the Sudeten Germans over the Austrian *Anschluss* and an expectancy that the same thing was going to happen to them—and soon—had not waned. On the contrary, the feeling seemed to be spreading, apparently spurred on by the radicals on both sides of the border. Minister Eisenlohr reported rumors to the effect that April 10, the day of an announced plebiscite for Austria, would be the day of *Anschluss* for the Sudetenland.[25] The *Turnverband* was said to be arming itself. The SdP flag was being unfurled and hung from churches and city halls in town after town, as the people celebrated the voluntary amalgamation of the other national parties, the *Bund der Landwirte* and the Christian Socialists, into the SdP.

Less than a week after his return to Prague, then, Henlein came to the mission in Prague with desperate complaints.[26] All along the borders, Reich party, SA, and SS units were spreading the word that *Anschluss* was coming on April 10, when German troops would march in. These units were also urging the population in the border area to form partisan units. In Böhmisch-Krumau, large numbers of people were having uniforms made in preparation for the coming invasion. Swastika flags were appearing everywhere. In Prague, radical German students were inciting people against the SdP, whose policies they said were only holding up union with Germany. "To avoid serious complications," the mission reported, "Konrad Henlein, who regards the situation as extremely dangerous, is asking for stringent measures to stop this propaganda." The SdP itself took steps to counter the radicalization. Its leadership denied the rumors as fast as they cropped up. It also sent out directives that during April emphasis would be put on internal consolidation and not on public rallies.[27] The SdP leadership seemed almost relieved, it was noted, that the Czechs had issued a ban on all meetings. But even this proclamation was a two-edged sword. The radio station in Leipzig was implying that the ban pertained only to the SdP, which in reality was not the case, and thus stirred up the people even more.[28]

On April 4, the SdP complained again about the illegal antics of local Reich party units on the border, which were now promising weapons deliveries to the Sudeten German populace.[29] The idea of setting up a uniformed, but unarmed volunteer service had originally come up in Henlein's talk with Hitler but had not been implemented. Now, some radicals were apparently reviving the idea—only this time there was talk of an armed militia. In Reichenberg and other towns, SdP people were building up an *Ordner* service along SS lines. They approached the consul in Reichenberg for arms, and when this was refused them, they expressed the intention of approaching SS formations across the border to arrange supplies and training. Minister Eisenlohr reported that the "key role in the psychological and organizatorial mobilization of these Sudeten German partisan units" was being played by one Rolf Hein, "who in the opinion of local Sudeten German units is an agent of the Reich German *Sicherheitsdienst*." [30] Berlin's response was that the SdP could temporarily drop the idea of setting up any kind of a volunteer service.[31]

Not only was Henlein having trouble keeping the SdP in line, his second task—negotiating with the Czechs—was actually increasing radicalization and dissent. Karl Hermann Frank's secretary, Dr. Kurt Eckert, returned from northern Bohemia, describing the situation there as "catastrophic and convulsive":

> All sectors of the population, from factory owners to the unemployed, are openly characterizing the Sudeten German party negotiations with the Czechoslovakian government—even if [the party] was striving for autonomy as its maximum goal—as treason to the people, which would cost Henlein his whole following. . . . The tension is so great that one shot would suffice for the Sudeten Germans in order to start a blood bath among the Czechs.[32]

Eckert's report was clearly exaggerated, but it serves if not as an exact description of the situation, then at least as a good indication of what Frank and the radicals were aiming for. He continued: "If the SdP would try to speak at all about the possibility of conciliation politics today, regardless of on what basis, it would unquestionably be hooted down." Eckert and Frank felt that "without the help of the Reich, it would be impossible to keep discipline," especially in light of the fact that the people were taking Hitler's words from his speech of February 20 (complaining about the ten million Germans left outside the Reich by Versailles) quite literally. Eisenlohr felt sufficiently alarmed about Eckert's report to ask that the Reich broadcast something to cool down the situation. He also recommended that the SdP and Reich agencies coordinate their commentaries on the speech which Henlein was preparing for delivery at the SdP convention in Karlsbad on April 24.[33] But coordination of a fifth column was not as easy as it might seem. In Berlin, VOMI was having troubles of its own, indicating that either someone was not following orders or—more likely—that there were no clear-cut orders to follow. On April 9 VOMI asked the top SA leadership to investigate the dangerous activities of some of its local units along the border: it had been reported that sixteen truckloads of SA men, thirty to a truck, were cruising the border near Friedland, yelling across, "Ein Volk, ein Reich, ein Führer." [34] VOMI also felt constrained to warn the Propaganda Ministry against any commentaries on the radio apart from the official news.[35]

The same day that VOMI was urging the SA to bring its radical personnel to heel, Henlein was once again turning to the Reich for help. He requested a meeting with either the foreign minister or the state secretary to discuss the critical situation in the Sudetenland, perhaps hopeful that the mounting crisis would at last produce some meaningful results.[36] But if Henlein thought that the heightened tension and increased radicalization would now move Hitler to some kind of action, he was sadly mistaken. This time not even the foreign minister received him. He had to be content to see Lorenz at VOMI.[37] Still left to his own devices, Henlein continued his precarious balancing act. With his radical followers on the one side and the Czechoslovak government on the other, Henlein jacked up his demands in a speech at the SdP congress in Karlsbad on April 24 and 25, 1938, but he still insisted that autonomy was the maximum goal.[38] Rejecting the governmental proposal for the solution of the minorities problem as embodied in the Minorities Statute, Henlein put forth his own plan—the Eight Demands of the Karlsbad Program. The Eight Points were disguised to look like autonomy, but if actually realized, would have been tantamount to union with Germany. The eighth point demanded freedom to embrace "German *Volkstum* and the German *Weltanschauung.*" There could be little doubt what "German *Weltanschauung*" was. The program was admirably conceived: guaranteed to be rejected by the Czechs, yet obvious in its purpose to any Sudeten German who cared to read between the lines. In short, Henlein had managed exactly what Hitler had asked for in March, behaving as if willing to negotiate with the Czechs without actually bringing about any solution to the crisis. Eisenlohr commented on the speech: "It can be said in general that Henlein has succeeded in keeping a path for negotiations with the government open without disappointing his followers. In the latter case, the tone of German radio and press has probably been decisive." [39] For once, some degree of coordination had been achieved between the various Germandom agencies.

Despite the escalating internationalization and radicalization, Hitler still had not set down a definite plan for precipitate action to solve the Czechoslovak problem. One indication of this was his remark to General Alfred Jodl, probably soon after the Austrian *Anschluss,* that he was in no hurry to handle the Czech question. First, he would have to digest Austria.[40] Another indication was a conversation which Hitler had with General Wilhelm Keitel on April 22 about military contingency plans for attack on Czechoslovakia (the so-called *Fall Grün* "Operation Green").[41] Three alternatives came under discussion. The first, sudden attack without warning, Hitler rejected out of hand as too dangerous in light of world opinion. Rather, preparations should be made for the other two eventualities. The first of them, war after diplomatic discussions had led to a crisis, was the less favorable since it would give the enemy time to prepare. Hitler favored the third alternative: quick action after an incident—say, perhaps the murder of the German minister, Eisenlohr (!). While Hitler, for political and strategic reasons, would have preferred this third contingency, it remained just that—a proposal. He did not establish any concrete program for engineering such an incident; nor did he give any indication when he hoped to act decisively. From this point on, as in the past, the führer remained the improviser and his position only evolved under the pressure of events, although he made sure that military contingency plans took every eventuality into consideration.

Hitler was partly holding back at this point because of Mussolini's plans in the Mediterranean. He made this most plain in a conversation with his *Wehrmacht* adjutant, Major Rudolf Schmundt, just before the führer's visit to Rome in early May of 1938.[42] If Mussolini considered his work completed, Hitler noted—*i.e.*, if after Italy's difficult time with Abyssinia and the involvement in Spain, Mussolini had no desire to keep France and Britain busy in the Mediterranean—then Czechoslovakia would have to wait. As Schmundt recorded it: "If yes, Czechia distant future . . . return with empty pockets." If Mussolini did intend to extend his African imperium, however, then "return with Czechia in the bag." Disturbed by Ribbentrop's aggressive language during Hitler's visit, the duce and his foreign minister, Count Ciano, resisted German offers of a military alliance, which meant that war between the Western powers and Italy did not appear a likelihood. Hitler, it seemed, did return to Germany with empty pockets.[43] With the failure of this contingency, the führer was temporarily stymied; but no sooner had he returned from Italy, than hope presented itself from another direction. While the conference in Rome had been going on, Henlein was once again in London, for the first time since October of 1937, carrying out his instructions to "woo" the English.[44] This task was certainly more attractive to him than trying to keep order back home. The English seemed to believe everything he said or at least were overjoyed to hear his moderate language. Moreover, the publicity certainly did not hurt

Henlein's position at home. On the one hand, it could possibly strengthen his moderate image with the Czechs; on the other, the promise of English help toward a peaceful solution of the Sudeten problem might help Henlein check the overeager radicals within his own party. At any rate, Henlein once again achieved success in England: he conferred with Harold Nicolson, an influential conservative MP; renewed his contact with Vansittart and Christie; and even managed to impress the skeptical Churchill to some extent.[45] On his way back home, Henlein stopped off at the Obersalzberg to report to Hitler on the junket.

By this time, the English were clearly coming around to the point of view that the Sudeten problem could be solved with a little effort and good will. On May 7, the British ambassador to Berlin, Sir Neville Henderson, had told Ernst Woermann, head of the Europe section of the AA political department, that the British would push hard for a settlement. He added, "the situation is so, that the French would act for the Czechs and Germany for the Sudeten Germans. England would help Germany in this case . . . ."[46] That same day, Henderson gave Woermann a personal memorandum:

> His Majesty's Government in the United Kingdom are now urging the Czechoslovak Government to seek without delay a solution of this problem on comprehensive lines by direct negotiations with the Sudeten Germans. His Majesty's Government wish to inform the German Government of this and to express the hope that the German Government will be ready to use their influence to promote a settlement.[47]

Three days later, Henderson's assistant, Sir Ivone Kirkpatrick, confided to Otto von Bismarck of the AA political department, "if the German government would inform the English government confidentially of what solution it was striving for, then he believed to be able to assure, that the English government would exert such pressure in Prague that the Czechoslovak government would be forced to accept the German wishes."[48]

These remarks by highly placed British officials offered a golden opportunity for Hitler to take the Sudeten problem, or rather the problem of the further existence of Czechoslovakia, in hand. But still he did not do so; nor did he have to. The British offers to help by pressuring the Czechs meant that events could proceed on the steam still inherent in the situation. Eventually, the friction resulting from

British pressure from one direction and the gradual raising of the ante by the Sudeten Germans on the other might well produce enough tension so that others, in a panic, would do what Hitler always preferred: create a crisis situation which he could then exploit. A second directive on Operation Green, prepared and submitted on May 20 by the *Wehrmacht* on Hitler's instructions, clearly reveals the führer's intention to let the Czech problem stew for the time being. The directive again defined the political contingencies under which Hitler felt he might attack Czechoslovakia:

> It is not my intention to smash Czechoslovakia through military action without provocation in the near future, unless an irreversible development of the political situation within Czechoslovakia compels me to or if political developments in Europe create a particularly favorable opportunity which may never again return.[49]

More dramatic proof for Hitler's improvisational approach to political decisions could not be found. On the one hand, the statement seems to suggest that intervention might be far less remote than the Hossbach memorandum in late 1937 had anticipated: Hitler now felt that he might have to take action even if he was not planning to do so at this time—if events should seem to compel him to action. On the other hand, the führer had not really moved appreciably closer to making a final decision than in his conversation with Major Schmundt in April of 1938, which had stressed Mussolini's plans as vital to the course Germany would follow: he still let his decision rest on what others might or might not do.

Hitler could not have known it, but his wait-and-see approach was already making others extremely nervous at this point. On May 21, just a day after the new Operation Green directive had been secretly prepared, a dramatic event caused Hitler to alter his stance once again: the Czechs mobilized. The entire maneuver had come as a response to alarming reports of German troop movements in the direction of the Czech border. After a weekend of frenetic diplomatic inquiries indicated that the German military activity posed no immediate threat to Czechoslovakia, the brief crisis ended with a flurry of newspaper reports on how firm action had stopped Hitler short. In reality, however, the upshot of the crisis was neither a relieved West nor a chastened Hitler. Frightened by visions of impending war, the English now pushed even harder to force a "solution" of the Sudeten situation. Even more important, Hitler—furious over the affront and apparently in an attempt to save face—once again secretly changed his approach to Operation Green. On May 30, he stated: "It is my irreversible decision to destroy Czechoslovakia through military action in the foreseeable future." [50] But even if his resolve were acquiring new urgency, Hitler remained the improviser, without concrete plans. The directive continued:

> It is the responsibility of the political leadership to await or to bring about the appropriate time politically and militarily.
> An irreversible change in conditions within Czechoslovakia or other political events in Europe which create a surprisingly favorable opportunity which may never reoccur can cause me to act precipitately.

During the ensuing month, Hitler's position evolved still further, perhaps as the Czech "affront" worked on his pride. By June 18, his intentions had become still clearer, to the point where he was willing to project a tentative date for action. "The solution of the Czech question on my own is the short range goal of my political intent. I am determined to exploit any favorable political opportunity to realize this goal after October 1." [51] By the summer of 1938, then, events had moved so far that Hitler apparently would take advantage of the first chance he got *after October 1* (the date when military preparations could be completed) to handle Czechoslovakia. For Hitler, the "foreseeable future" was now pinned down, taking into account the traditional autumn deadline for war in Central Europe as imposed by the exigencies of the harvest season and the weather.

The several directives that Hitler issued in the spring of 1938 not only show an evolving stance on the dictator's part toward *when* he would tackle the Czech problem, they also shed light on Hitler's changing attitudes toward the *methods* he might choose. In the Operation Green directive of May 20, Hitler had stated that the development of political conditions *within* Czechoslovakia might conceivably prompt him to take swift action. This was something new. The previous November he had still spoken only in terms of the general international situation, projecting the possibility of Mediterranean war or civil war in France. Now he spoke primarily in terms of a Czech internal crisis—a crisis which would almost certainly involve the Sudeten Germans and their activities. Apparently, Henlein's offer to the führer was finally bearing fruit: what Hitler was contemplating here bore a very close resemblance to the fifth column alternative proposed earlier by Henlein.

While Henlein's cooperation was important to the potential success of such a fifth column approach, it was even more essential that there was some kind of Reich agency which could coordinate the internal undermining of the Czech state. By the summer of 1938, again without any real effort on his part, Hitler had that too: for by this time, the *Volksdeutsche Mittelstelle* had taken official and virtually complete charge of ethnic German affairs.[52] During the spring and summer of 1938, as the Sudeten crisis was approaching its apogee, VOMI reached that position of dominance in *Volkstum* affairs which men in Germandom work, both radicals and traditionalists, had dreamed about for years. VOMI was rapidly expanding its mandate as the increasingly tense international situation demanded more discipline and control in relations between the Reich and German minorities. Its warnings to the SA and especially to the Propaganda Ministry on its excesses in April of 1938, reflected a developing self-confidence. Lorenz was now present at all meetings where Germandom abroad was discussed: for example, he had been present during Hitler's conference with Henlein in March. The AA, too, had learned to respect the VOMI organization. Sudeten Germans coming to the mission in Prague with complaints and requests were invariably referred to VOMI. Even officials of foreign governments who had occasion to discuss minority problems while in Berlin knew where to turn—as, for example, Prime Minister von Daranyi of Hungary, who requested conversations with Lorenz in April of 1938.[53] On April 30, 1938, Hess directed all ministries to consult with VOMI before allocating any funds in connection with ethnic Germans.[54] In May, Lorenz issued definite orders to the Germans in Poland to get together: he was no longer merely serving as mediator in the quarrels.[55] With regard to Czechoslovakia and the Sudeten Germans, VOMI was busy setting up the mechanism for a controlled fifth column. Henlein had returned from his junket to England in May to meet a less than encouraging situation at home. The national hysteria which had followed the Austrian *Anschluss* continued undiminished. Minister Eisenlohr reported from Prague: "Hardly anyone thinks any longer of autonomy, on however comprehensive a scale. The overwhelming majority, in fact almost the whole population, hopes for *Anschluss* with the German Reich and expects it in the immediate future." [56] In light of this feeling and the radical activity which undoubtedly accompanied and encouraged it, it was imperative that Henlein, with the help of VOMI, establish some effective control mechanisms. On June 3, 1938, Henlein met with Lorenz and set up a system whereby Henlein could give orders to his party, down to the *Kreisleiter* level, in case of emergency. Together they established a network of agents, each responsible for a certain *Kreis* within Czechoslovakia and each stationed on the German border as close to his assigned Sudeten *Kreis* as possible. In the event that Czechs cut off communication, these men would relay messages to VOMI. In Bad Elster a central command post was set up, through which Henlein, should he have to operate from Reich soil, could pass on orders through these same agents.[57] At the same meeting, Henlein, still in the dark as to Hitler's exact intentions, asked Lorenz what he should do if the Czechs should suddenly give in to all his conditions and in turn demand that he enter the government. Lorenz, presumably just as ignorant of Hitler's plans, did not answer the question. So Henlein volunteered a suggestion: he would say yes, with the condition that the Czechs change their foreign policy and "the Czechs will never accede to that." [58] Thus, without Hitler's instructions and perhaps without his knowledge, VOMI and Henlein were already setting up a working fifth column, not only by constructing a command mechanism, but also by making elementary political decisions. To further solidify its political connections with the SdP, VOMI sent a "legal advisor," Dr. Herbert Kier, to work with the SdP negotiating team. On June 14, Kier arrived in Prague and "immediately entered the inner councils of the SdP." [59]

It is difficult to pinpoint exactly why VOMI was establishing a bureaucratic mechanism for the Sudeten fifth column at this particular juncture. Possibly it was acting on its own, just as it had in the past as it gained authority and initiative in *Volkstumspolitik*. The chaotic state of Sudeten politics combined with the tense international situation certainly invited such intervention. On the other hand, Lorenz and Henlein met so soon following Hitler's May 30 directive—four days afterward—that it is logical to suspect some connection. There is no evidence, however, to ascertain how much VOMI might have known at this point about Operation Green. If Lorenz were familiar with the directive, then he may have drawn his conclusions from the phrase that it was "the responsibility of the political leadership to await or to bring about the appropriate time [for intervention] politically and militarily." Hitler seemed to be committing himself more and more to a fifth column approach, without in any way deviating from his policy of letting others do the work for him: his vague call to action was an open invitation to further initiative in Sudeten politics, albeit within a slightly narrowed framework. Whatever Lorenz's knowledge of Hitler's directive might have been, he was certainly acting in a manner consistent with the führer's mood, even if at root he may have merely intended to expand the activity of his agency.

By the summer of 1938, VOMI had achieved such a dominant position in ethnic German affairs, that Hitler at last moved to recognize the fact. On July 2 Hitler commissioned the *Volksdeutsche Mittelstelle* "with the unified coordination of all state and party offices, as well as with the utilization of funds at the disposal of all agencies for ethnic German and borderland questions." [60] It was a momentous decision. Hitler had at last intervened personally and definitively to centralize the hitherto freely competitive field of Germandom politics. No longer could anyone and everyone pursue his own policies with regard to German minorities, confidently claiming the führer's mandate. From now on it was clear that only one agency would act under the führer's orders in ethnic German affairs.[61] It was also clear that VOMI would have the means to act: funds from the various Germandom agencies now under its complete control totalled some fifty to sixty million marks per year—the equivalent of the whole AA budget! [62]

Other high Nazi leaders quickly recognized VOMI's authoritative position. On July 6 Ribbentrop, in his capacity as plenipotentiary of the NSDAP for foreign policy questions, named Lorenz as his deputy.[63] At the same time, VOMI acted to elbow out its competition, at least as far as the Sudeten German question was concerned. When, on July 15, State Secretary Weizsäcker of the AA asked SS-*Oberführer* Behrends of VOMI how the negotiations between Henlein and Milan Hodža (the Czech foreign minister) were going, Behrends replied evasively. The *Volksdeutsche Mittelstelle* had received no information for the longest time, Behrends assured him—and this with VOMI's own man on the negotiating team.[64] VOMI also almost immediately began to extend its activities into broader and broader areas, including ethnic German economic interests.[65] On July 7, Behrends was directed to take a seat on the board of directors of the *Deutsche Stiftung*, a quasi-public trust which had widespread investments in ethnic German settlements all over Europe.[66]

By recognizing VOMI's predominance, Hitler not only ended the Germandom struggle simply by extending recognition to the victor; he also assured himself of the vital command mechanism he would need to effectively manipulate a fifth column and undermine Czechoslovakia from within. It soon became clear, however, that regardless of how powerful VOMI might have become, there were too many other dynamic forces at work for the Sudeten crisis to be simply "steered." Despite VOMI's success in shaping an institutionalized fifth column in the Sudetenland, it was not successful in totally dampening and coordinating the activities of the independent radicals. The dilemma seemed to be organizing and disciplining the foreign ethnic groups to act radically, yet not letting them become too overtly radical. Even with a network of agents and channels of command, independent activities still could flourish. For example, on June 9, 1938, SS-*Obergruppenführer* Lorenz reported to the AA that the SdP was distributing leaflets in Czech, urging all citizens to disobey the state. He could not find out where the leaflets were coming from. Karl Hermann Frank seemed to think they originated with the Gestapo; the Gestapo denied it. One of Frank's colleagues thought that perhaps military intelligence was behind the pamphlets, but the War Ministry denied such allegations. The Czechs were claiming that Hans Krebs was the guilty party; yet Krebs was just as vociferous in his denials. Finally in light of the stir the incident was causing, Henlein was asked to conduct an investigation of the problem.[67] Such uncontrolled radical activities did not only originate on the local level. Minister Eisenlohr complained that Walter Wannemacher, senior editor of the main SdP organ, *Die Zeit*, had revealed some odd directives for party journalistic activity to Erwin F. Stranik, Prague representative of the *Berliner Tageblatt*:

> Reports on Czechoslovakia cannot be inflammatory enough. . . . No negotiations between the SdP and the government would take place. Demand for autonomy long since outdated. Even if the government should offer it, SdP would refuse. . . . To Stranik's objection that he had the opposite instructions from the *Berliner Tageblatt*, Wannemacher replied that all authoritative Reich

agencies approved his [Wannemacher's] position. Stranik should not bother to learn any Czech any more, since German entry could be expected imminently.

In reporting the incident, Eisenlohr complained that these instructions violated the guidelines which he had received and recommended that the *Volksdeutsche Mittelstelle* be informed at once.[68]

Thus, even though a relative international calm set in during the summer months after the Czech mobilization crisis, there was no lack of frenetic activity just beneath the surface of official international relations: forces continued to keep the Sudeten pot boiling. All the while, confident that others would keep things going for him, Hitler continued his wait-and-see approach. He was right. While the führer seemed to be doing nothing, others—for a variety of reasons—felt compelled to do something. Among them were the British. By this time ranking British officials, warned by the opposition of Hitler's fall deadline, were determined to engineer a solution to the Sudeten problem before September. They had somehow concluded that unless a settlement were reached by the annual Nazi Party Day, Hitler himself would act. Henderson, the British ambassador in Berlin, wrote of this possibility to Lord Halifax: "It may be taken for granted that Herr Hitler at Nuremberg will define Germany's standpoint in Sudeten question." Henderson urged action, arguing that Hitler might otherwise alter what he would accept for a solution. Henderson feared that Hitler might say "that [because the] British . . . failed to bring Beneš to reason, Germany claims her inalienable right to secure herself in her own way the lives and interests of her German brethren across the frontier." [69] Henderson's appeal seems to have converted Halifax, for he in turn wrote to Campbell, his representative in Paris: "It seemed clear from information at our disposal . . . that Herr Hitler was greatly preoccupied with Czechoslovakia and that he was moving to a point where he would determine, if he had not already done so, to secure a settlement by the end of September . . . ." [70] The British seemed determined, then, to solve the Sudeten problem before Nuremberg and were convinced that internationalization was the way to do it. On August 3 Lord Walter Runciman, the former ship-building tycoon, with few credentials for the task awaiting him, arrived in Prague to mediate between the Czechs and the Sudeten Germans. He, too, was impressed by the urgency of the situation. "If an accommodation is not reached, I fear an awkward speech at Nuremberg," he wrote Halifax. "There is very little time to be lost: barely a fortnight before the Nuremberg oration." [71] Apprehensive of delay, sure of a Hitler "deadline," confident that the problem could be solved somehow, the British pushed the Czechs to make concessions. But still the negotiations produced nothing in the way of agreement. People in both the Sudeten German and Czech camps were polarized in their positions. As the deadlock continued, it was not only the British who felt compelled to move: many in the Sudeten German party were itching to act as well. Hitler's wait-and-see approach had heightened already existing tensions within the SdP.

With the strengthening of the radical undercurrent in the SdP, a rift began to develop between some of the more moderate members of the Sudeten German negotiating team and Karl Hermann Frank. During July, Dr. Herbert Kier, VOMI's man on the scene, reported that many Sudeten SdP leaders were afraid that a solution of the Sudeten German problem by force would lead to a frightful massacre of the population. "The concern was so great that the leaders had expressed the urgent hope that a violent solution would not be undertaken." They had hesitated to give this warning themselves, however, for fear of giving the impression that they lacked personal courage.[72] One member of the SdP, Karl Hermann Frank, did not shy away from violent solutions, regardless of the consequences. His constant remarks to this effect were bothering other members of the negotiation team, such as Ernst Kundt, Gustav Peters, Alfred Rosche, and Wilhelm Sebekowsky. During party deliberations, Frank was constantly dropping bombs like the following: "It's all a matter of complete indifference what's being negotiated. Things would come about completely differently." Each time he made such statements, he would refer ominously to the special sources of information at his disposal. Kundt, especially, was disturbed by Frank's constant "indiscretions." If there were any basis to what Frank said, he complained, then what was the point in continuing the negotiations? If Frank were lying, on the other hand, then there was the danger that the Sudeten Germans would get the blame if the negotiations were broken off. By this time, the Runciman mission was in Czechoslovakia and it would not do if the English lord got the impression that the Sudeten leaders were not seriously seeking a peaceful solution.[73] To complicate matters even further, the negotiating team, and everyone else for that matter, had lost touch completely with their leader, Konrad Henlein. He had secreted himself somewhere and could only be reached through one man—Karl Hermann Frank.[74] The negotiations in Prague were now reaching a critical stage as Beneš himself stepped in to take over the talks on the Czech side.[75] Beneš's appearance immediately raised the specter which Henlein had feared all along and which had prompted his question to Lorenz in July: what if the Czechs now gave in entirely and caught the Sudeten German negotiating team in a trap? This question also bothered the members of the negotiating team. Henlein was apparently not to be had for an answer, so Kundt, speaking for his colleagues, turned desperately to Ribbentrop via the German mission in Prague. But Ribbentrop was not helpful either. He expressed the desire not to be approached so often by the Sudeten German party for advice. Henlein had received his instructions; there was no reason for people to keep appearing from Prague to get decisions on specific questions. Henlein and his people would simply have to help themselves. Ribbentrop declined to do anything more than repeat verbally the last instructions he had heard Hitler give—over five months before: "Always negotiate and do not let the thread break; but always demand more than the opposing side can offer." [76]

There are several possible reasons why Henlein secluded himself and kept his negotiators in the dark. He may by now have known too much. In an interview with Colonel Christie in Zurich on August 13, arranged by Henlein's liaison man in London, Walter Brand, Henlein had spoken for the first time about the possibility of war.[77] (By this time Henlein was under the close scrutiny of the SD, on express orders from Heydrich.)[78] Had Hitler revealed more to Henlein than would have been commensurate with intensive bargaining, then it made sense to keep in the background and allow the uninitiated negotiating team to keep an honest face in the negotiations, with no risk of betraying compromising information. It is also possible that Henlein did not know enough—that Hitler had not as yet revealed to the Sudeten leader any details of what he intended to do. In this case, it is quite possible that Henlein's nerves were not up to the strain of Hitler's wait-and-see policy: consequently, he had absented himself totally from the public eye, while hoping that eventually Hitler would step in and resolve the contradictions for him. By late August, it suddenly appeared that Hitler was about to do just that. On August

26, Hitler revealed to Karl Hermann Frank that he had decided on war.[79] At the same time, he ordered Frank to provoke incidents in Czechoslovakia. It was significant that now, when Hitler finally informed the top leadership that it was war he was after, it was the more radical SdP leader whom he told first. Frank must have been delighted. As for Henlein, however much he wanted Hitler to step in and rescue the Sudeten Germans, it is unlikely that he wanted war at this point: he simply did not have the stomach for it. It was probably for this reason that Henlein sent his liaison man, Friedrich Bürger, scurrying to Munich on August 29 with orders to see Hitler immediately.

Henlein had been conferring with various British officials about certain English proposals which, if implemented, might be a way to avoid war. He had spoken with Lord Runciman on August 18 and again on August 22 in Marienbad with Frank Ashton-Gwatkin, Runciman's assistant on the mission. In this second conversation, Ashton-Gwatkin had made proposals which Frank termed "dangerous for us." Once more, on August 28, just after Frank returned from Berlin, Henlein spoke again with Ashton-Gwatkin.[80] But if Henlein now was relaying any concrete English proposals through Bürger, Hitler was having none of them. England was bluffing, Hitler assured Bürger, to gain time. No, he would not meet with any English minister; England would not attack, and even if it did, it would find Germany armed and ready. Now is the most favorable time for an attack on Czechoslovakia, Hitler went on, by December it would be too late. By then, they [the Czechs] would have arrested Henlein. As for Henlein, the führer wanted to see him on the first or second day in September.[81] The date turned out to be ideal for Henlein: on August 31, Ashton-Gwatkin once again spoke with Henlein, urging the Sudeten leader to see Hitler and to relay a message from Runciman to the effect that Anglo-German relations could be greatly improved if Hitler would facilitate settlement of the Sudeten problem.[82]

Armed with the latest British proposal, Henlein himself went to Berchtesgaden to see the führer on September 1. Hitler informed him that since the English had agreed to make it an international problem [!], he [Hitler] was going to take the situation in hand. As Henlein later revealed, Hitler informed him that the "finishing off" [*Erledigung*] would come in September. In the meantime Henlein should continue negotiating. Now Henlein knew for certain, if he had not

before, that Hitler was determined to have war. The revelation must
have discomforted him: he wanted Hitler's intervention; but war was
another thing. Yet the Sudeten leader was not in a position to protest
too much either and he certainly must have known that all too well.
As Hitler dismissed Henlein, he is reputed to have said, "Long live the
war—even if it lasts two to eight years." [83]

Henlein returned to Czechoslovakia to inform the relieved
English that Hitler really did not want war: Henlein was becoming an
accomplished liar. Now, it seemed at long last that his troubles were
solved. All he had to do was carry on his negotiating game for a little
while longer and the führer would intervene. But once again, events
overtook him—and perhaps Hitler, too. This time it was the Czechs
who acted. Under immense pressure from the British and acting under
threat of war, Beneš began to make wide ranging concessions to the
Sudeten Germans—concessions which were approaching the fulfill-
ment of the Karlsbad program which Henlein still insisted to be his
basis for negotiations. Some of these concessions Beneš offered to the
Sudeten German negotiating team on August 30 as Henlein was
leaving for Berchtesgaden. The new offer came very close to matching
the Karlsbad demands, but not quite.[84] Consequently, on September
2, the Sudeten negotiators rejected the proposal. Then, less than a
week later, on September 7, Beneš dropped his so-called Fourth Plan
in the laps of the Sudeten Germans.[85] As Henlein had feared, it was all
there: complete acceptance of everything the SdP had demanded. Dr.
Alfred Rosche and Dr. Rudolf Schickedanz, both members of the
negotiating team, spoke in terms of 95 percent of their demands
having been satisfied.[86] Even Frank, totally dumbfounded, mentioned
the figure 90 percent. "The new government proposal," he said,
"covers all the basic demands raised in Karlsbad." [87] What was
Henlein to do? If he refused to accept, he and his party would lose the
moral advantage and bear the brunt of blame for not wanting to settle
the Sudeten question peacefully. There must have been another worry
in the back of his mind, too. He still presumably did not know
precisely when the führer would act. For all he knew, the Czech
capitulation might even have caused the führer to change his mind.
Not to accept might well leave Henlein high and dry. On the other
hand, to accept entailed risks as well. The Sudeten population was in
a decidedly radical mood. Again, as in March and April, rumors were
circulating and everywhere incidents were flaring up. Reports came

into Chemnitz, in Saxony, that in the Czechoslovakian town of Weipert SdP auxiliaries were removing all Czech names from street signs and stores. The local SdP office claimed to have orders to provoke incidents constantly, leading to a high point by the following Tuesday (September 12).[88] Apparently, Frank was carrying out his instructions well. Given this growing radicalism, there was no telling what would happen if Henlein accepted the proposals. Again there was the führer to consider. Were he still bent on war, to accept the Czech plan might well eliminate the possibility of the very incident Hitler was looking for to provoke it and Henlein was scarcely in a position to provoke the wrath of the führer.

There was still one possible "out." The Nuremberg Party Day was coming up in a week (Henlein was already in Nuremberg awaiting the occasion) and surely Hitler would make his intentions known in the course of that annual celebration. All sides were expecting precipitate action on the part of the Reich—action to be signalled by the führer's speech on September 12. If the SdP could only delay until then, something was sure to break. Fortunately, another propitious incident just "happened" to give the SdP the very excuse it needed to stall the Czechs. On September 7, Frank had sent his deputies Fritz Köllner, Franz May, and Hans Neuwirth to the town of Mährisch-Ostrau to investigate charges that the Czechoslovak State Police had arrested and mistreated some local Germans, accusing them of spying and smuggling weapons. Frank was afraid that the police would extract "false" confessions of plots to incite an armed uprising. While the three men were investigating the situation, Franz May got himself struck by a policeman in the course of a demonstration. All three were taken to the gendarmerie.[89] It was an episode reminiscent of the one in Teplitz-Schönau the previous year. It is not possible to say with certainty whether the incident came as a result of heightened tensions or whether it was staged from the start. In all likelihood, the incident was not perpetrated in direct response to the Czech offer, for it came on the same day. There was no time for Henlein, in Nuremberg, to issue any such directive; he had probably not as yet even received word of the proposal. If the encounter had been stage-managed, then it was probably Frank's doing (after all, Hitler had ordered him to stage incidents), perhaps to set the stage for the radical solution which he personally favored. Whether staged by Frank or not, or for what purpose, considering the widespread radical activity on the part of the SdP rank and file, the incident certainly comes as no surprise. At any rate, the SdP leaders immediately seized upon it as a drowning man seizes a life raft. They broke off negotiations until such time as the Czechs would apologize and bring the guilty parties to justice. The Czechs complied and negotiations were rescheduled—for September 13, the day after Hitler's speech.[90]

As the Party Day approached, speeches by Goebbels and Göring on September 10 added fuel to the flames. Göring's slanderous attack on the Czechs was so vituperous that it put even the crudities of Goebbel's rhetoric in the shade.

> We know, [Göring screamed], that it's intolerable how that little fragment of a people down there—no one knows where they came from—constantly persecutes and molests a cultural people. We do know though that it is not just these half-pints. Behind them stands Moscow, behind them stands the eternal Jewish-Bolshevik fiend. In the face of this ridiculous attempt to intimidate us, I would like to assure one thing: we have always been warriors but never cowards [*Schiesser aber niemals Scheisser*].[91]

Then, on September 12, Hitler himself spoke.[92] He, too, ranted on about Beneš and the Czechs. As his speech built to a crescendo, everyone waited for him to reach that final stage of apoplexy where he would confront the world with something irreversible—an ultimatum, a demand for a plebiscite. But nothing of the sort happened: Hitler still left the door to peace, as well as his options, open.

Next day Henlein and his associates left Nuremberg for Eger. Hitler had still not found, or created, that incident which might never reoccur. If he were going to war with Czechoslovakia, as he had indicated to the Sudeten leaders, the moment apparently had not yet come. Now the SdP leaders were faced with the necessity of reopening negotiations after they had already been offered everything they had ever asked for. As they reached the frontier, news reached them that disturbances were flaring up all over the place. No doubt the fragmentary reports made the situation sound even more serious than it was. Henlein, possibly confused and in need of instructions, decided not to cross the border into Czechoslovakia, but instead went to Selb, a town in Bavaria close to the border, where VOMI had set up headquarters. Frank and the others went on to Eger, where they learned that martial law had just been declared in parts of western Bohemia.[93] Frank, apparently, more decisive and willing to act on his own than Henlein, or conceivably with Henlein's knowledge and consent, responded by picking up the phone and calling Prime Minister Hodža in Prague. The Sudeten radical gave the Czechs a six hour ultimatum: repeal martial law, remove the state police from Sudeten German areas, confine troops to barracks, and turn police functions over to the Sudeten Germans.[94] It looked as if the moment of truth had finally come. An uprising had broken out in the Sudetenland; the Sudeten leaders were delivering an ultimatum to the Czechs. This seemed to be the incident which Hitler had sought, the incident which would serve as a pretext for war. But was it? It is unlikely that Hitler, working through Henlein and Frank, conspired to incite a general uprising at this point. The time was not ripe for Operation Green to go into effect and an incident sparking war had to come almost immediately before the *Wehrmacht* moved. Hitler had warned Henlein on September 1 that he would handle the entire situation in September, but at a conference on Operation Green held in Nuremberg at the beginning of the Party Day celebration, October 1 was still the tentative target.[95] In addition, if Hitler were behind the uprising on September 12 and 13, he probably would not have made the speech he did, leaving the door open for peace. There is some indication that Hitler was taken by surprise by this new turn of events. On September 13, the Czechs supposedly monitored the following conversation between Henlein and Hitler, in which Hitler sounded very worried:

> HITLER: You have presented the Czech government with an ultimatum? Was it well considered? What will you do if the ultimatum expires unanswered?
>
> HENLEIN: I will immediately dissolve the negotiating delegation and break off talks with the Czech government.
>
> HITLER (after a period of silence): Good, Henlein, very good! Excellent! An excellent idea! [96]

If such a conversation did take place and if Hitler did not precipitate the uprising, it is conceivable that Frank precipitated the incidents on his own, either falsely assuming that Hitler's speech would be a signal to action or perhaps even attempting to force the führer's hand, and that Henlein, his hand forced, went along. It is also possible that the two had already learned of martial law as they approached the border and decided together on precipitate action. After all, if Hitler did not signal action at Nuremberg, then the Sudeten leaders would be faced once again with negotiating with the Czechs after all their demands had been met: a rather ludicrous prospect which would have exposed to the world the insincerity of the whole negotiating process. But here again there are inconsistencies. The disturbances were far too sporadic and localized for that. Given the complex communications network which Henlein and Lorenz of the *Volksdeutsche Mittelstelle* had set up, had the Sudeten leadership really wanted to instigate an insurrection, it would have been far different from those spasmodic outbursts which occurred during the night after Hitler's speech.

Given the situation as a whole, it is likely that the actions of Henlein and Frank on September 13 were improvised, rather than planned in advance. The most plausible explanation is that the demonstrations were what they appeared to be: spontaneous, scattered outbreaks, probably by people frustrated and disappointed that Hitler had not used the annual Party Day speech to signal their "deliverance." Aware that Hitler would probably take action soon, Henlein and Frank were then confronted with a sudden unrest which seemed too good to pass up. If the uprisings were on a large scale—which they were not, but might have appeared to be from the perspective of Selb and Eger—then to do nothing would be to admit losing control of the party, an unforgivable crime to Hitler, who valued nothing more in his paladins than that they had "conquered and held" their *Gaue*. To exploit the unrest, on the other hand, and to put themselves at the head of it might give the führer the chance to act he seemed to be waiting for. Why else would he have been ordering incidents recently in the Sudetenland? These are some of the thoughts which must have been bothering both Frank and Henlein at this point. At any rate, they immediately began to push the situation for all it was worth. Frank had already returned to Czechoslovakia; now—on September 14—Henlein crossed the frontier as well. No sooner had the time limit run out on the ultimatum—also on the 14th—than Henlein dissolved the negotiating team, officially broke off talks with the Czechs, and recrossed the border to set up operations in Selb. Confident now that Hitler would act, Frank announced to the party leaders still with him in Eger: "On the basis of the powers given me by Konrad Henlein, I dissolve the Sudeten German party. No one is empowered any longer to issue any announcements in the name of the SdP. I am going through Asch to the führer's headquarters." [97] With that, he left.

These were all gestures inviting a dramatic climax of some sort. It quickly began to dawn on the Sudeten leaders, however, that the whole maneuver was falling on its face. Hitler had *not* acted. Worse yet, the uprising, at the head of which the SdP leaders had hastened to place themselves, had fizzled completely. After one day of violent outbursts, the Sudeten areas suddenly quieted down, probably as a result of resolute Czech action: the government had declared martial law in some areas and sent in troops. [98] This left the Sudeten leaders high and dry. On the evening of September 14, Eisenlohr reported from Prague:

> The leadership staff of the SdP is sitting in Asch as a kind of revolutionary committee without a revolution, without contact with the rest of the Sudeten German territory, and without contact with Henlein, who is supposed to be somewhere in the neighborhood of Asch.

Eisenlohr also indicated that the SdP leaders had counted—incorrectly—on Reich intervention. "SdP command has directed party members to leave Prague in the expectation of a German air raid within 48 hours, and, apparently, has gone under this assumption in the attempt to unleash a revolt." [99] From any viewpoint, the episode was a total failure for the SdP leadership. Henlein, having fled across the border with his coterie, appeared doomed as leader of his people. Resentment immediately began to set in among the masses of the Sudeten Germans as soon as the word got out that Henlein had left them in the lurch. [100] No doubt Henlein's own contemptuous remarks about Krebs's ignominious flight to Germany in 1933 must have come back to mind. Senator Ludwig Frank, SdP leader in Marienbad, went so far as to say he "would have nothing to do with the insurrection." [101]

At this point, ironically, it was once again a third party rather than Hitler or Henlein, who stepped in to resolve the apparent impasse. On the morning of September 14, a telegram arrived from London: the prime minister, Neville Chamberlain, proposed a meeting between himself and Hitler. He would discuss any German proposal, *including plebiscite,* something that not even Hitler had mentioned publicly up to this point. [102] Hitler had once again left the door open and, once again, the British had obligingly stepped in. The fiasco of the "revolt-that-never-was" had been resolved in a way which no one could have predicted and in a manner which precluded the necessity of that "incident which might never return" which was to have triggered Operation Green. With that it was only a matter of time until the Sudetenland became a part of the Reich: for plebiscite meant *Anschluss.* In Selb, Henlein heard of the unprecedented step taken by Chamberlain and immediately telegraphed Hitler:

> Chamberlain will probably suggest *Anschluss.*
> In case you approve this, *mein Führer,* I take the liberty of making two suggestions as the first step to a solution:
> 1.) No plebiscite, but immediate annexation of areas with over 50 percent German populace
> 2.) Occupation of this area within 24 hours (48) by German troops . . . .[103]

It was an interesting suggestion—the last one which Henlein would make to Hitler: the last one, really, which he needed to make. In the course of his talks with Chamberlain, Hitler would make use of it. Right up to the end, Hitler proved himself amenable to being "educated" by his subordinates, and by his enemies.

The Sudeten crisis continued for several weeks, bringing the world to the brink of another great war. Nor were the surprises over. Hitler, by now sure of British and French acquiescence at almost any price, pushed the situation for all the traffic would bear. Still without a plan of action, he allowed himself to settle temporarily, under the influence of his ally Mussolini, for a victory without war. But as the world watched anxiously during the talks at Godesberg, then at Munich, the man who had been center stage for months faded almost unnoticed into the background of the international crisis. Konrad Henlein had gotten his wish: he and his people had become a "factor in National Socialist Reich policy." Now, ironically, he no longer mattered. Doomed to remain a weak provincial *Gauleiter,* he would soon be eclipsed by his deputy, Karl Hermann Frank. On September 15, after Chamberlain's first trip to Germany was announced to the world, Henlein had issued a proclamation which concluded with the words:

> We want to live as free German people!
> We want peace and work again in our homeland!
> We want to go home to the Reich! [104]

Henlein's statement contained a contradiction. Traditionally, no Sudeten German would have said "homeland" and "Reich" in the same breath, simply because the Sudeten homeland had never been a part of the modern German Reich. The very concept of ethnic German implied that one lived outside the Reich. But Henlein was no longer a traditionalist; he had long since abandoned the idea that the interests of his people lay outside the German Reich. In making this proclamation, then, he set the seal on a process that destroyed the ethnic integrity of the Sudeten Germans. From this point on, their interests would be relegated to minor importance in the face of the needs of the larger entity of which they would soon be a part. Several weeks after Henlein's proclamation the Sudeten Germans did go to the Reich and from that moment on their fate would be inextricably linked with that of Hitler's Germany. With its destruction came the end of a German Sudetenland as well.

XI

Summary

IN the end, it is no simple matter to assess responsibility for the events leading to destruction of the Czechoslovakian state. In the labyrinthine tangle of Sudeten German and Reich German politics from 1933 to 1938, there is ample evidence to implicate all factions in the fate of the Czech republic. As the complex interrelationship of Reich and Sudeten Germandom politics unravels, however, it does seem clear that as far as the Sudeten Germans are concerned, it is oversimplifying the developments to speak in terms of malevolent and deliberate cooperation with Hitler throughout the 1930s with the goal of destroying the Czech state. The tragedy of the Sudeten Germans lies in the fact that they completely misjudged the nature of the power structure in the Third Reich; that they sought to use National Socialist Germany and wound up in the end being used themselves as tools in a radically expansive Reich foreign policy. Although the leading political figures in the Sudetenland and the Sudeten population itself eventually functioned as a fifth column for Hitler, they had not always done so. Only after a protracted series of political struggles involving both Reich and Sudeten leaders—struggles which men like Konrad Henlein, leader of the Sudeten unity movement, never really understood—was a crisis situation reached which prompted Hitler to show a strong hand as political decision maker and in turn impelled the Sudeten leadership to cast its lot with the political designs of the Third Reich. As for Hitler's role in these political developments, it is again an oversimplification to speak in terms of a long range, carefully delineated plan for exploiting the Sudeten population in the interest of destroying the Czech state. As a political decision maker, Hitler seldom appears to have made detailed blueprints of any kind. As numerous scholars have pointed out, the political atmosphere of the Hitlerian regime often resembled a kind of "bureaucratic state of nature"—in which political "free enterprise," duplication of function, and intense personal rivalries, as well as fragmentation of power prevailed. In the wings, as it were, stood Hitler, the ultimate opportunist, ready when conditions demanded it of him or were unmistakably propitious to seize control of a given situation and make a binding decision. This pattern of decision making emerges most clearly as the Sudeten crisis develops.

The Sudeten problem, in short, cannot be interpreted primarily in terms of Hitlerian plotting and manipulation. Even before Hitler's accession to power in 1933, *Volkstumspolitik* or "ethnic German politics" had commanded the interest and involvement of many Germans in the Reich. There were politicians in Germany who had a long standing concern for the welfare of Germans living abroad and people of German descent living as citizens of other states—men who had been active on the behalf of ethnic Germans for decades and continued to play this role after 1933. This particular faction in Germandom politics I have termed the "traditionalists." Politically this group was composed of a variety of conservative activists who tended to treat ethnic Germans not so much as tools of Reich foreign or domestic policy but as unique population groups with viable interests and goals of their own. Although not National Socialists, and in some cases anti-Nazi, these traditionalists were able to function in Hitler's regime for quite some time, in part because they spoke the same *völkisch* language as the Nazis, in part because their chief spokesmen and most effective leaders, Hans Steinacher and the Haushofers (General Karl and his son Albrecht), had very close relations with Hitler's deputy, Rudolf Hess. Although not Nazis themselves, Steinacher and the Haushofers continued to pursue their Germandom activities after Hitler's seizure of power, partly in the hopes of "educating [their] masters" to the needs of the ethnic Germans. What authority and protection these men enjoyed was derived from a compliant Hess, who had as little notion of what the traditionalists were trying to achieve as the traditionalists themselves had of the ultimate thrust of the National Socialist revolution. The traditionalists had as their power base two organizations: the *Volksbund für das Deutschtum im Ausland* (VDA), an organization which had traditionally functioned as a cultural, social, and charitable liaison between Germany and Germans living abroad, and the *Volksdeutscher Rat* ("Ethnic German Council" or VR), a quasi-official institution created by Steinacher and the Haushofers shortly after

Hitler came to power. Both organizations became prime targets for a second kind of Germandom activist: National Socialists, who out of a combination of personal ambition and ideological commitment found *Volkstumspolitik* an especially attractive area of political involvement. Generally these Nazi politicos regarded the ethnic Germans not as objects of brotherly concern but as tools to be manipulated in a radical German expansionist foreign policy.

Initially, the Reich National Socialist Germandom faction was dominated by three men: Ernst Bohle, Alfred Rosenberg, and Baldur von Schirach. Ernst Bohle was an ethnic German enthusiast who dreamed of building his power base, the *Auslandsorganisation* (AO) into a command post controlling a network of National Socialists all over the world where German communities existed. Alfred Rosenberg, party ideologist and self-styled racial authority, operated from within his own power base, the *Aussenpolitisches Amt.* One of the first to enter the field of Germandom politics, Rosenberg was also one of the first casualties of that struggle. Almost by accident, Baldur von Schirach, Hitler Youth leader, also involved himself in Germandom politics. Schirach's activity is an example of the strong appeal of *Volkstumspolitik,* even for those whose main political concerns related only tangentially to the problems of Germans living abroad. These three major National Socialist activists involved initially in Germandom politics were far from united in their goals. They did share one characteristic, however. All three were rather prominent figures in the Nazi hierarchy, and as such needed to be somewhat circumspect in their propensity to be radical so as not to publicly compromise the regime.

Although the traditionalists and the National Socialist factions were the principal protagonists in the Germandom struggle, there were also a number of radical splinter groups which vied for power and influence in ethnic German affairs. Some of these splinter groups, like the *Sudetendeutscher Heimatbund* (SHB), were composed of irredentist ethnic Germans living in exile in the Reich. Due to the often chaotic and highly personalized power constellations in Nazi Germany, such groups could cause trouble out of all proportion to their size. Lacking the official status which would have imposed some discretion on their political activities, these small unofficial groups often behaved with reckless impunity and contributed in no small way to exacerbating the Sudeten.question and radicalizing *Volkstumspoli-*

tik. Given the differences of temperament, political philosophy and methods of their leaders, it is no surprise that all three of these groups—traditionalists, official National Socialist organizations, and radical splinter groups—soon found themselves in fierce competition with one another.

In the Sudetenland a similar tripartite power struggle developed. Here the "traditionalists" were those men who grouped around a young, new political leader, Konrad Henlein, who in 1933 founded a political movement, the Sudeten German *Heimatfront* (SHF), dedicated to creating a united Sudeten German community in the face of what was regarded as Czech oppression. Most of these men, like their counterparts in Germany, were passionately nationalistic, but for the most part non-Nazi activists. Many of them had emerged from the ranks of the *Kameradschaftsbund* (KB), a secret society founded on the political philosophy of Viennese sociologist Othmar Spann. Although racist and pan-German, the *Kameradschaftsbund* members in the leadership circle around Henlein were too intellectual and elitist in orientation to be at ease with the plebeian mass movement of National Socialism and ultimately with the former National Socialists who eventually joined the Henlein movement in large numbers. Again as in Germany, a second group involved in Sudeten ethnic politics was composed of National Socialists, many of whom flocked to the Henlein movement after the Sudeten National Socialist Party (DNSAP) was dissolved in 1933. These men were only peripherally concerned with the unity of their fellow Sudeten Germans: their main concern was to promote the union of the Sudetenland with Germany, which of course entailed the destruction of Czechoslovakia. Finally, there were a number of small conspiratorial groups and circles, radical in nature, many of which operated underground within the growing Henlein movement. The continued activity of these Sudeten radicals was aimed at steering the Henlein movement in the direction of irredenta. Although not quite as open, this Germandom rivalry in the Sudetenland was every bit as acrimonious as that in the Reich, the difference being that while in Germany the struggle was carried out largely among various official and quasi-official agencies, in the Sudetenland the rivalry became internalized for the most part within the right-wing Henlein movement itself.

For several years after 1933, traditionalists and Nazis in Germany fought for the most part on even terms. The fact that Hitler

needed and demanded a quiescent foreign policy during this period
initially worked in favor of the traditionalists and against the radicals.
Moreover, the natural advantage that the radicals may have had in
being National Socialists in a Nazi regime was mitigated by the fact
that they fought among themselves as much as with the traditionalists.
Ernst Bohle, for example, was never accepted by the powerful
Gauleiter and was eventually overshadowed by a new rival on the
Germandom scene, Joachim von Ribbentrop, Hitler's main foreign
policy consultant. Rosenberg, more an ideologist than a bureaucratic
infighter, was his own worst enemy. But as the Germandom struggle
continued, and as increasingly it became clear that the quiescent
period in Nazi foreign policy would not continue indefinitely, the
traditionalists discovered that the opposition was becoming considerably stronger. National Socialists on both sides of the border had
successfully begun to unite in their attacks against the traditionalists.
Out of fear and necessity the Reich traditionalists also looked across
the border into the Sudetenland for allies and for the opportunity to
show that their brand of *Volkstumspolitik* was the more viable. In the
Sudetenland, meanwhile, Henlein felt beset by rivals within his own
party and saw the overtures of Reich traditionalists like Hans
Steinacher as means of securing his position within the Sudeten
Germandom camp. By late 1934, then, radicals and traditionalists on
both sides of the border had cemented relationships with each other.
Increasingly what had been two separate sets of feuding camps
became one larger struggle of international dimensions: with two
distinct factions, Reich-Sudeten traditionalists and Reich-Sudeten
National Socialists at war with one another over the formulation of
Germandom policy. This merging of forces was to have tremendous
implications both for German foreign policy in general as well as for
German-Czech relations.

The traditionalists at first saw their cross-frontier endeavors
vindicated. Henlein's party, with immense financial aid from Steinacher, emerged from the Czech national elections in May of 1935 with
the largest number of votes of any party in the country. His
movement—now renamed the Sudeten German party (SdP)—had
clearly become the dominant political organization in the Sudeten
community. Steinacher rejoiced. But although they perhaps did not
realize it at the time, the traditionalists—in order to score a
success—had violated one of their cardinal principles: they had

blurred the line they had so carefully tried to draw between Reich politics and the affairs of ethnic Germans. This distinction had served as a barrier, albeit a fragile one, to the internationalization of the Sudeten question. Now that this barrier had been eliminated, a new course of action was open to the radicals who would soon use internationalization of the Sudeten problem to very different ends.

The year 1935 brought with it new problems for the German traditionalists: their former bureaucratic power base, the *Volksdeutscher Rat,* was dissolved and replaced by a new party office, the *Volksdeutsche Mittelstelle* (VOMI). Although the traditionalists were now forced to work within the National Socialist fold, men like Steinacher did not regard this development as a total disaster for their non-National Socialist Germandom policies, mainly because VOMI was put under the leadership of Otto von Kursell, a man not unsympathetic to the traditionalist cause. An old party member, Kursell had impeccable National Socialist credentials, but was at the same time no fanatic. Working under Kursell's protection, the traditionalists were no longer so exposed to frontal attack by their Nazi rivals. At the same time, one of their most persistent opponents, Ernst Bohle, had been eclipsed by a rising new star on the Nazi firmament, Joachim von Ribbentrop. Because Ribbentrop initially had no interest in ethnic Germans, Steinacher and his associates felt that he posed no threat to traditionalist policies. But appearances were deceiving. Kursell's protection was not all it seemed; nor was Ribbentrop's ostensible harmlessness. The Kursell office might be a fortress against direct attack by other National Socialist organizations, but it was after all a party institution. As such, it virtually invited infiltration and subversion—perhaps the most effective methods of bureaucratic conquest within the Nazi state. Similarly, while Ribbentrop posed no immediate threat in his role as Hitler's foreign policy advisor, his presence in the field of foreign policy work and Germandom politics was like a walking time bomb: an extremely ambitious and radical man, in the not too distant future, Ribbentrop was to become one of the most aggressive proponents of violent Nazi imperialist expansion.

On the surface, Henlein had far more reason to feel optimistic in 1935, due to the rapid growth of his movement and his party's resounding electoral success. But again it was the case of a triumph which brought with it certain dangers. On the one hand, the greatly increased size of the Henlein party put it in a much better bargaining position vis-à-vis both the Czechs and Henlein's Sudeten German political opponents. On the other hand, the very influx of members which gave the Henlein movement political strength in the outside world also indicated that increased numbers of more radicalized Sudeten Germans, including former Sudeten National Socialists, were flocking into the movement with the hope of turning the party in a more radical direction. Although safer than ever from outside assault, the Henlein party was soon to face the even more difficult problem of conflict and schism within the movement itself. Moreover, by depending so heavily on Steinacher and the other German traditionalists for support in financing the election, Henlein was beginning to build a potentially dangerous political alliance with and reliance on a Germandom faction in the Reich whose own future appeared anything but secure. These were clouds on the horizon that both Reich and Sudeten traditionalists failed to see, blinded as they were by what appeared to be an encouraging vindication of the more moderate approach to Germandom politics.

During the course of the following year, ominous new developments seemed to indicate that a kind of turning point had been reached in the Germandom struggle. It was a year in which the balance of power and prestige would swing in Germany's favor; it was also a year during which Hitler began to venture more boldly into the international arena, as with his move to remilitarize the Rhineland. It was at this time that the Sudeten problem also became more of an international question. After a long period of relative indifference toward Germandom politics, Hitler showed a direct interest in the Sudeten problem for the first time during 1936 and surprisingly seemed to favor the traditionalists and their approach. Albrecht Haushofer, who had submitted plans for a nonaggression pact between Germany and Czechoslovakia—the price of which was to be cultural and economic equality for the Sudeten Germans—suddenly found himself commissioned by Hitler to open negotiations with the Czechs in November of 1936. The discussions led to nothing and were dropped under Hitler's orders several months later, but the experience had served to teach Hitler something. The Reich traditionalists had continued doggedly to pursue their Germandom activities even in the face of heavy fire from National Socialist Germandom organizations with the hope, as Haushofer had put it, of "educating [their] masters."

Now, at one point in the negotiations with the Czechs, Haushofer advised that if for any reason a nonaggression pact proved inadvisable, then the way to prevent it from reaching fruition would be to raise Sudeten demands to an unacceptable level—advice which Hitler would find occasion to follow several years later under quite different circumstances as the Sudeten problem reached the crisis point. The traditionalists were indeed "educating [their] masters" but in ways they never suspected. In the meantime, they had simply managed to bring the Sudeten question one step into the international arena.

Despite Hitler's ostensibly encouraging use of the traditionalists in the negotiations with Czechoslovakia, Reich and Sudeten traditionalists began to become aware that they were fighting a life and death struggle for political survival at this point. In a desperate attempt to secure their position, they also ventured further into the international arena. Henlein, using connections he had forged during the previous year, visited England in an attempt to convince influential Englishmen that the more moderate Sudeten cause was worthy of support and to strengthen his hand vis-à-vis the more radical forces within the Reich and the Sudetenland. Conditions within the Sudeten German party itself during 1936 also tended to make the Sudeten ethnic question less and less an internal Czech matter and more a matter of international concern. By the spring of 1936, intense personal rivalries and ideological quarrels within the Henlein movement—triggered by the activities of radicals with increasingly stronger connections in Germany—actually threatened to tear the party apart. In his desperation to resolve the crisis, Henlein sought to widen his own contacts in the Reich. His request brought in the *Volksdeutsche Mittelstelle* as referee to adjudicate the quarrels. Although the acrimony in the party was temporarily hidden through this arbitration, the price had been high indeed, for Henlein had become dangerously dependent on Reich agencies to keep his movement together for him.

It is astounding that throughout the period 1933 to 1936, as the struggle over Germandom politics in the Reich became increasingly bitter and intense, there is little evidence of either direction or interference on Hitler's part. Memoranda flooded into the Reich Chancellory and remained unanswered. Warring factions looked for binding decisions and found either silence or vague encouragement for both parties in the dispute. It is clear at this point that Hitler still had little interest in the Sudeten question and was perfectly content to let the Germandom rivalries go on without interference, at least as long as they did not threaten to compromise his regime. Only late in 1936 did Hitler show any personal interest in Czechoslovakia and the Sudeten Germans, and then only briefly, when he commissioned the traditionalist Albrecht Haushofer to explore the possibility of a nonaggression pact. Hitler's concern was short-lived and his motives ambiguous; the negotiations were allowed to lapse after only several months and the matter was not pursued further. However brief this flicker of interest on Hitler's part in the Czech republic, the traditionalists interpreted their involvement in the negotiations as a hopeful sign that their ideas and activities could influence National Socialist foreign policy. A nonaggression pact after all could well bring Czechoslovakia peacefully closer to the German sphere of influence and loosen the republic's ties with the Franco-Soviet alliance system. In reality, however, Hitler's passing interest in Czechoslovakia boded ill for the traditionalists, for it was only one symptom of what would be increased testing and probing on the führer's part as he began to seriously consider the alteration of the European status quo, by whatever means necessary.

In 1937, the ominous clouds that from time to time had threatened to complicate the traditionalists' involvement in the Germandom struggle suddenly brought disaster. Ironically, when defeat came for Steinacher and his colleagues, it was not as a result of the machinations of long time antagonists, but at the hands of an organization which only broke openly into ethnic German politics at a relatively late date: Heinrich Himmler's SS. There were a number of reasons why the SS became involved in *Volkstumspolitik*. Himmler liked to collect bureaucracies and the complex of agencies dealing with ethnic Germans represented another possible link in his chain of bureaucratic empire. The *Reichsführer* also was fascinated with *völkisch* and racial ideology and dreamed of vast territories in the East on which to settle a new racial elite of German peasant-farmers. What better raw material than the ethnic Germans who were already settled in these areas? Through its police activities, the SS had actually become involved in the Sudetenland as early as 1933, carrying out surveillance of refugees and more nefarious special political assignments or *Sonderaufträge*. Closely tied in with these activities was the role played by another organization in Himmler's empire, the

Sicherheitsdienst or SD—the ideological watchdog and secret service agency of the Nazi party. The SD, whose directors found the Spannist philosophy of many of the leaders in the Henlein movement especially repugnant, quickly became involved in the Germandom struggle on the side of the radicals in the Sudeten German party. Eventually as Himmler became more and more interested in foreign policy *per se,* the SS began to infiltrate all those organizations which dealt with foreign policy formulation, including Ribbentrop's agency, the *Dienststelle Ribbentrop,* the *Auswärtiges Amt* or "Foreign Office," and most ominously for the traditionalists, the *Volksdeutsche Mittelstelle* itself.

The traditionalists consistently underestimated the strength of these rivals in the Germandom struggle, partly because the SS and SD were so circumspect in their involvement in Germandom politics. Moreover, Steinacher and Henlein failed to anticipate how the many compromises and concessions they had felt compelled to make had left them particularly vulnerable to the political tactics used by the SS. By 1937, the SS had become more and more open in its attacks against the traditionalists and gradually undercut both Steinacher and Henlein's power bases. One of the traditionalists' few supporters in official National Socialist circles, Kursell, was ousted as director of the *Volksdeutsche Mittelstelle,* and replaced by a trusted Himmler associate, SS-*Obergruppenführer* Werner Lorenz. Steinacher's own power base, the VDA, was also infiltrated and his close colleagues were harassed. At the same time, a number of Sudeten German Party leaders, including Henlein's deputy, Karl Hermann Frank, began to take orders from the SS.

As Hitler's diplomatic successes continued during 1937, the stress on caution in Germany's international affairs lessened perceptibly. Now the radicals could act with far more impunity than before, and by the end of the year, the traditionalists were through. In October of 1937, at Himmler's insistence, Steinacher was sacked as VDA director and banned from any further activity in ethnic German affairs. The immediate grounds for this total fall from grace was Steinacher's unyielding insistence on the integrity of ethnic German communities, specifically the German ethnic group in South Tirol. High Nazi circles, which were working toward an alliance with Mussolini at this point, decided that it was no longer possible to tolerate Steinacher's stubborn and embarrassing interference on behalf of the South Tirolese. At this point, Henlein began fully to realize the implications of his decision to cast his lot with the traditionalist faction in Germandom politics. Just a month after Steinacher's dismissal, with radical dissent in his own party raging uncontrolled, Henlein caved in completely and on November 19 sent Hitler a letter inviting the German dictator to take the fate of the Sudeten Germans into his hands.

By the end of 1937, then, the long period of Germandom rivalry had come to an end, with the victory of the radical National Socialists. Without any consistent personal effort or involvement in the area of Germandom politics, Hitler found that the struggle of the various factions over the years had presented him with a considerable array of weapons which could be used were he to embark on a radical expansionist policy. There was a compliant political organization within Czechoslovakia, the Sudeten German party, capable of functioning as a fifth column, as well as a command agency to organize and discipline that fifth column from Berlin, the *Volksdeutsche Mittelstelle.* Organized and willing groups of cadres, the splinter groups in the Germandom struggle, were in a position to push the radicalization process on both sides of the border. The Sudeten problem itself had been removed from the context of Czech domestic politics and had been maneuvered into the international arena, where Hitler could deal with the question without compunction as German chancellor. Finally, Hitler was able to draw from an impressive bag of political "tricks" which had been developed over the years by both sides struggling for control of *Volkstumspolitik.* Ironically, some of the most important of these political gambits actually originated with the traditionalists, whose purpose in developing them of course was very much at odds with the use Hitler was now to make of them.

As the Sudeten crisis developed during 1938, Hitler skillfully drew upon this arsenal of weapons forged during the course of the Germandom struggle. But the various agencies and situations were more than just passive tools at the führer's disposal: they continued to exert a kind of dynamic of their own in determining the direction the Sudeten crisis was to take. Thus, even though Hitler turned his attention increasingly toward Czechoslovakia during 1938, he was often, albeit with skill and effectiveness, *reacting* as much as *initiating* for a good part of the time. Perhaps his most unique talent as a decision maker ultimately lay in being able to turn developments initiated by others to his own purpose.

Ultimately, the nature and length of the Germandom struggle, as well as the enormous impact of that struggle on the development and outcome of the Sudeten question, reveals a great deal about the nature of the Nazi regime. Both with regard to domestic politics and foreign policy decision making, its power structure was far looser and more fragmented than often portrayed. Throughout the battle over ethnic politics, its various factions demonstrated a great deal of diversity and political free enterprise. Even men like Steinacher who stood in opposition to so many ideals and goals of the official National Socialist leaders involved in Germandom work managed to maintain himself for an incredibly long time and actually exert some influence —even if not always what he may have intended—on the course the Sudeten crisis was to take. Nazi foreign policy formation appears to have been to a large extent a haphazard affair, generated by competitive friction within the system—which might suggest that prior studies have been somewhat too Hitler-centric and have underestimated the plurality inherent within the Nazi system at this time. On the other hand, as this study indicates, one must be careful not to carry this characterization too far. Whatever the limits on his power, Hitler was still the dictator, and it would be an error to trivialize his authority. The plurality in the Nazi system, and particularly in the realm of *Volkstumspolitik,* existed because of a specific set of circumstances, including an initial need to mask ultimately radical goals. Hitler's Social Darwinistic approach to government also played a role here. Ultimately, however, when Hitler did bring his full attention to bear on the Sudeten question, there was little doubt as to who was in charge. Although the dynamic resulting from political free enterprise continued apart from Hitler's close control and supervision even after he had taken charge of the Sudeten crisis, this is not so much evidence of the dictator's helplessness as far more testimony to his political prescience. Hitler well knew that there was a dynamic inherent within the National Socialist revolution which would eventually dovetail with his own intention radically to alter the face of Europe. In the early years of his regime, when necessity imposed caution, he found it advisable to rein in that dynamic. The Röhm affair in 1934 was the most dramatic example of this; in the realm of *Volkstumspolitik,* the equivalent was the periodic admonition to the radicals to restrain themselves in their activities. Later, when the conditions for a more aggressive foreign policy became more propitious, Hitler needed only to loosen the reins judiciously, confident that ensuing events would move in the right direction and provide him with the opportunities he needed. It was the revolutionary vision and dynamic of National Socialism, then, as encompassed in the ceaseless activity and endless dreams of the Nazi political "entrepreneur," which allowed Hitler to be the successful opportunist he was and obviated the need for any blueprint for aggression. That the traditionalists in the Germandom struggle did not realize this until it was too late—if, indeed, they ever realized it—was both their tragedy and their folly.

The long struggle and ultimate defeat of the traditionalists reveals much about the role of such conservatives in a totalitarian state. Initially, it would appear, conservatives—to the extent that they function within the idiom of the system—can continue to generate policy and influence the course of events; perhaps these men would even seem to be one of the only viable sources of resistance to such a regime. In the end, however, the role of the conservative opposition working within the system would seem to have its limits. For once a certain stage of radicalization has been reached, both the influence and the powers of resistance on the part of such men become increasingly ineffectual. The very fact that they have been used to the idiom of the system, used to speaking the same kind of language as those in power, blinds them to this loss of effectiveness until it is too late: eventually they and their ideas become pawns to be manipulated for the benefit of the regime.

Key to Abbreviations

AA	*Auswärtiges Amt*
AO	*Auslandsorganisation der* NSDAP
BdA	*Bund der Auslandsdeutschen*
BdL	*Bund der Landwirte*
BDO	*Bund Deutscher Osten*
BFHB	*Bund der Freunde der Hitlerbewegung*
DAF	*Deutsche Arbeitsfront*
DAI	*Deutsches Auslandsinstitut,* Stuttgart
DAWG	*Deutsche Arbeits- und Wirtschaftsgemeinschaft*
DNB	*Deutsches Nachrichtenbüro*
DNP	*Deutschnationale Partei*
DNSAP	*Deutsche Nationalsozialistische Arbeiterpartei* (Sudeten)
DPAA	*Deutschpolitisches Arbeitsamt*
HJ	*Hitlerjugend*
KB	*Kameradschaftsbund*
KdD	*Kreditanstalt der Deutschen*
NSDAP	*Nationalsozialistische Deutsche Arbeiterpartei* (Reich German)
NSBO	*Nationalsozialistische Betriebszellenorganisation*
NSHB	*Nationalsozialistischer Hochschullehrerbund*
NSLB	*Nationalsozialistischer Lehrerbund*
NSStB	*Nationalsozialistischer Studentenbund*
OSSA	(Cover company under control of *Auswärtiges Amt*)
PROMI	Propaganda Ministry
RFSS	*Reichsführer* SS (Himmler)
RJF	*Reichsjugendführung*
RMdI	*Reichsministerium des Innern*
SD	*Sicherheitsdienst*
SdL	*Sudetendeutscher Landstand*
SdP	*Sudetendeutsche Partei*
SHB	*Sudetendeutscher Heimatbund*
SHF	*Sudetendeutsche Heimatfront*
SPD	*Sozialdemokratische Partei Deutschland*
VDA	*Verein* (later, *Volksbund*) *für das Deutschtum im Ausland*
VOMI	*Volksdeutsche Mittelstelle*
VR	*Volksdeutscher Rat*

APPENDIX B

Major Reich Germandom Organizations*

TRADITIONALISTS	NATIONAL SOCIALISTS	RADICAL SPLINTER GROUPS
Volksbund für das Deutschtum im Ausland (VDA), 1933— originally, *Verein für das Deutschtum im Ausland* (1881) Dr. Hans Steinacher	*Auslandsorganisation* (AO), 1933— Ernst Bohle	*Sudetendeutscher Heimatbund* (SHB), 1919— Hans Beer
	Aussenpolitisches Amt der NSDAP, 1933— Alfred Rosenberg	*Emigres*, 1933— Hans Krebs Karl Viererbl Leo Schubert Rudolf Jung
Kulturabteilung: *Auswärtiges Amt* (AA) Friedrich Stieve	*Reichsjugendführung* (RJF) Baldur von Schirach	
	Dienststelle Ribbentrop, 1933—	
	Bund Deutscher Osten (BDO), 1933— Alfred Rosenberg	
Volksdeutscher Rat (VR), 1933 —Karl and Albrecht Haushofer Hans Steinacher	*Buro Kursell*, 1936 —Otto von Kursell Franz Wehofsich *Volksdeutsche Mittelstelle* (VOMI), 1937 —Werner Lorenz Hermann Behrends	

*Arrows indicate organizational evolution

APPENDIX C

Sudeten Germandom Organizations*

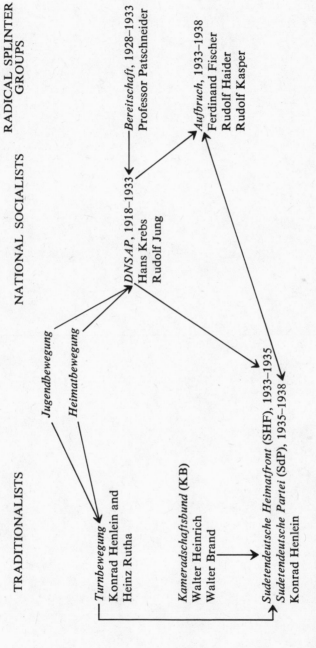

TRADITIONALISTS

Turnbewegung
Konrad Henlein and
Heinz Rutha

Kameradschaftsbund (KB)
Walter Heinrich
Walter Brand

Sudetendeutsche Heimatfront (SHF), 1933–1935
Sudetendeutsche Partei (SdP), 1935–1938
Konrad Henlein

Jugendbewegung

Heimatbewegung

NATIONAL SOCIALISTS

DNSAP, 1918–1933
Hans Krebs
Rudolf Jung

**RADICAL SPLINTER
GROUPS**

Bereitschaft, 1928–1933
Professor Patschneider

Aufbruch, 1933–1938
Ferdinand Fischer
Rudolf Haider
Rudolf Kasper

*Arrows indicate membership flow

Notes

CHAPTER I

1. The most recent proponent of the view that Henlein was a covert Nazi from the outset is Johann Wolfgang Brügel, *Tschechen und Deutsche* (Munich, 1967); typical of Sudeten apologist literature is Walter Brand, *Die sudetendeutsche Tragödie*, Ackermann-Schriften für Kultur, Wirtschaft, und Politik, no. 1 (Lauf bei Nuremberg, 1949). Radomir Luža, *The Transfer of the Sudeten Germans: A Study of Czech-German Relations, 1933–1962* (New York, 1964) provides a more balanced interpretation but still emphasizes the affinity of Henlein's movement for National Socialism.

2. John W. Wheeler-Bennett, *Munich: Prologue to Tragedy* (Toronto, 1948); Boris Celovsky, *Das münchener Abkommen von 1938*, Quellen und Darstellungen zur Zeitgeschichte, no. 3 (Stuttgart, 1958); Helmuth K. G. Rönnefarth, *Die Sudetenkrise in der internationalen Politik: Entstehung, Verlauf, Auswirkung*, Veröffentlichungen des Instituts für europäische Geschichte Mainz, vol. 21 (Wiesbaden, 1961), 2 vols.; Keith Eubank, *Munich*, 1st ed. (Norman, Oklahoma, 1963).

3. In 1933 there were slightly over ten million Germans scattered throughout Central and Eastern Europe, as well as in countries overseas. For a breakdown by country, *see* Hans-Adolf Jacobsen, *Nationalsozialistische Aussenpolitik 1933–1938* (Frankfurt/Main, 1968), pp. 160–1.

4. On the German *Volksgruppe* in Latvia *see* Hans von Rimscha, "Zur Gleichschaltung der deutschen Volksgruppen durch das Dritte Reich. Am Beispiel der deutschbaltischen Volksgruppe in Lettland," *Historische Zeitschrift*, 182, no. 1 (1956): 29–63; in Rumania, Jacobsen, *Aussenpolitik*, p. 570ff.; in Poland, Theodor Bierschenk, *Die deutsche Volksgruppe in Polen 1934–1939*, Beihefte zum Jahrbuch der Albertus-Universität, no. 10 (Kitzingen/Main, 1954) and Richard Breyer, *Das deutsche Reich und Polen 1932–1937* (Würzburg, 1955), esp. pp. 220–71.

For general treatments of *Volksgruppen* from a contemporary viewpoint *see* Max Hildebert Boehm, *Volkstheorie und Volkstumspolitik der Gegenwart*, Wissenschaftliche Forschungsberichte zum Aufbau des neuen Reiches, no. 4 (Berlin, 1935) and Paul Rohrbach, *Deutsches Volkstum als Minderheit* (Berlin, 1926).

5. Martin Broszat, "Die völkische Ideologie und der Nationalsozialismus," *Deutsche Rundschau*, 84 *(January 1958): 53–68.*

6. *Ibid.*, p. 59.

7. *Ibid.*, p. 60.

8. In the case of Czechoslovakia and the Weimar republic *see* Dagmar

Perman, *The Shaping of the Czechoslovak State: Diplomatic History of the Boundaries of Czechoslovakia 1914–1920*, Studies in East European History, vol. 7 (Leiden, 1962), pp. 176–81.

9. Rönnefarth, *Sudetenkrise*, 1: 87.

10. Thomas Masaryk, *Die Weltrevolution: Erinnerungen und Betrachtungen 1914–1918*, trans. Camill Hoffman (Berlin, 1925), p. 81; Brügel, *Tschechen*, p. 151.

11. Brügel, *Tschechen*, pp. 64–5.

12. Elisabeth Wiskemann, *Czechs and Germans: A Study of the Struggle in the Historic Provinces of Bohemia and Moravia*, 2nd ed. (London, New York, 1967), pp. 84–5; Brügel, *Tschechen*, pp. 75–6.

13. Wiskemann, *Czechs*, pp. 140–96.

14. *Ibid.*, p. 208.

15. Brügel, *Tschechen*, pp. 128, 145, 194–5.

16. There were 3.5 million ethnic Germans living in Czechoslovakia in 1933; Hungary, with the next highest German population, had only 800,000. Jacobsen, *Aussenpolitik*, p. 161.

17. On this early quiescent period of National Socialist foreign policy, Charles Bloch, *Hitler und die europäischen Mächte 1933/34: Kontinuität oder Bruch?*, Hamburger Studien zur neueren Geschichte, no. 4 (Frankfurt/Main, 1966); Karl Dietrich Bracher, "Das Anfangsstadium der Hitlerschen Aussenpolitik," *Vierteljahrshefte für Zeitgeschichte*, 5 (January 1957): 63–76, esp. 65.

18. Jacobsen, *Aussenpolitik*, p. 246.

19. On Hitler's world view, Gerhard L. Weinberg, *The Foreign Policy of Hitler's Germany: Diplomatic Revolution in Europe, 1933–36* (Chicago, 1970), pp. 1–24; Jacobsen, *Aussenpolitik*, pp. 1–6.

20. There are a number of studies which emphasize this aspect of the Third Reich. The pioneer study is Hannah Arendt, *The Origins of Totalitarianism* (Cleveland, 1958); also Robert Koehl, "Feudal Aspects of National Socialism," *American Political Science Review*, 54 (1960): 921–33; most recently, Edward Peterson, *The Limits of Hitler's Power* (Princeton, 1969).

Joseph Nyomarkay, *Charisma and Factionalism in the Nazi Party* (Minneapolis, 1968), pp. 26–47, examines Hitler's use of the role of referee in quarrels between his subordinates as a tool to stay in power. John McRandle, *The Track of the Wolf: Essays on National Socialism and Its Leader, Adolf Hitler* (Evanston, Illinois, 1965), goes so far as to say that Hitler's role as referee in his paladin's quarrels was actually the motor force of the Nazi regime; Hitler's foreign policy was nothing more than a function of using this technique to stay in power.

CHAPTER II

1. On the "conservative revolutionary" in Germany *see* Klemens von Klemperer, *Germany's New Conservatism: Its History and Dilemma in the*

Twentieth Century (Princeton, 1957); Fritz Stern, *The Politics of Cultural Despair* (New York, 1965); Armin Mohler, *Die konservative Revolution in Deutschland 1918–1932* (Stuttgart, 1950); Kurt Sontheimer, *Antidemokratisches Denken in der Weimarer Republik* (Munich, 1962).

2. Donald H. Norton, "Karl Haushofer and the German Academy, 1925–1945," *Central European History*, 1 (March 1968): 80–97; on the activities of OSSA and the *Vereinigte Finanzkontore*, Grünau (AA) to OSSA, November 7, 1933 (Bundesarchiv, Koblenz [hereafter BA]/R2-15678/25–29). On the political mobilization of *Volkstum* groups, Hans-Adolf Jacobsen, *Nationalsozialistische Aussenpolitik 1933–1938* (Frankfurt/Main, 1968), pp. 160–251.

3. Jacobsen, *Aussenpolitik*, p. 165.

4. Hans Steinacher, unpublished calendar notes (hereafter cited as Steinacher, "Notizen"), April 29, 1933, Jacobsen Collection, Bonn.

5. Among others, Jaroslav César and Bohumil Černý, "Německá irredenta a Henleinovci v ČSR v letech 1930–1938" [German irredenta and the Henleinists in the CSR in the years 1930–1938], *Československy Časopis historický*, 10, no. 1 (1962): 1–17; Ralph Bischoff, *Nazi Conquest through German Culture* (Cambridge, Mass., 1942), pp. 91–2.

6. The changing of *Verein* to *Volksbund* is usually pointed out as symptomatic of *Gleichschaltung, e.g.,* Johann Wolfgang Brügel, *Tschechen und Deutsche* (Munich, 1967), p. 247. The request to change the name of the organization had already been made by *Reichsminister* Külz in 1932. Jacobsen, *Aussenpolitik*, p. 165, n. 2.

7. These thoughts were expressed in the resignation of the young VDA director of academic work, Ernst Neumann, who protested the *Verein*-orientation of the organization under Otto Gessler. Open letter to the *Hessische Volkswacht*, April 12, 1933.

8. In an interview with the author on November 1, 1968, Steinacher characterized his work as *volklich* rather than *völkisch*. This is a distinction in terms which traditionalists were not making in the 1930s. Terminology notwithstanding, Steinacher's whole career is evidence of the very real differences between the NS *völkisch* (etatist) and the traditional *volklich* (ethnic-oriented) approaches. Some scholars, including some writing in the thirties, have recognized this difference in thrust: Jacobsen, *Aussenpolitik*, pp. 163–164; Mohler, *Konservative Revolution*, pp. 77–9; Hans von Rimscha, "Zur Gleichschaltung der deutschen Volksgruppen durch das Dritte Reich," *Historische Zeitschrift*, 182, no. 1 (1956): 41ff.; *Verpflichtendes Erbe* (Kiel, 1954), pp. 29–32; Max Hildebert Boehm, *Volkstheorie und Volkstumspolitik der Gegenwart*, Wissenschaftliche Forschungsberichte zum Aufbau des neuen Reiches, no. 4 (Berlin, 1935), p. 37.

Unfortunately, too many contemporary critics of the VDA, as well as modern scholars, have looked only at the common *völkisch* heritage of the NS and the traditionalists and have dismissed these ideological differences as insignificant or superficial: an analysis which denies or distorts the role of "conservative opposition" played—albeit in the end unsuccessfully—by men like Steinacher. Brügel, *Tschechen,* pp. 247, 249; Gerhard L. Weinberg, *The Foreign Policy of Hitler's Germany* (Chicago, 1970), p. 225, n. 82.

9. Jacobsen, *Aussenpolitik,* p. 164; Boehm, *Volkstheorie,* p. 38; Hermann Ullman, "Die Jugend in den Volksgruppen," *Andreas Hofer: Jahrbuch des VDA* (Berlin, 1935), pp. 30–41.

10. Fischer (AO) *Aufzeichnung,* October 22, 1937 (Politisches Archiv des Auswärtigen Amtes [hereafter PA]/Chef-AO/vol. 94). On Steinacher's early career, R. Wichterich, *Volksdeutscher Kampf. Dargestellt am Lebensweg Dr. Steinachers* (Cologne, 1936).

11. Steinacher, "Notizen," November 15, 1933.

12. Speech at the VDA *Mainzer-Tagung,* May 19, 1934, VDA Wirtschaftsunternehmen, *Volksdeutscher Durchbruch* (Berlin, 1934), p. 16.

13. Steinacher telegram to Hitler, May 22, 1933, requesting an audience (BA/R43II/1406).

14. Jacobsen, *Aussenpolitik,* p. 164.

15. Martin Broszat, "Die völkische Ideologie und der Nationalsozialismus," *Deutsche Rundschau,* 84 (January 1958): 57.

16. Rudolf Hess to Steinacher, June 2, 1933 (BA/R43II/1408C).

17. The VDA "Bilanz am 31. Dezember 1934" showed a budget of RM 2,527,820.68 (BA/R57/DAI/675). *See also* unsigned report on VDA school activities of October 17, 1933 (PA/Kult A/VDA/vol. 19). On subsidies to the VDA from the Interior Ministry, Frick to the *Landesregierungen,* February 24, 1933 (BA/Schumacher Sammlung/355); Hermann Kügler (Ribbentrop's former representative to the VR) to Professor Hans-Adolf Jacobsen, September 9, 1966, part of a private document collection made accessible to the author by Professor Jacobsen (hereafter cited as Jacobsen Collection, Bonn). On AA subvention of VDA work, VDA (*Leiter der Hauptabteilung Verwaltung und Finanzen* [Director of the main department for administration and finance]), to AA, n.d. requesting a sum in Czech crowns to be sent through the consulate in Kaschau [Košice] (PA/Kult A/VDA/vol. 15).

18. Jacobsen, *Aussenpolitik,* pp. 160–220.

19. Rosenberg to Heinrich Lammers (*Reichsminister* and chief of the Reich Chancellory) on March 24, 1933 (BA/R43II/1406). Steinacher also claimed that Rosenberg was in competition for leadership of the VDA in 1933 and that if Gessler had continued in this post, it would have been only a short time until the Nazis took over. Interview with the author, November 1, 1968.

20. Jacobsen, *Aussenpolitik,* p. 175.

21. Ursula Michel, "Albrecht Haushofer und der Nationalsozialismus" (Ph.D. diss. University of Kiel, 1964), pp. 8–9, characterizes General Karl Haushofer's relation to Hess as an "odd feeling of friendly responsibility toward the young war comrade; a feeling difficult to describe but characteristic of Karl Haushofer, who recognized and valued Hess's uprightness without, however, failing to recognize his instability and need for dependence."

22. *Ibid.,* p. 126; Donald H. Norton, "The Influence of Karl Haushofer on Nazi Ideology" (Ph.D. diss., Clark University, 1963).

23. Michel, "Haushofer," pp. 132, 149. For deliberations on the form the VR was to take, Albrecht Haushofer to his father (National Archives Microcopy T-253, Roll 59, Frames 516174–75 [hereafter NA, T-253/Roll/Frame]).

24. From Berlin, May 30, 1933, as quoted in Michel, "Haushofer," p. 153; *see also* pp. 131–2 for her insights into Albrecht Haushofer's overestimation of political chances of the VR.

25. Steinacher, unpublished manuscript [hereafter cited as "Lebensaufzeichnungen"], as quoted in Michel, "Haushofer," p. 148, n. 203; Jacobsen, *Aussenpolitik,* p. 190.

26. (NA, T-253/46/1500087–88.)

27. (PA/VIA/Volksdeutscher Rat/vol. 1/Deutschtum 7.)

28. *Ibid.* Already prior to this, the Hitler Youth and the *Studentenschaft* were rivalling the VDA. Gerhard Krüger (chairman of the *Studentenschaft*) to Seebohm, April 5, 1933 (BA/Schumacher Sammlung/355).

29. Jacobsen, *Aussenpolitik,* pp. 165–70.

30. *Ibid.,* p. 72.

31. Two contemporary official works on the AO and Bohle are Emil Ehrich (Bohle's adjutant), *Die Auslandsorganisation der NSDAP,* Schriften der Deutschen Hochschule für Politik, no. 13 (Berlin, 1937); Leitung der AO der NSDAP, *Jahrbuch der Auslandsorganisation der NSDAP 1939* (Berlin, 1939).

32. Biographical data on Bohle is taken from his *curriculum vitae* submitted in an application for a position with the *Abteilung für Deutsche im Ausland,* Bohle to Rudolf Schmeer, April 4, 1933 (BA/Schumacher Sammlung/293); Hermann Degener, ed., *Wer Ist's,* 10th ed. (Berlin, 1935), p. 158.

33. In his application, Bohle refers to his "fluent mastery of the English language both written and spoken" and to his "thorough knowledge of the English mentality" (BA/Schumacher Sammlung/293).

34. This department had been created through a *Verfügung* of Gregor Strasser, dated May 1, 1932, to encompass "all local groups, outposts, and individual members of the NSDAP which are located outside the boundaries of Germany, the Saar, Danzig, and Austria." Jacobsen, *Aussenpolitik,* p. 91.

35. Founded on June 6, 1932, after it had been decided that only Reich Germans could belong to the NSDAP abroad, the *Bund* consisted of citizens of other countries who were sympathetic to National Socialism. *Satzung des "Bundes der Freunde der Hitler-Bewegung,"* June 14, 1932 (PA/Chef AO-53).

36. Apparently Rosenberg's eccentric racial ideas, which were well known to many foreigners, disqualified him from running an organization that operated so much abroad—especially at a time when Hitler was trying to foster a conservative image in matters of foreign policy. Jacobsen, *Aussenpolitik,* p. 98.

37. The organization had been made an independent *Gau* by Strasser, *Verfügung,* dated November 21, 1932 (BA/Schumacher Sammlung/292).

38. Bohle to Schmeer, April 4, 1933 (BA/Schumacher Sammlung/293).

39. Schmeer to Bohle, April 6 and 19, 1933; *Anordnung* #21/33; Schmeer *Ernennung,* May 8, 1933. (BA/Schumacher Sammlung/293).

40. Emil Ehrich, one of Bohle's closest collaborators, characterizes him: "In his openness, he lacked any inclination toward conspiracy and deviousness. Often he appeared amateurish and frivolous, but at the same time he showed a considerable diplomatic aptness in dealing with conflicting people or tendencies, or in [being able to] rise above them. He took almost childlike pleasure in a certain amount of publicity. In his private life, he was as unprepossessing as possible; right up to the end he lived in a rented house in Berlin. He was certainly no *Bonze*." Jacobsen, *Aussenpolitik*, p. 118.

41. Jacobsen, *Aussenpolitik*, p. 100.

42. *Verfügung des Stellvertreters des Führers*, October 3, 1933 (BA/Schumacher Sammlung/293).

43. *Rundschreiben* no. 54, October 10, 1933. *Ibid.*

44. *Reichsgesetzblatt*, 1, no. 135, December 2, 1933 (Berlin, 1933): 1016. In 1934 the law was changed to make the office of *Stellvertreter des Führers* a government as well as a party position. *Reichsgesetzblatt*, 1, no. 71, July 3, 1934 (Berlin, 1934): 529.

45. Bohle to Hess, December 4, 1933 (PA/Chef AO-49).

46. *Ibid.*

47. *Verpflichtendes Erbe*, p. 40.

48. Andrew Gladding Whiteside, *Austrian National Socialism before 1918* (The Hague, 1962), p. 37ff.

49. Its headquarters was in Vienna; SHB leaders were Hubert Partisch and Professor Anton Clement. Beer, *Mitteilung*, December 30, 1933 (PA/Kult VIA/vol. 13).

50. Wolf *Aufzeichnung*, August 30, 1927 (PA/Politik 6 Sonderakte/Sudetendeutscher Heimatbund [hereafter SHB]/1).

51. For example, the encounter at Bad Schandau, Saxony, October 19, 1930, in César and Černý, "Německá irredenta," p. 3.

52. Czech verbal note, November 14, 1933; also Altenburg (AA) *Aufzeichnung*, February 8, 1935, which reiterates all Czech complaints about the SHB since 1928 (PA/Politik 6 Sonderakte/SHB/2).

53. SHB (Grass) to Police Presidium in Eberswalde, February 24, 1933 (PA/Politik 6 Sonderakte/SHB/1).

54. *Geheimes Stattspolizeiamt* to AA, May 10, 1933; AA to Gestapo, May 26, 1933. *Ibid.*

55. Frick to SHB, May 9, 1933 (PA/Politik 6 Sonderakte/SHB/1).

56. Koch telegram to AA, October 5, 1933 (PA/Pol. IV/Politik 6/Nationalitätenfrage, Fremdvölker/vol. 22).

57. César and Černý, "Německá irredenta," p. 8.

58. Jacobsen, *Aussenpolitik*, pp. 69, 169, 173; Beer to Willy Meerwald, April 28, 1934 (BA/R43II/125).

59. Beer, *Mitteilung*, October 7, 1933 (PA/Politik 6 Sonderakte/SHB/2).

60. Hüffer *Aufzeichnung*, November 4, 1933; Beer's *Denkschrift*, October 1933, "Sudetendeutsche Arbeit" (PA/Kult VIA/Deutschtum in der Tschechoslowakei/vol. 13).

61. Beer to Hüffer, November 25, 1933; Czech verbal note, November 14, 1933 (PA/Politik 6 Sonderakte/SHB/2).

62. Meerwald to Beer, January 6, 1934 (BA/R43II/125/BA259).

63. Beer to Meerwald, "Ein Jahr nationalsozialistischer Staatsführung und Volkstums-Arbeit im Osten" (BA/R43II/125/BA273–281).

64. In a meeting between Steinacher and Köpke of the AA it was decided: "the *Sudetendeutscher Heimatbund* has no tasks beyond the border but is here only to encompass the Sudeten Germans in the Reich. It is subordinate to the *Volksdeutscher Rat* with regard to ethnic German policy" (Goeken note, March 19, 1934 [PA/Kult VIA/Volksdeutscher Rat/vol. 1/Deutschtum 7]).

65. Beer to Meerwald, May 8, 1934 (BA/R43II/125/BA269); Beer to Hess, June 9, 1934 (BA/R43II/125/BA295).

66. Kersken to Meerwald, June 21, 1934 (BA/R43II/125/BA311).

67. Jacobsen, *Aussenpolitik*, p. 263ff.

68. The *Bund der Auslandsdeutschen* was another small organization, the leaders of which showed stubborn independence even after the VR claimed authority over its activities: *e.g.*, the German envoy in Prague complained that the BdA was sending compromising, inflammatory literature to Sudeten Germans in Czechoslovakia, including the *Rektor* of the German University —an institution especially vulnerable to Czech pressure. Koch to AA, September 11, 1933 (PA/Kult VIA/Deutschtum 1/Tschechoslowakei/vol. 13).

69. Paul Seabury, *The Wilhelmstrasse: A Study of German Diplomacy in the Nazi Era* (Berkeley, 1954); Jacobsen, *Aussenpolitik*, pp. 20–44; Heinz Sasse, "Das Problem des diplomatischen Nachwuchses im Dritten Reich," *Forschungen zu Staat und Verfassung: Festgabe für Fritz Hartung* (Berlin, 1958), pp. 459–84.

70. Quoted in Joachim Leuschner, *Volk und Raum: Zum Stil der nationalsozialistischen Aussenpolitik*, Kleine Vanderhoeck no. 58 (Göttingen, 1958), p. 39.

71. Jacobsen, *Aussenpolitik*, p. 26f.

72. Many German diplomats tried to distance themselves from Nazi foreign policy, claiming that NS "para-diplomatic" agencies deprived them of all power and effectiveness: *e.g.*, Erich Kordt, *Nicht aus den Akten* (Stuttgart, 1950), pp. 91–2. However, *see* Leonidas Hill, "The Wilhelmstrasse," *Political Science Quarterly*, 82 (December 1967): 546–70, for the similarity of goals (if not means) between AA officials and Hitler; Charles Bloch, *Hitler und die europäischen Mächte 1933/34: Kontinuität oder Bruch?*, Hamburger Studien zur neueren Geschichte, no. 4 (Frankfurt/Main, 1966), p. 7ff., for evidence that Hitler's initial foreign policy had the support of both the conservatives and the wider German public.

73. Even the German resistance to Hitler in 1938 did not think in terms of an independent Czechoslovakia but in terms of a peaceful integration of that country into the German sphere of influence. *Denkschrift* composed jointly by members of the resistance, Kordt, *Akten*, p. 362.

74. Jacobsen, *Aussenpolitik*, p. 32.

75. This cooperation was pointed up in a series of conferences, March

27–28, 1934 at the AA in which Steinacher, Koch, and high Foreign Office officials participated, Hüffer *Aufzeichnung*, March 28, 1934 (PA/Kult VIA/ Deutschtum in der Tschechoslowakei/vol. 18).

76. Jacobsen, *Aussenpolitik*, pp. 181–2.

CHAPTER III

1. For an overview of the mechanics of *Volkstum* work in Czechoslovakia in the early 1920s, balance the pro-German accounts, particularly Josef Pfitzner, *Sudetendeutsche Einheitsbewegung*, 2nd ed. (Karlsbad, Leipzig, 1937), against those favoring the Czechs, such as Josef Fischer, Vaclav Patzak, and Vincenc Perth, *Ihr Kampf: Die wahren Ziele der Sudetendeutschen Partei* (Karlsbad, 1937), pp. 49–80. *See also* Hans Neuwirth, "Der Weg der Sudetendeutschen von der Entstehung des tschechoslowakischen Staates bis zum Vertrag von München," *Die Sudetenfrage in europäischer Sicht*, Veröffentlichungen des Collegium Carolinum, vol. 12 (Munich, 1962), pp. 142–3.

2. Robert G. L. Waite, *Vanguard of Nazism: The Free Corps Movement in Postwar Germany, 1918–1923* (New York, 1969), pp. 206–7, 239–54.

3. Pfitzner, *Einheitsbewegung*, pp. 62–5; Neuwirth, in *Sudetenfrage*, pp. 142–3; Ronald M. Smelser, "*Volkstumspolitik* and the Formulation of Nazi Foreign Policy: The Sudeten Problem, 1933–1938" (Ph.D. diss., University of Wisconsin, 1970), 138–43.

4. Neuwirth, in *Sudetenfrage*, p. 142.

5. There are widely divergent opinions regarding the meaning and potential of the early postwar youth movement in Czechoslovakia. Emil Franzel emphasizes the presence of varying currents within the movement to show that it had a democratic, federalist, European potential, as well as nationalist-totalitarian tendencies: "Die Politik der Sudetendeutschen in der Tschechoslowakei 1918–1938," in Helmut Preidel, ed., *Die Deutschen in Böhmen und Mähren. Ein historischer Rückblick*, 2nd ed. (Gräfelfing bei Munich, 1952), p. 359. On the other hand, Jaksch points out that strong antidemocratic impulses from the Reich, combined with the fact that Sudeten Germans in the youth movement tended to identify democracy with alien rule, undermined any democratic tradition present. Wenzel Jaksch, *Europas Weg nach Potsdam* (Stuttgart, 1958), p. 237.

6. Franzel in Preidel, ed., *Die Deutschen*, p. 357; Pfitzner, *Einheitsbewegung*, pp. 35–37; Fischer *et al., Ihr Kampf*, p. 63ff.; Hans Schmid-Egger, "Die Gründung der Tschechoslowakei und die Sudetendeutschen," in Hans Schmid-Egger, ed., *Umbruch in Mitteleuropa: Beiträge zur Geschichte der böhmischen Länder in der Zeit von 1848 bis 1948* (Munich, 1960), pp. 9–12.

7. Pfitzner, *Einheitsbewegung*, p. 73.

8. *Ibid.*, p. 38ff.

9. Andrew Gladding Whiteside, *Austrian National Socialism before 1918* (The Hague, 1962). For the best NS treatments, *see* Alois Ciller, *Vorläufer des*

Nationalsozialismus (Vienna, 1932) and Alois Ciller, *Deutscher Sozialismus in den Sudetenländern und der Ostmark* (Hamburg, 1944). (Ciller, who Germanized his name from Cihula, was active in the Bohemian National Socialist movement as early as 1902. Whiteside, *Austrian National Socialism*, p. 82). Hans Krebs, *Kampf in Böhmen* (Berlin, 1936).

10. Whiteside, *Austrian National Socialism*, p. 83.

11. *Ibid.,* p. 86.

12. *Ibid.,* p. 121.

13. Written in 1918, it reached the third edition by 1922. For a short analysis, *see Ibid.* pp. 107ff. Jaroslav César and Bohumil Černý note that some personal animosity in the rivalry between Jung and Hitler stemmed from the fact that Jung had a university education, while Hitler did not. *Politika německých buržoazních stran v Československu v letech 1918–1938* [The politics of the German bourgeois parties in Czechoslovakia in the years 1918–1938], 2 vols. (Prague, 1962), 2:133, n. 188.

14. Jung's letter to Party Treasurer Franz Xaver Schwarz, October 22, 1936, in which Jung uses this lever in order to solicit help for his Sudeten colleagues who had fled to the Reich (BA/Schumacher Sammlung/313).

15. Koch emphasizes this tradition within the context of a generational conflict in the DNSAP. Report to AA, November 8, 1933 (PA/Pol. II/Politik 6/Nationalitätenfrage, Fremdvölker/vol. 22). Franzel in Preidel, ed., *Die Deutschen*, pp. 359–60; Whiteside, *Austrian National Socialism*, p. 112f.

16. Whiteside, *Austrian National Socialism*, pp. 65, 85.

17. A copy of the party program, "Parteigrundsätze der Deutschen Nationalsozialistischen Arbeiterpartei. Beschlossen auf dem letzten gemeinsamen Parteitage für die Sudeten-und Alpenländer zu Wien, 5. Mai 1918," can be found in Ciller, *Vorläufer*, pp. 140–5.

18. According to *Ibid.* p. 109, the Chancellory was set up in Salzburg, August 7, 1920. Present were Hitler and Anton Drexler, representing the Reich; Hans Knirsch and Rudolf Jung, the Sudetenland; Walter Riehl and Ferdinand Ertl, Austria.

19. Jaroslav César and Bohumil Černý, "Německa irredenta a Henleinovcí v ČSR v letech 1930–1938," [German irredenta and the Henleinists in the CSR in the years 1930–1938], *Československy Časopis historický*, 10, no. 1 (1962):6. On May 19, 1932, Krebs invited Gregor Strasser to attend the DNSAP Party Day in Tetschen (BA/Schumacher Sammlung/313).

20. Gustav Peters, "Erinnerungen aus den Jahren 1885 bis 1935," unpublished manuscript, made available by the Collegium Carolinum Munich, pp. 208–10, comments that both Krebs and Jung wrote far too much and in doing so gave a distorted picture of the Sudeten situation, not to mention delivering to the Czechs good material for accusation. In fact, Krebs's brochure *Paneuropa oder Mitteleuropa* (Munich, 1931) was used against him during the postwar trial which resulted in his being sentenced to death. *Anklageschrift gegen die Abgeordneten und Senatoren der Sudetendeutschen Partei*, Dokumente und Quellen aus Böhmen und Mähren, vol. 1 (Munich, 1962); 12–13. This volume is a bad, but important translation of the

original Czech protocol of the postwar trials against the Sudeten Germans; it unfortunately does not include the appendix of original documents constantly mentioned in the text itself.

Peters, active in the *Deutschpolitisches Arbeitsamt* (DPAA) and the *Deutsche Arbeits- und Wirtschaftsgemeinschaft* (DAWG) and a member of the SdP after 1935, died before he could complete the second part of his memoirs.

21. On *Volkssport*, see Koch to AA, November 8, 1933 (PA/Pol. IV/Politik 6/Nationalitätenfrage, Fremdvölker/vol. 22). Also in imitation of the NSDAP, the DNSAP introduced the *Ordnerdienst* in April 1933 to protect their meetings, and in July, the attempt was made to introduce a Voluntary Labor Service (*Freiwilligen Arbeitsdienst*). César and Černý, *Politika*, 2:184–6.

22. César and Černý, "Německá irredenta," p. 6. Jung supposedly made a number of trips to Germany during the second half of 1931 to pave the way for cooperation between the DNSAP and the NSDAP. If this is true, he was violating his own guidelines during this period, which were to keep any contacts with the Reich at a minimum, so as to obviate any Czech crackdowns on the party's activities. In *Politika*, 2:145, César and Černý claim that as early as 1930, Krebs and Jung discussed with Hitler in Berlin the basis of further common action. On December 30, 1930, both men supposedly had a two hour conference with Hitler, and the next day Jung shared the stage with Goebbels in the *Sportpalast*.

23. Ciller, *Vorläufer*, pp. 140–5.

24. The DNSAP decided at their Party Day in Dux, in 1919, to conform to the new situation—*i.e.,* the Czechoslovakian state. In 1920, they sent five elected representatives into the House of Deputies in Prague. By 1928 they had eight representatives and four senators. Koch report to the AA, November 8, 1933 (PA/Pol. IV/Politik 6/Nationalitätenfrage, Fremdvölker/vol. 22). On national self-administration, see César and Černý, *Politika*, 2:136.

25. Krebs, *Kampf in Böhmen*, p. 197; Pfitzner, *Einheitsbewegung*, p. 55, claimed that at the time of the Party Day in Tetschen on May 29, 1932, there were 1,024 *Ortsgruppen* with 61,000 members and 250,000 "sympathizers" (*Anhänger*).

26. Figures in *Völkischer Beobachter*, no. 155, June 3, 1932 (BA/Schumacher Sammlung/313).

27. Elisabeth Wiskemann, *Czechs and Germans*, 2nd ed. (London, New York, 1967), p. 199.

28. Koch to AA, November 8, 1933 (PA/Pol. IV/Politik 6/Nationalitätenfrage, Fremdvölker/vol. 22).

29. "Collaboration between the NSDAP in Germany and in Czechoslovakia," *Regierungspräsident* in Oppeln to the Prussian Interior Minister, April 25, 1931 (BA/Schumacher Sammlung/313). In reaction to the dangers confronting it, the party by late 1932 was emphasizing much more strongly quiet organizational work rather than noisy propaganda displays in public. César and Černý, *Politika*, 2:134–5, n. 195.

30. César and Černý, *Politika*, 2:130–138; *see also* the DNSAP account in Hans Krebs, ed., *Der Volkssportprozess* (Aussig, 1932).

31. For example, in August of 1932, during the *Volkssport* trial, the Czech prosecutor triumphantly presented the court with a letter from the NS-*Studentenbund* in Munich to one of the accused, Rudolf Haider, purportedly asking him for a report. This was given as evidence that Haider was engaging in relations with an illegal organization abroad, thus violating the Law for the Protection of the Republic. On August 25, 1932, Hans Krebs wrote to Phillipp Bouhler, chief of the Party Chancellory in Munich, asking either him or Gregor Strasser to look into the case. He complained that, given Haider's exposed situation, it was inexcusably irresponsible that the NSStB in Munich should write such a letter. (BA/Schumacher Sammlung/313).

32. Koch to AA, January 11, 1933 (PA/Pol. IV/Politik 6/Nationalitätenfrage, Fremdvölker/vol. 22).

33. Koch reported, April 16, 1933: "In other respects, I hear from the provinces that the influx into the National Socialist party is still enormous. Aside from the events in Germany and radio transmissions, it is just the persecution to which the party has been exposed which accounts for this." *Ibid.* On May 24 he added: "Namely, among the youth, the revolution [*Erhebung*] in Germany has reverberated strongly. The enthusiasm for the ideas of National Socialism and for its leader, Hitler himself, is great." Quoted in César and Černý, *Politika*, 2:180, n. 107.

34. Koch to AA, February 25, 1933. (NA, T-120/3523/E643565).

35. Johann Wolfgang Brügel, *Tschechen und Deutsche* (Munich, 1967), p. 244ff.; Krebs gives the full text of the last press declaration of the DNSAP in *Kampf in Böhmen,* p. 213.

36. Franzel in Preidel, ed., *Die Deutschen,* pp. 359–60.

37. Koch to AA, November 8, 1933 (PA/Pol. IV/Politik 6/Nationalitätenfrage, Fremdvölker/ vol. 22).

38. For the text of the government pronouncement *see* Ernst Nittner, ed., *Dokumente zur sudetendeutschen Frage 1916–1967,* rev. ed. (Munich, 1967), pp. 125–6, No. 74.

39. Its full name according to Pfitzner, *Einheitsbewegung,* p. 72, was "Preparedness to work for youth education and popular enlightenment in the Czechoslovak Republic" (*Bereitschaft zur Arbeit für Jugenderziehung und Volksbildung in der Tschechoslowakischen Republik*).

40. Wiskemann, *Czechs,* pp. 137–38; Fischer *et al., Ihr Kampf,* pp. 44–5; César and Černý, *Politika,* 2:133–4.

41. Fischer *et al., Ihr Kampf,* pp. 44–5.

42. Ernst Nittner, *Der böhmisch-mährische Raum als Objekt des Hitlerischen Imperialismus,* Sonderdruck (Munich, 1960), p. 13, maintains: "[*Aufbruch*] was a supernationalistic circle; it was anti-Semitic, anticlerical, imperialistically oriented; in short, one could say that these men were latter day *Schönerers.*"

43. "Memorandum über die Entwicklung der Opposition in der SdP," unsigned, dated May 25, 1936 (Státní Ústředni Archiv, Prague [hereafter SUA]/5-HS-OA-#14).

44. César and Černý, *Politika,* 2:225, n. 46, estimate that the *Heimatfront*

in Moravia had 11,361 members organized in 193 *Ortsgruppen*; of this membership, only 41.5 percent were former DNSAP members. This is one indication that the majority of the SHF membership came from the non-NS Right.

45. Rudolf Jahn, ed., *Sudetendeutsches Turnertum* (Frankfurt/Main, 1958), p. 65ff.

46. Both Fischer *et al., Ihr Kampf,* pp. 39–41, and Franzel in Preidel, ed., *Die Deutschen,* p. 358, give Rutha and Henlein credit for reforming the *Turner* movement. Henlein, it should be noted, was greatly impressed with the *Sokol*; he had visited a *Fest* in Prague in 1926. Pfitzner, *Einheitsbewegung,* p. 77.

47. Rudolf Jahn, *Konrad Henlein: Leben and Werk des Turnführers* (Karlsbad, Leipzig, 1938), esp. pp. 65–6.

48. *Ibid.,* pp. 68–72, 80–94.

49. *Ibid.,* pp. 94–8.

50. Anton Altrichter, *Der Volkstumskampf in Mähren,* ed. Gaupresseamt Niederdonau der NSDAP, Niederdonau Schriftenreihe für Heimat and Volk, no. 4 (St. Pölten, 1940), p. 30.

51. Jahn, *Henlein,* pp. 113–18.

52. Though the core of his SHF support came from the *Turners,* Henlein tried to divorce the *Turnverband* itself from politics in order to protect the *Turner* movement from persecution should his Front be dissolved by Czech authorities. At his press conference on October 10, 1933, one week after he proclaimed the founding of the SHF, Henlein denied that the *Turnverband* had any complicity in his actions. (SUA, Prague/Fond SdP #1/vol. 1).

53. On the *Kameradschaftsbund* and its significance, Brügel, *Tschechen,* pp. 239–40; Boris Celovsky, *Das münchener Abkommen von 1938,* Quellen und Darstellungen zur Zeitgeschichte, no. 3 (Stuttgart, 1958), p. 107f.; César and Černý, *Politika,* 2:202–11; Fischer *et al., Ihr Kampf,* pp. 9, 38ff., 42ff., 54ff.; Emil Franzel, *Sudetendeutsche Geschichte* (Augsburg, 1958), p. 362f. and Franzel in Preidel, ed., *Die Deutschen,* p. 362; Václav Král, ed., *Die Deutschen in der Tschechoslowakei 1933–1947* (Prague, 1964), p. 15; Kurt Nelhiebel, *Die Henleins gestern und heute: Hintergründe und Ziele des Witikobundes* (Frankfurt/Main, 1962); Neuwirth, in *Sudetenfrage,* p. 144, n. 46, and p. 149; Věra Olivová, "Kameradschaftsbund," *Z Českých Dějin: Sborník prací in memoriam Prof. dr. Václava Husy* (Prague, 1966), pp. 237–68; Wiskemann, *Czechs,* pp. 137–8; and most recently, John Haag, "'Knights of the Spirit': The Kameradschaftsbund," *Journal of Contemporary History,* vol. 8, no. 3 (July 1973): 133–54.

54. Othmar Spann, *Der wahre Staat* (Leipzig, 1921).

55. Quoted in Fischer *et al., Ihr Kampf,* p. 9.

56. Peters, "Erinnerungen," p. 266, maintained that if Spann's ideas, with which the Dollfuss regime sympathized, could have been successfully realized in Austria, it would have been a tactical success for the *Kameradschaftsbund.* In fact, the regime did incorporate many of Spann's ideas, but this influence and the regime itself were extremely short-lived.

57. Neuwirth, in *Sudetenfrage,* p. 144.

58. Fischer *et al., Ihr Kampf,* pp. 38–9; Franzel in Preidel, ed., *Die Deutschen,* p. 362.

59. Franzel, *Sudetendeutsche Geschichte,* p. 362.

60. One rare piece of documentation on this technique of infiltration includes two letters from Walter Brand, one of the top KB leaders and an intimate of Konrad Henlein. November 14, 1931, Brand writes to the *Bezirksverband Niederland* of the *Bund der Landwirte* (BdL) that the BdL is planning a *Gau* business office (*Gaugeschäftsstelle*) in Rumburg and that he would like to apply for the job. At the same time, he writes to his father, requesting that he contact someone who can give a recommendation. He asks that his role in the KB and its organ, *Die junge Front,* be kept in the background. (SUA/Presidium zemeského úřadu v Praze/53372).

61. Franzel in Preidel, ed., *Die Deutschen,* p. 362.

62. Report of November 8, 1933 (PA/Pol. IV/Politik 6/Nationalitäten-frage, Fremdvölker/vol. 22). Wiskemann, *Czechs,* p. 136, points out that while the Sudeten Nazis were in favor of the expansion of the Reich, the KB people clung to an "Austrian allegiance."

63. For general comments on the differences, see Fischer *et al., Ihr Kampf,* p. 43; Walter Brand, *Die sudetendeutsche Tragödie,* Ackermann-Schriften für Kultur, Wirtschaft, und Politik, no. 1 (Lauf bei Nuremberg, 1949), pp. 43–4.

64. Klemens von Klemperer, *Germany's New Conservatism: Its History and Dilemma in the Twentieth Century* (Princeton, 1957), pp. 129–33.

65. "Report of the Deliberations of the Working Committee of the All-German Union." Remarks of Hans Knirsch in Frankfurt, September 24, 1920. In Koloman Gajan and Robert Kvaček, eds., *Deutschland und die Tschechoslowaksi 1918–1945* (Prague, 1965), pp. 56–7, No. 6.

66. Wiskemann, *Czechs,* pp. 137–38.

67. Klemperer, *Conservatism,* pp. 124–33; *Ibid.,* p. 137.

68. Smelser, *"Volkstumspolitik,"* pp. 203–6, for details on the negotiations.

69. Holzhausen in Prague to AA, October 23, 1933, refers to Knirsch's remarks (PA/Kult VIA/Deutschtum in der Tschechoslowakei/vol. 13).

70. *Ibid.*

71. Krebs supposedly tried to sabotage the negotiations with Henlein, embittered that he was not to get a leading role in the new organization. César and Černý, *Politika,* 2:198, n. 183.

72. Henlein's birth certificate, with the 1941 changes, has been preserved (SUA, Prague/40K/#68).

73. Henlein's official biographer was Karl-August Deubner, *Der Politiker Konrad Henlein* (Bad Fürth/Munich, 1938).

74. A fair sampling of the limits of Henlein's philosophical horizons can be obtained from Willi Brandner, ed., *Konrad Henlein: Reden und Aufsätze zur völkischen Turnbewegung 1928–1933,* (Karlsbad, 1934).

75. Fischer *et al., Ihr Kampf,* pp. 51–2.

76. Franzel in Preidel, ed., *Die Deutschen,* p. 364.

77. Fischer *et al., Ihr Kampf,* p. 17.
78. Franzel in Preidel, ed., *Die Deutschen,* p. 364.
79. Fischer *et al., Ihr Kampf,* p. 52.

CHAPTER IV

1. Henry Picker, ed., *Hitler's Tischgespräche im Führer Hauptquartier 1941–1942,* (Bonn, 1951), pp. 47, 69, 85, 176.
2. Gerhard L. Weinberg, *The Foreign Policy of Hitler's Germany* (Chicago, 1970), pp. 109–10.
3. Already in February of 1933, Hitler assured Mastný, the Czech ambassador to Berlin, that no contacts existed between the NSDAP and the Sudeten radicals, and emphasized his desire to be a good neighbor. *See* U.S. Government Printing Office, *Documents on German Foreign Policy,* Series C, vol. 2 [hereafter *DGFP,* C, II], no. 68, Köpke *Aufzeichnung,* November 15, 1933; *DGFP,* C, II, no. 15, Hohen-Aesten to Groesche, October 17, 1933, and no. 91, Lammers to AA, November 30, 1933.
4. Heinrich Lammers in the Reich Chancellory transmitted Hitler's wishes to Foreign Minister von Neurath, December 14, 1933 (BA/R43II/1406). Aid was limited to financial assistance and was to be distributed through the legation in Prague to a network of confidantes—all with the utmost discretion. Hüffer *Aufzeichnung,* December 19, 1933 (BA/ Schumacher Sammlung/313).
5. Knirsch told Koch, the minister to Prague, of Hitler's statement. Koch to AA, December 17, 1933 (BA/Schumacher Sammlung/313).
6. Hans-Adolf Jacobsen, *Nationalsozialistische Aussenpolitik 1933–1938* (Frankfurt/Main, 1968), p. 175.
7. Hüffer *Aufzeichnung,* March 28, 1934 (PA/Kult A/Deutschtum in der Tschechoslowakei/vol. 18). Goeken *Vermerk,* March 19, 1934 (PA/Kult A/VR/vol. 1/Deutschtum 7).
8. Dr. Hans Neuwirth, a member of the inner circle of the Sudeten German party and a confidant of Steinacher in the VDA claims that Hess did have an understanding for the exigencies of Germandom work but did not have the will to act decisively. Interview with the author, November 6, 1968. This agrees with Albrecht Haushofer's assessment of Hess; *see* Chapter 2, n. 24.
9. A good summary of the traditionalist approach to *Volkstumspolitik* can be found in a document labelled "Grundsätzliches" ("The Basics"), ostensibly prepared by Albrecht Haushofer for his father. (BA/Haushofer Nachlass/944b).
10. VDA to *Hofrat* Pollow, May 9 and June 1, 1934 (PA/Kult A/VDA/vols. 10 and 11, respectively). On October 1, 1934, Count Bethusy-Huc at the consulate in Brünn, who had just been commissioned by Bürger to pay out a sum of 45,220 crowns, complained in a report to the AA that it was inadvisable that such sums for unknown purposes be paid through the consulate. (PA/Kult VIA/Deutschtum in der Tschechoslowakei/vol. 15).

11. Exchange of letters between Hess and Lammers: H. to L., February 12; L. to H., February 17; H. to L., March 8; L. to H., March 14; H. to L., March 27, 1934 (BA/R43II/1406).

12. Stieve to Hess's staff, September 1934 (PA/Kult VIA/Deutschtum in der Tschechoslowakei/vol. 15).

13. Hans Steinacher, "Notizen," February 24, 1934. Jacobsen Collection, Bonn.

14. Goeken *Vermerk*, March 19, 1934 (PA/Kult A/VR/vol. 1/Deutschtum 7).

15. Hüffer *Aufzeichnung*, March 28, 1934 (PA/Kult A/Deutschtum im Ausland/vol. 18).

16. Bürger interview with the author, January 9, 1969; Hans Steinacher, "Lebensaufzeichnungen," pp. 217–20, 378; Steinacher, "Notizen," April 28, 1934.

17. Albrecht Haushofer and Hermann Ullmann were also in attendance. Steinacher, "Lebensaufzeichnungen," pp. 217–20; Radomir Luža, *The Transfer of the Sudeten Germans* (New York, 1964), p. 74, n. 43, errs in the date (January) of the meeting; Steinacher, "Notizen," April 28, 1934.

18. Friedrich Bürger, interview with the author, January 9, 1969.

19. Druffel (AA) report, n.d. (PA/Kult A/2VDA/vol. 9).

20. Druffel to AA, August 29, 1934 (PA/Kult VIA/Deutschtum in der Tschechoslowakei/vol. 15).

21. Jacobsen, *Aussenpolitik*, pp. 107–8; Bormann's *Ausführungsbestimmungen* ("instructions for execution"), in his *Rundschreiben*, February 24, 1934 (BA/Schumacher Sammlung/293).

22. Jacobsen, *Aussenpolitik*, p. 200.

23. *Ibid.*, pp. 468–9.

24. (PA/Kult A/VDA/vol. 11.)

25. (NA, T-253/51/150824.)

26. Kersken to VDA, September 17, 1934, also referred to this compromise (PA/Kult A/VDA/vol. 11).

27. Ursula Michel, "Albrecht Haushofer und der Nationalsozialismus" (Ph. D. diss, University of Kiel, 1964), p. 196, n. 22; also p. 33 of her Document Addenda, No. 54, Albrecht Haushofer to his father Karl, August 15, 1934.

28. (PA/Kult VIA/Deutschtum 1/vol. 18.)

29. Jacobsen, *Aussenpolitik*, p. 106. The "Territorial" *Gauleiter* were not willing to recognize someone as their equal merely because of his title. At this point, Bohle could not claim the same level of power because his AO did not correspond to a *Land Gau* and was not to be given this status until April of 1935, *ibid.*, p. 109.

30. *Ibid.*, p. 106, n. 33. It is interesting to note that Goebbels originally tried to recruit Steinacher. Steinacher, "Notizen," July 13, 1933: "He said I should not mess around with other ministries. Do everything through him. Has no connection with our question."

31. Jacobsen, *Aussenpolitik*, p. 200.

32. For Kersken's position on Bohle's proposal, Kersken to Bohle, February 27, 1934 (PA/Chef AO-49); Jacobsen, *Aussenpolitik*, p. 202. For further evidence of VDA confidence in Kersken and Kersken's willingness to protect the VDA: VDA to Kersken, October 18, 1933 (NA, T-253/58/515629–30). Kersken to *Grenzamt Gau Bayrische Ostmark,* November 24, 1933, *ibid.,* 515627. Kersken to VDA, September 17, 1934, Berlin Document Center [hereafter BDC], Research Division, Ordner 355. On Kersken, BDC file Kersken.

33. "Zusammenarbeit zwischen VDA and HJ," signed by F. Kemper of the HJ and Dr. Knüpfer of the VDA-*Jugend,* for the area of Baden, Karlsruhe, October 8, 1933 (NA, T-253/58/515845). The original agreement, on a national level, was signed by Dr. Schöneich for the VDA and Schirach for the RJF on May 6, 1933. A copy is in International Military Tribunal, *Trial of the Major War Criminals before the International Military Tribunal* [hereafter cited as *IMT*] 42 vols. (Nuremberg, 1947–49), 38: 101–2.

34. (PA/Kult VIA/2VDA/vol. 10.)

35. RJF *Verordnungsblatt,* no. 119, April 10, 1934 (PA/Kult A/2VDA/vol. 10.): Steinacher interview with the author, November 1, 1968. At one point, Steinacher even asked for support from the AA, specifically from Rödiger. Rödiger began a note to Hess strongly supporting the VDA, then thought the better of it, opting for a vaguely positive statement. Steinacher to Rödiger, April 25; Rödiger to Hess, April 26, 1934 (PA/Kult A/2VDA/vol. 10).

36. Jacobsen, *Aussenpolitik,* p. 205. In connection with Czechoslovakia, the posts in Breslau, Dresden, and Regensburg were especially important. Memorial Library, The University of Wisconsin, holdings in manuscript form, "Arbeitsbericht 1934 der Abteilung 'Ausland der RJF'," particularly the section "Bereich Mitte-Ost."

37. Such institutional conflict was not always just a matter of competency but sometimes resulted from personal animosity. Friedrich Heiss, RJF member and publisher of *Volk und Reich,* apparently jealous when Steinacher refused to put him on the VR, declared "war to the bloody end." Heiss to Steinacher, March 28, 1934 (NA, T-253/58).

38. Hillebrand *Denkschrift,* November 26, 1936 (NA, T-253/59).

39. (BA/Haushofer Nachlass/955b).

40. (Státní Ústřední Archiv [hereafter SUA], Prague/5-HS-OA-#14.)

41. Rudolf Sandner (*Hauptstelle der SHF*) to Franz Jannausch, November 8, 1933 (SUA, Bratislava/PR-#245).

42. Graf Pfeil report (consulate in Reichenberg) to AA, November 15, 1933 (PA/Kult VIA/Deutschtum in der Tschechoslowakei/vol. 13).

43. Koch report of May 30, 1934 (PA/Pol. II/Politik 5/Innere Politik, Parlaments- und Parteiwesen/vol. 9); *Aussenamt* of the *Deutsche Studentenschaft* (Zimmermann) to Stieve, June 28, 1934 (PA/Kult A/Deutschtum in der Tschechoslowakei/vol. 15): *Abteilung Ausland* of the RJF to AA, March 8, 1934 (PA/Pol. II/Politik 5/Innere Politik, Parlaments- und Parteiwesen/vol. 9). Contrast the negative view of Henlein's activities in the

Zimmermann and *Abteilung Ausland* reports with positive VDA reactions: Steinacher to AA, July 28, 1934 (PA/Kult A/Deutschtum in der Tschechoslowakei/vol. 15).

44. (SUA, Prague/40-k-#68.)

45. *Reichsgeschäftsleitung* Böhmisch-Leipa, apparently intercepted by the SHF, *ibid.*

46. In December of 1933, Brand, Kundt, Dr. Fritz Köllner, and Sebekowsky, all KB members in the top echelon of the new movement were arrested and confined for several months. Luža, *Transfer,* p. 73.

47. For biographical material on Frank, see (SUA, Prague/28-PK-#53); Czechoslovakian Information Ministry, *Česky Národ Soudí K. H. Franka* [The Czech people try K. H. Frank], (Prague, 1947); *Zpověd K. H. Franka* [The confessions of K. H. Frank], with a foreword by and under the technical collaboration of Karl Vykusy (Prague, 1946).

48. Friedrich Bürger interview with the author, January 9, 1969; Hans Neuwirth interview, November 6, 1968; Gustav Peters in his unpublished "Erinnerungen," pp. 272, 323. It is difficult to assess the degree to which Frank was Henlein's "gray eminence": adequate documentation is not available. Statements on the part of other former Sudeten German leaders should be taken *cum grano salis,* in light of the convenient temptation to make of him a scapegoat.

49. *Anklageschrift gegen die Abgeordneten und Senatoren der Sudetendeutschen Partei* (Munich, 1962); interviews with Friedrich Bürger, January 9, 1969, and Dr. Hans Neuwirth, November 6, 1968, also Dr. Hans Steinacher, November 1, 1968.

50. *Anklageschrift,* pp. 36–7.

51. One remark by an AA official illustrates both the extent of the backing behind emigrés like Krebs as well as Hess's indecisiveness in combatting them: "the führer's deputy had been against the appointment of Sudeten German immigrants [to Reich posts] from the very beginning, but had not been able to put across this point of view." Rödiger *Aufzeichnung,* September 21, 1934 (PA/Kult A/Deutschtum in der Tschechoslowakei/vol. 15).

52. Kersken's *Denkschrift* "Zur sudetendeutschen Volkspolitik und deren Möglichkeiten" with two *Anlagen,* June 19, 1934 (BA/R43II/125). Steinacher, "Lebensaufzeichnungen," p. 222.

53. (NA, T-253/49/503733).

54. Bürger interview, January 9, 1969.

55. (NA, T-253/51/505825.)

56. Steinacher, "Notizen," March 1 and 3, 1934; Steinacher, "Lebensaufzeichnungen," p. 221.

57. For the Hitler memo (BA/R43II/125); memo to Meerwald, May 22, 1934 (PA/Kult A/VDA/vol. 11).

58. Goeken *Vermerk,* March 19, 1934 (PA/Kult A/VR/vol. 1/Deutschtum 7); Kersken to Meerwald, June 21, 1934 (BA/R43II/125); Karl Haushofer, *Denkschrift* "Daseinsfrage des V.R.," July 24, 1934 (NA, T-253/51/505887-889).

59. Kersken to *persönlichen Referent* of the führer, June 21, 1934 (BA/R43II/125/BA311).

60. *Anklageschrift*, p. 60; apparently, Krebs's propaganda activities were not limited to the written word. At the request of the mission in Prague, the AA (Lorenz to PROMI, March 20, 1934) was moved to ask the Propaganda ministry for phonograph records supposedly made by Krebs containing propaganda. PROMI to AA, March 24, denied the existence of such records (PA/Politik 6/Nationalitätenfrage, Fremdvölker/vol. 22).

61. Renthe-Fink *Aufzeichnung*, January 31, 1935 (PA/Kult A/Deutschtum in der Tschechoslowakei/vol. 17).

62. *Anklageschrift*, p. 46.

63. Hüffer *Aufzeichnung*, June 22, 1934 (NA, T-120/3523). Krebs to Bibra, October 14, 1936, *Anklageschrift*, p. 56.

64. Köpke (AA) to Koch, June 18, 1934 (NA, T-120/3523).

65. Kersken to Rödiger (AA), June 19, 1934 (PA/Kult VIA/Deutschtum in der Tschechoslowakei/vol. 15).

66. Hüffer *Aufzeichnung*, December 19, 1933 (BA/Schumacher Sammlung/313).

67. Jacobsen, *Aussenpolitik*, p. 200; Frick to *Landesregierungen*, February 24, 1933 (BA/Schumacher Sammlung/355).

68. Steinacher, "Lebensaufzeichnungen," p. 226.

69. Hans Neuwirth *Denkschrift* "Südosten," May 20–25, 1934 (NA, T-253/46).

70. *Anklageschrift*, pp. 54–8. Hess *Verfügung*, December 7, 1933, establishing the *Kontrollstelle* (NA, T-120, 3523). Krichbaum is sometimes incorrectly rendered as "Kriechbaum."

71. Kügler (Ribbentrop's man on the VR) to Jacobsen, September 9, 1966. Documents in the Jacobsen Collection, Bonn.

72. RJF (Teichmann, *Volksgruppenreferent im Abteilung Ausland*) to AA, November 30, 1933 (PA/Pol. IV/Politik 6/Nationalitätenfrage, Fremdvölker/vol. 22).

73. Hans Neuwirth interview, November 6, 1968.

74. VDA to AA via Gestapo, August 11, 1934 (PA/Pol. IV/Politik 6/Nationalitäten, Fremdvölker/vol. 23).

75. Kundt to Holzhausen, December 7, 1933, *ibid.*

76. Koch report, June 9, 1934 (PA/Kult A/Deutschtum in der Tschechoslowakei/vol. 15).

77. Wilhelm Kaiser to Hitler, July 20, 1934, (PA/Pol. IV/Politik 6/Nationalitätenfrage, Fremdvölker/vol. 23).

78. Dietrich Orlow, *The History of the Nazi Party: 1919–1933* (Pittsburgh, 1969), p. 84.

79. Neuwirth, "Südosten" (NA, T-253/46).

80. (BA/R43II/125.) There seems to be no other evidence that backs up Krebs's claim that there was a meeting on May 11 such as the one described here.

81. Kersken, "Zur sudetendeutschen Politik und deren Möglichkeiten," June 19, 1934 (BA/R43II/125).

82. There appears to be no record of Hitler having issued such a decree, just as there seems to be no concrete evidence that Krebs's May 11th meeting with the führer ever really took place. However Hess's orders of March 13, 1934, seem to be very similar to those described in Kersken's paper and attributed to Hitler. Hüffer *Aufzeichnung,* March 28, 1934 (PA/Kult A/ Deutschtum in der Tschechoslowakei/vol. 18). Goeken *Vermerk,* March 19, 1934 (PA/Kult A/Volksdeutscher Rat/Deutschtum 7/vol. 1).

83. Johann Wolfgang Brügel, *Tschechen und Deutsche* (Munich, 1967), p. 249f.

84. Meerwald to Hess, June 15, 1934 (BA/R43II/125).

CHAPTER V

1. The VR had only succeeded to date in subordinating a few minor Germandom organizations such as the *Bund Deutscher Osten* and the *Bund für Volkstum und Heimat*—a meager showing for almost a year's work. Hans-Adolf Jacobsen, *Nationalsozialistische Aussenpolitik 1933–1938* (Frankfurt/ Main, 1968), p. 184.

2. Hans Steinacher, "Notizen," July 30, 1934, Jacobsen Collection, Bonn; also Hans Steinacher interview with the author, November 1, 1968.

3. Steinacher, "Notizen," September 18, 1934; Steinacher, "Lebensaufzeichnungen," pp. 227–28. Friedrich Bürger (alias Walter Schmidt), in his deposition to the Collegium Carolinum, Munich, no. 202, has set the date of the meeting with Hess in 1935. In an interview with the author on January 9, 1969, he admitted that this date was in error. The meeting referred to is the one on September 18, 1934.

4. Steinacher, "Lebensaufzeichnungen," pp. 227–8.

5. SHF *Hauptleitungssitzung* of September 20, 1934 (SUA, Prague/ 2KKH/#6).

6. Henlein interview of October 6, 1934, with *Večer* (PA/Pol.II/Politik 5/Innere Politik, Parlaments- und Parteiwesen/vol. 9). Henlein's *Rundschau* stated on October 7 that the SHF had nothing to do with Krebs, the SHB, or with any other political office in Germany or Austria (PA/Kult A/Deutschtum in der Tschechoslowakei/vol. 15).

7. Koch report, October 22, 1934, with text of Henlein's speech (PA/Pol.IV/Politik 6/Nationalitätenfrage, Fremdvölker/vol. 23).

8. Koch's report, October 23, 1934 (NA, T-120/3523).

9. Radomir Luža, *The Transfer of the Sudeten Germans* (New York, 1964), p. 73; also SHF *Hauptleitungssitzung,* October 23, 1934, where Rosche is supposed to be coopted eventually into the *Hauptrat* of the SHF (SUA, Prague/2KKH/#6).

10. Luža, *Transfer,* p. 75f.

11. Steinacher, "Notizen," January 17, 1935.

12. Luža, *Transfer,* pp. 73, 77.

13. SHF *Hauptleitungssitzung*, November 5, 1934 (SUA, Prague/2KKH/ #6).

14. Luža, *Transfer*, p. 77f.

15. *Ibid.*

16. Graf Pfeil to AA, November 29, 1934 (PA/Kult A/ Deutschtum in der Tschechoslowakei/vol. 16).

17. Koch to AA, November 22, 1934 (PA/Pol.IV/Politik 6/Nationalitätenfrage, Fremdvölker/vol. 23).

18. *Zpověd K. H. Franka* [The confessions of K. H. Frank], foreword by Karl Vykusy (Prague, 1946), p. 30; Helmut K. G. Rönnefarth, *Die Sudetenkrise in der internationalen Politik*, Veröffentlichungen des Instituts für europäische Geschichte Mainz, vol. 21 (Wiesbaden, 1961), 2:103–4, n. 31; Hans Neuwirth, interview with the author, November 6, 1968.

19. SHF *Hauptleitungssitzungen* of November 5 and 12, 1934 (SUA, Prague/2KKH/#6).

20. Jacobsen, *Aussenpolitik*, p. 213f.

21. *Ibid.*, pp. 108f., 215f. For Ribbentrop, *ibid.*, p. 298.

22. Bohle to AA (PA/Kult VIA/Deutschtum 1/vol. 18).

23. Steinacher, "Notizen," October 14–15, 1934.

24. *Ibid.*, October 22, 1934.

25. Hess to Karl Haushofer, October 23, 1934. Haushofer *Nachlass*, Hartschimmelhof, Jacobsen Collection, Bonn.

26. Steinacher, "Notizen," January 9, 1935.

27. Albrecht Haushofer to his father, January 18, 1935. Quoted in Ursula Michel, "Albrecht Haushofer und der Nationalsozialismus" (Ph.D. diss., University of Kiel, 1964), Document Addenda, nos. 57, 35.

28. Jacobsen, *Aussenpolitik*, p. 219.

29. Steinacher, "Notizen," February 1, 1935.

30. Haushofer to Hess, February 3, 1935, Haushofer *Nachlass*, Jacobsen Collection, Bonn.

31. Steinacher, "Notizen," February 1, 1935; Jacobsen, *Aussenpolitik*, p. 220.

32. Steinacher, "Notizen," December 13, 1934.

33. Bohle to AA, February 23, 1935 (PA/Kult A/ Deutschtum in der Tschechoslowakei/vol. 17).

34. Hess to all *Gauleiter*, *Anordnung* 51/35, March 21, 1935 (BA/Schumacher Sammlung/355).

35. Steinacher, "Notizen," December 19–20, 1934.

36. Steinacher, "Lebensaufzeichnungen," pp. 226–7.

37. Jacobsen, *Aussenpolitik*, p. 201. Hilgenfeldt and Bohle had collaborated before against Steinacher. Steinacher, "Notizen," June 16, 1934: "Being heavily bombarded from four sides" in reference to moves by Hilgenfeldt, Bohle, Frick, and Schirach, all of whom accused the VDA of aiding elements beyond the border hostile to the party.

38. Jacobsen, *Aussenpolitik*, p. 801.

39. *Ibid.*, p. 802.

40. Hitler's major foreign policy speech on May 21, 1935, particularly stressed his interest in peace, offered bilateral nonaggression pacts, promised to observe the Lucarno Treaty, and expressed disinterest in Austria. Gerhard L. Weinberg, *The Foreign Policy of Hitler's Germany* (Chicago, 1970), p. 209.

41. Bürger to Rödiger, April 15, 1935; April 30, 1935 (PA/Kult A/ Deutschtum in der Tschechoslowakei/vol. 17).

42. *Ibid.*

43. Krichbaum to RMdI, May 6, 1935 (PA/Kult A/Deutschtum in der Tschechoslowakei/vol. 18).

44. Hess, *Anordnung* 66/35 (BA/Schumacher Sammlung/293).

45. Hess, *Anordnung* 85/35, *ibid.*

46. Steinacher, "Notizen," January 20, 1935.

47. Kersken to Rödiger (AA), September 18, 1934; Stieve to Kersken, September 1934 (PA/Kult A/Deutschtum in der Tschechoslowakei/vol. 15).

48. Hess to Neurath, February 5, 1935 (PA/Kult A/Deutschtum 1/vol. 18).

49. Jacobsen, *Aussenpolitik*, p. 200, n. 8.

50. Hüffer *Aufzeichnung*, March 28, 1934 (PA/Kult A/Deutschtum in der Tschechoslowakei/vol. 18).

51. Koch report, June 25, 1934 (PA/Kult A/Deutschtum in der Tschechoslowakei/vol. 15).

52. Steinacher, "Notizen," December 16–17, 1934.

53. Burmeister, *Staatssekretär* in the Finance Ministry, kept the minutes (BA/R2/15678).

54. Steinacher, "Lebensaufzeichnungen," pp. 229–30.

55. A Koch report to this effect had already been sent to the AA on February 1, so Steinacher may be erring in his dates (PA/Kult A/Deutschtum in der Tschechoslowakei/vol. 17).

56. Hans Neuwirth interview with the author, November 6, 1968; *Zpověd K. H. Franka*, p. 45.

57. Steinacher, "Lebensaufzeichnungen," p. 230; Karl Haushofer to Hess, May 7, 1935, Haushofer *Nachlass*, Jacobsen Collection, Bonn.

58. *See* Johann Wolfgang Brügel, *Tschechen und Deutsche* (Munich, 1967), p. 259.

59. Koch to Stieve, September 20, 1934 (PA/Kult A/Deutschtum in der Tschechoslowakei/vol. 15).

60. In this case Dr. Patschneider apparently received support from Karl von Loesch, head of the German *Schutzbund.*

61. Elisabeth Wiskemann, *Czechs and Germans*, 2nd ed. (London, New York, 1967), pp. 247–8.

CHAPTER VI

1. Johann Wolfgang Brügel, *Tschechen und Deutsche* (Munich, 1967), pp.

265–9; Radomir Luža, *The Transfer of the Sudeten Germans* (New York, 1964), pp. 80–1. The distribution of seats was arranged so that the SdP received forty-four, the Czech Agrarians forty-five mandates.

2. Brügel, *Tschechen*, p. 268. Brügel also denies that the general Sudeten German population was pro-Hitler, maintaining that they were probably thinking in terms of autonomy, p. 267ff. He does claim, however, that Henlein was Hitler's loyal paladin from the very beginning and led his people step by step into the führer's grip.

3. Koch to AA, May 22, 1935. *DGFP*, C, IV, p. 187.

4. Brügel, *Tschechen*, p. 72. His remarks apply to an earlier period but are still valid in 1935.

5. Erich von Hoffmann in *Die Sudetenfrage in europäischer Sicht*, Veröffentlichungen des Collegium Carolinum, vol. 12 (Munich, 1962), p. 252.

6. Edward Peterson, *The Limits of Hitler's Power* (Princeton, 1969), p. 86. Himmler finally fired Vollert in 1943 as unreliable. The following year Vollert was arrested as part of the resistance.

7. Hans Steinacher "Notizen," May 20, 1935, Jacobsen Collection, Bonn. Steinacher's somewhat pejorative reference to Karl Haushofer illustrates the fact that Steinacher had indeed been the driving force behind VR activities, while the general played a more passive role.

8. The VDA and VR had become so closely intertwined because of Steinacher that they were virtually indistinguishable both in the minds of their opponents and, apparently, in Steinacher's mind also.

9. Hans-Adolf Jacobsen, *Nationalsozialistische Aussenpolitik 1933–1938* (Frankfurt/Main, 1968), p. 221.

10. Steinacher, "Notizen," June 20, 1935.

11. Jacobsen, *Aussenpolitik*, pp. 110, 592.

12. *Ibid.*, p. 298.

13. *Ibid.*, pp. 252–318; Eugene Davidson, *The Trial of the Germans* (New York, 1966), pp. 147–67. Ribbentrop began building up his office after Hindenburg had named him Reich plenipotentiary for Disarmament Questions, April 24, 1934.

14. Jacobsen, *Aussenpolitik*, pp. 284, 290f., 301ff. Ribbentrop worked closely with the SD, *ibid.*, p. 290.

15. Davidson, *Trial*, pp. 148, 156, 158.

16. Jacobsen, *Aussenpolitik*, p. 413ff.; Gerhard L. Weinberg, *The Foreign Policy of Hitler's Germany* (Chicago, 1970), pp. 210–16.

17. Letter from Kügler to Professor Hans-Adolf Jacobsen, September 9, 1966, now in the Jacobsen Collection, Bonn.

18. Steinacher, "Notizen," July 16–17, 1935.

19. Jacobsen, *Aussenpolitik*, p. 224f.

20. Hans Steinacher interview with the author, November 1, 1968.

21. Steinacher, "Notizen," August 1–2, 1935.

22. *Ibid.*, August 3, 1935.

23. Schirach to Steinacher, June 18, 1935 (BA/R43II/1407).

24. *See* the following telegrams: Steinacher to Hess, June 18; Steinacher

to Schirach, June 18; Schirach to Lammers, June 25; Thomsen (Reich Chancellory) to Schirach, June 20, 1935 (BA/R43II/1407).

25. Steinacher interview with the author, November 1, 1968; Hillebrand to Haushofer, February 12, 1941 (BA/Haushofer Nachlass/955a).

26. Steinacher to Haushofer, June 27, 1935, Haushofer Nachlass, Hartschimmelhof, Jacobsen Collection, Bonn.

27. Steinacher, "Notizen," July 3, 1935.

28. *Ibid.*, September 6–7, 1935.

29. Jacobsen, *Aussenpolitik*, pp. 225–34, esp. 226f.; BDC file on Kursell; Robert Koehl, *RKFDV: German Resettlement and Population Policy 1939–1945*, Harvard Historical Monographs, No. 31 (Cambridge, Mass., 1957), p. 37, n. 8.

30. Jacobsen, *Aussenpolitik*, p. 226.

31. *Ibid.*, pp. 226, 231.

32. *Ibid.*, p. 230.

33. *Ibid.*

34. *Ibid.*, p. 605.

35. *Ibid.*, p. 228f.

36. "Memorandum über die Entwicklung der Opposition in der SdP", unsigned, May 25, 1936 (SUA, Prague/5-HS-OA/#14). The *Aufbruch* people thereupon availed themselves of the title of a journal formerly published by their KB opponents, *Die junge Front*.

37. César and Černý, *Politika německých buržoaních stran v Československu v letech 1918–1938* [The politics of the German bourgeois parties in Czechoslovakia in the years 1918–1938], 2 vols. (Prague, 1962) 2:275f. Some SdP members thought the telegram, which had been composed by Henlein, Brand, and Neuwirth, to be too conciliatory. It went unanswered. Helmut K. G. Rönnefarth, *Die Sudetenkrise in der internationalen Politik*, Veröffentlichungen des Instituts für europäischer Geschichte Mainz, vol. 21 (Wiesbaden, 1961), 1:141f.

38. SdP *Hauptleitungssitzung*, May 23, 1935 (SUA, Prague/2KKH/#6).

39. Luža, *Transfer*, pp. 73, 77.

40. Věra Olivová, "Československo a německo ve třicátých letech" ["Czechoslovakia and Germany in the 1930s"], in *Československý Časopis historický*, no. 6 (1968): 887–8; cf. Rönnefarth, *Sudetenkrise*, 1:142–8; Brügel, *Tschechen*, pp. 270–1. The Czech-Soviet alliance of June of 1935 was also a blow to this scheme. Beneš's election to president of the republic in December ended any real possibility of a coalition. The SdP and the Czech Agrarians had failed to unite on a candidate in the elections, Karel Kramář (Kramář, the first minister president of Czechoslovakia, was the very embodiment of extreme Czech nationalism). Rönnefarth, *Sudetenkrise*, 1:150f.

41. César and Černý, *Politika*, 2:318.

42. Stein (legation in Prague) to AA, August 26 and 28, 1938 (NA, T-120/3523).

43. Stein to AA, August 31, 1935 (NA, T-120/3527).

44. *See* Rönnefarth, *Sudetenkrise*, 1:142–50.

45. "Rundbrief an die Mitarbeiter aus den Gründungtagen der Bewegung," *Konrad Henlein Spricht,* Bücherei der Sudetendeutschen Heimatfront, Series I, no. 2 (Karlsbad, Leipzig, 1937), p. 18ff.

46. Luža, *Transfer,* p. 86.

47. The Czech prime minister, Hodža, contributed further to this process when he announced on December 5, 1935, that the government refused to recognize the SdP as the sole representative of the Germans in Czechoslovakia. Boris Celovsky, *Das münchener Abkommen von 1938,* Quellen und Darstellungen zur Zeitgeschichte, no. 3 (Stuttgart, 1958), p. 115.

48. Luža, *Transfer,* p. 80; also p. 59, n. 53.

49. Rönnefarth, *Sudetenkrise,* 1:163; Steinacher interview, November 1, 1968.

50. Interesting evidence of such pressures are the remarks by Gerhard Fuchs, *Gegen Hitler und Henlein,* Schriftenreihe der Kommission der Historiker der DDR und der ČSSR, no. 4 (Berlin, 1961), p. 169; Gerhard Fuchs, "Zur Behandlung der sudetendeutschen Frage (1933–1938) in der westdeutschen Geschichtsliteratur," *Probleme der Geschichte des Zweiten Weltkrieges* (Berlin, 1958), 2:147f.

A concrete illustration of the internal class dissention is Peters's criticism of the proposed "Wirtschaftsprogramm der SdP" prepared by Janovsky. Peters, a leader of the business-oriented faction of the party, felt that the report was too hard on business. Gustav Peters to Henlein, October 14, 1937 (SUA, Prague/40K/#71).

51. "Memorandum über die Entwicklung der Opposition in der SdP," unsigned, dated May 25, 1936 (SUA, Prague/5-HS-OA/#14). In time, both KB and *Aufbruch* became generic epithets hurled at political opponents who had nothing to do with either organization.

52. SdP *Hauptratssitzung,* July 4, 1935 (SUA, Prague/2KKH/#6).

53. Remarks by Otto von Stein (German diplomat in Prague) on the SA-*Standarte* 134 in Plauen. Stein to AA, September 25, 1935 (NA, T-120/3523).

54. Altenburg to RMdI, PROMI, and *Reichsministerium für Wissenschaft, Erziehung und Volksbildung,* November 14, 1935 (PA/Pol. IV/Politik 6/Nationalitätenfrage, Fremdvölker/vol. 24).

55. Koch report, June 15, 1934 (PA/Kult A/Deutschtum in der Tschechoslowakei/vol. 15).

56. Goeken (AA) to Dr. Rudolf Fricke (a Steinacher colleague), October 15, 1935, (*ibid.,* vol. 18).

57. Josef Suchy, in charge of education in the SdP, made a deal with the NSDAP *Parteischulung* to receive materials. Similar connections existed between the *Reichsbund für Leibesübungen* and the *Turnschule* in Asch, as well as the *Reichsnährstand. Zpověd K. H. Franka* [The confessions of K. H. Frank], foreword by Karl Vykusy (Prague, 1946), p. 36f.; *IMT,* 32: 10; *Anklageschrift gegen die Abgeordneten und Senatoren der Sudetendeutschen Partei* (Munich, 1962), p. 46; Luža, *Transfer,* p. 100.

58. (BA/Schumacher Sammlung/313.)

59. Wagner to Reich-Prussian Interior Ministry, April 9, 1936 (PA/Inland IIg/220/vol. 1).

60. Heinburg (AA) *Aufzeichnung*, November 13, 1936, quoted in Brügel, *Tschechen*, p. 284.

61. Peterson, *Hitler's Power*, pp. 428–51.

62. Otto von Stein to AA, August 31, 1935 (NA, T-120/3523); Rönnefarth, *Sudetenkrise*, 1:159–61.

63. Gustav Peters, "Erinnerungen aus den Jahren 1885–1935," unpublished manuscript in the Collegium Carolinum, Munich, pp. 329–30; Friedrich Bürger interview with the author, January 9, 1969.

64. July 8, 1936 (BA/Schumacher Sammlung/313).

65. Steinacher, "Notizen," November 4, 1935.

66. *Ibid.,* November 22, 1935.

67. For complaints about attacks from the *Rumburger Zeitung*, "Sudetendeutscher Dienst," an SdP newsletter distributed in Berlin, December 10, 1935 (SUA, Prague/41-T/#80); also "Sudetendeutsche Pressebriefe," Prague, January 24, 1936, no. 20, p. 4 (SUA, Litoměříce).

68. Steinacher, "Notizen," November 23, 1935. Steinacher believed the assurances to have come from Lammers (Reich Chancellory). Steinacher interview, November 1, 1968.

69. Krebs to Wiedemann (Hitler's adjutant), December 9, 1935, asking for the opportunity to thank the führer personally for his appointment and at the same time to discuss the Sudeten problem. The meeting did not take place. *Aktennotiz,* Wiedemann for Meerwald (also *Reichskanzlei*), December 11, 1935 (BA/R43II/1407).

70. Dieter Ross, *Hitler und Dollfuss,* Hamburger Beiträge zur Zeitgeschichte, vol. 3 (Hamburg, 1966), p. 189ff.; cf. Weinberg, *Foreign Policy*, p. 103f.

71. Weinberg, *Foreign Policy*, p. 215f.

72. *Ibid.,* p. 235f.

CHAPTER VII

1. Gerhard L. Weinberg, *The Foreign Policy of Hitler's Germany* (Chicago, 1970), Chapter 11.

2. *Ibid.,* p. 270.

3. Boris Celovsky, *Das münchener Abkommen von 1938,* Quellen und Dartstellungen zur Zeitgeschichte, no. 3 (Stuttgart, 1958), p. 132.

4. Weinberg, *Foreign Policy*, pp. 315–21.

5. On the efforts of Sudeten leaders to secure aid and sympathy in England, *see* Celovsky, *Abkommen*, p. 114ff.; Radomir Luža, *The Transfer of the Sudeten Germans* (New York, 1964), p. 86ff.; Johann Wolfgang Brügel, *Tschechen und Deutsche* (Munich, 1967), p. 264ff.

6. Walter Brand, *Die Sudetendeutsche Tragödie*, Ackermann-Schriften für Kultur, Wirtschaft, und Politik, no. 1 (Lauf bei Nuremburg, 1949), p. 38.

7. Steinacher, "Notizen," July 8, 1935, Jacobsen Collection, Bonn.

8. Laurence Thompson, *The Greatest Treason; the Untold Story of Munich* (New York, 1968), p. 22. Thompson was the first scholar who succeeded in interviewing Christie.

9. *Ibid.*, p. 275. Colonel Christie denied having ever been a member of the Secret Service, as had been commonly assumed. His only contact, he claimed, was with his friend Vansittart.

10. *See Völkischer Beobachter*, no. 345, December 12, 1935.

11. *Zpověd K. H. Franka* [The confessions of K. H. Frank], foreword by Karl Vykusy (Prague, 1946), p. 24.

12. *Ibid.*

13. Stein to AA, August 21, 1935 (NA, T-120/3523).

14. Telegram from Woermann (AA) to Prague legation, June 10, 1936 (PA/Pol. IV/Politik 6/Rassenfrage, Fremdvölker, Nationalitätenfrage [hereafter RFN]/vol. 1).

15. Telegram from Eisenlohr (Prague) to AA, July 15, 1936, *ibid.*

16. Luža, *Transfer*, p. 87. These remarks coincided with the Nazi propaganda campaign which was also harping on the theme of the "Bolshevisation" of Czechoslovakia: a fact which takes some of the credence from the SdP claim to be working independently. On the other hand, a great many conservatives, including Czechs, were very wary of the Russian alliance, and showed great sympathy with the anticommunist line.

17. *Ibid.*, p. 87f.

18. Brügel, *Tschechen*, p. 286f.

19. Neurath *Aufzeichnung*, August 14, 1936; Stein report, July 21, 1936. Both in (PA/Pol. IV/Politik 6/RFN/vol. 1).

20. Brügel, *Tschechen*, p. 287.

21. Luža, *Transfer*, p. 87.

22. Neurath *Aufzeichnung*, August 14, 1936 (PA/Pol. IV/Politik 6/RFN/vol. 1).

23. Altenburg *Aufzeichnung*, October 9, 1936, quoted in Koloman Gajan and Robert Kvaček, eds., *Deutschland und die Tschechoslowakei 1918–1945* (Prague, 1965), p. 99f., Document 26.

24. Stieve to Prague legation, February 1, 1937 (PA/Inland IIg/222/Deutschtum/vol. 3).

25. *Ibid.*

26. Celovsky, *Abkommen*, p. 118f. Brand was an ideal man for the job. The radicals wanted him out of the way anyway, and Brand's English language abilities were the best of any of Henlein's collaborators. Brand later extended his activities to Paris as well.

27. Gerhard L. Weinberg, "Secret Hitler-Beneš Negotiations in 1936–37," *Journal of Central European Affairs*, 19, no. 1 (1960): 368–74; Robert Kvaček, "Ceskoslovensko německá jednání v roce 1936" [The Czechoslovak-German negotiations in 1936], *Historie a vojenství* (1965), pp. 721–54; *see also* accounts in Brügel, *Tschechen*, p. 355ff.; Celovsky, *Abkommen*, p. 88f.; Weinberg, *Foreign Policy*, pp. 316–21.

28. Weinberg, "Negotiations," p. 366f.

29. *Ibid.*, p. 368.

30. Brügel, *Tschechen*, p. 355. A personal factor was also involved in Trauttmansdorff's Germandom activities: he seems to have had visions of becoming a kind of social attaché in Prague. Note also Trauttmansdorff's letter to Celovsky, in *Abkommen*, p. 97f. For Beneš on Trauttmansdorff, *see Memoirs of Dr. Beneš* (London, 1954), p. 15.

31. Trauttmansdorff's report, January 9, 1937, "Bericht über die Verhältnisse in der Tschechoslowakei," Library of Congress, Manuscript Division, Washington, D.C., Albrecht-Haushofer folder, no. 11249; also Brügel, *Tschechen*, p. 355.

32. Weinberg, "Negotiations," p. 369f.

33. *Ibid.*, p. 370ff., for Haushofer report to Hitler. I follow Weinberg in my assessment of Hitler's marginal comments.

34. Weinberg, *Foreign Policy*, p. 320.

35. Quoted in Weinberg, "Negotiations," p. 371, n. 24.

36. Ursula Michel, "Albrecht Haushofer und der Nationalsozialismus" (Ph.D. diss., University of Kiel, 1964), pp. 132, 149.

37. "Memorandum über die Entwicklung der Opposition in der SdP," p. 6f. (SUA, Prague/5-HS-OA/#14.)

38. *Ibid.*, p. 7.

39. *Ibid.*

40. *Ibid.*

41. *Ibid.*

42. Luža, *Transfer*, p. 89.

43. Protocol of the *Hauptratssitzung*, May 28, 1936 (SUA, Prague/2KKH/#6).

44. "Memorandum über die Entwicklung der Opposition in der SdP," pp. 10–11 (SUA, Prague/5-HS-OA/#14). Also BDC file on Meckel.

45. In *Tagung* of the *Hauptrat* and *Klubvorstand* of the SdP in Eger, June 11, 1936 (SUA, Prague/2KKH/#6).

46. Eisenlohr to Renthe-Fink, June 13, 1936 (PA/Pol. IV/Politik 6/RFN/vol. 1).

47. "Gedächtnisprotokoll über die Bereinigung der sudetendeutschen Angelegenheiten", unsigned, June 9, 1936; telegram from Renthe-Fink to Prague, June 11, 1936, both *ibid.*

48. (SUA, Prague/2KKH/#6.) Mediation was not limited to high levels in the SdP but also went on among the rank and file. For example, the adjutant of *Reichssportführer* Graf v. d. Schulenburg was to travel to Asch to settle quarrels there between the *Turnverband* and the *Sportverein.* Eisenlohr to AA, Telegram 139, December 2, 1936 (PA/Pol. IV/Politik 6/RFN/vol. 2).

49. Hans-Adolf Jacobsen, *Nationalsozialistische Aussenpolitik 1933–1938* (Frankfurt/Main, 1968), p. 231.

50. Franz Wehofsich interview with the author, November 19, 1968; BDC file on Wehofsich.

51. "Verlauf der Einigungsverhandlungen Konrad Henlein-Rudolf Kas-

per," June 12, 1936, which is Kasper's own account of the negotiations which he passed on to Kursell (SUA, Prague/5-HS-OA/#14) and also (PA/Pol. IV/Politik 6/RFN/vol. 1). Henlein explained his position in the meeting of the party *Hauptrat* and *Klubvorstand* on June 11. On July 8, at a *Hauptleitungssitzung* of the SdP, Henlein appointed Brand head of his private chancellory and made Frank his deputy (SUA, Prague/2KKH/#6)

52. Altenburg, Wehofsich, Krebs, and Frank were present. Altenburg *Aufzeichnung,* July 25, 1936 (PA/Pol. IV/Politik 6/RFN/vol. 1).

53. Lierau in Reichenberg was busy writing Krebs to this effect: for example his letter of July 16, 1936, referred to in *Anklageschrift gegen die Abgeordneten und Senatoren der Sudetendeutschen Partei* (Munich, 1962), pp. 47–8.

54. Jaroslav César and Bohumil Černý, *Politika Německízch buržoaních stran v Československu v letech 1918–1938* [The politics of the German bourgeois parties in Czechoslovakia in the years 1918–1938] 2 vols. (Prague, 1962), 2:370, n. 166.

55. *Ibid.,* p. 363, n. 146.

56. Neurath put his account of the meeting on paper that same day (PA/Pol. IV/Politik 6/RFN/vol. 1).

57. Altenburg *Aufzeichnung,* August 17, 1936, *ibid.*

58. Eisenlohr telegram to AA, October 6, 1936, (*ibid.,* vol. 2); Altenburg *Aufzeichnung,* October 9, 1936 (SUA, Prague/AA-I/98-29-#D49858) quoted in Koloman Gajan and Robert Kvaček, eds. *Deutschland und die Tschechoslowakei,* p. 99f., Document 26.

59. Brügel, *Tschechen,* p. 259.

60. Altenburg *Aufzeichnung,* February 15, 1937; Altenburg to *Personalabteilung,* September 26, 1936 (PA/Pol. II/(Verschluss)/Pog Tschech./vol. 1).

61. Unsigned *Aufzeichnung,* September 7, 1936 (PA/Inland IIg/221/vol. 2). Telegram from Eisenlohr to AA, February 6, 1937 (PA/Pol. II/(Verschluss)/Pog Tschech./vol. 4).

62. VDA to AA, February 3, 1936, requesting that 9,560 crowns be passed on to SdP delegate Köllner (PA/Kult A/VDA/vol. 15).

63. Grünau (AA) to Reich Finance Ministry, March 9, 1936 (PA/Inland II/63-01 OSSA/#079-80).

64. Renthe-Fink *Aufzeichnung,* January 22, 1936, Jacobsen Collection, Bonn. The request for funds was granted February 3 by the Finance Ministry. Luža, *Transfer,* p. 100.

65. Altenburg *Aufzeichnung,* October 9, 1936 (PA/Pol. IV/Politik 6/RFN/vol. 2); Altenburg *Aufzeichnung,* October 16, 1936, and letter from Altenburg to Krüger (Ley's representative), November 17, 1936 (PA/Pol. II/(Verschluss)/Pog Tschech./vol. 1).

66. Altenburg (?) to Gritzbach (*Stabsamt* General Göring), February 13, 1937 (PA/Pol. II/(Verschluss)/Pog Tschech./vol. 1).

67. Luža, *Transfer,* pp. 91–2.

68. Helmut K. G. Rönnefarth, *Die Sudetenkrise in der internationalen Politik,* Veröffentlichungen des Instituts fur europäischer Geschichte Mainz, vol. 21(Wiesbaden, 1961), I:156.

69. In terms of discontent, economic dislocation, and radicalization, the summer of 1936 appears in retrospect to be a watershed. One sign of this was the rapid multiplication of contacts with the Reich after that point. Walter Brand, *Tragödie,* p. 35; Gustav Peters, "Erinnerungen aus den Jahren 1885–1935," unpublished manuscript in the Collegium Carolinum Munich, pp. 329–330; Friedrich Bürger interview with author, January 9, 1969.

70. Steinacher was again feeling increasingly threatened, as he confided to Henlein, "Notizen," August 13, 1936.

71. Renthe-Fink *Aufzeichnung,* March 24, 1936; AA to Eisenlohr, March 26; Willuhn (Reich Chancellory) to Reichs-Aussenminister Neurath, April 7, 1936; Lammers (Reich Chancellory) to AA, April 29 (all in PA/Pol. II/(Verschluss)/Pog Tschech./vol. 12). Celovsky, *Abkommen,* p. 107, n. 1, referring in surprise to Jung's low party number (85), draws the conclusion that Jung must have been a long time member of the NSDAP. Celovsky fails to recognize the tactic of bestowing such numbers *ex post facto* as a mark of privilege. Actually, Krebs, Jung, and Schubert were made party members in November of 1935 *as of April 1, 1925* with the numbers 85, 86, and 87 respectively, along with the Golden Party Emblem. Jung *Denkschrift,* undated (BA/Schumacher Sammlung/313).

As part of Henlein's campaign to solicit Hitler's recognition, in July 1936 he sent the führer a copy of the book, *Sudetenland,* with a handwritten dedication. Meissner sent the book to Hitler's adjutant, Schaub, on July 17 with a printed thank-you note for Hitler's signature. Brügel, *Tschechen,* p. 594, n. 73. If Henlein thought he would get a reaction from the führer with such niceties, he was to be sadly disappointed.

72. Rönnefarth, *Sudetenkrise,* 1:156.

CHAPTER VIII

1. SS racial ideology and settlement policies were set down perhaps most completely by Ulrich Greifelt during the war in "Die Festigung deutschen Volkstums als zentrale Ostaufgabe" (RKFDV Stabshauptamt, n.d. but after June 1941). (NA, T-74/10/38180), 4ff.; also "Planungsgrundlagen für den Aufbau der Ostgebiete" (Planungsabteilung des RKFDV, n.d.). (NA, T-74/15/38668ff.)

2. Steinacher had a glimmering of what was to come. He wrote as early as 1934: "A whole new domestic political power grouping is in the works. We shall not remain unmolested. The SS is pushing to the fore." Hans Steinacher, "Notizen," August 4, 1934, Jacobsen Collection, Bonn. He subsequently added to the entry: "In June I received an officer of the SS who was to inquire what I thought about ethnic resettlement. I declined sharply." Despite these misgivings, Steinacher seems to have treated the SS as just one more power constellation and was not initially aware of the magnitude of the threat.

3. Schlomo Aronson, "Heydrich und die Anfänge des SD und der Gestapo 1931–1935" (Ph.D. diss. Freie Universität, 1967); George Browder,

" 'SIPO' and SD, 1931–1940. Formation of an Instrument of Power" (Ph.D. diss., University of Wisconsin, 1968); Hans Buchheim, *SS und Polizei im NS-Staat* (Duisdorf, 1964).

4. Aronson, "Heydrich," p. 186.

5. *Ibid.,* p. 185.

6. Friedrich Zipfel, "Gestapo und SD in Berlin," *Jahrbuch für die Geschichte Mittel- und Ostdeutschland,* vol. 10 (1961): 272; also Hess *Anordnung* of October 20, 1934, Rudolf Hess, *Anordnungen des Stellvertreters des Führers,* collection of all *Anordnungen* issued prior to March 31, 1937 and still valid at that date (Munich, 1937), p. 661.

7. Aronson, "Heydrich," pp. 288–318; Browder, " 'SIPO' and SD," p. 96ff.

8. Browder, " 'SIPO' and SD," p. 98f.

9. Hess *Verfügung* of December 7, 1933. Hess, *Anordnungen des Stellvertreters,* pp. 26–7.

10. BDC file on Krichbaum (sometimes misspelled Kriechbaum). Walter Schellenberg claimed that Krichbaum was an old acquaintance of Heydrich, who had "slipped" [*eingeschleust*] him into the job. Helmuth Groscurth, *Tagebuch eines Abwehroffiziers 1938–1940,* Quellen und Darstellungen zur Zeitgeschichte, vol. 19 (Stuttgart, 1970).

11. Krichbaum Gestapo questionnaire, March 15, 1937. BDC file on Krichbaum.

12. Aronson, "Heydrich," p. 150ff.

13. Steinacher, "Lebensaufzeichnungen," p. 226f.; also letter from Krebs to Krichbaum, December 12, 1937, *Anklageschrift gegen die Abgeordneten und Senatoren der SdP* (Munich, 1962), p. 58.

14. Reports from Krichbaum to the Interior Ministry, May 6, 1935, containing detailed information on VR members Hermann Ullmann, Friedrich Bürger, Hans Neuwirth, and Hans Rückel (VDA-*Landesleiter,* Bavaria); also report on Hanns Beer. All the reports are sharply negative except the one on Beer, which is extremely positive. (PA/Kult A/Deutschtum in der Tschechoslowakei/vol. 18).

15. Hanns Beer *Mitteilung* of ʼOctober 7, 1933, as newly named *Reichstreuhändler* of the SHB (PA/Politik 6 Sonderakte/Sudetendeutscher Heimatbund/vol. 2).

16. Neuwirth statement to the Czech People's Court, *Anklageschrift,* p. 38.

17. *See* Gestapa Darmstadt to Staatspolizeistellen, Kreisämter and Polizeiämter, October 7, 1935, BDC Research Division, Ordner 313, p. 153; also Heydrich to Wolff in Himmler's personal staff, February 2, 1938, BDC file on Rudolf Haider.

18. *See* letter from Wilhelm Kaiser to Hitler, July 20, 1934 (PA/Pol. IV/Politik 6/Nationalitätenfrage, Fremdvölker/vol. 23).

19. *See* reports from Agent Go.1 to Gestapo Dezernat II 1A2 of January 19 and February 14, 1935 (BA/R58/347-10/RSHA). Dezernat II 1A2 was in charge of "SPD, SAP, Reichsbanner, Freie Gewerkschaften, Sportverbände

der verbotenen Organisation," Aronson, "Heydrich," p. 298. See also August Heissmayer, chief of the SS *Personalamt, Rundschreiben* of July 12, 1935, warning against SS people crossing into Czechoslovakia on the grounds that they would get arrested (BA/NS2/38 RuSHA/vol. 50).

20. Steinacher, "Notizen," September 24, 1935.

21. Aronson, "Heydrich," p. 426, n. 78.

22. Bohumil Černý, *Most k novému životu. Německá emigrace v ČSR v letech 1933–1939* [Bridges to a new life. The German emigrés in the CSR in the years 1933–1939] (Prague, 1967), pp. 138–51; Charles Wighton, *Heydrich, Hitler's Most Evil Henchman* (London, 1962), pp. 115–18; Rene Sonderegger, *Mordzentrale X: Enthüllungen und Dokumente über die Auslandstätigkeit der deutschen Gestapo,* Kulturpolitische Schriften, no. 5 (Zurich, 1936), pp. 50–77. Naujocks used the alias "Müller." One of his companions was SD man Werner Göttsch who later would become involved with SD activities in Slovakia. BDC file on Werner Göttsch; also Jörg Hoensch, *Die Slowakei und Hitlers Ostpolitik,* Beiträge zur Geschichte Osteuropas, vol. 4 (Cologne, Graz, 1965), pp. 186, 190, 223f.

23. Jürgen Runzheimer, "Der Ueberfall auf den Gleiwitzer Sender," *Vierteljahrshefte für Zeitgeschichte,* 10, no. 4 (October 1962): 408–26.

24. Hans Buchheim, *Anatomie des SS-Staates,* 2 vols. (Munich, 1967), 1:60.

25. Černý, *Most,* discusses the left-wing German emigrés in Czechoslovakia and SD activities.

26. Wighton, *Heydrich,* p. 102f.

27. Hermann Raschhofer, *Die Sudetenfrage: ihre völkerrechtliche Entwicklung vom ersten Weltkrieg bis zur Gegenwart* (Munich, 1953), pp. 162–3, n. 1.

28. "Memorandum über die Entwicklung der Opposition in der SdP," May 25, 1936 (SUA, Prague/ 5-HS-OA/#14).

29. Viererbl had a regular column entitled "Auslandsdeutsche Rundschau" in the NS-*Monatshefte.* Typical of his attacks on the KB and political Catholicism are the September and December issues, 1935, and the January through April issues, 1936.

30. *Der Spannkreis* (BA/DA/195), pp. 1–24.

31. *Ibid.,* p. 23.

32. The document was probably prepared by Alfred Schweder, one of the earliest SD men, personally recruited by Heydrich. Schweder, who is the author of *Politische Polizei,* was deputy director of the problem area (*Sachgebiet*) "Politischer Katholizismus" by 1939. Information on his activities is from Friedrich Zipfel, "Gestapo und SD," p. 275f., n. 37.

33. Walter Schellenberg, *Memoiren,* ed. Gita Petersen (Cologne, 1956), p. 57.

34. Heydrich to *Persönlicher Stab,* RFSS, March 10, 1938, in BDC file on Viererbl.

35. Lurtz to *Bundeskanzleramt,* July 29, 1936, quoted from Johann Wolfgang Brügel, *Tschechen und Deutsche* (Munich, 1967), p. 318f.

36. Letter from Karl Goerdeler to an American friend, quoted in Hans Gisevius, *Bis zum bitteren Ende,* 2 vols. (Zurich, 1946), 2:362.

292   *The Sudeten Problem, 1933–1938*

37. Heydrich to RFSS *Persönlicher Stab,* June 27, 1941; Brehm to Gestapo *Leitstelle* Kattowitz, May 28, 1943. BDC file on Brehm.

38. Brehm to SS-WVHA, December 2, 1943, *ibid.*

39. Brehm to Hess, October 7, 1938, *ibid.*

40. Heydrich to RFSS *Persönlicher Stab,* June 27, 1941, *ibid.*

41. Brehm to Willich, SD-*Hauptamt,* May 8, 1940. BDC Research Division, Ordner 457. Also BDC file on Liebl; BDC Mappe Polizei-Liste SD/RFSS, 12.

42. *Lebenslauf,* BDC file on Kasper.

43. Fritz Tittmann to Party Treasurer Schwarz, March 22, 1939, *ibid.*

44. *Lebenslauf, ibid.*

45. Tittmann *Bescheinigung* on Kasper, December 20, 1939. Kasper later cashed in on both his contacts in the Reich. After April 1939 he became SS-*Standartenführer, Abteilungsleiter* in the DAF (Ley's Labor Front), and special deputy for ethnic German work in the *Volksdeutsche Mittelstelle. Ibid.*

46. When the remainder of Czechoslovakia was occupied on March 15, 1939, Meckel was promoted to SS-*Standartenführer* and, on Heydrich's personal recommendation, was assigned to the SD-*Hauptamt.* Meckel, *Lebenslauf*; Meckel to SS-*Oberführer* Kelz, SS-*Hauptamt,* September 13, 1939, all in BDC file, Meckel. *See also* Chapter VII, n. 43.

47. A list of the sixty-five names is included with a letter from Brehm to Willich, SD-*Hauptamt,* May 8, 1940. BDC Research Division, Ordner 457.

48. Hans-Adolf Jacobsen, *Nationalsozialistische Aussenpolitik 1933–1938* (Frankfurt/Main, 1968), p. 261. Another example of infiltration was the gradual takeover of the Gestapo in Prussia. Aronson, "Heydrich," p. 247f.

49. Jacobsen, *Aussenpolitik,* pp. 276–80, 284, 303, 702–3.

50. *Ibid.,* p. 290. Also *Dienststelle Ribbentrop* (no signature, but probably Ribbentrop himself) to Dr. Best (Gestapo), May 5, 1937 (PA/Dienststelle Ribbentrop/343864).

51. Likus (SS) *Notiz,* December 19, 1936 (PA/Dienststelle Ribbentrop/343927-28).

52. Jacobsen, *Aussenpolitik,* pp. 284, 308.

53. "Aufzeichnung über den Einsatz des SD im Ausland," dated August 8, 1940 (PA/Inland IIg/83-78/71).

54. *See* BDC file on Lierau.

55. Lierau to SS-*Hauptamt,* June 11, 1935, *ibid.*

56. See Heydrich to Himmler, April 2, 1936, *ibid.*

57. This information comes from an interview with Friedrich Bürger (January 9, 1969). On Bibra as Bohle's protégé, *see* Jacobsen, *Aussenpolitik,* pp. 475, 517. On Chamier, see his BDC file; also Steinacher, "Lebensaufzeichnungen," p. 349.

58. *Anklageschrift,* pp. 56–7; also (PA/Inland IIg/225/vol. 6).

59. Letters of October 25 and November 12, 1936, Gerhard L. Weinberg, "Secret Hitler-Beneš Negotiations in 1936–37," *Journal of Central European Affairs,* 19, no. 1 (1960):369.

60. Albrecht Haushofer to his father Karl, February 13, 1938 (BA/Haushofer Nachlass/833).

61. Henlein had complained pointedly about the paper in his conversation with Foreign Minister von Neurath in Berlin during the Olympic Games. *See also* Steinacher, "Lebensaufzeichnungen," p. 349f. Typical of the newspaper's position, which was almost identical to that of *Aufbruch,* is an article of July 17, 1936 (*Rumburger Zeitung,* no. 170, p. 1), praising a labor-oriented local SdP leader who resigned from the party in the wake of the pro-KB settlement of party disputes.

62. Between December 17, 1936, and February 4, 1937, the *Rumburger Zeitung* carried verbatim no less than six major speeches by Hitler, Göring, and Rosenberg. *See* no. 301, December 12, 1936, p. 7; no. 2, January 1, 1937, p. 5; no. 16, January 20, 1937, p. 5; no. 25, January 30, 1937, p. 5; no. 26, January 31, 1937, p. 3; no. 29, February 2, 1937, p. 7.

63. Hans Neuwirth interview with author, November 6, 1968.

64. There is no direct documentation on SD support of the newspaper. Evidence on the SD connections comes to us almost entirely through eyewitness accounts or is circumstantial. Nevertheless there is compelling reason to believe that the contention is a valid one. The strongest single piece of evidence is probably the case of Kursell's dismissal, *see* nn. 88–89; also Kursell's own testimony, Jacobsen, *Aussenpolitik,* p. 232. Both Hans Neuwirth (in an interview with the author on November 6, 1968) and Hans Steinacher (in an interview with the author on November 1, 1968 and in his "Lebensaufzeichnungen," p. 349f.) have attested to SD backing of the paper and its attacks. Moreover, the circumstances surrounding the attempts to ban the newspaper in Germany and Henlein's futile pleas for that ban while on his visit to the Reich, indicates that the paper had *very* powerful backers. This would also account for the fact that its information seemed to come from high places in the Reich. In addition, after Goebbels had proclaimed the ban, it was the *police* network (*i.e.,* Himmler) which foiled the order by not passing it on.

65. Hans Neuwirth interview, November 6, 1968.

66. Steinacher, "Lebensaufzeichnungen," p. 350.

67. *Rumburger Zeitung,* no. 262, November 1, 1936, p. 3, in an article entitled "Die Klassenkämpfer des Geistes an der Arbeit."

68. Of a circulation of 2,000, 1,500 copies went to the Reich. Neurath *Aufzeichnung,* August 14, 1936 (PA/Pol. IV/Politik 6/RFN/vol. 1).

69. Hans Steinacher interview, November 1, 1968.

70. Ribbentrop, isolated as ambassador in London, would have enough problems just holding on to his own inside line to Hitler. Between November of 1936 and November of 1937, he made eleven trips to Berlin. Eugene Davidson, *The Trial of the Germans* (New York, 1966), p. 158.

71. *See* Chapter 7, n. 56.

72. On the *Abwehr*-SD relationship, *see* Karl Heinz Abshagen, *Canaris: Patriot und Weltbürger* (Stuttgart, 1950), pp. 107, 138–9, 180; Oscar Reile, *Geheime Ostfront: Die deutsche Abwehr im Osten 1921–1945* (Munich-Wels, 1963), pp. 193, 250ff.; Heinrich Orb, *13 Jahre Machtrausch: Nationalsozialismus,* (Olten, Switzerland, 1945), pp. 75f., 365ff.; also Paul Leverkuehn,

German Military Intelligence, trans. R. H. Stevens and C. FitzGibbon (London, 1954).

73. For the text of the agreement, *see* Gerd Buchheit, *Der deutsche Geheimdienst* (Munich, 1966), p. 456, n. 21; 170ff.

74. Abshagen, *Canaris,* pp. 123, 185–90. Also Lahousen testimony, IMT, *Trial of the Major War Criminals before the International Military Tribunal* (Nuremburg, 1947–49) 2:411f.

75. Groscurth, *Tagebuch,* entry for October 6, 1938, notes that Canaris was completely disregarded in the festivities following the Sudeten union and resented it "since [he] had discovered Henlein three years ago and propped him up. . . ." (BA/N104/1 Groscurth).

76. Report on Lierau accompanying Heydrich's letter to Himmler, recommending that Lierau be excluded from the SS. BDC file on Lierau.

77. Abshagen, *Canaris,* p. 141f.

78. In a review of the year 1935, written approximately August of 1938, Groscurth describes his position in the *Abwehr.* "Privates Tagebuch Gros-curths," p. 2, courtesy of the *Institut für Zeitgeschichte,* Munich. Groscurth shared the views of his chief; along with Hans Oster, Groscurth was later one of the officers most actively pursuing the overthrow of the Nazi regime. Abshagen, *Canaris,* p. 123.

79. Groscurth wrote in 1938: "Domestically, too, there was endless friction, above all with the Gestapo. It was very difficult to aid Henlein, who until 1938 was completely rejected by many political agencies." Groscurth, "Privates Tagebuch," p. 2. That Groscurth had good connections with Henlein's movement becomes clear in a letter from the *Büro Kursell* (Jenkner) to Altenburg (AA), November 16, 1936; the writer mentions that since Kursell has no way of testing a certain Sudeten leader's reliability, he's going to consult Groscurth for an expert opinion (PA/Pol. II/(Verschluss)/Pog Tschech./vol. 1).

80. Kersken *Denkschrift,* June 19, 1934 (BA/R43II/125). Bürger told the author, on January 9, 1969, that he had been on "best terms with Groscurth."

81. Except where otherwise indicated, details on the *Rumburger Zeitung* affair come from Steinacher's "Lebensaufzeichnungen," pp. 349–51.

82. See *Rumburger Zeitung* articles January 17, 1937, no. 14, p. 1; January 23, 1937, no. 20, p. 2; January 28, 1937, no. 23, p. 3.

83. Steinacher, "Lebensaufzeichnungen," p. 351.

84. Viererbl memo to Rosenberg, February 4, 1937 (BA/NS8/117).

85. Steinacher wrote of Wehofsich in 1935: "I have to give Wehofsich to Kursell. Necessary. Whether Wutschi [Wehofsich's nickname] will be able to be loyal and hold the line? Whether his career will be more important to him than character." Steinacher, "Notizen," December 21, 1935. A year later (on November 28, 1936), Steinacher had his answer: ". . . Wehofsich . . . is hanging his head. Wants to keep connection with Bohle."

86. Davidson, *Trial,* p. 158.

87. Aronson, "Heydrich," p. 423, n. 37.

88. The complaint included three other newspapers: *Deutsche Landpost,*

Sudetendeutsche Tageszeitung, and *Rigasche Post*—indicating that the *Rumburger Zeitung* was perhaps not the only paper through which the SD was working. Kursell to Wiedemann, December 17, 1936 (BA/NS10/34/281–282).

89. Jacobsen, *Aussenpolitik,* p. 232.

90. *Ibid.;* also Albrecht Haushofer to his father, January 19, 1937, quoted in Ursula Michel, "Albrecht Haushofer und der Nationalsozialismus" (Ph.D. diss., University of Kiel, 1964), Document Addenda, nos. 61, 31.

91. Haushofer to Hess (NA, T-253/56/512012-13).

92. Hess to Neurath, January 27, 1937 (PA/Inland IIg/222/Deutschtum/vol. 3). Also Jacobsen, *Aussenpolitik,* p. 234f.

93. On Lorenz, *see* Robert Koehl, *RKFDV: German Resettlement and Population Policy 1939*–1945, Harvard Historical Monographs, no. 31 (Cambridge, Mass., 1957), pp. 37–9; Jacobsen, *Aussenpolitik,* p. 236f.

94. On Behrends, *see* his BDC file; also Jacobsen, *Aussenpolitik,* p. 237f.

95. Gisevius, *Bis zum bitteren Ende,* 1:165; also Orb, *Machtrausch,* p. 90f. Behrends had been transferred to the SD-*Hauptamt* on January 13, 1934, as an *Untersturmführer.* By April 20, 1934, he had made *Hauptsturmführer.* Then, in rapid succession on June 15, *Sturmbannführer;* July 4, *Obersturmführer. Dienstalterliste der Schutzstaffel der NSDAP, 1. Dezember, 1938* (Berlin, 1938).

96. On at least two occasions, Lorenz assured Steinacher of his support. Steinacher, "Notizen," February 8 and March 12, 1937.

97. After explaining his ideas to Lorenz on March 12, Steinacher wrote: "Apparently I hadn't made myself clear enough." *Ibid.,* March 12, 1937.

98. *Ibid.,* March 15, 1937.

CHAPTER IX

1. Hans-Adolf Jacobsen, *Nationalsozialistische Aussenpolitik 1933–1938* (Frankfurt/Main, 1968), pp. 246–8.

2. Hans Steinacher interview with the author November 1, 1968; Steinacher, "Notizen," January 22, 1937 Jacobsen Collection, Bonn; Albrecht Haushofer folder no. 11249, Library of Congress, Manuscript Division, Washington, D.C.

3. Jacobsen, *Aussenpolitik,* p. 249.

4. DAI (either Strölin or Csaki) memo on conference with Lorenz, April 23, 1937 (BA/R57/vorl. 163–7).

5. Stieve *Aufzeichnung* (for Mackensen), May 20, 1937 (PA/Kult A/VDA/vol. 17).

6. Jacobsen, *Aussenpolitik,* p. 247f.

7. *Ibid.,* p. 246.

8. Steinacher, "Notizen," February 13, 1937.

9. *Ibid.,* June 23, 1937.

10. Jacobsen, *Aussenpolitik,* p. 249.

11. Rödiger report (AA), September 27, 1937 (BA/R57/vorl. 163–7).

12. Proclamation of the *Reichsorganisationsleiter,* September 2, 1937 (BA/Schumacher Sammlung/355).

13. Rödiger (AA) report, September 27, 1937 (BA/R57/vorl. 163–7).

14. Steinacher, "Notizen," August 13, 1937; also "Lebensaufzeichnungen," p. 387.

15. Trauttmansdorff's "Bericht über die Verhältnisse in der Tschechoslowakei," January 9, 1937, in Library of Congress, Manuscript Division, Washington, D.C., Albrecht Haushofer folder no. 11249.

16. Lierau (Reichenberg) to AA, January 30, 1937 (PA/Kult A/ Deutschtum in der Tschechoslowakei/vol. 22).

17. *See* Jacobsen, *Aussenpolitik*, p. 241.

18. *See* "Abschlussprotokoll über die Verhandlungen mit der deutschen Volksgruppe aus Rumänien," Behrends, April 24, 1937. VOMI recognized the Fabritius group. *See* telegram from Twardowski (AA) to Bucharest legation, May 11, 1937. Both in (PA/Inland IIg/223).

19. "Stellungnahme zum Bericht über die Prüfung der VFK für die Geschäftsjahre 1936 und 1937," unsigned, p. 24 (PA/Inland IId/64–01/9/vol. 193).

20. *Rundschreiben* no. 36/37 of the *Reichsorganisationsleiter der NSDAP,* July 27, 1937 (BA/R43II/124a).

21. Unsigned, undated "Notiz" (PA/Inland IId/64–03).

22. Jacobsen, *Aussenpolitik*, p. 236.

23. *Zpověď K. H. Franka* [The confessions of K. H. Frank], foreword by Karl Vykusy (Prague, 1946), p. 26.

24. Telegram from Twardowski to Prague Legation, June 17, 1937, and Eisenlohr reply of June 18 (PA/Kult VIA/Deutschtum in der Tschechoslowakei/vol. 23).

25. VOMI to *Deutsches Auslandsinstitut,* June 30, 1937 (BA/R57/163–7).

26. Telegram of Langmann (AA) to Prague legation, June 30, 1937 (PA/Kult VIA/Deutschtum in der Tschechoslowakei/vol. 24).

27. Eisenlohr report, July 11, 1937 (included in letter of Krebs to Altenburg, July 12) (PA/Pol. IV/Politik 6/RFN/vol. 4).

28. Altenburg *Vermerk,* July 15, 1937 (PA/Pol. IV/Politik 6/RFN/vol. 4); Altenburg to Legation Secretary von Halem in Prague, July 15, 1937, in Koloman Gajan and Robert Kvaček, eds., *Deutschland und die Tschechoslowakei* (Prague, 1965), pp. 129–30, Document 494305.

29. Krebs to Altenburg, July 15, 1937 (PA/Pol. IV/Politik 6/RFN/vol. 4).

30. Twardowski, "Notiz," August 18, 1937 (PA/Inland IIg/223).

31. Vogt (SdP Office for Nationalities and League of Nations Questions) letters to Henlein, November 24 and December 7, 1936 (SUA, Prague/ 22ANV/#37).

32. Fries "Notiz," August 23, 1937 (PA/Inland IIg/223).

33. *Die Zeit*, Prague, September 10, 1937 (PA/Kult VIA/Deutschtum in der Tschechoslowakei/vol. 24).

34. *Zpověď K. H. Franka*, p. 26; also SdP *Hauptleitungssitzung* (SUA, Prague/2KKH/#6).

35. Altenburg *Aufzeichnung*, March 3, 1937 (PA/Pol. IV/Politik 6/ RFN/vol. 3).

36. *Ibid.*

37. Eisenlohr telegram to Heinburg (AA), April 25, 1937 (PA/Pol. IV/Politik 6/RFN/vol. 4).

38. *Zpověď K. H. Franka,* p. 26.

39. Lierau to AA, October 7, 1937, quoted in Gajan and Kvaček, eds., *Deutschland und die Tschechoslowakei,* Document 49313-15.

40. *See* Bormann *Rundschreiben*, November 13, 1937 (BA/Schumacher Sammlung/355).

41. Fischer (AO) *Aufzeichnung*, October 22, 1937 (PA/Chef-AO/vol. 94).

42. Jacobsen, *Aussenpolitik*, p. 427.

43. *Ibid.,* p. 249.

44. *Ibid.*

45. Telegram from Steinacher to Hitler, October 21, 1937 (BA/R-43II/1408C/RK16485B).

46. *Vermerk* (Röhrecke in the Reich Chancellory), November 3, 1937, *ibid.*

47. Ursula Michel, "Albrecht Haushofer und der Nationalsozialismus" (Ph.D. diss., University of Kiel, 1964), p. 157.

48. Behrends to AA, December 2, 1937 (PA/Kult A/vol. 17).

49. Friedrich Bürger to Groscurth, October 21, 1937 (BA/R-43II/1408C/RK17988B).

50. Bürger to Lammers, November 4, 1937. The letter contains the names of others who received copies, *ibid.*

51. On Rutha, *see* letter from Krebs to Fritz Wiedemann (Reich Chancellory), October 9, 1937, with accompanying report (PA/NS10/34/2-7).

52. Rutha had been vice-president of the *Deutscher Völkerbundliga* and also of the European Nationalities Congress; board member of the *Verband der deutschen Volksgruppen Europas.* Taken from his obituary (SUA, Prague/22ANV/#36).

53. Franz Wehofsich interview with the author, November 19, 1968. Wehofsich claimed that Kreissl, Krebs's man in Czechoslovakia, had smuggled suspenders into Rutha's cell with which he then hanged himself.

54. On the Teplitz-Schönau incident, *see* Altenburg *Aufzeichnung*, November 6, 1937, *DGFP, D, II,* #9; also Helmut K. G. Rönnefarth, *Die Sudetenkrise in der internationalen Politik*, Veröffentlichung des Instituts fur europäische Geschichte Mainz, vol. 21 (Wiesbaden, 1961), I:171ff.; *cf.* Johann Wolfgang Brügel, *Tschechen und Deutsche* (Munich, 1967) p. 327f.

55. Quoted in Radomir Luža, *The Transfer of the Sudeten Germans*, (New York, 1964), p. 103, n. 93.

56. Eisenlohr report, October 22, 1937, *Akten zur deutschen Auswärtigen Politik* (Baden-Baden, 1950), Series D, vol. II, #5. Hereafter *ADAP.*

57. Eisenlohr report, October 24, 1937. *Ibid.,* #6.

58. Eisenlohr telegram to Heinburg (AA), April 25, 1937 (PA/Pol. IV/Politik 6/RFN/vol. 4).

59. "Aussprache Konrad Henleins mit Herrn Ministerpräsidenten Dr. Hodža," September 16, 1937 (SUA, Prague/28PK/#52).

60. *See* record of conversation with Lorenz (probably Dr. Strölin of the *Deutsches Auslandsinstitut*), November 18, 1937 (BA/R57/vorl. 163–7).

61. Text in *ADAP*, D, II, #23 (November 19, 1937). Note that Henlein quite possibly did not write the letter to Hitler himself but had it composed. The real writer remains anonymous. Rönnefarth, *Sudetenkrise*, 2:82, n. 8, suggests that neither Henlein nor Frank were *wortgewandt* enough to have written the document.

62. Goebbels broke off the campaign abruptly on November 3. Mackensen *Aufzeichnung*, November 3, 1937. *ADAP*, D, II, #11.

63. Gustav Peters, "Erinnerungen aus den Jahren 1885–1935," manuscript in the Collegium Carolinum, Munich, p. 364.

64. "Niederschrift über die Besprechung in der Reichskanzlei am 5. November 1937 von 16.15 bis 20.30 Uhr," *IMT*, 25:386; *ADAP*, D, I, #19. *Cf.* A. J. P. Taylor, *The Origins of the Second World War* (New York, 1963), p. 128ff.

65. See Boris Celvosky, *Das münchener Abkommen von 1938.* Quellen und Darstellungen zur Zeitgeschichte, No. 3 (Stuttgart, 1958), pp. 91–93.

CHAPTER X

1. In this context *see* Keith Eubank, "Konrad Henlein, the Sudeten Question and British Foreign Policy," *The Historical Journal*, 12, 4 (1969):674–97.

2. Schmidt *Aufzeichnung*, November 19, 1937. *ADAP.*, D, I, #31.

3. *Notiz für den Führer*, January 7, 1938. *ADAP*, D, I, #93. Erich Kordt regarded this document as Ribbentrop's "political testament," *Nicht aus den Akten* (Stuttgart, 1950), p. 175.

4. Letter to Trauttmann, ambassador to China, June 30, 1938, quoted in Boris Celovsky, *Das münchener Abkommen von 1938*, Quellen und Darstellungen zur Zeitgeschichte, no. 3 (Stuttgart, 1958), p. 156, n. 8; also Weizsäcker *Aufzeichnung*, n.d., but beginning of June 1938, *ADAP*, D, II, #259.

5. A. J. P. Taylor, *The Origins of the Second World War* (New York, 1963), p. 138; Alan Bullock, *Hitler, a Study in Tyranny*, rev. ed. (New York, 1961), pp. 361–7.

6. On Austria, *see* Jürgen Gehl, *Austria, Germany and the Anschluss 1931–1938* (London, 1963).

7. Eisenlohr to AA, March 31, 1938, *ADAP*, D, II, #112.

8. *Ibid.*

9. Jonak and Kasper were expelled. *See* report in the *Reichspost* (Vienna), December 5, 1937 (BA/Schumacher Sammlung/313).

10. Altenburg *Aufzeichnung*, December 9, 1937 (PA/Inland IIg/225/vol. 6). The ban on *Aufbruch* in Czechoslovakia had been lifted in 1937.

11. VOMI (Stier) to Burmeister (Finance Ministry), (BA/R2/15718/for-

merly F.6642); Hencke (Prague) to Chef AO, March 4, 1938, Jacobsen Collection, Bonn.

12. Spahn (AO) memo (for Bohle), March 1, 1938; also unsigned *Aufzeichnung* (AO), undated but approximately at the same time as the memo. Both in (PA/Chef-AO/Tschechoslowakei/121).

13. Eisenlohr to AA, December 6, 1937 (PA/Kult A/Deutschtum in der Tschechoslowakei/vol. 25).

14. Eisenlohr to *Staatssekretär* AA, March 11, 1938 (PA/Pol. IV/Politik 6/RFN/vol. 6/#226).

15. Otto von Bismarck (AA) to Eisenlohr, March 14, 1938, *ibid.*, #228.

16. Mackensen (AA) to Eisenlohr, March 17, 1938; Groscurth (*Abwehr*) to AA, March 14, 1938. Both in PA/Inland IIg/226/vol. 7).

17. Eisenlohr to AA, March 18, 1938 (PA/Chef-AO/Tschech./121).

18. Eisenlohr to AA, March 16, 1938 (PA/Inland IIg/226/vol. 7).

19. Eisenlohr to AA, February 4, 1938 (PA/Kult A/Deutschtum in der Tschechoslowakei/vol. 25).

20. Capra *Vermerk* of February 12, 1938, Jacobsen Collection, Bonn.

21. Quoted in Keith Robbins, *Munich 1938* (London, 1968), p. 190.

22. Henlein to Ribbentrop, March 17, 1938, *ADAP*, D, II, #89.

23. On the meeting between Henlein, Frank and Hitler see, "Vortragsnotiz über meine Besprechung mit dem Führer der Sudetendeutschen Partei, Konrad Henlein und seinem Stellvertreter, Karl Hermann Frank," unsigned, in files of *Staatssekretär, ibid.,* #107.

24. Erich Kordt, *Akten*, pp. 207–8; Ribbentrop's account of the meeting, *ADAP*, D, II, #111, *Aufzeichnung*, March 31, 1938. Ribbentrop had written the following names in the margin of Henlein's letter to him (*see* n. 21): "Frank, Kundt, Samilkowski,/Sebekowsky?/Künzel, Neuwirth. (Kameradschaftsbund) Span [*sic*], Kreisel [*sic*], Casper, Brehm." Over Frank's name he had written *forciert*; over Kundt's *kein Vertrauen*. The group was almost equally divided between KB and *Aufbruch* people.

25. Eisenlohr to AA, March 31, 1938 (PA/Inland IIg/226/vol. 7).

26. Hencke to AA, March 31, 1938, *ibid.*

27. *See* n. 25.

28. VOMI (Luig) to PROMI (Krieg), April 8, 1938 (PA/Pol. IV/Politik 6/RFN/vol. 8).

29. Eisenlohr to AA, April 4, 1938 (PA/Chef AO/Tschech./121).

30. Eisenlohr to AA, April 1, 1938 (PA/Inland IIg/226/vol. 7).

31. Weizsäcker (*Staatssekretär* in AA) to Prague, April 6, 1938, *ADAP*, D, II, #118.

32. Eisenlohr paraphrases Eckert's comments and also includes recommendations of his own in a report to Ribbentrop, April 9, 1938, *ibid.*, #123.

33. *Ibid.*

34. Luig (VOMI) to *Oberste SA-Führung*, Munich, April 9, 1938, *ADAP*, D, II, #125.

35. Luig to Krieg (PROMI), April 8, 1938 (PA/Pol. IV/Politik 6/RFN/vol. 8).

36. Eisenlohr to AA, April 8, 1938, *ibid.*

37. Telegram from Weizsäcker to Prague, April 11, 1938, *ibid.*

38. For a copy of the Eight Demands, *ADAP*, D, II, #135.

39. Eisenlohr to Berlin, April 26, 1938, *ibid.*, #138.

40. Celovsky, *Abkommen*, p. 157.

41. Schmundt *Aufzeichnung*, "Grundlage zur Studie 'Grün'. Zusammen-fassung der Besprechung Führer-Gen. Keitel am. 21.4," April 22, 1938, *ADAP*, D, II, #133.

42. Schmundt *Aufzeichnung*, April 1938, "Erwägung des Führers", *ibid.*, #132.

43. Helmut K. G. Rönnefarth, *Die Sudetenkrise in der internationalen Politik*, Veröffentlichung des Instituts fur europäische Geschichte Mainz, vol. 21 (Wiesbaden, 1961), 1:256ff.

44. Henlein left on May 12 for two days. Weizsäcker *Aufzeichnung*, May 12, 1938, *ADAP*, D, II, #155; Laurence Thompson, *The Greatest Treason* (New York, 1968), p. 69f.

45. In a letter to a Lieutenant Colonel Kurt Graebe, who passed the information on to the AA, May 24, 1938 (PA/Kult A/Deutschtum in der Tschech./vol. 26); Herbert von Dirksen (London) to AA, June 10, 1938, *ADAP*, D, II, #250; interview with Friedrich Bürger (who had spoken with Henlein upon his return to Berlin), January 9, 1969.

46. Woermann to embassy in Rome, May 7, 1938, *ADAP*, D, II, #149.

47. Annex to Woermann letter of May 7, 1938 to Rome, *ibid.*, #150.

48. Otto von Bismarck *Aufzeichnung*, May 10, 1938, *ibid.*, #151.

49. "Entwurf für die neue Weisung 'Grün'," annex to note from General Wilhelm Keitel to Hitler, May 20, 1938, *ibid.*, #175.

50. Annex to *Oberkommando der Wehrmacht*, "Weisung für Plan 'Grün'," May 20, 1938, *ibid.*, #221.

51. From Part I of new draft for "Operation Green." Prepared by General Staff for Hitler's signature, *ibid.*, #282.

52. Hans-Adolf Jacobsen, *Nationalsozialistische Aussenpolitik 1933-1938* (Frankfurt/Main, 1968), p. 241ff.

53. Erdmannsdorf (Budapest) to AA, April 11, 1938 (PA/Inland IIg/227/vol. 8).

54. Hess to Frick (Interior Ministry), cc. to other ministries, April 30, 1938 (BA/R2/15718/formerly F. 6642).

55. Jacobsen, *Aussenpolitik*, p. 245.

56. On May 13, *DGFP*, D, II, #276. British observers diverged somewhat from Eisenlohr's assessment of the general mood at this time. Newton to Halifax, July 26, 1938, Prague: report states that moderate elements are gaining ground in the SdP. General conclusion is that the majority of Sudeten Germans are still for *Anschluss*, but not an overwhelming majority, E. L. Woodward and Rohan Butler, eds., *Documents on British Foreign Policy 1919-1939*, 2 vols. (London, 1949), Third Series, vol. II, #549, p. 9. Hereafter *DBFP*.

57. Lorenz *Aufzeichnung*, June 3, 1938, *ADAP*, D, II, #237.

58. *Ibid.,* #238.

59. Eisenlohr to AA, June 18, 1938 (PA/Staatssekretär/Tschechoslowakei/vol. 1).

60. (PA/Inland IIg/232/vol. 13).

61. Jacobsen, *Aussenpolitik*, p. 243.

62. Records show the following breakdown: Ministry of the Interior, 17–18 million; AA, 15–16 million; *Deutsche Stiftung* und OSSA, 12–15 million; PROMI, 3 million; plus miscellaneous others. (PA/Inland IIg/226/Deutschtum/vol. 7), March, 19, 1939, Appendices A and B.

63. Ribbentrop *Anordnung* #18, July 6, 1938 (PA/Handakten Hewel/11).

64. Weizsäcker *Aufzeichnung*, July 15, 1938 (PA/Staatssekretär/Tschechoslowakei/vol. 2).

65. Altenburg (AA) to Hencke (Prague), June 20, 1938, relaying that VOMI has expressed the desire that the electric works in Troppau remain in German hands (PA/Pol. IV/Politik 6/vol. 11).

66. Stieve (AA) to VOMI, July 7, 1938 (BA/R2/15718/formerly F. 6642).

67. Lorenz to AA, June 9, 1938, *ibid.*

68. Eisenlohr to AA, May 18, 1938, *ADAP*, D, II, #164. On May 20, VOMI sent word to Eisenlohr that Wannemacher be reprimanded, *DGFP*, D, II, #176, pp. 303–4.

69. Henderson to Halifax, August 25, *DBFP*, Third Series, II, #689, p. 156.

70. Halifax to Campbell (Paris), August 25, *DBFP*, Third Series, II, #691, p. 159. Neurath, the former German foreign minister, knew better and told Henderson so: "His Excellency [Neurath] replied that after six years' close association he knew Herr Hitler pretty well and that, unless he had greatly changed, he did not believe that he would burn his boats at Nuremburg. Herr Hitler preferred to do things in his own way and not as he was expected to do." *DBFP*, Third Series, II, #757, pp. 224–6. This apparently did not impress the British very much, although Neurath had characterized Hitler's approach to decision making most accurately.

71. Runciman to Halifax, August 24, *DBFP*, Third Series, II, #680, pp. 149–50.

72. Weizsäcker *Aufzeichnung*, July 21, 1938 (PA/Staatssekretär/Tschechoslowakei/vol. 2). The British also noted that the mood of the Sudeten Germans was tending toward moderation, partly because of irritation at the fruitless negotiations, partly out of disappointment that the Reich was not offering more support. *DBFP*, Third Series, II, #566, pp. 29–33.

73. Woermann *Aufzeichnungen*, August 13–14, 1938, (PA/Staatssekretär/Tschechoslowakei/vol. 2).

74. *Ibid.*

75. Hencke to AA, August 20, 1938, *DGFP*, D, II, #378, pp. 596–8; Hencke to AA, August 24, 1938, *ibid.,* #386, pp. 614–17; Hencke to AA, August 26, 1938, *ibid.,* #391, pp. 624–5.

76. Altenburg *Aufzeichnung*, August 18, 1938 (PA/Inland IIg/229/vol. 10).

77. Walter Brand, *Die sudetendeutsche Tragödie*, Ackermann-Schriften für Kultur, Wirtschaft, und Politik, no. 1 (Lauf bei Nürnberg, 1949), p. 42.

78. Walter Schellenberg, *Memoiren*, ed. Gita Petersen (Cologne, 1956), p. 57.

79. Helmut Groscurth, *Tagebuch eines Abwehroffiziers 1938–1940*, Quellen und Darstellungen zur Zeitgeschichte, vol. 19 (Stuttgart, 1970), p. 104. As late as the end of July, Hitler had not betrayed his intentions to Frank. On the occasion of the international *Turnfest* in Breslau he had told Frank and the Sudeten delegation, "Have patience and wait." *Zpověd K. H. Franka* [The confessions of K. H. Frank], foreword by Karl Vykusy (Prague, 1946), p. 39. Thompson, *Treason*, without giving the source quotes Hitler (p. 121) as saying: "Don't get impatient. Go home. Stand by your tasks. Stand together. Obey Henlein."

80. Newton to Halifax, August 19, 1938, *DBFP*, Third Series, II, #652, p. 122; Runciman to Halifax, August 23, *ibid.*, #674, p. 142; Appendix II, "Conversations with Herr Henlein" and "Memorandum on the Sudeten German Question and Lord Runciman's Mission," *ibid.*, pp. 656–9; Troutbeck to Halifax, August 29, 1938, *ibid.*, #706, pp. 177–8. Also Hencke to AA, August 24, 1938, *DGFP*, D, II, #387, pp. 617–18.

81. Groscurth, *Tagebuch*, pp. 108–9; Schmidt (Friedrich Bürger) Deposition #202, Sudetendeutsches Archiv, Munich.

82. Newton to Halifax, September 1, 1938, *DBFP*, Third Series, II, #731–732, pp. 199–201.

83. Groscurth, *Tagebuch eines Abwehroffiziers*, pp. 111–12. Apparently Henlein did not give up completely in his attempts to dissuade Hitler. Bürger maintained that later, just after the Party Day, Henlein "returned depressed; he had tried to convince Hitler that a military solution was not necessary. Hitler had answered, *he needed a trial run for his young Wehrmacht.*" Bürger Deposition, #202, Sudetendeutsches Archiv, Munich. Also *Zpověd K. H. Franka*, p. 42.

84. Hencke to AA, August 30 and September 1, 1938, *DGFP*, D, II, #407; pp. 660–1; #417, pp. 675–6.

85. See annex of Hencke to AA, September 8, 1938, *ADAP*, D, II, #440.

86. Telegram #339 Hencke to AA, September 8, 1938, *ibid.*, #441.

87. Telegram #340 Hencke to AA, September 8, 1938, *ibid.*, #442.

88. Weizsäcker *Aufzeichnung*, September 10, 1938 (PA/Staatssekretär/Tschechoslowakei/vol. 3).

89. Rönnefarth, *Sudetenkrise*, 1:485f. Rönnefarth blames Frank for creating the incident.

90. Hencke to AA, September 9, 1938, *ADAP*, D, II, #446.

91. Göring and Goebbel's speeches quoted in *Völkischer Beobachter*, September 11–12, 1938. Portion here quoted from Johann Wolfgang Brügel, *Tschechen und Deutsche* (Munich, 1967), p. 464.

92. *Adolf Hitler Reden und Proklamationen 1932–1945*, ed. Max Domarus, 2 vols. (Würzburg, 1962–3), 2:897–906.

93. Rönnefarth, *Sudetenkrise*, 1:492ff.

94. Altenburg *Aufzeichnung,* September 13, 1938, *ADAP,* D, II, #467.

95. Schmundt notes on conference, September 9–10, 1938, *DGFP,* D, II, #448, pp. 727–30.

96. Koloman Gajan and Robert Kvaček, eds., *Deutschland und die Tschechoslowakei* (Prague, 1965), p. 143, Document 44. Rönnefarth sees the ultimatum as Frank's work, *Sudetenkrise,* 1:493.

97. Hans Neuwirth, *Aussage* no. 201/VI, 5f., Sudetendeutsches Archiv, Munich; Walter Brand claimed to have overheard a conversation between Frank and Hitler. Frank pleaded for tanks and troops. Hitler replied that Frank should wait; that the time was not yet ripe. Thompson, *Treason,* p. 142.

98. The Czechs had proclaimed martial law in parts of Bohemia. Altenburg Memorandum, September 14, 1938, *DGFP,* D, II, #472, p. 757.

99. Eisenlohr to AA, September 14, 1938, *ADAP,* D, II, #481.

100. Hencke reports of September 17, 1938; Toussaint report of the same date. *ADAP,* D, II, #513, #515, #520.

101. Pierre Buk (F. C. Weiskopf), *La Tragédie tchécoslovaque de Septembre 1938 a Màrs 1939, avec des documents inédits du Livre blanc tchécoslovaque* (Paris, 1939), p. 27.

102. Kordt (London) to AA, September 13, 1938, *ADAP,* D, II, #470.

103. Henlein to Hitler, September 15, 1938, *ibid.,* #489.

104. *Ibid.,* #490.

Bibliography

A. PRIMARY SOURCES

1. Archives, Unpublished Documents
a. BERLIN DOCUMENT CENTER (BDC)—Personal files on:
    Sigismund von Bibra
    Friedrich Brehm
    Fritz von Chamier
    Werner Göttsch
    Rudolf Haider
    Rudolf Kasper
    Heinrich Kersken
    Wilhelm Krichbaum
    Otto von Kursell
    Otto Liebl
    Walter von Lierau
    Rudolf Meckel
    Karl Viererbl

    BDC Research Division, Ordners 313, 355, 457 Mappe Polizeiliste SD/RFSS 12

b. BUNDESARCHIV, KOBLENZ (BA)
    Schumacher Sammlung / 292, 293, 313, 355
    R43II (Reichskanzlei) / 124a, 125, 1406, 1407, 1408c
    DA / 195 (Der Spannkreis. Gefahren und Auswirkungen)
    Haushofer Nachlass / 944b, 955a, 833
    R2 / 15678 (Finanzministerium) 25–29, 15718
    R58 / 347–10 / RSHA
    NS2 / 38 RuSHA / vol. 50 (RSHA)
    N104 / 1 Groscurth (Groscurth Nachlass)
    NS8 / 117 (NSDAP)
    R57 / vorl. 163–7; DAI 675 (Deutsches Auslandsinstitut)
    NS10 / 34 / 2–7 (NSDAP), 281–282
c. INSTITUT FÜR ZEITGESCHICHTE, Munich
    "Privates Tagebuch Groscurths," unpublished manuscript

d. LIBRARY OF CONGRESS, Manuscript Division, Washington, D.C.
Albrecht Haushofer folder no. 11249

e. NATIONAL ARCHIVES MICROCOPY (NA), Alexandria, Virginia
    T-74 / Office of the Reich Commissioner for the Strengthening of
    Germandom
    T-120 / German Foreign Ministry Records
    T-175 / Records of the Reichsführer SS and Chief of the German Police
    T-253 / Records of Private German Individuals

f. POLITISCHES ARCHIV DES AUSWÄRTIGEN AMTES, Bonn (PA)
    Kulturabteilung: (Kult A = Kult VIA):
    Kult A / Deutschtum in der Tschechoslowakei / 13, 15, 16, 17, 18, 22–26
    Kult A / Deutschtum 1 / Tschechoslowakei / 13
    Kult A / Deutschtum im Ausland / 18
    Kult A / Deutschtum 1 / 18
    Kult A / Volksdeutscher Rat / Deutschtum 7 / vol. 1
    Kult A / VDA / 9, 10, 11, 13, 15, 17, 19
    Kult A / 2VDA / 9, 10
    Politische Abteilung:
    Pol. IV / Politik 6 / Nationalitätenfrage, Fremdvölker / 22, 23, 24
    Pol. IV / Politik 6 / Rassenfrage, Fremdvölker, Nationalitätenfrage
        [RFN] / 1, 2, 3, 4, 6, 8, 11, 12
    Politik 6 Sonderakte / Sudetendeutscher Heimatbund [SHB] / 1, 2
    Pol. II / (Verschluss) / Pog Tschech / 1, 4, 5, 12
    Pol. II / Politik 5 / Innere Politik, Parlament und Parteiwesen / 9
    Politik—Inland:
    Inland IId / 63-01 OSSA / 079-80
    Inland IId / 64-01 / 9 / 193
    Inland IId / 64-03
    Inland IIg / 220 / 1 (Deutschtum)
    Inland IIg / 221 / 2   ”
    Inland IIg / 222 / 3   ”
    Inland IIg / 223 / 4   ”
    Inland IIg / 225 / 6   ”
    Inland IIg / 226 / 7   ”
    Inland IIg / 227 / 8   ”
    Inland IIg / 229 / 10   ”
    Inland IIg / 232 / 13   ”
    Inland IIg / 82-01 / Geschäftsgang
    Inland IIg / 83-78 / 71
    Staatssekretär:
    Tschechoslowakei 1, 2, 3
    Dienststelle Ribbentrop
    Chef AO:
    49 (Korrespondenz mit Stellvertreter des Führers-Stabsleiter)
    53 (Die oberste Leitung der AO: Schriftwechsel)

94 (VDA)
121 (Tschechoslowakei)
Handakten Hewel: 11
g. STÁTNÍ ÚSTŘEDNI ARCHIV, Bratislava (SUA, Bratislava)
PR245
h. STÁTNÍ ÚSTŘEDNI ARCHIV, Litoměřice (SUA, Litoměřice)
Sudetendeutsche Pressebriefe
i. STÁTNÍ ÚSTŘEDNI ARCHIV, Prague (SUA, Prague)
Fond SdP #1 / vol. 1
5-HS-OA #14
40K-#68, #71
41-T #80
28PK- #52, #53 (SdP records)
2KKH- #6 (SdP records)
22ANV / #36, #37 (SdP records)
11HS / STF / #24
Presidium zemeského úřadu v Praze / 53372
j. SUDETENDEUTSCHES ARCHIV & COLLEGIUM CAROLINUM, Munich
Deposition #200 / Gustav Peters manuscript, "Erinnerungen aus den Jahren 1885–1935"
Deposition #201 / Hans Neuwirth, "Zeugnis—Schrifttum zur sudetendeutschen Geschichte"
Deposition #202 / Walter Schmidt (Friedrich Bürger), "Aufzeichnung über die Beziehungen Konrad Henleins zu Adolf Hitler 1936–1938"
Deposition #203 / Walter Brand, "Aufzeichnung über die Tatigkeit von Dr. W. Brand in London und Paris in den Tagen der tschechischen Mobilmachung Ende Mai 1938"
k. UNIVERSITY OF WISCONSIN, Memorial Library
Karl Nabersberg, "Arbeitsbericht für das Jahr 1934 der Abteilung 'Ausland' in der Reichsjugendführung", copy #6
1. MISCELLANEOUS
JOHANN GOTTFRIED VON HERDER INSTITUT, Marburg
INSTITUT FÜR AUSLANDSBEZIEHUNGEN, Stuttgart
INTERVIEWS:
Walter Brand—November 11, 1968
Friedrich Bürger—January 9, 1969
Hans Neuwirth—November 6, 1968
Hans Steinacher—November 1, 1968
Franz Wehofsich—November 19, 1968
JACOBSEN COLLECTION, Bonn
Documents in private possession of Professor Hans-Adolf Jacobsen, including Haushofer papers
Hans Steinacher, unpublished calendar notes ("Notizen"), transcribed by Professor H.-A. Jacobsen

2. Published Documents

Brandner, Willi, ed. *Konrad Henlein: Reden und Aufsätze zur völkischen Turnbewegung. 1928–1933.* Karlsbad: K. H. Frank, 1934.

Czechoslovakian Ministry of Information. *Česky Národ Soudí K. H. Franka* (The Czech people try K. H. Frank). Prague: 1947.

Dienstaltersliste der Schutzstaffel der NSDAP. 1. December 1938. Berlin: 1938.

Documents on British Foreign Policy. 1919–1939. Edited by E. L. Woodward and Rohan Butler. Third Series. 2 vols. London: His Majesty's Stationery Office, 1949. (DBFP)

Documents on German Foreign Policy 1918–1945. Series D (1937–1945). Washington, D.C.: U.S. Government Printing Office, 1949–1951. (DGFP)

———. Series C (1933–1937). Washington, D.C.: U.S. Government Printing Office, 1957–1963. (DGFP)

Domarus, Max, ed. *Adolf Hitler. Reden und Proklamationen 1932–1945.* 2 vols. Würzburg: Verlagsdruckerei Schmidt, 1962–1963.

Ehrich, Emil. *Die Auslandsorganisation der NSDAP.* Schriften der Deutschen Hochschule für Politik II, no. 13. Berlin: Dünnhaupt, 1937.

Gajan, Koloman and Kvaček, Robert, eds. *Deutschland and die Tschechoslowakei 1919–1945. Dokumente über die deutsche Politik.* Prague: Orbis, 1965.

———, eds. *Germany and Czechoslovakia, 1919–1945.* Prague: Orbis, 1965.

Germany, Auswärartiges Amt. *Akten zur deutschen Auswärtigen Politik.* Series D. Baden-Baden: Impremerie Nationale, 1949–. (ADAP)

Germany, Reichsminister des Innern. *Reichsgesetzblatt.* Berlin: Reichsverlagsamt, 1934.

Henlein, Konrad. *Konrad Henlein Spricht. Aufruf, Pressekonferenz Böhmisch-Leipa.* Bücherei der Sudetendeutschen Heimatfront, Series I, no. 2. Karlsbad: K. H. Frank, 1937.

Hess, Rudolf. *Anordnungen des Stellvertreters des Führers.* Munich: Eher Verlag, 1937.

International Military Tribunal. *Trial of the Major War Criminals before the International Military Tribunal.* 42 vols. Nuremburg: Secretariat of the Military Tribunal, 1947–1949. (*IMT*)

Král, Václav, ed. *Die Deutschen in der Tschechoslowakei 1933–1947.* Prague: Academie, 1964.

———, ed. *Das Abkommen von München. 1938.* Prague: Academie, 1968.

Leitung der Auslandsorganisation der NSDAP. *Jahrbuch der Auslands-Organisation der NSDAP. 1939.* vol. 1. Berlin: Gauverlag der Auslands-Organisation der NSDAP, 1939.

Nittner, Ernst, ed. *Dokumente zur sudetendeutschen Frage 1916–1967.* rev. ed. Munich: Ackermann-Gemeinde, 1967.

Picker, Henry, ed. *Hitlers Tischgespräche im Führer Hauptquartier 1941–1942.* Bonn: Athenaeum, 1951.

Woodward, E. L. and Butler, Rohan, eds. *Documents on British Foreign Policy. 1919–1939.* Third Series. 2 vols. London: His Majesty's Stationery Office, 1949.

Zpověď K. H. Franka. Foreword by and under the technical collaboration of Karl Vykusy. Prague: A. S. Cil, 1946.

3. Memoirs, Apologia

Beneš, Eduard. *Memoirs of Dr. Beneš.* London: Allen and Unwin, 1954.

Gisevius, Hans. *Bis zum bitteren Ende.* 2 vols. Zurich: Fretz and Wasmuth, 1946.

Groscurth, Helmuth. *Tagebuch eines Abwehroffiziers 1938–1940.* Quellen und Darstellungen zur Zeitgeschichte, vol. 19. Stuttgart: Deutsche Verlagsanstalt, 1970.

Kordt, Erich. *Nicht aus den Akten. Die Wilhelmstrasse in Frieden und Krieg. Erlebnisse, Begegnungen und Eindrücke 1928–1945.* Stuttgart: Union Deutsche Verlagsgesellschaft, 1950.

Masaryk, Thomas. *Die Weltrevolution: Erinnerungen und Betrachtungen 1914–1918.* Trans. Camill Hoffman. Berlin: E. Reiss, 1925.

Orb, Heinrich. *13 Jahre Machtrausch: Nationalsozialismus.* Olten, Switzerland: Otto Walter, 1945.

Schellenberg, Walter. *Memoiren.* (ed.) Gita Petersen. Cologne: Verlag für Politik und Wirtschaft, 1956.

Steinacher, Hans. "Lebensaufzeichnungen." Unpublished manuscript.

4. Newspapers, Periodicals

Aufbruch: Das Blatt der Kommenden.
Berliner Tageblatt.
Die junge Front.
Nationalsozialistische Monatschefte.
Rumburger Zeitung.
Schwarzes Korps.
Sudetendeutsche Pressebriefe.
Sudetendeutsche Rundschau.
Der Tag (Aussig).
Volk und Führung.
Völkischer Beobachter.
Der Weg.
Die Zeit (Prague).

B. SECONDARY SOURCES

1. Unpublished Materials (*Dissertations, Manuscripts*)

Aronson, Schlomo. "Heydrich und die Anfänge des SD und der Gestapo 1931–1935." Ph. D. dissertation, Freie Universität (Berlin), 1967.

Browder, George. " 'SIPO' and SD, 1931–1940. Formation of an Instrument of Power." Ph. D. dissertation, University of Wisconsin, 1967.

Michel, Ursula. "Albrecht Haushofer und der Nationalsozialismus." Ph. D. dissertation, University of Kiel, 1964.

Norton, Donald H. "The Influence of Karl Haushofer on Nazi Ideology." Ph. D. dissertation, Clark University, 1963.

Smelser, Ronald M. "*Volkstumspolitik* and the Formulation of Nazi Foreign

Policy: The Sudeten Problem, 1933–1938." Ph. D. dissertation, University of Wisconsin, 1970.

2. Books

Abshagen, Karl Heinz. *Canaris. Patriot und Weltbürger.* Stuttgart: Union Deutsche Verlagsgesellschaft, 1950.

Altrichter, Anton. *Der Volkstumskampf in Mähren.* Niederdonau Schriftenreihe für Heimat und Volk, no. 4. Edited by Gaupresseamt Niederdonau der NSDAP. St. Pölten: St. Pöltner Zeitungsverlag, [1940].

Anklageschrift gegen die Abgeordneten und Senatoren der Sudetendeutschen Partei. Dokumente und Quellen aus Böhmen und Mähren, vol. 1. Munich: 1962.

Arendt, Hannah. *The Origins of Totalitarianism.* Cleveland: World, 1958.

Bierschenk, Theodor. *Die deutsche Volksgruppe in Polen. 1934–1939.* Beihefte zum Jahrbuch der Albertus-Universität, no. 10. Kitzingen/Main: Holzner-Verlag, 1954.

Bischoff, Ralph. *Nazi Conquest through German Culture.* Cambridge: Harvard University Press, 1942.

Bloch, Charles. *Hitler und die europäischen Mächte 1933/34: Kontinuität oder Bruch?* Hamburger Studien zur neueren Geschichte, no. 4. Frankfurt/Main: Europäische Verlagsanstalt, 1966.

Boehm, Max Hildebert. *Volkstheorie und Volkstumspolitik der Gegenwart.* Wissenschaftliche Forschungsberichte zum Aufbau des neuen Reiches, no. 4. Berlin: Junker and Dünnhaupt, 1935.

Brand, Walter. *Die sudetendeutsche Tragödie.* Ackermann-Schriften für Kultur, Wirtschaft, und Politik, no. 1. Lauf bei Nuremberg: Rudolf Zitzmann, 1949.

Breyer, Richard. *Das deutsche Reich und Polen 1932–1937.* Würzburg: Holzner, 1955.

Brügel, Johann Wolfgang. *Tschechen und Deutsche.* Munich: Nymphenburger, 1967.

Buchheim, Hans, *Anatomie des SS-Staates.* 2 vols. Munich: Deutscher Taschenbuch Verlag, 1967.

———. *SS und Polizei im NS-Staat.* Duisdorf: Selbstverlag der Studiengesellschaft für Zeitprobleme, 1964.

Buchheit, Gerd. *Der deutsche Geheimdienst.* Munich: Paul List, 1966.

Buk, Pierre (Weiskopf, F. C.). *La Tragédie tchécoslovaque de Septembre 1938 à Màrs 1939, avec des documents inédits du Livre blanc tchécoslovaque.* Paris: Editions du Sagittaire, 1939.

Bullock, Alan. *Hitler: A Study in Tyranny.* rev. ed. New York: Harper and Row [Bantam], 1961.

Celovsky, Boris. *Das münchener Abkommen von 1938.* Quellen und Darstellungen zur Zeitgeschichte, no. 3. Stuttgart: Deutsche Verlagsanstalt, 1958.

Černý, Bohumil. *Most k novému životu. Německá emigrace v ČSR v letech 1933–1939* [Bridges to a new life. The German emigrés in the CSR in the years 1933–1939]. Prague: Lidova Demokracie, 1967.

César, Jaroslav and Černý, Bohumil. *Politika německých buržoazních stran v Československu v letech 1918–1938* [The politics of the German bourgeois parties in Czechoslovakia in the years 1918–1938]. 2 vols. Prague: CSAV, 1962.

Ciller, Alois. *Deutscher Sozialismus in den Sudetenländern und der Ostmark.* Hamburg: Hanseatische Verlagsanstalt, 1944.

—— *Vorläufer des Nationalsozialismus. Geschichte und Entwicklung der nationalen Arbeiterbewegung im deutschen Grenzland.* Vienna: Ertl Verlag, 1932.

Davidson, Eugene. *The Trial of the Germans.* New York: Macmillan, 1966.

Degener, Hermann, ed. *Wer Ist's.* 10th ed. Berlin: Arani, 1935.

Deubner, Karl-August. *Der Politiker Konrad Henlein: Schöpfer der sudetendeutschen Einheit.* Bad Fürth bei Munich, Leipzig, Vienna: Deutscher Hort-Verlag, 1938.

Eubank, Keith. *Munich.* 1st ed. Norman, Oklahoma: University of Oklahoma Press, 1963.

Fischer, Josef; Patzak, Vaclav and Perth, Vincenc. *Ihr Kampf: Die wahren Ziele der Sudetendeutschen Partei.* Karlsbad: Verlagsanstalt 'Graphia,' 1937.

Foustka, R. N. *Konrád Henlein: Neoficielní historie jeho strany.* [Konrad Henlein: Unofficial history of his party] Prague: Nakladatelství volné myšlenky, 1937.

Franzel, Emil. *Sudetendeutsche Geschichte: Eine volkstümliche Darstellung.* Augsburg: Adam Kraft, 1958.

Fuchs, Gerhard. *Gegen Hitler und Henlein. Der solidarische Kampf tschechischer und deutscher Antifaschisten von 1933 bis 1938.* Schriftenreihe der Kommission der Historiker der DDR und der ČSSR, no. 4. Berlin: Rütten and Loening, 1961.

Gehl, Jürgen. *Austria, Germany and the Anschluss 1931–1938.* London: Oxford University Press, 1963.

Gregor, A. James. *Contemporary Radical Ideologies. Totalitarian Thought in the Twentieth Century.* New York: Random House, 1968.

Hoensch, Jörg. *Die Slowakei und Hitler's Ostpolitik. Hlinkas Slowakische Volkspartei zwischen Autonomie und Separation 1938/1939.* Beiträge zur Geschichte Osteuropas, no. 4. Cologne, Graz: Böhlau Verlag, 1965.

Jacobsen, Hans-Adolf. *Nationalsozialistische Aussenpolitik 1933–1938.* Frankfurt/Main: Alfred Metzner Verlag, 1968.

Jahn, Rudolf. *Konrad Henlein: Leben und Werk des Turnführers.* Karlsbad, Leipzig: Adam Kraft Verlag, 1938.

—— ed. *Sudetendeutsches Turnertum.* Frankfurt/Main: Heimreiter Verlag, 1958.

Jaksch, Wenzel. *Europas Weg nach Potsdam.* Stuttgart: Deutsche Verlagsanstalt, 1958.

Klemperer, Klemens von. *Germany's New Conservatism: Its History and Dilemma in the Twentieth Century.* Princeton: Princeton University Press, 1957.

Koehl, Robert L. *RKFDV: German Resettlement and Population Policy 1939–1945.* Harvard Historical Monographs, no. 31. Cambridge, Mass.: Harvard University Press, 1957.

Krebs, Hans. *Kampf in Böhmen.* Berlin: Volk und Reich Verlag, 1936.

———. *Paneuropa oder Mitteleuropa?* Nationalsozialistische Bibliothek, No. 29. Munich: Franz Eher Verlag, 1931.

——— ed. *Der Volkssportprozess. Ein Tatsachenbericht nach den stenographischen Protokollen und den Zeitungsmeldungen über die Brünner Gerichtsverhandlungen vom 8. August bis 14. September 1932.* Aussig: DNSAP, 1932.

Leuschner, Joachim. *Volk und Raum: zum Stil der nationalsozialistischen Aussenpolitik.* Kleine Vandenhoeck, No. 58. Göttingen: Vandenhoeck and Ruprecht, 1958.

Leverkuehn, Paul. *German Military Intelligence.* Trans. R. H. Stevens and C. FitzGibbon. London: Weidenfeld and Nicolson, 1954.

Luža, Radomir. *The Transfer of the Sudeten Germans: A Study of Czech-German Relations, 1933–1962.* New York: New York University Press, 1964.

McRandle, John. *The Track of the Wolf: Essays on National Socialism and Its Leader, Adolf Hitler.* Evanston, Ill.: Northwestern University Press, 1965.

Mohler, Armin. *Die konservative Revolution in Deutschland 1918–1932.* Stuttgart: Friedrich Vorwerk Verlag, 1950.

Molisch, Paul. *Die sudetendeutsche Freiheitsbewegung in den Jahren 1918–1919.* Vienna, Leipzig: Wilhelm Braumüller, 1932.

Nelhiebel, Kurt. *Die Henleins gestern und heute: Hintergründe und Ziele des Witikobundes.* Frankfurt/Main: Röderberg Verlag, 1962.

Neumann, Franz L. *Behemoth: The Structure and Practice of National Socialism. 1933–1944.* 2nd [rev.] ed. New York, Toronto: Oxford University Press, 1944.

Nittner, Ernst. *Der böhmisch-mährische Raum als Objekt des Hitlerischen Imperialismus.* Sonderdruck. Munich: Ackermann-Gemeinde, 1960.

Nyomarkay, Joseph. *Charisma and Factionalism in the Nazi Party.* Minneapolis: University of Minnesota Press, 1968.

Orlow, Dietrich. *The History of the Nazi Party: 1919–1933,* Pittsburgh: University of Pittsburgh Press, 1969.

Perman, Dagmar. *The Shaping of the Czechoslovak State: Diplomatic History of the Boundaries of Czechoslovakia, 1914–1920.* Studies in East European History, Vol. 7. Leiden: C. J. Brill, 1962.

Peterson, Edward. *The Limits of Hitler's Power.* Princeton: Princeton University Press, 1969.

Pfitzner, Josef. *Sudetendeutsche Einheitsbewegung.* 2nd ed. Karlsbad and Leipzig: K. H. Frank, 1937.

Preidel, Helmut, ed. *Die Deutschen in Böhmen und Mähren: Ein historischer Rückblick.* 2nd ed. Gräfelfing bei Munich: Edmund Gans Verlag, 1952.

Raschofer, Hermann. *Die Sudetenfrage: ihre völkerrechtliche Entwicklung vom ersten Weltkrieg bis zur Gegenwart.* Munich: Isar Verlag, 1953.

Reile, Oscar. *Geheime Ostfront: Die deutsche Abwehr im Osten 1921–1945.* Munich-Wels: Welsermühl, 1963.

Robbins, Keith. *Munich: 1938.* London: Cassells, 1968.

Rönnefarth, Helmuth K. G. *Die Sudetenkrise in der internationalen Politik: Entstehung, Verlauf, Auswirkung.* Veröffentlichungen des Instituts für europäische Geschichte Mainz, vol. 21. 2 vols. Wiesbaden: Franz Steiner Verlag, 1961.

Rohrbach, Paul. *Deutsches Volkstum als Minderheit,* Berlin: Engelmann, 1926.

Ross, Dieter. *Hitler und Dollfuss. Die deutsche Oesterreich-Politik 1933–1934.* Hamburger Beiträge zur Zeitgeschichte, vol. 3. Hamburg: Leibnitz, 1966.

Schmid-Egger, Hans, ed. *Umbruch in Mitteleuropa. Beiträge zur Geschichte der böhmischen Länder in der Zeit von 1848 bis 1948.* Munich: Ackermann-Gemeinde, 1960.

Schubert, Günter. *Anfänge nationalsozialistischer Aussenpolitik.* Cologne: Verlag Wissenschaft und Politik, 1963.

Seabury, Paul. *The Wilhelmstrasse: A Study of German Diplomacy in the Nazi Era.* Berkeley: University of California Press, 1954.

Sonderegger, René. *Mordzentrale X: Enthüllungen und Dokumente über die Auslandstätigkeit der deutschen Gestapo.* Kulturpolitische Schriften, no. 5. Zurich: Reso-Verlag, 1936.

Sontheimer, Kurt. *Antidemokratisches Denken in der Weimarer Republik.* Munich: Nymphenburger Verlag, 1962.

Spann, Othmar. *Der wahre Statt.* Leipzig: Quelle and Meyer, 1921.

Stern, Fritz. *The Politics of Cultural Despair.* New York: Doubleday, 1965.

Taylor, A. J. P. *The Origins of the Second World War.* New York: Fawcett, 1963.

Thompson, Laurence. *The Greatest Treason: The Untold Story of Munich.* New York: William Morrow, 1968.

Verpflichtendes Erbe: Volkstum im Ringen um seinen Bestand und seine Anerkennung. Kiel: Ferdinand Hirt, 1954.

Volksdeutscher Durchbruch. Aufrufe und Bekenntnisse zur gesamtdeutschen Verbundenheit. Berlin: VDA Wirtschaftsunternehmen GmbH, 1934.

Waite, Robert G. L. *Vanguard of Nazism: The Free Corps Movement in Postwar Germany, 1919–1923.* New York: Norton, 1969.

Weinberg, Gerhard L. *The Foreign Policy of Hitler's Germany: Diplomatic Revolution in Europe, 1933–36.* Chicago: University of Chicago Press, 1970.

Wheeler-Bennett, John W. *Munich: Prologue to Tragedy.* Toronto: Macmillan, 1948.

Whiteside, Andrew Gladding. *Austrian National Socialism before 1918.* The Hague: M. Nijhoff, 1962.

Wichterich, R. *Volksdeutscher Kampf. Dargestellt am Lebensweg Dr. Steinachers.* Cologne: 1936.

Wighton, Charles. *Heydrich. Hitler's Most Evil Henchman.* London: Odhams Press, 1962.

Wiskemann, Elisabeth. *Czechs and Germans. A Study of the Struggle in the*

Historic Provinces of Bohemia and Moravia. 2nd ed. London, New York: St. Martin's Press, 1967.

3. *Articles*

Bracher, Karl Dietrich. "Das Anfangsstadium der Hitlerschen Aussenpolitik." *Vierteljahrshefte für Zeitgeschichte* 5 (January 1957), 63–76.

Broszat, Martin. "Die völkische Ideologie und der Nationalsozialismus." *Deutsche Rundschau* 84 (January 1958), 53–68.

Bürger, Friedrich. "Henleins 'Geheimbericht' vom November 1937." *Sudetenland* no. 3 (1967), 185–9.

César, Jaroslav and Černý, Bohumil. "Německá irredenta a henleinovci v ČSR v letech 1930–1938" [German irredenta and the Henleinists in the CSR in the years 1930–1938]. *Československo časopis historický* 10 (1962), 1–17.

Eubank, Keith. "Konrad Henlein, the Sudeten Question and British Foreign Policy." *The Historical Journal* 12, 4 (1969), 674–97.

Franzel, Emil. "Die Politik der Sudetendeutschen in der Tschechoslowakei 1918–1938." *Die Deutschen in Böhmen und Mähren. Ein historischer Rückblick.* Helmut Preidel. 2nd ed. Gräfelfing bei Munich: Edmund Gans Verlag, 1952. 333–372.

Fuchs, Gerhard. "Zur Behandlung der sudetendeutschen Frage (1933–1938) in der westdeutschen Geschichtsliteratur." *Probleme der Geschichte des zweiten Weltkrieges* 2 (1958): 145–58.

Haag, John. " 'Knights of the Spirit': The Kameradschaftsbund." *Journal of Contemporary History*, vol. 8, no. 3 (July 1973): 133–54.

Hill, Leonidas. "The Wilhelmstrasse in the Nazi Era." *Political Science Quarterly* 82 (December 1967): 546–70.

Koehl, Robert. "Feudal Aspects of National Socialism." *American Political Science Review*, 54 (1960), 921–33.

Kvaček, Robert. "K historii Henleinovi Sudetoněmecké strany" [On the History of Henlein's Sudeten German Party] *Dějepis ve škole. Časopis pro dějepis, ústavu ČSR a SSSR* 4 (May, 1957): 193–200; (June 1957): 241–49.

———. "Československo-německá jednání v roce 1936" [The Czechoslovak-German negotiations in 1936] *Historie a vojenství* (1965): 721–54.

Neuwirth, Hans. "Der Weg der Sudentendeutschen von der Entstehung des tschechoslowakischen Staates bis zum Vertrag von München." *Die Sudetenfrage in europäischer Sicht.* Veröffentlichungen des Collegium Carolinum, vol. 12. Munich: Verlag Robert Lerche, 1962. 122–79.

Norton, Donald H. "Karl Haushofer and the German Academy, 1925–1945." *Central European History* 1 (March, 1968): 80–97.

Olivová, Věra. "Československo a německo ve třicátých letech" [Czechoslovakia and Germany in the 1930s]. *Československo časopis historický* 16 (1968): 881–91.

———. "Kameradschaftsbund." *Z Českých Dějin: Sborník prací in memoriam Prof. Dr. Vaclava Husy* Prague: Universita Karlova, 1966. 237–68.

Rimscha, Hans von. "Zur Gleichschaltung der deutschen Volksgruppen durch das Dritte Reich. Am Beispiel der deutschbaltischen Volksgruppe in Lettland." *Historische Zeitschrift* 182, no. 1 (1956): 29–63.

Runzheimer, Jürgen. "Der Ueberfall auf den Gleiwitzer Sender." *Vierteljahrshefte für Zeitgeschichte* 10, no. 4 (October, 1962): 408–26.

Sasse, Heinz. "Das Problem des diplomatischen Nachwuchses im Dritten Reich." *Forschungen zu Staat und Verfassung: Festgabe für Fritz Hartung.* Berlin: Duncker and Humbolt, 1958. 459–84.

Ullmann, Hermann. "Die Jugend in den Volksgruppen." *Andreas Hofer: Jahrbuch des VDA.* Berlin: Grenz- and Ausland Verlag, 1935. 30–41.

Weinberg, Gerhard L. "Secret Hitler-Beneš Negotiations in 1936–37." *Journal of Central European Affairs* 19 (1960): 368–74.

———. "The May Crisis, 1938." *Journal of Modern History* 29, no. 3 (September 1957), 213–25.

Zipfel, Friedrich. "Gestapo und SD in Berlin." *Jahrbuch für die Geschichte Mittel- und Ostdeutschland* 10 (1961): 263–92.

Index

Kügler, Hermann, 104, 125, 264, 278, 282
Kuehn-Luetzow, Count, 146
Kühne, Lothar, 179–180
Külz (Reichsminister), 263
Künzel, Franz, 45, 299
Kulturverband, 61
Kundt, Ernst, 91, 103, 232–233, 277–278, 299
Kursell, Otto von, 21, 127–129, 140, 158, 171, 183–184, 186–188, 195, 248, 252, 283, 288, 293–295

Labor Front. *See Reichsarbeitsfront*
Labor Unions (Sudeten), 47–48, 50, 136, 153–154, 177, 196, 273
Lammers, Heinrich, 203, 264, 274–275, 283, 285, 289, 297
Landständische Jungmannschaft, 45
Langmann, Otto, 296
Lany (Czech Secret Service), 112
League of Nations, 16, 108, 141, 148, 160, 203, 296
Lehmann, Emil, 46, 90
Leitgen, Alfred, 106, 125
Ley, Robert, 161, 168, 177, 288, 292
Liebig, Theodor, 112
Liebl, Otto, 56, 154, 176, 197, 200, 292
Lierau, Walter von, 88–89, 136, 174–175, 181–182, 185, 195, 288, 292, 294, 296–297
Likus, Rudolf, 179–181, 292
Loesch, Karl von, 281
Lorenz, Werner, 157, 177, 188–189, 190–193, 195–198, 201, 203, 205, 207, 214, 217, 222, 227–230, 233, 239, 252, 278, 295, 298, 300–301
Ludendorff, Erich, 175
Luig, Wilhelm, 202, 299
Lurtz (Austrian consul), 291

Mackensen, Hans-Georg von, 295, 298–299
Mährisch-Trübauer Verband, 47
Malypetr, Jan, 132
Masaryk, Jan, 147
Masaryk, Thomas, 8, 103, 131, 262
Mastný, Vojtěch, 150, 191–192, 274
Matis (SdP radical), 153
May, Franz, 236
Meckel, Rudolf, 155, 178, 287, 292

Meerwald, Willy, 34–36, 88, 97–98, 266–267, 277, 279, 285
Meissner, Otto, 289
Metzner, Adolf, 156
Ministry for Germans Abroad (proposals for), 21, 28, 128
Moeller van den Bruck, Arthur, 6
Mussolini, Benito, 100, 143, 201–202, 223, 225, 241, 252

Nabersberg, Karl, 80
Nationalsozialistische Betriebszellenorganisation (NSBO), 27
Nationalsozialistische deutsche Arbeiterpartei (NSDAP), 21, 23, 25, 27, 29–30, 49–50, 94, 125–127, 129, 137–138, 168, 220, 231, 265
Nationalsozialistische Studentenschaft, 23, 265, 276
Nationalsozialistischer Lehrerbund (NSLB), 77
Nationalsozialistischer Studentenbund, 56, 271
Naujocks, Alfred, 171, 291
Neumann, Ernst, 263
Neurath, Constantin von, 39, 73, 111–112, 124, 148, 159, 182, 203, 213–214, 274, 281, 286, 289, 293, 295, 301
Neuwirth, Hans, 75, 87–89, 93–95, 103, 107, 112, 170, 185, 195, 236, 268, 272, 274, 277–278, 280–281, 283, 290, 293, 299, 303
Newton, Basil, 300, 302
Nicolson, Harold, 224
Nieland, Hans, 25–26

Oberländer, Theodor, 125, 193
Ortsgruppe Auswärtiges Amt der NSDAP (proposed), 27
OSSA, 16, 263, 288, 301
Oster, Hans, 294

Papen, Franz von, 79
Partisch, Hubert, 266
Patschneider, Dr. (*Bereitschaft*), 55, 91, 112, 114, 281
People's Party (Slovakia), 132
Peters, Gustav, 136, 232, 269–270, 272, 277, 284–285, 289, 298
Pfeiffer, Heinz, 182–183, 186
Pfeil, Graf, 103, 276, 280